ALL
ABOUT
THE
STORY

ALL ABOUT THE STORY

News, Power, Politics, and
The Washington Post

LEONARD DOWNIE, JR.

PUBLICAFFAIRS
NEW YORK

PublicAffairs
Hachette Book Group
1290 Avenue of the Americas, New York, NY 10104
www.publicaffairsbooks.com
@Public_Affairs

Printed in the United States of America
First Edition: September 2020

Published by PublicAffairs, an imprint of Perseus Books, LLC, a subsidiary of Hachette Book Group, Inc. The PublicAffairs name and logo is a trademark of the Hachette Book Group.

The Hachette Speakers Bureau provides a wide range of authors for speaking events. To find out more, go to www.hachettespeakersbureau.com or call (866) 376-6591.

The publisher is not responsible for websites (or their content) that are not owned by the publisher.

Print book interior design by Linda Mark.

Library of Congress Cataloging-in-Publication Data
Names: Downie, Leonard, Jr., author.
Title: All about the story : news, power, politics, and the Washington post / Leonard Downie Jr.
Description: First edition. | New York : PublicAffairs, 2020. | Includes index.
Identifiers: LCCN 2020007418 | ISBN 9781541742284 (hardback) | ISBN 9781541742260 (epub)
Subjects: LCSH: Downie, Leonard, Jr. | Journalists--United States--Biography. | Newspaper editors—United States—Biography. | Washington post.
Classification: LCC PN4874.D698 A3 2020 | DDC 070.92 [B]—dc23
LC record available at https://lccn.loc.gov/2020007418

ISBNs: 978-1-5417-4228-4 (hardcover), 978-1-5417-4226-0 (ebook)

LSC-C

10 9 8 7 6 5 4 3 2 1

For Mom and Dad, and Janice

Contents

Contents

Introduction

𝕴 HAVE VERY SELDOM WRITTEN ABOUT MYSELF during my more than a half century as a journalist. I was raised in the Midwest by parents who taught me modesty as a fundamental virtue. I always thought that my job was to tell the story, not to be the story.

I grew up in a working-class neighborhood in Cleveland, Ohio, attended public schools, and graduated from The Ohio State University in Columbus. All along the way, I wrote for and edited student newspapers, beginning in the fifth grade. I fell in love with journalism.

Eventually—and somewhat accidentally—I landed an unlikely summer reporting internship at the *Washington Post*, right in the heart of the Eastern journalistic establishment. Unexpectedly for me, I was hired as a full-time reporter at the end of that summer. Although I was the youngest journalist in the newsroom, I was already married and had a child. It could not have been a more improbable beginning for what became a long, exciting, and fulfilling journey.

I became an investigative reporter in my twenties, an editor on the Watergate story in my early thirties, and a foreign correspondent in London. I went on to lead the *Post* newsroom for twenty-four years— first as managing editor under the legendary Ben Bradlee and then as his successor as executive editor. I never became as famous as Ben was, and I never thought of myself as the story. Instead, as the top editor of the *Post*, I let the many momentous stories I oversaw to speak for themselves.

Nevertheless, people told me in recent years that I had a significant story of my own to tell. One of them, the redoubtable Bob Woodward, author of so many books himself, recalls, "I urged you to write your story because it was a remarkable, historic time to edit the *Post*. And you did it so well. Take us there."

I thought about that. After all, I directed coverage of the impeachment of President Bill Clinton, the 9/11 terrorist attacks on New York and Washington, and the wars in Afghanistan and Iraq, among other historic stories. I drove award-winning *Post* investigative journalism that brought about significant changes locally and nationally. I made decisions about reporting on the private lives of politicians and about revealing national security secrets. I dealt personally with presidents, prime ministers, and royalty. I clashed with government and corporate leaders over stories they opposed, and I agonized over whether some stories might endanger lives. I sometimes made mistakes that I still regret. More often, I believe, I produced journalism vital to American society. My mission was to seek the truth and hold the powerful accountable.

Much of my time at the *Post* turned out to be a golden age for American newspapers. They enjoyed all-time highs in readership, influence, and the advertising revenue that paid for it all. As the editor of one of the nation's leading newspapers, I was among those who set the agenda for what was news for many years.

By 2008, however, in what turned out to be my last year as the *Post*'s executive editor, everything was changing rapidly. News media, along with the rest of American life, were being transformed by the digital revolution. Print and broadcast news audiences were shrinking. Americans were being inundated with news, information, and opinion—factual and false—from countless cable channels, websites, and social media. New digital media were diverting advertising revenue away from newspapers, eroding their economic base. I was forced to begin to downsize the *Post* newsroom while trying to maintain the quality and impact of its journalism. But I was losing ground, and I was unhappily forced to retire as executive editor at the age of sixty-six.

I was not ready for leisure, and I am a lousy golfer. I decided to teach investigative journalism and write about the uncertain future of news and the deteriorating relationship between the American government and the press. Journalism had been my calling. My devotion to it had been an all-consuming, lifelong commitment—at times at a high cost to relationships and family. I was an outsider, a chronicler, and investigator rather than a player, always avoiding opinion or advocacy. Now, I was ready to get personally involved in the increasingly contentious political, philosophical, and practical issues of the role of the news media in our democracy. And I realized that my life and career were full of good examples and lessons.

This book is the story of my uncommon career in journalism, and what it illuminates about the past, present, and future of news. I will take the reader inside the *Post* to show how stories that helped shape history were initiated, reported, written, and edited in newsroom dramas usually hidden from public view. I will show how those stories illustrate values, habits, and issues of journalism that are relevant today.

I also will take the reader inside my own life as a journalist and visit the unexpected twists and turns in that journey from accidental intern to the top of the *Post* newsroom. Some of what I accomplished was serendipitous, as the reader will see, while I believe that much more of it was due to my unwavering pursuit of aggressive journalism that sought the truth and made a difference.

I will focus on turning points in my career. I will begin with when I cheekily decided to compete for the job of managing editor of the *Post*, number two at the time under Ben Bradlee, even though I was his opposite in background, personality, and style. I will double back to how I got there—all the way back to my roots and the beginnings of my journey. I'll tell next about my investigative reporting that led to the abolition of the dysfunctional local court system, my unexpected leadership of the Watergate story through the climactic months before President Nixon's resignation, my education on the job as a fledgling foreign correspondent, and my preoccupation with the sad story of Prince Charles and Princess Diana.

Then I will turn to my role in what the *Post* did in the quarter century while I was leading its newsroom: Confronting the Clintons. Responding to an ultimatum from the murderous Unabomber. Meeting the unprecedented journalistic challenge of the 9/11 terrorist attacks. Unsuccessfully wrestling with President George W. Bush's rationale for invading Iraq. Coping with our reporters' challenges and the dangers in aggressively covering the ensuing war and its aftermath. Investigating the CIA's secret extralegal war on terrorism. Exposing wrongs, such as the mistreatment of wounded veterans at the Walter Reed Army Medical Center, the abuse of children in the local government's care, and unwarranted shootings by Washington, D.C., police.

Along the way, I will invite readers to join me in considering difficult journalistic decisions. What should be reported about the private lives of politicians and other public figures? When does holding U.S. presidents accountable go too far—or not far enough? How can a newspaper editor decide what stories would or would not endanger human life or national security? How should an editor respond to requests by officials, all the way up to the president, to not publish some stories? How far should an editor go to protect reporters' confidential sources?

I will introduce the reader to some of the extraordinary journalists I was privileged to work with at the *Post* and describe what it was like to manage all that talent under unrelenting deadline and competitive pressures, demanding professional expectations, and persistent public scrutiny. I followed Ben Bradlee's credo: hire the best possible people and enable them to do their best work. In my case, that meant much more personal involvement in stories with editors and reporters throughout the newsroom. Someone had to make the final decisions, and the buck stopped with me.

As I was finishing this book, the COVID-19 pandemic became the biggest and most important news story for Americans at least since the

9/11 attacks. It challenged everything about journalism that I will be sharing with readers here, especially journalism that seeks truth and holds power accountable when doing so is most difficult, but also most needed.

That challenge deepened after the shocking killing of George Floyd, a forty-six-year-old black man, by a white Minneapolis police officer, Derek Chauvin, widely seen on videos taken by bystanders. Large multiracial crowds staged days and days of peaceful protests in cities across America against police killings of black citizens and persistent racism and socioeconomic inequality. They were accompanied at times by destructive looting and violent clashes with police. Meanwhile, the country continued to suffer from the deadly pandemic and its devastating economic impact.

Protests and scattered violence in Washington, in particular, reminded me that the underlying issues of race in America remained unresolved a half century after my reporting on the 1968 riots in the nation's capital, following the assassination of the Rev. Martin Luther King Jr. President Trump's belligerent response to the protests and to press coverage of both the unrest and the COVID-19 crisis reminded me of President Nixon, Vietnam War protests, and Watergate.

Journalists worked under the most trying conditions to report accurately and fully for the American people on the national crises of 2020. They literally risked harm, while enduring constant verbal attacks by Trump and his supporters. I will discuss this further at the end of the book. For the calling to which I have devoted my life, times like this are indeed all about the story.

Ben and Len

𝕴 MAY HAVE SUSPECTED WHY EXECUTIVE EDITOR Ben Bradlee had called me into his glass-walled newsroom office, the one made famous in the movie *All the President's Men*. I had heard the newsroom rumors that I was among those being considered to become the *Washington Post*'s next managing editor, running the newsroom under Ben and becoming most likely to eventually succeed him.

I tried not to think about it so that I could concentrate on my work as national news editor, especially as I was directing the newspaper's coverage of the 1984 presidential election campaign. But I was kidding myself. I couldn't stop thinking about it.

I felt I was ready for the job. I was forty-two, and I had been a reporter and an editor at the *Washington Post* for twenty years. At twenty-four, I was a Pulitzer Prize finalist for investigative reporting that transformed Washington's local court system. While in my early thirties, I edited many of the *Post*'s Watergate stories. Afterward, I managed the newspaper's large local news staff. I then became a foreign correspondent for several years as the

Post's bureau chief in London. I had been told that I was brought back to the newsroom to give me experience with national news.

The more I thought about it, the more I realized that I very much wanted to help lead the *Post*. I wanted to build on Ben's bold, cutting-edge approach to journalism to make the newspaper the nation's most aggressive and authoritative source of news.

In June 1984, it was still very much Ben's *Washington Post*. Despite some stumbles, he was still the Ben Bradlee of Watergate and the Pentagon Papers, who had created the modern *Washington Post* during nearly two decades as its top editor. He had survived the embarrassment of having to return the Pulitzer Prize awarded to the *Post* for a story fabricated by reporter Janet Cooke about a nonexistent eight-year-old heroin addict. He was still close to and supported by *Post* CEO Katharine Graham, despite her concerns about a post-Watergate letdown in the newsroom. He was about to put behind him what had become a dysfunctional relationship with his longtime managing editor, Howard Simons. After being told by Mrs. Graham that he would not succeed Ben as executive editor, Simons was leaving the *Post* to become curator of the Nieman Foundation at Harvard University.

Over the years, I'd had plenty of contact with Ben, mostly in newsroom meetings and on editors' retreats. He had watched me run the local and national news staffs. He had sent me to London. But we were not pals, and I was not one of his favorites. We were, in fact, very different.

Benjamin Crowninshield Bradlee was born into an old Boston family and attended St. Marks School and Harvard. He had recovered from polio and willed himself to walk again. He served with valor in battle as a junior officer on a destroyer in the Pacific in World War II. He spoke French fluently and lived for a time in Paris. Later he was a close friend of John F. Kennedy. At sixty-three, Ben was just as charismatic as Jason Robards had portrayed him to be in his Academy Award–winning performance in the 1976 movie *All the President's Men*. He had become a nationally recognized icon of charm and self-confidence. Ben and his much younger third wife, the glamorous *Post* feature writer Sally Quinn, were the most sought-after couple on the Washington social scene. In turn, they frequently entertained the capital's boldface names in their historic home in Georgetown, which once was owned by the son of Abraham Lincoln.

In the *Post* newsroom, Ben was the center of attention in his perfectly tailored suits and colorful Turnbull and Asser shirts with distinctive white collars. He charmed women and men alike with his jaunty manner, wise-ass wit, and salty language. He had a great eye for journalistic talent, and he befriended rising young stars in the newsroom, keeping himself in touch with the current zeitgeist. Being complimented by Ben with a clap on the shoulder made a *Post* journalist's day. Being ignored by him could be agony.

As executive editor, Ben made quick, instinctive, sometimes impulsive decisions—both about news stories and newsroom people—and left the details of carrying them out to others. He was mostly interested in national, foreign, and sports news, plus the irreverent Style section that he had created. He paid little attention to local or financial news, or to stories about ordinary people. He encouraged initiative and aggressive competition among reporters and editors for the front page—and for his approval. This became known inside and beyond the newsroom as "creative tension."

Ben had a short attention span and often impatiently cut off conversations in his office by pulling out a crossword puzzle or his nail clipper. Contrary to his tough-guy image, he avoided confrontations whenever he could, delegating to others the delivery of bad news. He hated firing people and almost never did it himself. Despite all of that, I thought that he was the most gifted natural leader that I had ever met.

I was the anti-Bradlee. During my early years at the paper my young Ivy League colleagues nicknamed me "Land Grant Len." I had attended the land-grant Ohio State University, becoming the first in my family to earn a college degree. Because I married at eighteen and had my first child at nineteen, I was not drafted during the Vietnam War. I had never been abroad until, at twenty-nine, I went to Europe and Israel on a traveling journalism fellowship that allowed me a leave of absence from the *Post*. My personal style tended toward Midwestern bland. My clothing was seen as so unfashionable that some in the newsroom said it must have come from J. C. Penney, rather than Raleigh's, the conservative men's store I frequented.

As the *Post*'s London bureau chief, I had interviewed numerous European leaders, hosted Prince Charles at dinner, covered his royal wedding, and appeared often on British television. But I had no public profile back in Washington and no social life to speak of, beyond friends at the *Post*. I was not a networker and had no posse in or outside the newsroom. As a somewhat antisocial outsider who had always been awkward at small talk, I usually attended only those Washington dinners and parties at which I was likely to pick up information useful to the newspaper. I limited the time I spent working in my office or traveling to conferences and news industry conventions. Instead, I spent much of my long work days roaming a newsroom that had doubled in size to nine hundred people. I returned there late at night and on weekends whenever a big story broke or something went amiss. At a sometimes significant cost to my family and personal life, the newspaper was paramount to me. As I think about it, I guess it *was* my life.

Yet both despite and because of the differences between Ben and me, I knew that I was respected throughout the newsroom for my past investigative reporting, my sure-handed editing, and my encouraging leadership. I was nationally known among investigative journalists, whose numbers had been growing rapidly after Watergate. As an editor, compared to Ben, I was hands-on almost to a fault, deeply immersed in nearly every news and personnel decision while running the local and national news staffs. I paid close attention to all my reporters and editors, and I was known not to play favorites, as Ben did. My evident enthusiasm for all kinds of good stories was contagious.

Despite our different backgrounds and styles, Ben and I were both fiercely competitive and determined to produce journalism that made a difference. We both preferred the unusually free-flowing, energetic newsroom culture Ben had created, in which anyone could run with an idea, reach the front page, and influence the course of the newspaper. We were dedicated to the pursuit of truth and detested lying and betrayal of trust, as sanctimonious as that may sound. We believed in separating news reporting and opinion, as quaint as that became in the digital age. We were both quintessential newspapermen who loved our work and lived for big stories.

Although I may have had an inkling when I went into Ben's office that day in 1984 that he would discuss the managing editor's job, I was completely unprepared for what he proposed. He talked briefly about how difficult it would be to replace Simons, a sensitive, people-oriented intellectual who had effectively complemented Ben for many years. They had become estranged after Watergate because the book and movie *All the President's Men* had made Ben famous while leaving Simons mostly in the shadows.

Ben told me that he had been unable to decide who should replace Simons: Style section editor Shelby Coffey, foreign news editor Jim Hoagland, or me. What if, Ben asked me, the three of us temporarily shared the job until he could decide which one of us he would keep as his managing editor?

Facing Ben across his big desk, I struggled with how to respond. Although I had heard rumors about Shelby and Jim being considered, the three of us had never talked about it.

Had Ben already discussed this with them? Did they want to do it? How would we go about it?

Shelby Coffey was a boyishly handsome, courtly Southern gentleman. He'd been raised in the comfortable family of a leading lawyer in Lookout Mountain, Tennessee, and gone to military school, from which he retained a disciplined personality. He smiled easily and oozed effortless charm that often captivated the people around him while hiding his real feelings and agenda. Shelby became an unusually talented story editor who had realized much of the potential for Ben's vision of the Style section. He brought out the best in its idiosyncratic writers, especially Sally Quinn. Because he and his physician wife, Mary Lee, had become close friends of Sally and Ben, Shelby was widely thought to be Ben's preference for managing editor, and thus to be his eventual successor.

Jim Hoagland also was from the South, but a different part of it. He'd grown up in Rock Hill, South Carolina, and earned a journalism degree at the state university. He learned French, studied at the University of Aix-en-Provence, and served in the U.S. Air Force for two years in Germany before trying his hand at journalism at the *International Herald Tribune* in Paris. He started at the *Post* in 1966 on the Metro staff, where he worked with me on one of my investigative reporting projects. Jim then served as a *Post* foreign correspondent in Paris, Beirut, and South Africa. His coverage of apartheid in South Africa won a Pulitzer Prize. Jim was foreign news editor by the time I was London bureau chief. He had become an urbane, tough-minded, sometimes imperious Franco-phile—an expert on foreign affairs with contacts around the world. Jim was as taciturn as Shelby was outgoing. He was neither charming nor convivial, but often quite intimidating.

My response to Ben's proposal was impulsive. Without thinking it through, I told him that I did not want to be part of a triumvirate with Shelby and Jim, even temporarily, even if it meant that I would never get the job. I said I didn't think it would work for the three of us or be good for the newsroom. Having three managing editors trying to direct the newsroom would have been confusing, and I knew that we each would want to do it differently. Ben thought for a moment, and then asked me to think about it some more.

As the day went on, I became increasingly distracted from my work. This is something I want, I told myself, and I am the best person for the job. Finally, I went back into Ben's office. I was nervous but determined. I told him that he should give the job only to me. Without disparaging Shelby or Jim, I pointed to my broader experience across the newsroom and what I had accomplished as an investigative reporter, a local news editor, a foreign correspondent, and a newsroom leader. I knew I could do the job. I wanted the job. This time, Ben said *he* would think about it.

WHAT I DID NOT KNOW—AND BEN MAY NOT HAVE YET KNOWN— was that he was not going to make the decision himself. It would be made by Donald Graham, Katharine Graham's son, who was then the *Post*'s thirty-nine-year-old publisher. As it happened, Ben, Don, and I had all started at the *Post*, at different times, as reporters on its local news staff. Our divergent paths since then had brought us together at what would be a turning point for me and the newspaper.

Don's maternal grandfather, the wealthy financier Eugene Meyer, had bought the then money-losing *Washington Post* at auction in 1933, when it was one of five daily newspapers in the nation's capital city. In 1946, after more than a decade of resuscitating it with his own money, Meyer turned control of the newspaper over to Philip L. Graham, who had married Meyer's daughter, Katharine, six years earlier.

Phil Graham, a charismatic, brilliant, restless man who was later diagnosed with bipolar disorder, greatly strengthened the *Post*, in part by buying the competing morning paper, the *Washington Times Herald*. That purchase considerably increased the *Post*'s circulation and advertising, eventually enabling it to overtake the previously dominant afternoon newspaper, the *Washington Star*. Phil Graham also bought *Newsweek* magazine on the recommendation of Ben Bradlee, who was then working at the news magazine as a reporter. Graham and Bradlee had known each other since the time when Ben first worked at the *Post*, from 1949 to 1952, as a flashy young crime reporter on the city staff. Graham gave Bradlee a finder's fee of what eventually became millions of dollars in *Washington Post* stock, and Bradlee soon became *Newsweek*'s star Washington bureau chief.

After a tumultuous period of erratic behavior that disrupted his marriage and the newspaper's leadership, Phil Graham committed suicide on August 3, 1963. Katharine Graham, unexpectedly but determinedly, took control of the *Post* in order to keep it in the family. While she focused on the business side of the paper, she turned to Bradlee to energize what she thought was an underperforming newsroom, which had long been led by managing editor Alfred Friendly. The editor of the paper, J. Russell Wiggins, had concentrated on its liberal-leaning editorial page, which had been the most influential part of the *Post*. Mrs. Graham, as we always called her, invited Ben to an exploratory lunch at Washington's F Street Club, at which he famously told her, "If Al Friendly's job ever opened up, I'd give my left one for it."

Mrs. Graham brought Ben back to the *Post* in August 1965 as deputy managing editor. In November, he replaced a disappointed Friendly, who returned to writing before eventually retiring. In 1968, after Wiggins retired, Ben took the title of executive editor. At his suggestion, Mrs. Graham hired someone else to be the editor of the editorial page, reporting separately to her. Although she freely kibitzed from time to time, she gave Ben, as the executive editor, complete independence in decision making about news coverage, ensuring that his decisions would never be influenced by advertisers, other business considerations, or government power.

Ben was soon working long hours remaking the newsroom and changing the face of the newspaper. He hired well-known, talented journalists from other newspapers, and he encouraged them to produce enterprising stories and vivid writing. He also enabled younger reporters to pursue stories that landed on the front page. I ended up being one of them.

In 1971, when I was put on the city desk as an editor for a while, Don Graham briefly worked as a local news reporter in his first job at the newspaper. Don knew that his mother and grandfather wanted him to take over the *Post* someday. He had been the editor of the student newspaper at St. Albans School, a college preparatory school in Washington, D.C., and of the *Daily Crimson* at Harvard. He was just eighteen when his father committed suicide, something he and I have never discussed during the nearly half century we've known each other. I can only imagine the impact on Don of his father's illness and death.

After graduation from Harvard, Don served as an enlisted man in public information for the 1st Cavalry Division of the U.S. Army in Vietnam. When he returned home, he surprised his mother by becoming a Washington, D.C., Metropolitan Police officer for seventeen months in an inner-city neighborhood to learn about the community. Mrs. Graham then told Don that she wanted him to start learning about the *Post*. He began by rotating through every department, beginning with the newsroom. He eventually knew virtually everyone at the *Post* by name.

Although the city reporters were not assigned to specific editors at the time, Don noticed that many of them sought me out to discuss their assignments and edit their stories. Soon, he did, too. He covered the police and fire departments and wrote a series of stories about alcoholism and family violence, informed by what he had seen as a police officer. He and Carl Bernstein, another young city reporter at the time, braved tear gas to cover the disruptive 1971 May Day anti–Vietnam War protests in downtown Washington. Don, who was unpretentious, wanted no special treatment, and he didn't get any from me. I edited, and sometimes rewrote, his stories, just as I would with any other reporter.

Don worked at *Newsweek* during much of the Watergate investigation, while I was second in command of the *Post*'s local news staff. We were thrown together again when Ben asked Don in August 1974 to spend a year fixing the leadership of the newspaper's sports department, which Ben had been unable to do. I had just become the top editor of the local news staff, and Don and I found ourselves comparing notes about managing our staffs. When Don later became the *Post*'s general manager, focusing on its production and business departments, he continued to discuss my management of the local news staff with me. We were both detail-oriented, and we sometimes reviewed the performance of each reporter and editor on my staff. We found that we had similar values and instincts. I began to get the feeling that I was being groomed.

In 1979, Mrs. Graham promoted Don from general manager to publisher of the newspaper, while she remained the corporation's CEO. Don was told by some people that he should have his own editor of the *Post*, as his mother had. But he was in no hurry to replace Ben, even after the Janet Cooke scandal. In fact, as Ben recalled in his memoir, *A Good Life*, Don was by Ben's side at every painful public discussion of it.

As the years went by, Don assured Ben that he would not have to retire at sixty-five, as top editors at the *New York Times* were required to do. Eventually, the two of them agreed that Ben could continue until he was seventy, just so long as he had someone strong working with him, ready to take over. At the same time, Don and his mother were concerned that the newspaper, despite all that had been accomplished under Ben and Howard Simons, was too uneven in quality. The newsroom had suffered somewhat from hubris and complacency in the aftermath of Watergate and the movie *All the President's Men*. Ben was becoming bored, as he later acknowledged. The staff was somewhat adrift and plagued by rivalries. That made the selection of a new managing editor critical for the Grahams.

Even before Simons had decided to leave for Harvard, Don and Mrs. Graham were discussing with Ben who should replace Simons and eventually succeed Ben if it worked out. Shelby Coffey always came up because of his success as editor of Style and his relationship with Ben. Jim Hoagland had impressed Mrs. Graham when he traveled with her on foreign trips. Bob Woodward had been in the conversation until he took himself out of the running. When he was the editor in charge of local news, while I was in London, Woodward had edited and approved Janet Cooke's fabricated story to be published and to be nominated for the Pulitzer Prize. The scandal cast a pall across the newsroom.

Don also did something that he told nobody else at the time. He secretly asked eight or nine of the senior *Post* journalists he most respected who they thought should become managing editor and, if successful, succeed Ben. He told me many years later that "their unanimous advice" was that it should be me. "They all trusted you" with the newspaper, he said in an interview for this book.

Eventually, Don and Ben agreed that Don should make the decision about the next managing editor. Ben could offer the job to the person Don chose.

When I did not hear anything for several weeks, I tried to focus on my work and the demanding election campaign season. Finally, Ben invited me out to lunch. Without preamble, he asked if I wanted to be his managing editor. I immediately said yes.

Characteristically, Ben did not talk much about how we would work together, except that we should be completely open with each other. He added that, starting on my first day on the job, I should chair the twice-daily editors' meetings and decide which of the stories they offered would go on the front page—decisions that would shape my mission for the newspaper day by day. It was what Howard Simons had been doing. Just like that, Ben was giving me the keys to the car and putting me behind the wheel.

Shelby Coffey soon left the *Post* to become editor of *US News and World Report* magazine, and, later, the *Dallas Times-Herald* and the *Los Angeles Times* newspapers. Jim Hoagland became a Pulitzer Prize–winning foreign affairs columnist for the *Post*, based first in Paris and, later, in Washington. Bob Woodward stayed on the *Post*'s staff as an investigative reporter and editor while he wrote a series of best-selling books.

I may not have been the partner whom Ben would have chosen, but we worked together remarkably well right from the start. We interviewed job candidates and made hiring decisions together. He attended most of my daily story conferences, which he enlivened with humor and seeded with suggestions. I dropped into his office, which was across from mine along the newsroom's north wall, whenever I needed advice. At the same time, I increasingly assumed most of the responsibility for the direction and content of the newspaper and the management of the newsroom.

My straightforward, aggressive, hands-on style soon became familiar throughout the staff. Without ever saying it in so many words, Ben clearly trusted me with the newspaper.

Bob Kaiser, one of my closest colleagues, who was then the *Post*'s national news editor, marked the changing of the guard as taking place in the early evening of June 14, 1985, after I had been Ben's managing editor for less than a year. TWA Flight 847, with 147 passengers and crew, 85 of them Americans, had been hijacked by Lebanese terrorists after its takeoff from Athens and forced to land in Beirut. It was the beginning of a three-day drama of violence and hostage taking, a big breaking story in a year of several hijackings. I was directing multistory coverage involving the foreign, national, and financial news staffs when Ben, with his suit jacket on, came over to Bob and me while we were conferring about the front page. It was still hours before deadline. "You guys have this under control," he told us, and he left for home.

A few years later, *The Washingtonian* magazine published a long profile of me, describing how I was "quietly but firmly taking editorial control of the *Washington Post*." The article's headline, in big type on a left-hand page, across from a full-page photograph of me holding a copy of the *Post*, was: "He's Not Bradlee."

BEN STILL HAD THE FINAL SAY ON DIFFICULT DECISIONS WE HAD to make about stories involving national security.

From December 1985 to May 1986, Ben and I tried to decide whether to defy President Ronald Reagan and senior intelligence officials by publishing a story by Bob Woodward and *Post* reporter Patrick Tyler about an important espionage secret that had been sold to the Soviet Union. A low-level National Security Agency employee named Ronald Pelton had told the Soviets how the NSA and the U.S. Navy, in a covert operation called Ivy Bells, had intercepted Soviet military communications transmitted through undersea cables. Pelton had been arrested and charged with espionage, but what he gave to the Soviets in exchange for a $35,000 payment was not publicly revealed.

In repeated conversations with Ben and me, the NSA's director, Lieutenant General William Odom, argued strongly against publication of our story because, he insisted, it would reveal an important national security secret. A former senior Central Intelligence Agency official lectured us on unanticipated adverse reactions the Soviet Union might have to the story's revelations. Senior White House officials elliptically argued that the story would tell the Soviets what the United States knew about what the Soviets knew.

As weeks became months, Ben and I see-sawed about whether to publish the story. Sometimes, I worried about what we might unintentionally reveal to the Soviets. Sometimes, Ben wondered wearily what purpose there was in such stories about national security secrets. At other times, one or both of us were ready to go ahead—figuring we would not really be telling the Soviets anything they did not already know—only to be given new reasons to delay by administration officials. Along the way, we removed some details from the story in response to some of their specific concerns.

In May, at a meeting at the University Club around the corner from the *Post* building in downtown Washington, Central Intelligence Agency director William Casey melodramatically warned Ben and me that he would recommend that the Justice Department prosecute us and the newspaper if we published the story. In fact, he added, he had just come from Justice, where he had referred, for possible prosecution, CIA complaints about the *Post* and four other news media outlets for publishing other, unspecified classified information. Justice officials later told *Post* lawyer Edward Bennett Williams that they had turned Casey down.

In response to Casey's bullying, Ben decided to publish a story about the prosecution threats Casey made during our conversation. Casey had not asked, nor had we agreed, that our meeting would be off the record. But the story did not include anything about Ivy Bells.

Casey also had told us that he was going to call President Reagan. The president, in turn, telephoned Katharine Graham at her home a few days later. She told Reagan that the executive editor would be making the decision.

While Ben was still trying to decide—as Pelton's trial for espionage was beginning—NBC News reported a fraction of what we knew, including the code name Ivy Bells. Then we published what, by that time, had become a truncated story, followed by more details in later stories.

Our subsequent reporting showed that the NSA had been negligent in allowing Pelton, who had financial problems, access to such sensitive information. I figured that this was the embarrassing national security failure that the agency did not want revealed. I believed that Ben and I had been had. I would not allow it to happen again.

In January 1988, Don Graham delivered his usual state-of-the-newspaper assessment at an annual retreat of *Post* editors at a Dorado Beach resort in Puerto Rico. He said the newsroom was doing well under Ben and me, and he hoped we would be together for a while longer. When the time came for a change, he added, the newspaper would be in good hands with me as Ben's successor. It was a subtle announcement that exploded back in the newsroom and reverberated around the city. Despite much anticipation and occasional media stories about the possibility that I might succeed Ben, the reality of it was still something of a shock to everyone, because I was so unlike him.

More than three years would pass before Ben retired. But the newsroom's future and the important decisions about its journalism and role in American life were already in my hands. Was I really ready? I did not then realize how much what I experienced and learned in the previous two decades had prepared me for what awaited in leading the *Post*. After all, I had literally grown up, professionally and personally, in its newsroom.

2

Accidental Intern

𝕴 FIRST WALKED INTO THE NOISY OLD NEWSROOM of the *Washington Post* on the fifth floor of the newspaper's unimposing building in downtown Washington in June 1964. I felt like a stranger in a strange land. I was just twenty-two years old, and I looked younger and a bit gawky. I had been to the nation's capital only once before, while on a school trip seven years earlier. I had never set foot inside the newsroom of any professional newspaper. And, as I soon discovered, no one in the *Post* newsroom was expecting me.

I had been led to believe that I had an appointment with the *Post*'s deputy managing editor, Ben Gilbert. But when I reached his office, Gilbert, a gruff, bespectacled, gray-haired man, said he had never heard of me. I reminded him of an agreement that I was told he had made with George Kienzle, the director of The Ohio State University's School of Journalism. The idea, Kienzle had told me, was to research and propose an OSU–*Washington Post* graduate journalism experience in Washington. To do it, I would be paid by the *Post* to spend the summer after my graduation closely observing the newsroom and its journalists. Gilbert said he recalled having dinner with Kienzle some months earlier, but he had gotten so drunk he didn't remember anything they'd discussed. There was nothing he could do for me.

I panicked. I told Gilbert, truthfully, that I had just settled my wife and our three-year-old son into a suburban apartment for the summer, and I had no income.

After thinking for a moment, Gilbert told me that the *Post*'s paid intern program for college students was about to start its second summer. The interns had already been chosen, he said, but the city news staff might be able to use another helping hand during the vacation season. I would have to convince the city editor, Dick Molloy, and one of his assistant editors, Steve Isaacs, that I could handle the work. Molloy seemed agreeable enough, if not overly enthusiastic, when he interviewed me about my professional experience, which included work as a writer and editor for Ohio State's alumni magazine and a summer internship in the public relations department of an insurance company.

Isaacs was more interested. A big man with a football lineman's body and a pugnacious manner, he was only twenty-six himself, the precocious Harvard-educated son of a prominent Louisville, Kentucky, newspaper editor. Isaacs was intrigued by my modest Midwestern background and my many years of student journalism in public schools and Ohio State. I was quite unlike the mostly privileged young people from elite Eastern private schools and colleges who had been selected to be *Post* interns that summer. I was relieved when Isaacs and Molloy convinced Gilbert that I should join the seven others when they arrived.

Most of the interns turned out to be the offspring of acquaintances of Gilbert and of *Post* managing editor Alfred Friendly, himself an Amherst alum with a tendency to hire graduates of Ivy League and other elite Eastern colleges. In fact, one of the interns, Robert Goldberg, was an Amherst graduate and the son of U.S. Supreme Court Justice Arthur Goldberg. Another, Harvard senior Michael Lerner, was the son of the noted scholar and writer Max Lerner. Leslie Cheek III was a graduate of both Harvard and the Columbia University Graduate School of Journalism. Yale graduate Robert Kaiser was the son of diplomat Philip Kaiser, the Deputy Chief of Mission in the American Embassy in London. In addition, Kaiser was returning to the newsroom after a *Post* internship the previous summer, which he had gotten through a family connection and his work on the *Yale Daily News*.

I had not come to Washington expecting that my first real job at a newspaper would be at the *Post*. This was just supposed to be a research assignment. I was planning to return to The Ohio State University's School of Journalism to get a master's degree. I did not anticipate what kind of stepping-stone to the future my accidental internship might be.

On the morning the other interns were expected to begin work, I was seated early at my assigned desk, near the long line of gray metal desks that formed the city desk. A young man in an old man's dark, pin-striped suit burst into the newsroom, slid onto the city desk in front of assistant city editor Roy Aarons, and announced: "Hi, Roy. I'm back." It turned out to be Bob Kaiser. He appeared to be very much at home.

Isaacs shrewdly sized up the situation. He calculated that Kaiser and I, because of our experience and eagerness, were the most likely interns to produce useful journalism for the *Post* that summer. He also guessed that we could be natural rivals because of our contrasting pedigrees—Kaiser's brash self-confidence and my low-key determination. Isaacs created a competition between us to determine who would have the most bylined stories in the *Post* by summer's end. We tied, with thirteen stories each. My very first story, about local bank workers hoarding commemorative John F. Kennedy half dollars to sell on the side to coin dealers, appeared at the top of the *Post*'s front page on June 26. It was my first investigative story for the newspaper.

The scruffy *Post* newsroom of that time was crowded with dirty gray desks cluttered with piles of paper, clunky black rotary phones, and manual typewriters. The air was smoky, and not all the cigarette butts made it into ashtrays. By day, the newsroom was bustling with work that seemed to me to be very important, accompanied by shouted orders from editors, ringing telephones, clacking typewriters, and calls of "copy" or "boy," summoning young copy boys, as they all were called then, to carry typed pages of stories in progress from reporters to their editors. There was a surprising amount of socializing and laughter before the pressure of deadlines arrived in the late afternoon and early evening. I found that it was not that much different from the atmosphere, on a much smaller scale, of the *Lantern* newsroom at Ohio State.

At night, the *Post* newsroom was populated by characters out of *The Front Page*. The night copy editors, who gave stories their final edits and headlines on deadline, imbibed from liquor bottles kept in their desk drawers. The curmudgeonly night city editor, Bill Brady, was a master of intimidating sarcasm when pointing out holes in stories. When he first called me "Ace" while editing a story of mine that survived his scrutiny, I felt complimented, until I heard him calling everyone Ace.

Harry Gabbett, a small, wiry man who was a witty artist with words, worked night rewrite, meaning he wrote stories based on information phoned in to him by reporters covering crimes, fires, and other breaking news out on the streets. Whenever I was assigned to call Gabbett with what I found at the scene of a crime or a fire, I was always afraid he would ask a question about a significant fact that I could not answer. Gabbett's most famous lead paragraph of a news story he wrote in the *Post* has been widely republished: "Paul (Race Horse) Mitchell, 57, of one address right after another, died on the street here yesterday—unexpectedly and after a long illness, but mostly from two bullet wounds."

Finished stories were sent through pneumatic tubes scattered throughout the newsroom to the print shop on the floor below, where they were set in hot metal type on ancient linotype machines. Through a series of processes, pages of type and artwork were cast into curved metal plates that were put onto the huge printing presses in the bottom of the building. When the presses started up to print the first pages of the *Post*'s earliest edition at about 10:30 each evening, the whole building shook. Feeling those tremors when working late in the newsroom was a thrill of which I never tired. Many years later, the old presses were replaced by modern successors in two new *Post* printing plants in the Washington suburbs. I missed them.

Despite our rivalry that summer, Bob Kaiser helped me become comfortable in the sometimes intimidating newsroom, where he already had that previous summer's experience under his belt. We enjoyed outperforming the other interns as we got to know each other in what would turn out to be the beginning of a lifelong journalistic relationship and personal friendship. Although he was almost a year younger than me,

Bob would become the big brother that I never had, as I was the oldest of four brothers. I was not surprised when Al Friendly offered Kaiser work as a part-time correspondent in the *Post*'s London bureau while he pursued a master's degree at the London School of Economics.

I didn't know what to expect when Friendly called me into his office at the end of the summer. Although he was in charge of the newsroom under editor J. Russell Wiggins, Friendly was a distant figure, with his office and conference room hidden behind a wall at the front of the newsroom. I couldn't have imagined that he would unknowingly determine the course of my life when he asked me if I wanted to work full-time as a reporter at the *Post*.

IT IS A TWENTIETH-CENTURY AMERICAN STORY. MY PARENTS, Leonard and Pearl Downie, were strong-willed, self-sufficient offspring of immigrants who had come to the United States just after the turn of the century.

My mother's father, Stephan Evenheimer, emigrated from Hungary. He worked in a steel mill in Cleveland, Ohio, before dying of cancer at age fifty-two when I was just three years old. My maternal grandmother, born Matilda Simader, was brought by her parents to the United States from Germany. Pearl was the oldest of their four daughters and one son, and she shared in the responsibilities of caring for her younger siblings. When she could, she spent much of her time by herself, reading.

My father's father, David Downie, grew up in Manchester, England. He ran away from home when he was seventeen and wound up fighting on the British side in the Boer War in South Africa. When he returned to Manchester, he married Margaret Ann Broome, an orphan raised by her aunt, whom he had known as a teenager. They came to the United States via Canada and settled in Cleveland, where my grandfather worked in an automobile factory. My father was their middle child, with an older brother and a younger sister.

Although he never learned to read music, Dad had a natural talent for singing and playing musical instruments, which he did all his life as a hobby. He also loved writing. He wrote news and sports stories and editorials for his high school newspaper, and poems that were published in

Cleveland's morning newspaper, the *Plain Dealer*. He met Pearl when she was doing his makeup for a high school musical. They fit together from the beginning. Dad was handsome, outgoing, and popular in school. Mom was softly beautiful and shy. During the Depression, they both worked, Mom in a drapery shop and Dad in a variety of jobs, including movie usher, roller skate messenger, and factory worker. They married when they finally could afford to, in 1940.

When World War II began, my father enlisted in the U.S. Army Air Force while my mother was pregnant with me. Sometime after I was born—on May 1, 1942—he reported to the Aviation Cadet Center at Adams Field in Little Rock, Arkansas. That left my mother with a newborn in Cleveland, supported by my father's military pay. Dad washed out of pilot training due to motion sickness. He wound up serving out the war at Adams Field as a leader and mentor to the young pilots who were trained there. He rose to second in command of the war-depleted 581st Army Air Force Unit as a sergeant. He edited the base newspaper, ghost-writing the base commander's column. After his discharge from active service, Dad served four years in the Air Force Reserve in Cleveland.

Mom and Dad had three more sons, my younger brothers Jerome, Brian, and Mark. Our parents taught us, by word and by example, the values of honesty, hard work, frugality, fairness, and modesty. We were active churchgoers. My father taught Sunday school, and I and my brothers were confirmed in the Evangelical and Reformed Church, which later merged into the United Church of Christ. I participated in church youth groups, and I even became a citywide Christian youth leader as a teenager. I remember it being more about my ego and the heady experience of leadership than my faith. After I left our family home, I drifted away from religion.

Dad first sold milk door-to-door after the war, then began delivering baked goods wholesale to food stores. Later, he sold flavoring ingredients to ice cream companies, eventually becoming well known in that industry. He was a natural salesman and enjoyed his work and meeting people. He was much more gregarious than I ever would be. He moonlighted for extra money as a bartender and waiter at glittering parties and banquets for Cleveland's leading catering company. He never complained about the long hours, although he was often exhausted at home. He would never know what might have been had he been able to go to college and try his hand at journalism.

Mom ruled the household and tightly managed the family budget. She insisted that I and my brothers change our own bed linens, keep our shared rooms clean, and take turns doing other household chores. Dad and Mom bought, fixed up, and moved us from one inexpensive old house to another in working-class neighborhoods on Cleveland's West Side. They did their own repairs, painting, and wallpapering. My dad also bought and repaired used cars for the family's use.

As far back as I can remember, I was a very independent child and something of a loner. I had few friends in my neighborhood or at school, but it never seemed to bother me. My first memory of an interest in journalism was when I tapped out a brief account of trivial family happenings on a toy typewriter almost as soon as I could read. After being given a reading and writing test in elementary school, I was put into a Cleveland Public Schools program for gifted children called Major Work. I spent the fifth and sixth grades with other Major Work students at Landon Elementary School in a single open classroom with its own well-stocked corner library. When our assignments were completed, we were free to read anything we wanted. We also wrote and presented to the rest of the class modest research projects on subjects of our choosing. Mine included a prize-winning, sixth-grade report about the St. Lawrence Seaway, which connected the Great Lakes to the Atlantic Ocean.

Most important for me, our English teacher started a little elementary school newspaper. I was one of the writers in the fifth grade and the editor-in-chief in the sixth grade. The first three-page, mimeographed issue of *The Landon Life*, published on January 19, 1953, contained my first article, about what it was like for the students in the rest of school to change rooms each semester. I still have a dog-eared copy. I was hooked on journalism at the age of eleven.

As a teenager, I was a newspaper carrier in my neighborhood, delivering a now-defunct afternoon newspaper, the *Cleveland Press*, then Ohio's largest-circulation daily. It was my first paying job, and it made me feel connected to newspapering. I read both the *Press* and the *Plain Dealer* every day and studied the history of the *Press* and the Scripps Howard chain that owned it. Dad took me one evening to an event where the well-known crusading editor of the *Cleveland Press*, Louis B. Seltzer, spoke about his memoir and the watchdog role of the press in a way that I found inspiring.

In my early teens, my mother gave me permission to take public transit downtown to the main Cleveland Public Library. The librarians allowed me to wander the stacks, where I could pull and read books that interested me. I remember particularly enjoying the writing of humorists James Thurber, an Ohioan, and Robert Benchley. I occasionally went to the nearby, cavernous Cleveland stadium and paid a dollar or two to sit in the bleachers and watch the Indians play baseball and the Browns play football, at a time when both teams were among the best in their sports. I looked older than I was, reaching my full height of nearly six feet before I was twelve years old.

I became a top student at Wilbur Wright Junior High School, but I was too clumsy to play sports, too gawky to attract girls, and too square to be socially popular. Instead, I excelled at journalism. In a pattern I would follow in high school and college, I worked on the junior high newspaper, the *Sky-Wrighter*. I first covered school sports and then edited the biweekly newspaper in the ninth grade. One of my fellow student journalists, and predecessor as editor of the *Sky-Wrighter*, was Donna Shalala. She went on to run cabinet departments in the Carter and Clinton administrations and became chancellor of the University of Wisconsin-Madison, president of the University of Miami, and a member of Congress from Florida. Like Donna, I seemed to take naturally to leadership, although I did not have her outgoing personality.

At John Marshall High School, I was even more preoccupied with its weekly student newspaper, the *Interpreter*. Again, I started by covering sports and finished by editing the newspaper in my senior year. Academically, I enjoyed and excelled at English, social studies, and math. Although I got on with students in my classes, I was still socially awkward. I was largely ignored outside class by the cliques of popular students who ate lunch at the same tables in the cafeteria and got together after school.

Yet still drawn to leadership, I ran for class president nearly every semester. I usually lost to the same person, a boy who was prominent in the school's most desirable clique. When I ran against him yet again in the final semester of our senior year, I unexpectedly won in the secret ballot election on a Friday. I guessed it was because the other 411 seniors knew that the class president would be given considerable responsibility for graduation activities, and they thought that I was less likely than my opponent to play favorites.

The losing candidate, now no longer class president when he most wanted to be, was so unhappy that he got into an angry argument with his steady girlfriend, Barbara "Bonnie" Lindsey, one of the most popular girls in our class. "I guess you'll want to go to the dance with Len Downie now," he told her. And she decided to do just that, asking me to be her date at the next night's big dance. Something improbable clicked between us, and we were inseparable throughout the rest of our senior year.

My parents and I were determined that I would go to college, even though they couldn't afford it. Fortunately, with good grades and better test scores, I became a National Merit scholar and was accepted to the several colleges to which I applied, including Princeton and Ohio State. Rice University offered me a full scholarship to major in mathematics. Had I accepted, it would have been a disaster once I had encountered college calculus. Instead, I applied for an Ed Bang scholarship to study journalism at Ohio State. It was awarded to one Cleveland high school journalist each year by the city's Board of Education from a fund honoring a beloved Cleveland sportswriter. A panel of local journalists selected me for the scholarship, which would cover part of the cost of attending Ohio State.

Then came the first big turning point in my life. During the summer after our high school graduation, Bonnie discovered she was pregnant. After much agonizing and discussions with our shocked and angry parents, we decided to marry and go to Ohio State together. Bonnie had to abandon her plans to attend a small, prestigious liberal arts college, Ohio Wesleyan, in the first of several sacrifices she would make for me and my drive to be a journalist.

OUR FIRST SON, DAVID, WAS BORN ON MARCH 1, 1961, IN THE Ohio State University Hospital. With financial assistance from Bonnie's parents, our new family of three lived in a university townhouse complex for married couples, located just across the Olentangy River from the main Ohio State campus. I began working weekends at the Columbus, Ohio, plant of American Bakeries, Dad's employer in Cleveland. I pulled loaves of bread out of hot ovens and packages of hot dog and hamburger buns off conveyor belts. My coworkers mockingly called me "the college boy." My mother assured me that it was character building.

At school, when I was not in class, I was in the newsroom of the *Lantern*, the daily student newspaper published by Ohio State's School of Journalism. It provided an essentially professional experience for its student reporters and editors. The advertising-supported paper was published five mornings a week, with a 1 a.m. press start, for a free circulation of 30,000 on the huge Ohio State campus. In addition to university news, it covered city and state stories affecting the university community, plus national and foreign news from wire services.

Once again, I started with sports, covering Ohio State's then national champion football and basketball teams, as well as writing a sports column. As a freshman and sophomore, I traveled with the teams to away games and worked alongside professional sports writers in Big Ten schools' stadium and arena press boxes. I interviewed major college coaches and star athletes in their locker rooms after games. It was a heady experience that deepened my attraction to journalism.

In November 1961, Coach Woody Hayes's undefeated football team was voted national champion in news media polls after it won the Big Ten championship, making it eligible to play in the Rose Bowl on New Year's Day. However, after two hours of sometimes tense debate that I witnessed, the university's faculty council voted 28–25 not to allow the university to accept the bowl invitation. The opponents of the bowl bid argued that it was an opportunity to keep football from becoming too important at Ohio State. It was the first and only time the university turned down the opportunity to send its football team to a bowl game.

That evening, thousands of students reacted by taking over High Street, the main thoroughfare connecting the university to downtown Columbus. Blocking traffic for hours, they noisily marched to the state capitol and back. They were joined along the way by townspeople, and shepherded, it appeared, by sympathetic local police.

I wrote all three stories that filled the front page of the *Lantern* the next morning: the top story about the faculty council vote, a sidebar about the council's debate, and a news story about the student demonstration. Around that time, other universities were beginning to have debates and demonstrations about free speech. At Ohio State, it was about football. I researched and wrote an honors thesis about the finances of Ohio State football and the university athletics program that it dominated. Woody Hayes granted me an interview, and he turned out to be more cooperative and less overbearing than I had experienced during his antagonistic post-game press conferences.

In April 1962, Ohio State had its first free speech controversy, which presented me with a challenge. I was editorial page editor of the *Lantern* at the time. As it happened, I was nearly alone in the *Lantern* newsroom when word came that the university president had locked out a speaker scheduled to appear on campus that evening. Phillip Abbott Luce, then a leftist activist, had been invited by a faculty member and a student group he advised to speak about Luce's opposition to the House Un-American Activities Committee (HUAC) and its crusades against Communist subversion in the country, a 1960s holdover from the McCarthy era.

Ohio State president Novice G. Fawcett, citing a restrictive speakers rule adopted by the university's board of trustees during the Red scares in the early 1950s, cancelled Luce's appearance. He ordered that the law school auditorium be locked an hour before the scheduled speech. Several hundred students soon congregated outside the auditorium. The professor who had invited Luce told the students they could instead listen to Luce at an off-campus house nearby. While I was there watching Luce speak to students gathered outside the house, some of them were stopped and questioned by the campus police chief, who showed up with some plainclothes officers. When I tried to interview the officers, I was pushed away.

I hurried back to the *Lantern* newsroom to write a front-page story about all of this for the next morning's edition. The next day, in a decision I only later realized was wrong, I sat down at my editorial page editor's desk and wrote a strongly worded editorial condemning what Fawcett had done as "a severe blow to academic freedom at Ohio State." Over two days, I had written both the front-page news story and the lead editorial about the same event! As it happened, there were no student demonstrations and only muted faculty protests, although the speakers rule was quietly rescinded four years later. (1966?)

In time, I came to understand and strongly believe in a strict separation between news reporting and editorial opinion, as practiced by the *Washington Post* and many, but not all, other newspapers. For decades to come, I would use my youthful mistake as an object lesson about ethics for the journalists I later led at the *Washington Post* and the students I taught after retiring from the newspaper.

In the first semester of my junior year, I worked as managing editor of the *Lantern*, directing much of its journalism and often overseeing the start of our old printing press at 1 in the morning. This was usually followed by beer and burgers with the remaining staff members at a nearby pub. It meant not spending much time with Bonnie and David during the week, which I tried to make up on weekends.

There also was the pressure of staying afloat financially, despite assistance from Bonnie's parents. No one in the *Lantern* newsroom was paid because it was technically a laboratory of the School of Journalism. I won additional scholarships, and I worked the summer between my sophomore and junior years as a paid intern writer for the public relations department in the Columbus headquarters of Nationwide Insurance. In January 1963, I was given the opportunity to work around my class schedule for the next eighteen months as the salaried assistant editor of the *Ohio State Monthly* alumni magazine. I wrote and edited articles, took and developed photographs, designed pages, and helped to oversee the magazine's production at a printing plant an hour's drive from Columbus. Again, my days away from home were long, but the job provided a measure of financial security for our family until I graduated in June 1964.

When I was hired by the *Post* at the end of my summer internship, the editors agreed that I could initially work as a beginning reporter while researching and writing a thesis to earn a master's degree from Ohio State, a goal that journalism school director George Kienzle had set for me. I would then go back to the Ohio State campus to take required courses and get my degree before returning to the *Post*. I wrote obituaries and did night reporting and story rewriting shifts at the newspaper. I completed my master's thesis about what was then a relatively new phenomenon: swarming hordes of reporters and radio and television technicians covering major news stories, especially political conventions and election campaign events. My research included my first political trip with the national press corps covering President Lyndon Johnson's reelection campaign in the boroughs of New York in the autumn of 1964.

Our second son, Scott, was born on June 8, 1965, in Cleveland, where Bonnie was staying with her parents while I finished my coursework at Ohio State. I went there for his birth and returned briefly to Columbus to receive my master's degree. Sadly, George Kienzle, the first of several significant mentors for me, had died of cancer in March.

Our family of four then moved back to Washington as I returned to the *Post* as a local news reporter with a starting salary of $105 a week. My father helped me find and buy a surprisingly inexpensive new house in a sprawling new suburban community in Bowie, Maryland, built by William Levitt—the latest of his affordable Levittown postwar planned communities in New York, New Jersey, Pennsylvania, and Maryland. It was a little more than a half hour's commute from downtown Washington, but it turned out to be a world away from what my life would become at the *Washington Post*.

3

Muckraker

WHEN I RETURNED TO THE *POST* NEWSROOM in the summer of 1965, investigative reporting had begun reappearing in American newspapers after decades of dormancy. It was reporting that went beyond daily news events to dig deeper into wrongdoing and societal problems. It held powerful people and institutions accountable. I knew what it was, but I had not expected to be learning how to do it relatively soon—just as I had not expected just a year earlier to be working at the *Post* at all.

For a while after my return, my week was divided between working in the newsroom on two weekdays, reporting from police headquarters on two weeknights, and covering criminal arraignments in Washington's D.C. Court of General Sessions on Saturdays. I was only vaguely aware of Ben Bradlee's recent takeover of the newsroom.

At police headquarters, I sat at the battered metal desk of the legendary Alfred E. Lewis, who had already covered the police for thirty of the fifty years he would spend on the beat for the *Post*. A small man with a self-deprecating manner, he usually wore a regulation blue police sweater and conversed with officers in their language. He was persistent in his pursuit of crime news, and perhaps overly friendly in his relationships with the police sources he depended on for stories. On June 17, 1972, Al would be the only reporter allowed by the police to go with them inside the Democratic National Headquarters in the Watergate Office Building as they investigated an unusual burglary there.

Al was known by everyone at the *Post* as "Uncle Al" for his mentoring of young reporters, like me, who passed through the night police beat. He was among the last of the newspaper "leg men" who gathered information on their beats and out in the streets but never wrote stories. Instead, Al telephoned the information he gathered to a rewrite man in the newsroom, who, on some occasions during my day shifts, was me. So many different rewrite men, including Harry Gabbett, ghostwrote stories under Al's byline that he once won a local Washington Newspaper Guild writing award for the richness and variety of the stories' writing styles.

I briefly overlapped with Al when I arrived at the press room at police headquarters each evening, so he could fill me in. After he left, I pulled out a typewriter bolted into a compartment inside his desk to write my stories. Whenever I forgot to put the typewriter back in the desk, I caught hell from Al. He thought that, by leaving it out for him to find when he got to work the next day, I was mocking the fact that he did not write his own stories.

I learned about my relatively new city from the police radio chatter, written crime reports, and occasional forays to the scenes of crimes and fires. I also learned how to extract information from police officers uninterested in and sometimes hostile to talking to a reporter they didn't know. In the Saturday arraignment court, I had to overcome my natural shyness to ask questions of prosecutors and lawyers whom I had never met before. I had started feeling at home in the *Post* newsroom, but I still felt like an outsider in police headquarters and the courthouse. Yet what I learned in those months would soon prove useful.

Among the police, court, and other stories that I pursued, often on my own initiative without assignment, was the suicide of a sixty-two-year-old U.S. Patent Office examiner in a police precinct cell, where he was being held for public intoxication. From my night police post, I also found and reported that numerous people had died, suffered injuries, or fallen seriously ill while jailed for public drunkenness in police and court lockups around Washington. I was beginning to do investigative reporting.

Steve Isaacs, now the city editor, took a particular interest in me and my work. He fancied himself a mentor for some of the newer city news staff reporters who were only a few years younger than he was. He occasionally took me to lunch at the hotel next door to the *Post*, where he always began the meal with two martinis. I did not join him in the drinking. Nevertheless he enjoyed entertaining me with juicy newsroom gossip, in a tone laced with self-importance and impatient ambition.

I was surprised when Isaacs told me that my work had attracted the attention of Ben Bradlee, who had covered police, crime, and the local court while he was a young *Post* reporter. He and Isaacs, who also had briefly covered the court, knew that the D.C. Court of General Sessions was dysfunctional in ways that had never been reported by the newspaper. And Ben Gilbert, by then deputy managing editor, knew from his local government contacts that President Lyndon Johnson's administration was eager to reform the plantation-like federal rule of the District of Columbia, including its courts.

Apparently at Ben's suggestion, Isaacs and Gilbert sent me to the Court of General Sessions to look around and determine what I might write about it. The *Post*'s beat reporter continued to cover trials and other daily news there.

I was a young-looking twenty-three-year-old in a cheap suit wandering the teeming hallways and courtrooms of the overcrowded old criminal court building. Mostly unnoticed, I occasionally ducked into stairwells to take notes. My outsider mien suited me well for this kind of reporting. And it still was costing the *Post* only my $105 weekly salary.

I found a Dickensian scene in the court's corridors. I saw whiskey, carried in coat pockets and lawyers' briefcases, being consumed in public, and empty bottles discarded in hallways and bathrooms. I watched money changing hands as shabbily dressed defense lawyers demanded payment in advance from criminal defendants assigned to them by the court, with bail bondsmen soliciting fees from relatives and lawyers of defendants seeking freedom on bail. I saw defense lawyers mingling with police officers and complaining witnesses, bargaining over cases outside the courtrooms. When I eventually began interviewing prosecutors, defense lawyers, and judges, I found that some of the lawyers, when paid enough by defendants, then went from courtroom to courtroom seeking judges who would reward their clients with the most lenient sentence if they pleaded guilty to reduced charges.

In the courtrooms, I noticed that few trials were being held. Most criminal misdemeanor cases were resolved in a few minutes with guilty pleas, or with charges dropped altogether. More serious felony cases were sent by prosecutors to the federal courthouse a few blocks away. Negotiations among prosecutors and lawyers went on noisily in courtrooms as other cases were being heard. Judges hurried everyone along to clear a court calendar overloaded with too many cases for too few judges who worked too few hours.

Some of the judges, all of whom were federal political appointees, appeared less competent to hold court than I would have been. In one criminal courtroom, I watched the veteran clerk do most of the work, day after day, rushing cases to pleas while the judge, sometimes visibly intoxicated, looked on. Another judge, the son of a liquor distributor who was a big contributor to the Democratic Party, was confined to traffic court because of his erratic behavior on the bench.

One judge demanded that I identify myself as I sat in his courtroom taking notes, but he refused to be interviewed afterward. Some of the judges who did talk to me defended the status quo. But two relatively new judges, Charles W. Halleck, son of a prominent Republican congressman, and Harold H. Greene, a former Justice Department lawyer, told me they found the court disturbingly dysfunctional.

Although they did not want to be quoted, they helped me better understand the court's problems and told me about alternatives they were trying. They refused to give criminal cases to lawyers they found to be unscrupulous. They turned down guilty pleas that appeared to be unjust and rebuked lawyers for giving their defendants bad advice. They worked late into evenings to hear more cases and hold more trials, making themselves unpopular among other judges, court clerks, marshals, and bailiffs.

I learned for the first time in my reporting relationships with them how to make and manage confidential sources.

Greene, a diminutive, cerebral, soft-spoken man who had written much of the Johnson administration's civil rights legislation while he was at the Justice Department, was particularly helpful. What I didn't know was that Greene was probably providing similar guidance to a young researcher named Harry Subin, who was secretly studying the court for the Justice Department. Subin was hidden away in a small office where I never noticed him.

I kept Isaacs and Gilbert apprised of my progress, and they allowed me more time to painstakingly compile statistics to support my reporting. In that long ago age before computerized records, I spent many weeks of long days in the court clerk's office going through a year's criminal case files, page by page, counting by hand how few had gone to trial and discovering what happened to those that didn't. I found which judges were sought out by lawyers and defendants for the most lenient sentences. As significant patterns emerged from my primitive data gathering, I realized that I was fascinated by what others might find tedious. I learned the value of laboriously going through records for investigative reporting. Later, in the digital age, it would be called database reporting and become a staple of investigative journalism.

When I felt I was ready, and Isaacs and Gilbert agreed, I organized and wrote a seven-day series of front-page stories about the court, which was published in early February 1966. With headlines that included "Justice Found Rarely in Hullabaloo Marking Court of General Sessions" and "Justice Is Speedy Here, But Is It Justice" and "D.C. Defendants Can Pick Their Judges," the stories made vividly clear how dysfunctional the court was.

Some General Sessions judges and lawyers were so angry about my stories that they complained to the *Post* and prodded the local bar association to investigate me and my sources at the court—none of which came to anything. Instead, a *Post* editorial characterized my articles as an "indictment" of the Court of General Sessions and called for reforms. U.S. Attorney General Nicholas deB. Katzenbach granted me an interview to say that there should be a wholesale overhaul of the city's federally run court system, which produced another front-page story. That made me feel that my work was important.

Then an extraordinary thing happened. Deputy Attorney General Ramsay Clark invited himself to an off-the-record lunch with Ben Gilbert and me in an executive dining room at the *Post*. He told us that the Johnson administration had decided to abolish the Court of General Sessions and ask Congress to replace it with a new Washington, D.C., court in a new building with new leadership and new judges chosen on merit. He then asked me if Harold Greene should be its chief judge.

I was taken completely by surprise. By now, I understood the ethical separation between reporting and expressing opinions. I hesitantly told Clark how much Judge Greene had helped me, mostly without being identified in the stories. But I added that it was not my place as a journalist to advise the Justice Department one way or the other about whether Greene should lead a reformed court. In my mind I was thinking, *I'm not even twenty-four years old, for heaven's sake.*

Before the year was out, the Johnson administration replaced some of the judges on the Court of General Sessions and appointed Harold Greene as its chief judge. He began making changes that significantly improved the court. In 1970, Congress would replace the Court of General Sessions with the present-day D.C. Superior Court in a new building, with Greene as its first chief judge.

Seeing the impact of the court series, Steve Isaacs decided to let me set my own agenda as a full-time investigative reporter, the only one on the *Post's* local news staff, so long as I produced more front-page stories.

I persuaded city officials to let me go inside the badly overcrowded D.C. Jail and write about what I saw and what the prisoners told me about troubling conditions there. When I went back six months later, the number of prisoners had been reduced by a third, bunk beds had been removed from the sleeping dormitories, visiting and mail privileges had been expanded, a new recreation yard had been created, and new procedures had been put in place to reduce sexual assaults. Reforms also followed my subsequent investigations of the city's lengthy pretrial jailing of criminal defendants who could not afford bail, the city's abysmal detention facilities for youth offenders, and the poor performance of the D.C. Parole Board.

I was learning how to do investigative reporting largely by doing it on my own at what felt like warp speed. I was going inside places I had never imagined entering and talking to people I had not expected to meet. I was reporting and writing stories that were making a difference. I was attracting attention from important people. Senator Joseph Tydings of Maryland and his staff, for example, were in regular touch with me as they used my stories' revelations as the basis for congressional hearings and legislative proposals for reforms of federally supervised District of Columbia legal institutions.

The *Post* had nominated my court series for the 1967 Pulitzer Prize in each of two categories, local reporting and investigative reporting. I did not receive the prize in either one, even though, I was told afterward, I had been selected as one of the three finalists in each of the categories. Rather than being too disappointed, I felt validated. I had discovered the power of investigative reporting that made a difference. I had found my calling.

I WAS THE YOUNGEST OF A RELATIVELY SMALL NUMBER OF INVEStigative reporters at ambitious local newspapers scattered around the country in the 1960s. We were the vanguard of a long-overdue revival of the muckraking in magazines, books, and a few newspapers that had helped bring about significant change in the United States.

From roughly 1902 to 1912, investigative journalists such as Lincoln Steffens, Upton Sinclair, Ida Tarbell, and David Graham Phillips exposed turn-of-the-century corruption in national and local governments and in private businesses, including the monopolistic and largely unregulated oil, railroad, banking, insurance, and food-processing industries. They helped create the political climate for President Theodore Roosevelt's trust busting, the congressional passage of the Pure Food and Drug Act, and the ratification of the Seventeenth Amendment to the Constitution, which authorized popular election of the U.S. Senate. When their reporting revealed corruption by Roosevelt's political allies, he tried (unsuccessfully) to curb them in a 1906 speech comparing "these reckless journalists" to the Man with the Muckrake always focused on "the filth on the floor" in John Bunyan's *Pilgrim's Progress*. Instead, they proudly became known as "muckrakers."

Investigative journalism largely faded away during the two world wars, the Great Depression, the Korean War, and amidst the suppression of dissent during the McCarthy era. Except for a few journalistic rebels and syndicated columnists, most reporters and their news organizations devoted themselves to so-called objective coverage of events and official pronouncements. More skeptical reporting gradually revived with the demise of McCarthy's red-baiting and the upheaval of the civil rights, counterculture, and anti–Vietnam War movements. Reporters in such cities as Miami, Philadelphia, Indianapolis, Chicago, and Houston had begun investigating wrongdoing in local law enforcement, the courts, and other local agencies, just as I was doing in Washington.

I won an award for the court series from the Federal Bar Association, which is composed of lawyers and judges working in the federal courts and government. Ben accompanied me to the award luncheon. As we walked through downtown Washington, I had my first real conversation with him. He seemed pleased with the court series and its impact and recognition, although lukewarm about some of my other stories that, in his words, "opened up cans of worms." Ben had not had much experience with investigative reporting at that point, and he did not seem very interested in it. His priority was strengthening the *Post*'s national news performance and raising its profile, with his eye on competing someday with the *New York Times*.

However, as I later learned, it was Ben Bradlee's style to let the people in the newsroom whom he liked most take charge of the things he was less interested in. He expected them to work hard to please him. That left plenty of room for the headstrong Steve Isaacs, who had become metropolitan news editor, to chart his own course. Steve aggressively expanded coverage of the city and suburbs and fought for the importance of that coverage in the newspaper and the newsroom. In turn, Isaacs encouraged initiative by the young, mostly male reporters he thought were the best on his staff, including me.

As my investigative reporting gained recognition, I became accepted by other "Isaacs's Boys" who sat at desks around mine. It was then that, as the only state university graduate in the group, I was christened "Land Grant Len" by Dan Morgan, a plummy-voiced Harvard graduate who had been hired in 1963 and would be sent to West Germany as a foreign correspondent in 1968.

For a while, Bob Kaiser, my friendly rival from our summer internship, sat at the desk next to mine after he came back from London in 1967, and before he was sent to Saigon to report on the Vietnam War in 1969. Bob mixed more easily with the newsroom's old-timers. He helped me to navigate the distance I was covering so quickly in my work life. What sometimes came across to others as elitist arrogance on Bob's part felt to me more like reassuring guidance from someone more worldly than I was.

Nearby was Carl Bernstein, who had started at the *Washington Star* as a copy boy at the age of sixteen and began writing stories while he was still a teenager. When the *Star* did not hire him as a full-time reporter, because he had dropped out of the University of Maryland, he briefly became a star reporter at the Elizabeth, New Jersey, *Journal* before the *Post* hired him in 1966. Bernstein was our group's connection to the counterculture of the 1960s, which, at first, I experienced only vicariously.

While each of the other Isaacs's boys had beat assignments covering the city government, Isaacs also let them follow leads into investigative stories. Bernstein and Kaiser worked together to expose a notorious slum landlord, which led to his becoming a test case of the city's housing inspection system. We enjoyed our work and camaraderie, even as we heard that we appeared somewhat self-important to newsroom veterans.

Outside of work, we didn't see that much of one another. The others, childless twentysomethings (some single, some married), lived in the city, whereas I went home to my wife, Bonnie, and our two young sons in Bowie. Some of them, including Steve Isaacs, and their wives ventured out to visit us there. These visits were Bonnie's primary connection with the world in which I worked and spent so much time.

IN 1967, WHEN I WAS TWENTY-FIVE, I WAS CONTACTED BY A young lawyer at a large local law firm who had noticed my investigative stories. He represented, pro bono, a number of low-income black homeowners in inner-city Washington and inner-suburban neighborhoods who had been swindled by unscrupulous home improvement contractors.

Grifters going door to door had talked the victims into overpaying for shoddy home improvements with loans secured by high-interest second mortgages on their homes, which they unwittingly signed. The mortgages were then sold to finance companies that threatened foreclosure if the homeowners fell behind on often exorbitant payments. The lawyer, who wanted to be a confidential source, pointed me to more than a hundred lawsuits that he and legal aid lawyers had filed on behalf of victims in local and federal court against home improvement contractors and finance companies.

This opened a new door to investigative reporting for me. Lawsuits detailing allegations of wrongdoing turned out to be information goldmines. Each lawsuit's allegations and court record, including sworn affidavits, depositions, and court testimony, could be reported without risk of libel if the story was accurate and fair. Alleged victims and perpetrators named in the case records, along with their lawyers, could be contacted for interviews and illustrative examples.

Taking advantage of what was in the lawsuits required more laborious time spent digging into records, but what I found made it all worthwhile. The information in the legal records led me and David Jewell, a more experienced *Post* reporter who worked with me on this investigation, to numerous bilked homeowners in Washington, several predatory home improvement contractors and mortgage brokers, and a big, Philadelphia-based finance company that profited from the fraud.

I went into the homes of low-income African Americans in neighborhoods where I had never been before. I interviewed them in detail and asked to see whatever papers they had from the fraudulent transactions. Their stories disturbed and motivated me. A blind woman and her elderly mother who thought they were paying $900 for a water heater and radiator owed $7,500 on a second mortgage loan that they did not know they had signed. A retired couple wound up with a $15,000 mortgage-secured debt for cheap aluminum siding, some fresh paint and a new front door. Families lost their homes through foreclosure when they couldn't maintain payments on the second mortgages. The journalistic expression "giving voice to the voiceless" came alive for me.

I also learned how to prepare for and carry out confrontational interviews with the targets of investigative stories—in this case, the home improvement contractors, mortgage brokers, and finance company executives whom Jewell and I were able to find. We did our homework for each interview with information from lawsuits, corporate records, and victims' stories. Jewell, an aggressive interviewer, enjoyed these confrontations and emboldened me to ask tougher questions than I might have otherwise. I came to see that the often evasive and sometimes angry responses we got from these targets only strengthened the stories we wrote.

Federal investigations, criminal prosecutions, and consumer protection legislation followed our nine-part series of stories headlined "Homeowners Lost Millions in Mortgage Schemes," which the *Post* published in the autumn of 1967. It won a national award for financial reporting.

While working on those stories, I noticed that people who owned their own modest homes in those low-income neighborhoods were in the minority. Their homes were usually better maintained than nearby dilapidated houses and small apartment buildings where renters lived. I wondered who owned those rental properties.

I decided to focus on the rundown Shaw neighborhood, just blocks northeast of the *Washington Post*'s downtown building. City planners were considering spending federal money on an experimental urban renewal project in Shaw. The existing homes would be improved rather than being torn down and replaced. That meant that absentee landlords would be given government subsidies to upgrade their buildings, or they could sell them to developers and nonprofit groups that would be given the subsidies to renovate them. Either way, it would be a windfall for the slum landlords.

Who were they?

The answer lay inside the rows of file cabinets in the D.C. Recorder of Deeds office that held the paper records for every piece of real estate in the city. For several months in the winter of 1967–1968, I methodically read and took notes on all the deeds and mortgages for the hundreds of houses and apartment buildings in Shaw. With the help of the clerks in the office, I was once again mired in records. But I also was learning more than I ever expected about real estate and banking.

I found that the majority of Shaw's residential buildings, nearly 700 properties that were home to as many as 10,000 Shaw residents, were owned by just twelve Washington landlords. They had bought many of the houses and buildings at low prices with low-interest mortgage loans during the early 1960s, just before Shaw was designated to be an urban renewal area. They had spent the bare minimum on upkeep and were often cited by city housing inspectors for being slow to make repairs, if they made them at all. And they stood to make millions from any Shaw urban renewal project. Some of them already had gained profits of 25 percent to 100 percent selling similar slum properties to the government in a nearby teardown urban renewal area.

Once again, I was fascinated by what I was finding in the documents at the Recorder of Deeds. I leavened the solitary days by interviewing Shaw residents, city housing officials, and the relatively few slum land-lords who would speak to me. Most refused, even when I showed up at their little offices unannounced.

One day, I noticed that I was not alone in the rows of file cabinets at the Recorder of Deeds. A tall young man was taking notes on record after record in the files of Shaw properties a few rows of file cabinets behind me. I saw that he went to lunch at the same time every day, and that he left his notebooks on top of the file cabinet where he had been working.

I'm an investigative reporter, I thought, and he left those notebooks in a public place in a public building. During several of his lunch breaks, I looked through the notebooks. He was doing the same thing I was doing, but he was weeks and weeks behind me. It then dawned on me that he was working with the standard issue notebooks used by reporters at the *Washington Star*, the afternoon newspaper that still competed vigorously with the *Post*. Reporters there must have had the same idea about who might profit from urban renewal of the Shaw neighborhood.

I speeded up my records work, my analysis of the patterns that I had found, my sampling of D.C. housing inspectors' complaints about the slum landlords, my interviews, and my background research on urban renewal projects in Washington. I wrote as quickly as I could and warned my editors to hurry because the *Star* might be working on the same thing.

The *Post* began my five-part series with a front-page story on Sunday, March 24, 1968, headlined "Slum Landlords Buy Up Shaw Houses." I had made sure that it contained the most important themes of the series, the best data I had developed, voices from Shaw tenants, scenes inside their homes, and the names and thumbnail sketches of the twelve slum land-lords who owned the most homes in Shaw.

On Monday, when my second story appeared on The *Post's* front page, I found out that the tall man in the Recorder of Deeds office had indeed been working on the same story for months with another *Star* reporter. They'd had a similar idea for an investigative series about Shaw, and they had just been getting ready to write. Their editor was furious and told them to forget it. As word spread through both newsrooms, I had to ad-mit that I was pleased.

Just a week after the Shaw series ended in the *Post*, the assassination of the Reverend Martin Luther King ignited widespread rioting and burn-ing in Washington neighborhoods, including Shaw, which was the most devastated. I was pressed into the *Post's* coverage of the riots and the ensuing federal occupation of the capital city. Soon after the troops had left the city, I was asked to use my investigative reporting experience to reconstruct it all for a *Washington Post* book.

As soon as I could, I returned to looking into the causes of misery in those neighborhoods. I followed the money trail for the financing of slum landlords and other exploitive speculators in inner-city properties that led to Washington's venerable savings and loan industry, which then was a leading source of home mortgages in the city. I dived back into land and court records.

I found that speculators were buying inner-city homes at low prices and selling them with big markups to African American families. The speculators also obtained inflated mortgages for the home buyers, who were unable to obtain mortgages to buy homes in any other way. Other speculators, some with insider connections in the savings and loans, were siphoning money from inflated mortgage loans for buildings they rented out or were supposed to be renovating or constructing. By poring over 15,000 land and mortgage records, 900 lawsuits, and various other financial records, I found numerous loan transactions that should have been illegal under District of Columbia and federal law.

As the investigation mushroomed, I was joined by Jim Hoagland, who was a much better writer than I was. We found black families who had lost their homes, their life savings, or both. We found houses and apartment buildings abandoned throughout inner-city neighborhoods by speculators who milked them dry through mortgage loans, leaving some of the government-insured savings and loans that held those mortgages in financial jeopardy. We found savings and loans supposedly run by leading citizens that had been virtually taken over by slum real estate speculators.

One day, while I was writing one of the stories for what became a ten-part series, Ben Bradlee appeared at my desk, startling me. For the first time during the nearly four years that I had worked in the newsroom, Ben asked me what I was working on. I nervously began what would have been, for me, a typically long-winded answer. Ben, who had a notoriously short attention span, cut me off.

"I've got some guys in my office who represent the savings and loans in town," Ben said. "They told me that if we run your stories, they are going to pull all their advertising. I told them to get the hell out of my office."

I could feel my heart pounding during what became too long a pause. Then Ben put his hand on my shoulder and said, "Just get it right, kid."

The series, titled "Mortgaging the Ghetto," was published in the *Post* from January 5 to January 14, 1969. It triggered several government investigations that led to reforms.

All the savings and loan advertisements disappeared from the newspaper immediately. Nobody, including Ben, ever said another word about it. Much later, after doing some investigating in the advertising department, I found that the industry had pulled all its ads for an entire year, costing the newspaper hundreds of thousands of dollars, at a time when that was real money and the newspaper was dependent on such advertising.

I never forgot Ben's self-confident decisiveness, his trust in his journalists, and his complete independence from the newspaper's advertising department, whatever the cost. There was no doubt in my mind that the *Washington Post* was where I wanted to work for the rest of my career.

4

Washington Burning

𝕴N EARLY APRIL 1968, WASHINGTON WAS ON fire. Hundreds of stores and other buildings in predominantly African American neighborhoods throughout the city were looted and set ablaze in days of rioting after the April 4 assassination of Martin Luther King Jr. in Memphis, Tennessee. Flames and smoke filled the sky. Thousands of federal troops moved into and occupied the capital city to help police take back control of the streets, but not before most of the commercial thoroughfares of black Washington were destroyed.

The rioting posed an unprecedented challenge for the *Washington Post*, only three years into the Ben Bradlee era. And it presented a new test and learning experience for me, as I turned twenty-six.

The year 1968 was one of upheaval in the United States: The assassinations of King and Senator Robert F. Kennedy. Riots in dozens of American cities after King's death. The Tet Offensive and the worst weeks for American deaths in the Vietnam War. A growing and increasingly militant antiwar movement at home. Bloody clashes between police and protesters at the Democratic

National Convention in Chicago. Student takeovers of campus buildings at Columbia University in New York. Shootouts between police and black power activists in Cleveland, Ohio, and Oakland, California.

Yet even though there had been deadly riots in black neighborhoods in Detroit and Newark and disturbances in dozens of other American cities during what became known as "the long, hot summer of 1967," the upheaval in the nation's capital in 1968 was a shock. Many Washingtonians, including those in the *Post* newsroom, had not expected it to happen in our city.

African Americans made up an estimated two-thirds of D.C.'s population of about 850,000 people. Many of them lived in middle-class enclaves. But many others were confined to deteriorating lower-income neighborhoods where they often felt victimized by white landlords and shopkeepers. The police force was predominantly white, and, until late 1967, the District of Columbia was governed by three federally appointed commissioners overseen by congressional committees controlled by openly racist white Southern congressmen.

At the *Post*, deputy managing editor Ben Gilbert was an active advocate of racial harmony and self-government for the District of Columbia. He had been a pioneer in hiring and encouraging a few journalists of color at the *Post*. Sometimes, however, he downplayed coverage of clashes between the police and black residents, along with other racial incidents, which he feared could lead to more serious trouble. By the mid-1960s, Gilbert was involved in behind-the-scenes efforts by local leaders and the Johnson administration to avoid or tamp down unrest that could harm the city and jeopardize the possibility of self-government.

Bob Kaiser, who was then covering the city government, had inadvertently tested the *Post*'s willingness to report accurately on racial tensions in April 1967. He wrote a story about a secret meeting of the three D.C. commissioners to discuss the late-night arrest of Marion Barry, who had moved to Washington as a young leader of the Student Nonviolent Coordinating Committee, known as SNCC. Police had stopped Barry after midnight one night for jaywalking and then arrested him after an exchange of words. The commissioners and community leaders were concerned about reports that angry black men were gathering at the SNCC offices on 14th Street NW, a major black neighborhood thoroughfare, and threatening to riot in protest. After Barry was released, he met with and calmed down his supporters.

Gilbert opposed putting Kaiser's story on the *Post*'s front page. But Ben Bradlee overruled him. After a loud argument about the story in the middle of the newsroom, everyone on the staff understood what had happened. Ben was in charge now, and there would be no more such sacred cows.

As it happened, I had been the first *Post* reporter to write about Marion Barry after he came to Washington, where he later would become the city's four-term mayor. I had interviewed him in January 1966, when he helped lead a SNCC-backed one-day boycott by black riders of the privately owned D.C. Transit bus system, which had forced it to rescind a citywide fare increase. Barry never forgot that story during the ensuing decades when we were in frequent contact, sometimes in serious disagreement about *Post* coverage of personal misbehavior that bedeviled him in his public life.

In November 1967, President Johnson defied the congressional committees overseeing the city government and replaced the three commissioners with an appointed African American mayor, Walter E. Washington, and an appointed city council. Ben Gilbert was a close friend of Mayor Washington's, who had been a well-regarded D.C. public housing official. Gilbert tried unsuccessfully to stop Ben and Steve Isaacs from publishing an exclusive story about the appointment being imminent, for fear Johnson would delay or abandon it out of pique.

Joseph A. Califano Jr., President Johnson's liaison with the District of Columbia government, telephoned Katharine Graham to ask her to intercede with Ben, but she refused. Her stance marked a significant break from her late husband's way of operating vis-à-vis involvement in civic and national affairs, a change that Ben had strongly urged on her. In the newsroom, I remember how demonstrably proud Isaacs was of the scoop by veteran local reporter Elsie Carper, and how pleased he was to be backed up by Ben.

With the encouragement of the White House and the Justice Department, Mayor Washington then appointed former New York City police officer and Syracuse police chief Patrick V. Murphy to the newly created position of D.C. director of public safety, in charge of supervising the city's police, fire, and civil defense departments. Murphy was known as a reformer of police practices in New York and Syracuse and while serving in the Johnson administration's Justice Department. He now had authority over the well-meaning but cautious D.C. police chief, John Layton, with a mandate to improve relations between the city's police force and its black community.

Murphy defied the congressional oversight committees, who had protected the status quo in the police department, by promoting Jerry Wilson, another college-educated police reformer, as assistant chief for field operations, in charge of preventing and controlling civil disorders. Wilson had drawn up a riot response plan for Layton that would have ruled out shooting looters who didn't pose a danger to others, including the police.

I took time away from my Shaw project to cover Murphy after he came to Washington, because of my experience writing about law enforcement reform. I was interested in Murphy's philosophy of diversifying the police force, training officers in community relations, and using minimum force in making arrests and dispersing disorderly crowds. I talked to and wrote about Murphy so often that he offered me the job of being his spokesman. I could not decide if that was flattering or an embarrassing sign of too close a relationship with a source. I turned Murphy down and went back to work on Shaw.

What I didn't know at the time was that federal and city officials were quietly working on a contingency plan—called "Operation Cabin Guard"—for how they could respond to rioting in Washington with less loss of life and property than there had been in cities like Detroit and Newark in the summer of 1967. The police would be ordered to avoid deadly force whenever possible, and the military would be brought in to help restore and maintain order in the capital city. The officials were especially concerned about a Poor People's Campaign march and encampment that King had planned for Washington in the summer of 1968.

The Operation Cabin Guard plan identified elite military units that could be quickly deployed onto the city's streets. They were racially integrated and had black soldiers in key command positions. The Old Guard (3rd Infantry Regiment) at nearby Fort Meyer and the 91st Engineer Battalion at Fort Belvoir, both in suburban Virginia, had protected the Pentagon during massive anti–Vietnam War demonstrations in October

1967. The 82nd Airborne Division at Fort Bragg, North Carolina, had been commended for its restraint while deployed during the deadly rioting in Detroit, in contrast to the Michigan National Guard. The 503rd Military Police Battalion at Fort Bragg had been deployed during the integration of the University of Mississippi in 1962 and the Selma, Alabama, march and demonstrations in 1965. In February and March of 1967, officers of each of the designated military units toured the police precincts in Washington where they would be deployed if it became necessary.

Ben Gilbert, who knew about those preparations, also had a plan for the newspaper. If a major riot occurred in Washington, Steve Isaacs would mobilize dozens of *Post* journalists to go into the streets. A reporter and a photographer would be teamed in each of the radio-equipped cars normally reserved for the newspaper's photographers and advertising salespeople. Gilbert prepared detailed instructions for them, which included the following:

> A hand moving quickly into a pocket to pull out a [press] pass may be misunderstood. Thus, we have designed our own pass, which can be hung around the neck for easy identification. . . .
> Our fleet model photographic cars without any ornamentation look like official cars and can be targets. They are now being repainted two-tone and "unstandardized" in other ways. . . .
> We are seeking the broadest possible perspective in our reporting of racial unrest and find that inter-racial teams are especially valuable in riot situations.

Meanwhile, from March 24 to March 28, 1968, my series of articles about the slum landlords of the Shaw neighborhood was published on the front page of the *Post*. But I did not have my usual opportunity to pursue follow-up stories. A week later, Shaw's 7th Street NW commercial corridor was destroyed when Washington burned.

ON THE NIGHT OF THURSDAY, APRIL 4, 1968, THE INTERSECTION of 14th and U Streets NW—a commercial center of black Washington in the 1960s—was as usual filled with people changing buses, shopping, or just hanging out, as the news spread. Martin Luther King Jr. had been shot to death by an unidentified white assassin at the Lorraine Motel in Memphis, Tennessee. In the first minutes of shocked silence, the atmosphere at 14th and U became, in the words of one witness, "ominous—like before a hurricane strikes."

When he heard about King's assassination, Stokely Carmichael, the militant former national chairman of the Student Nonviolent Coordinating Committee, went to the nearby SNCC headquarters on 14th Street and rounded up workers who had gathered there. Accompanied by a growing number of angry African American teenagers and young adults, they went up and down 14th Street, forcing stores, carryout restaurants, barber shops, and movie theaters to close out of respect for King.

By 10:30 p.m., people began breaking store windows and jumping through them to grab watches, jewelry, radios, and televisions. Carmichael hurried into a waiting car that sped off. As late night turned into early morning, hundreds of looters swarmed from store to store. Responding police made some arrests but could not control the situation. By 3 a.m., the Operation Cabin Guard military units had been put on alert.

On Friday, bigger crowds gathered in the streets as thousands of students poured out of schools. Daylight looting and setting of fires spread from the 14th Street corridor to 7th Street NW, the commercial main street of the Shaw neighborhood, and other places in black neighborhoods, reaching within blocks of both the Capitol and the White House downtown.

President Johnson's personal representative, Deputy Attorney General Warren Christopher, and the designated "Task Force Washington" commander, Gen. Ralph E. Haines Jr., toured the city with Murphy and found that the looting and arson were overwhelming police and firefighters. On their recommendation, with Mayor Washington on the telephone call, the president signed the order for what became a twelve-day military occupation of Washington, with 13,600 federal and D.C. National Guard troops. Not since the Civil War had that many troops occupied an American city.

At the *Post*, Ben took active charge of the newspaper's response to King's assassination. He rushed reporters to Memphis, assigned additional stories, and cleared advertising out of Friday's newspaper to make room for all the news. He tore up the front page and moved back the next morning's printing and delivery schedule. Steve Isaacs, who'd become the metropolitan news editor, sent the first local *Post* reporters and photographers into the streets to cover the rioting. Ben went up to the roof of the *Post* building, ten blocks southwest of 14th and U, and saw the fires and smoke rising over the city. Banner headlines on Friday's front page read: "King Assassinated in Memphis: Shouting Crowds Smash Stores in District."

At police headquarters a dozen blocks away, a joint city and federal Task Force Washington command post was set up. The Johnson administration sent former Undersecretary of Defense Cyrus Vance to work as a federally paid consultant to Mayor Washington to coordinate strategy with Christopher, General Haines, and Murphy.

Vance brought with him a book of lessons he had learned from his experience in a similar role during the 1967 Detroit riots. They included making liberal use of tear gas and mass arrests to subdue rioters, while sharply reducing the use of guns by police and the military. A citywide dusk-to-dawn curfew, which was imposed for six consecutive nights during the ensuing military occupation of Washington, was to be fairly and strictly enforced. All soldiers were given written orders on wallet-sized cards that emphasized courtesy and restrained use of force. Most of the troops never loaded their guns.

Before order was fully restored, 1,100 buildings in what became known as the city's riot corridors were damaged or destroyed by looters and fires. Nearly 300 businesses were affected along 14th Street NW alone. Proportionately, 7th Street NW in Shaw was hit the hardest, with 200 of its 250 businesses destroyed.

Yet there were only twelve riot-related deaths throughout the city, seven of them in fires, compared with forty-three during the 1967 riots in Detroit. Six of the dead in Washington included police officers, firefighters, and soldiers. Most of the 1,190 injuries were not serious; many were from smoke or tear gas inhalation. An estimated 20,000 people were involved in the riots; more than 7,600 men, women, and children were arrested. There was almost no shooting.

With authority from Bradlee and Gilbert, Isaacs mobilized more than one hundred *Washington Post* reporters, columnists, photographers, and editors, fourteen of them African Americans, to cover the rioting and its aftermath of burned-out blocks of buildings. *Post* reporters and photographers roamed the streets in the radio-equipped cars. The reporters radioed in running accounts of what they saw on the streets and heard in interviews, while typists at the city desk in the newsroom recorded it all in memos to be shared by everyone who needed the information. The photographers periodically returned to the *Post* building to drop off their film.

Bob Maynard, a reporter from the *Post*'s national staff who later became one of the nation's most prominent African American journalists and the editor and owner of a newspaper in Oakland, California, unwittingly attracted an avid audience around the city desk when he radioed in vivid reports in his unhurried deep baritone.

"The flames are now rising, six, eight, now fifteen feet high," he related in one transmission, which has since been often quoted:

> The entire store is being engulfed, while looters, mostly children, race in and out of burning buildings, strangely unaware of the danger. . . .
>
> My car is now being surrounded by four gentlemen, all of them apparently hostile. Now there are eight of them, bouncing the car up and down. I shall leave the air momentarily, until things settle down. . . .
>
> There are four policemen ducking for cover right beside my car. . . . They are down on one knee behind the hood and trunk . . . with guns drawn and cocked . . . aiming over the car at the roof above us. . . . I am now getting onto the floor under the dashboard as fast as I can. . . . Over and out.

I was neither as brave nor as spell-binding as Maynard when I was sent out onto the streets with a cautious African American *Post* photographer. We got as close to the violence in our car as we dared. We sometimes were briefly but frighteningly trapped in smoke and tear gas. I called in details of what we witnessed, but I doubted that my reports were very useful.

I contributed much more once the federal occupation was under way. I was assigned to cover the command center at police headquarters, down the hall from the Task Force Washington war room, where a large wall map of the city showed trouble spots and troop concentrations. This same command center would again become vital for the city and important for me nine years later when terrorism would strike Washington and I would be deciding how the *Post* should respond to it.

I reported from the command center during the rioting that the federal officials were, in effect, managing the crisis, even though they showed as much deference as possible to Mayor Washington and city police officials. Christopher and Vance did most of the talking at end-of-the-day, late-night, and early-morning press conferences. Murphy and Jerry Wilson were occasionally spotted on the streets monitoring the police and conferring with military units.

AS THE OCCUPATION OF WASHINGTON ENDED, BEN GILBERT made an agreement with the Frederick A. Praeger Publishing Company to produce a *Washington Post* book about the riots, occupation, and aftermath, as quickly as possible. Gilbert turned to me and an African American *Post* reporter, Jesse W. Lewis Jr., to do most of the work. My task was to reconstruct the rioting from its beginning on the evening of April 4 through the ensuing military occupation, as close to hour-by-hour as possible, until April 16, when the last troops left town. Lewis was assigned to report on conditions in the city that spawned the riots and to find and interview some of the people who looted stores and set fires, which he did.

I wrote six of the book's twelve chapters, based on all the notes, news stories, and photographs from the *Post* journalists who covered the riots, plus my own interviews at military bases with troops and their commanders who had occupied the city. Telling an engaging, authoritative story about those twelve days required more exacting, finely detailed research and a more descriptive narrative form of writing than I had ever done for the newspaper. Working on that book opened a new door that I would occasionally walk through with great satisfaction throughout my life.

Gilbert guided me on the research, and our editor at Praeger, Lois Decker O'Neill, mentored me on the writing. From the *Post* reporters' notes, their answers to my questions, and my own reporting, I put together the first and only complete account of the sequence of events, the performance of the police and the military, and the roles of everyone, from Stokely Carmichael to police, city, and federal officials.

OUR BOOK, *TEN BLOCKS FROM THE WHITE HOUSE: ANATOMY OF the Washington Riots of 1968*, was published, in both hardcover and paperback, before the end of 1968. The authors were listed on the cover as "Ben Gilbert and the staff of *The Washington Post*," even though Gilbert wrote very little of it. Inside, he noted in the acknowledgments that "two writers stand out because their contribution to the work was so large that, in fairness, their names should have been listed with mine on the cover. They are Leonard Downie Jr. and Jesse W. Lewis Jr."

I was not concerned about the formal recognition because I had learned so much from the experience. When, on the tenth anniversary of the riots in April 1978, the *Washington Post* published a lengthy excerpt in its Sunday magazine of what I wrote in the book, the byline was all mine, in large type.

More important, Praeger's Lois O'Neill was impressed by my work. She asked me if I wanted to write a book on my own. I was still only twenty-six, and authoring a book was something that had never occurred to me. After some thought, I told her, yes, I would like to write a book about criminal courts.

5

A Reluctant Editor

By the summer of 1970, I was very comfortable as an investigative reporter at the *Post*. I had the freedom to choose my own subjects, and I could take whatever time I needed for my reporting and writing. I had little contact with editors until my stories were ready for them to work on.

There was a big difference between being a reporter and an editor. Reporters could go wherever news happened, witness events, interview people, write stories, and see their names in print. As an investigative reporter, I also enjoyed more independence, the thrill of detective work, original research, and the possibility of making a difference with what I wrote.

Editors were comparatively anonymous and mostly confined to the newsroom, where they experienced newsgathering vicariously. Yet their roles were just as important. They were the reporters' sounding boards for ideas and assignments, enablers of their writing, and arbiters of their stories' accuracy, fairness, and readability. I appreciated what my editors did for me, particularly in smoothing out my rather rough writing. But I was not eager to be one of *them*.

So I was completely blindsided when Andy Barnes asked me to join him in the dreary cafeteria on the second floor of the *Post* building for coffee one morning that summer. He and I had been friends almost since he'd arrived at the *Post* as a local reporter in 1966. Barnes was a Harvard man with large eyeglasses, a full head of unruly hair, and a big smile. He liked to show off his erudition, especially in literature, leavened by an almost apologetic hearty laugh. He was affable, well-mannered, and a very capable journalist, who years later would become the editor and then CEO and chairman of the *St. Petersburg Times*, one of the country's best regional newspapers.

Earlier in 1970, Barnes had become the low-key deputy to the high-strung Harry Rosenfeld, who had replaced Steve Isaacs as the metropolitan news editor. Rosenfeld, a broad-faced, bespectacled man of fifty at the time, came to the *Post* from the *New York Herald Tribune*, where he was a foreign news editor, which also became his first job at the *Post*. He was intelligent, intense, blustery, self-centered, and ambitious. He was very much a New Yorker who knew little about the Washington area.

As he wrote many years later in his memoir, Rosenfeld wanted to demonstrate to Ben Bradlee that he could "run a larger operation" by taking over the metropolitan staff, even though he "did not have an intense interest in local news or the background." He believed that Ben thought Steve Isaacs was running his staff in a disorganized, mercurial way that allowed his favored young reporters, including me, far too much freedom in choosing their own story assignments and, too often, the opportunity to goof off.

I never had the opportunity to ask Ben what he really thought. But I knew that Isaacs, headstrong as always, had presented a newsroom reorganization plan to senior editors of the *Post* at an off-site meeting. His plan would divide the newsroom into topic beats that would cut across its traditional local and national news divide. It would give Isaacs control over much of the new structure. He had proudly shown his proposal to me before leaving for the day-long meeting at a rural riverfront property that Ben had bought in West Virginia. Those of us back in the newsroom soon heard that Ben had summarily rejected the proposal, which embarrassed and angered Isaacs. During a touch football game later in the day, the big, burly Isaacs forcefully blocked Ben to the ground. Big mistake.

Ben exiled Isaacs to the *Post*'s Sunday magazine, and he put Rosenfeld in charge of the metropolitan staff. Rosenfeld made clear from the outset that he was determined to instill more discipline, break up cliques, and increase productivity. Our little group of remaining Isaacs's boys was one of his targets. Initially I was left alone to finish most of an investigation in suburban Prince George's County. Real estate developers connected to county officials had profitably transformed large swaths of the county's farmland into poorly constructed garden apartments that were rapidly deteriorating and overwhelming schools and government services.

My three-part Prince George's series had not yet been edited and published, as it would be later, when I went down to the *Post* cafeteria that morning with Andy Barnes. He surprised me by asking if I wanted to become an editor, specifically day city editor on the metropolitan staff, supervising coverage of the District of Columbia.

"But I've never been an editor," I said.

"Doesn't matter," Barnes responded.

"But I love being an investigative reporter."

"Doesn't matter," Barnes repeated firmly. "You don't have a choice. You will do this."

Barnes was transmitting an order from Rosenfeld, and it was nonnegotiable.

Although I tried to hide it from him, I was very upset. My life outside the *Post* had been in turmoil for some time. My wife, Bonnie, had left me for a *Post* colleague and had taken our two sons with her, eventually moving out of town. Our teenage marriage had been fragile for a long time. My devotion to the newspaper and the child care demands on Bonnie had put her educational and professional ambitions on hold, and we had other personal issues. Our late-developing social life with *Post* colleagues after a move from suburban Bowie to a popular neighborhood in the District of Columbia had not improved our relationship. We sold the house and divorced.

For the first time in my life, I was living alone. I briefly saw a psychiatrist to deal with my resulting anxiety. At the same time, I was working late nights and early mornings on my book about criminal courts for Lois O'Neill at Praeger. I already had banked a small advance on royalties, and I had done the necessary research and travel on my own time. I soon found a small apartment in the funky Adams Morgan inner-city neighborhood of Washington, across the street from a bigger, much nicer building where Carl Bernstein happened to live. His first marriage to a *Post* reporter also had ended.

Bernstein was a night owl who could look down from his apartment to see me typing away at a small table in front of a window in my apartment below. On a night or two when he saw me finally move away from my typewriter, he telephoned to invite me out to one of the few inexpensive restaurants still open at that hour. Carl seemed exotic to me, with his hi-fi immersion in both classical and rock music, his effortless attraction to women, and his happy-go-lucky, almost Bohemian lifestyle. By contrast, I was lonely, working as an investigative reporter by day and writing a book at night, far away from what had been my family.

Later that year, Bernstein gave me the name and the telephone number of Gerry Rebach, who had been his prom date and dance partner at the high school they'd attended in suburban Montgomery County, Maryland. She was now a popular French teacher at a Washington junior high school. Gerry was much more outgoing and sophisticated than I was. She had lived in France during her junior year abroad and traveled elsewhere overseas. We began dating, and we eventually moved in together.

At the *Post*, neither Harry Rosenfeld nor I had any idea what kind of editor I would be. I think we were both surprised by how quickly I took to shaping and line-editing reporters' stories. I saw how much I could learn about the craft from the better writers among them. I also realized how much I could influence the content of each day's newspaper with my reporters' stories and the ways in which I directed and edited them. In addition, I began what would be my long professional relationship with Don Graham.

Meanwhile, I finished my book, *Justice Denied: The Case for Reform of the Courts*, which was published by Praeger early in 1971. It sold enough copies to cover my advance on royalties and then some. The paperback rights were bought by Penguin, which republished it a year later. I was now really an author.

ALTHOUGH I WAS NOT DIRECTLY INVOLVED FROM MY SEAT ON the city desk, the thunderclap of the publication of the Pentagon Papers stories by the *New York Times* and the *Washington Post* in June 1971 would reverberate throughout my career.

What became known as the Pentagon Papers was a secret, 7,000-page study of U.S. involvement in Vietnam commissioned by President Johnson's secretary of defense, Robert McNamara, and carried out by the Defense Department. It documented a history of missteps and lies by the Truman, Eisenhower, Kennedy, and Johnson administrations as they escalated American involvement in what became the costly, lost-cause Vietnam War. Military analyst Daniel Ellsberg, who had worked on the classified study and evolved into an opponent of the war, spirited a copy out of his office safe at the Rand Corporation in Los Angeles and painstakingly photocopied it page by page over many weeks. After he failed to find interest in it among several Washington officials and politicians, the report made its way to the *New York Times*.

The first anyone else knew about this was when the *Times* published its first story on June 13, 1971. President Richard Nixon, who was already worried about mounting American opposition to the war, asked the Justice Department to seek a court order stopping the *Times* from publishing top-secret information that, his administration argued, could cause irreparable harm to the United States. An injunction was granted stopping publication, for the first time in American history, after three days of *Times* stories.

Ellsberg then gave 4,000 pages of the study to *Post* national editor Ben Bagdikian, who also had once worked at Rand. As depicted in the 2018 film *The Post*, Ben Bradlee had Bagdikian bring the papers to his George-town home, where he assembled a group of *Post* reporters and editors to produce a story for the next day's newspaper. The *Post*'s lawyers and some of its business executives tried to persuade Katharine Graham to stop publication because of the risks of criminal prosecution, loss of the licenses of television stations the *Post* owned, and damage to the news-paper's first sale of shares to the public. But after a tense day of listening to arguments as the journalists worked, Mrs. Graham told Ben in an eve-ning telephone call to his Georgetown home from hers, "Okay. . . . Let's go. Let's publish."

Most of us in the newsroom knew little about all of that, even after we saw in the next morning's newspaper the first of several days of *Post* stories about the Pentagon Papers. We never saw what went on at the Bradlee home among Ben, the journalists, the lawyers, *Post* business ex-ecutives, and Mrs. Graham. She was still a distant figure to me. There was no sign that Don, a reporter on my city staff, was involved.

Those rushed *Post* stories about the Pentagon Papers were not the best possible accounts of what was in the report, but they put a marker down. The *Post* also was forced to stop publishing and to join with the *Times* in the case that soon went to the U.S. Supreme Court.

On June 30, 1971, the *Post's* then managing editor, Eugene Patterson, a World War II tank commander who had previously won a Pulitzer Prize crusading for civil rights as the editor of the *Atlanta Constitution*, stood up on a desk in the middle of the *Post* newsroom. As we gathered around him, he announced that the Supreme Court had ruled 6–3 that the newspapers could resume publication of stories about the Pentagon Papers. The federal government was not justified under the First Amendment to engage in prior restraint of publication. And the government never did it again.

The *Post* and the *Times* resumed their series of stories about the Pen-tagon Papers. Even while the Supreme Court appeal was still pending, other newspapers around the country had also started writing about por-tions of the study circulated by Ellsberg. I could feel in the newsroom a sense that the *Post* was moving up in class.

The Supreme Court decision would underpin American freedom of the press ever afterward. Publication of the Pentagon Papers, along with the growing antiwar movement in the country and increasingly skeptical media coverage of the war on the ground in Vietnam, accelerated the erosion of what had been a cozy relationship between the press and the government. I was still primarily focused on local news. But the Nixon administration's efforts to stop publication of the Pentagon Papers—and the decision by Ben and Mrs. Graham to defy it—would loom large for me and the newspaper a little more than a year later.

DESPITE HOW MUCH I SURPRISED MYSELF BY ENJOYING MY FIRST stint as an editor, I was restless. I still missed being a reporter, and I aspired to work on the *Post*'s national news staff, which continued to get most of Ben's attention. I needed another credential, and I wanted to write another book.

A few years earlier, I had been turned down for a one-year Nieman Fellowship for journalists at Harvard University, despite being selected as a finalist at an unusually young age. While I may have manifested a Charlie Brown–like refusal to stop running for class president in high school, I did not try again for the Nieman. I felt slighted by the Harvard academics on the Nieman committee, whose members apparently had been underwhelmed by their interview with me.

Without intending to, Andy Barnes gave me an alternative and an idea. In a casual conversation one day, he told me about the Alicia Patterson Fellowship, which at that time paid qualifying journalists to travel for a year doing research and writing about a subject of their choosing. Barnes and his wife, Molly, had been fellows in 1969, studying urban problems in Europe and Africa.

I decided that the fellowship would be a good opportunity to build on my reporting about the damage done by real estate speculators in Washington and its suburbs. In my application for the fellowship, I proposed studying this phenomenon in cities across the United States. I also proposed evaluating the then fashionable alternative of planned suburban "new towns," such as Columbia, Maryland, and Reston, Virginia, in the United States, as well as those in Europe and Israel. It would give me the opportunity to travel abroad with Gerry, visit with my two sons on our way across the United States, and begin a new book.

I won one of the Alicia Patterson fellowships. Gerry and I took leaves of absence from our jobs, got married, and set off in August 1971. While traveling, with Gerry's translation help, I wrote Alicia Patterson newsletters about urban blight, suburban sprawl, and what turned out to be new town development growing pains in the United States and overseas in Israel, France, Italy, Sweden, and Britain.

My American research, plus my investigative reporting for the *Post*, would be incorporated into my next book, *Mortgage on America: The Real Cost of Real Estate Speculation*, for which I had already signed a contract with Lois O'Neill at Praeger. As it turned out, I would not finish the book and see it published until 1974, because I would become quite busy upon my return to the *Post*.

In the last weeks of the fellowship year, Gerry and I were staying for a few weeks in a married students' apartment at the London School of Economics at the beginning of the school's 1972 summer break. I wrote to the *Post*'s then new managing editor, Howard Simons, about what I wanted to do when I returned to the newsroom. I proposed that I write about urban affairs on the national staff, including investigative stories.

Simons responded that it had already been decided that I would succeed Andy Barnes as Harry Rosenfeld's deputy. It was the worst news I could have received. I had tolerated Harry's bluster when I was day city editor, because I could mostly ignore him while I went about my work. I figured that I would not be able to ignore him as his deputy.

Not long after that news began to sink in, came a mystery. The newspaper delivered to the door of our London apartment, the *International Herald Tribune*, was half-owned by the *Post*. On its front page that Monday, June 19, 1972, was a story from the *Post*, with the bylines of Carl Bernstein and Bob Woodward, about a burglary at the Democratic National Committee's headquarters in the Watergate Office Building in Washington. The story reported that one of the burglars, James McCord, was on the payroll of President Richard Nixon's reelection committee.

It raised a lot of questions for me: *Why would anyone break into the Democrats' headquarters? What was the connection with Nixon's reelection committee? Why was Bernstein still working at the* Post*? Who was Bob Woodward?*

Although Bernstein was a friend and an unusually talented reporter and writer, I knew that he often got into trouble at the newspaper. He had sometimes disappeared off the radar while on an assignment and never seemed to finish stories that didn't interest him. Steve Isaacs had once found him asleep on a couch in the *Post*'s city government bureau. Carl had left rental cars charged to the *Post* in commercial garages for weeks on end, running up enormous auto rental and garage bills. And that was just what I knew about him. If Harry Rosenfeld had fired him while I was gone, it would not have surprised me.

And Woodward? Whoever he was, he must have been hired while I was away on the fellowship.

As Gerry and I prepared to return to Washington and my dreaded new job, I didn't think that much more about the strange burglary.

6

Inside the
Watergate Story

WALKING BACK INTO THE *WASHINGTON POST* newsroom in July 1972 was like stepping out of a black-and-white film into a Technicolor movie. The gray, cramped, old newsroom had disappeared while I was away. On the spacious fifth floor of a greatly expanded building, under construction when I had left, was a vast, brightly lit, wide-open newsroom brimming with brilliant colors. I found out that Ben Bradlee had helped design it as an expression of the unlimited possibilities he envisioned for the newspaper.

That shiny new newsroom would become the setting for a new direction in American journalism. It began inauspiciously, a few weeks before my return, with what President Richard Nixon's White House called "a third-rate burglary." What the *Post* then did would profoundly change how the nation's media confronted abuses of public and private power.

It is a story that has been told many times in a variety of ways. But I want to tell it my way from the inside of the *Post* newsroom, more fully and accurately than I have seen before. I will tell what I learned from my role and how I believe it shaped me as an editor and leader. And I will show what Watergate's impact was on the *Post* newsroom and American journalism, and what is still relevant about it today.

The beginning of the story is familiar. Five men with bugging equipment were arrested at 2:10 a.m. on Saturday, June 17, 1972, inside the offices of the Democratic National Committee on the sixth floor of the Watergate Office Building. The building was one of six in the exclusive Watergate complex—two office buildings, a hotel, and three apartment buildings—on the east bank of the Potomac River near the Kennedy Center, eight blocks west of the White House.

Hours after the arrests, Joseph Califano, the general counsel of the Democratic Party, who was also one of the *Post*'s outside lawyers, telephoned *Post* managing editor Howard Simons to tell him about the burglary. Simons alerted Harry Rosenfeld, who then called Barry Sussman, the District of Columbia editor on the metropolitan news staff, at his home just after 8:30 a.m.

Sussman was a beefy, pipe-smoking man with wavy dark hair and a nervous smile. He had an encyclopedic memory and an unusually analytical, sometimes wildly imaginative, even conspiratorial, mind, which was well-suited to the detective work of investigative journalism. He left most of the routine city news to his assistant editors so that he could concentrate on the unexpected stories dug up by his most resourceful reporters. As soon as Sussman heard about the Watergate burglary, he guessed it would be anything but a routine local story.

From home, Sussman first telephoned veteran police reporter Al Lewis and sent him to the Watergate Office Building. He then summoned his favorite district staff reporter, Bob Woodward, on his day off, to meet Sussman in the *Post* newsroom. In just nine months at the newspaper, Woodward, then twenty-nine, had mined the city's bureaucracy on his own for investigative stories ranging from violations of food and drug safety regulations to misuse of Medicaid funds. His story about a corrupt U.S. Civil Service Commission official was displayed on the front page of that very day's *Washington Post*. Without any formal training, Woodward instinctively developed reporting skills that are still taught today.

Somehow, Al Lewis arrived at the Watergate Office Building that morning with the acting chief of police. He accompanied the chief past the already assembled media throng and through police lines into the building. Another officer who recognized Lewis let him ride up a freight elevator to the sixth floor. He sat at a desk in the Democratic National Committee's offices for the rest of the day, observing and interviewing the investigating officers, crime lab technicians, and FBI agents. There is no substitute for going to the scene of a story.

Once Sussman arrived in the *Post* newsroom, Lewis called him periodically to report what he had found. The five burglars all had worn suits and surgical gloves, and they had hundred-dollar bills in their pockets. They had carried burglary tools, cameras, eavesdropping equipment, pen-sized mace dispensers, and a walkie-talkie. As Sussman suggested, Lewis asked the police to help him draw a floor plan of the offices. He even brought back to the newsroom signed copies of the police officers' reports of the arrests, which were later given to me. I still have them.

Sussman sent Woodward to the D.C. Court of General Sessions for the arraignment of the five arrested burglars. When Woodward heard one of them, James McCord, tell the judge in a quiet voice that he had worked for the CIA, Woodward figured he was no ordinary burglar.

Meanwhile, Carl Bernstein had been called into the newsroom that Saturday by Metro's Virginia editor, Tom Wilkinson, as punishment for not having finished a long-assigned story. He began hanging around the city desk, clearly interested in the intriguing burglary. With Wilkinson's agreement, Sussman assigned Bernstein to work the telephones to try to find out who the burglars were.

Ten Metro reporters produced three stories about the Watergate burglary for the Sunday, June 18, edition of the *Washington Post*. Simons, who also had come in from home, stopped by Sussman's desk to tell him that the main story, under the byline of Alfred E. Lewis, was going on the front page. An accompanying story by Bernstein, reporting what he and other reporters were able to find out about the burglars, appeared on an inside page. Although no one noticed at the time, it was a year to the day since the *Post* had published its first stories based on the copies of the Pentagon Papers it had obtained on June 17, 1971.

Sussman brought Woodward and Bernstein back to the newsroom on Sunday to continue reporting. The first Watergate story with their joint byline—about burglar James McCord being a salaried security coordinator for President Nixon's reelection committee—appeared in the *Post* on Monday, June 19. Woodward, working with other reporters, continued to produce follow-up stories, including one describing the initial connections between the Watergate burglars and E. Howard Hunt, a consultant in the Nixon White House, and G. Gordon Liddy, a former White House staffer and a Nixon reelection committee official. Bernstein had been sent back to reporting in Virginia.

But Simons, concerned about initial competition on the story from the *New York Times* and the *Washington Star*, soon ordered Sussman to create and lead a full-time Watergate investigative team. He even allowed Sussman to include Bernstein on it. With Ben Bradlee away on vacation until mid-August, Simons was the top editor most involved in the Watergate story during the summer. He talked to Sussman and Rosenfeld about it every day.

I WAS NOW BACK IN THE NEWSROOM. MY OFFICIAL TITLE WAS deputy Metro editor, and I was given one of the glass-walled offices for senior editors that lined the perimeter of the newsroom. It was right next to Harry Rosenfeld's. The metropolitan news staff—Metro in newsroom lingo—covered news in the District of Columbia, its rapidly growing suburbs in Maryland and Virginia, and the rest of those two states. I would be sharing responsibility with Rosenfeld for all that news and Metro's more than one hundred editors and reporters.

Despite my misgivings when I was in London, the job turned out to be the best thing that could have happened. Rosenfeld and I got along much better than I'd anticipated. Almost from the beginning, I plunged deeply into supervision of all of the Metro staff and its stories, learning as I went, while Rosenfeld was immersed in Watergate. As he found he could trust my judgment, Rosenfeld included me among the editors who reviewed Watergate stories before their publication. Watergate was a Metro staff story because it began with a local burglary.

Sussman sent Bernstein to Miami, where four of the Watergate burglars lived. Bernstein managed to talk a local prosecutor's chief investigator into showing him a $25,000 check from a Nixon fundraiser, Kenneth H. Dahlberg, that had been deposited in the Miami bank account of one of the burglars, Bernard Barker. Back in the newsroom that same evening, Woodward tracked down and telephoned Dahlberg, a Minneapolis businessman. Dahlberg confirmed that the check was his, given to the Nixon reelection committee. He said that he had no idea how it got into Barker's account. Woodward wrote the top of the story, and Sussman filled in background paragraphs, as he often did. They finished just in time for the late-night deadline for the largest-circulation print editions of the August 1 *Post*.

In response to the Dahlberg check story, Congress initiated several limited investigations, which eventually led, many months later, to the creation of the Senate Watergate Committee. The FBI also was investigating, although federal prosecutors did not initially follow its leads very far into the Nixon White House. The story also triggered the first of many White House denials of any involvement in the "third-rate burglary," and, behind the scenes, its first efforts to limit or thwart Justice Department and congressional investigations.

Many years later, when he worked at Harvard's Nieman Foundation, Sussman wrote, "The case is pretty strong that the Dahlberg check story was the single biggest contribution the *Washington Post* made in the course of the scandal." In fact, there was much more to come. But Woodward and Bernstein's work with Sussman on that story marked the real beginning of what became the most famous reporting partnership in American journalism.

BERNSTEIN, THEN TWENTY-EIGHT, AND WOODWARD, TWENTY-nine, were initially wary of each other. They had strikingly different personalities, political leanings, and work habits, all of which I would get to know well. Woodward was conservative, meticulous, and self-contained. Bernstein was liberal, impulsive, and somewhat madcap. They often argued about the details and meaning of their reporting and writing about Watergate in both the *Post* and their two subsequent best-selling books. But these two young bachelors shared a determination to work flat out, with little rest, under Sussman's hard-driving direction.

Bob Woodward grew up as the son of a judge in a western suburb of Chicago. He graduated from Yale, where he had joined the Naval Officer Reserve Training Corps. In the last assignment of his five years in the navy, he was sent to Washington as a communications liaison officer between the Pentagon and the White House. In 1969, Lieutenant Woodward met an assistant director of the FBI named Mark Felt, who was a generation older, while they both were waiting for appointments near the Situation Room in the lower level of the West Wing of the White House. They struck up a relationship that Woodward continued to cultivate over the years, occasionally contacting Felt for career advice and information about the government. Woodward's natural ability to form such relationships and the care he took to maintain them over time would become one of his great strengths as a reporter.

Woodward turned his back on acceptance to the Harvard Law School and, on a whim, showed up at the *Washington Post* in August 1970, seeking a starting job in journalism. He was sent to Harry Rosenfeld, who gave Woodward a two-week tryout. None of Woodward's stories were judged acceptable for publication. But Rosenfeld helped him get a job at a suburban Maryland weekly newspaper. Under the guidance of its aggressive editor, Woodward soon was prowling the suburban county's government offices. He found and wrote stories about small scandals, some of which the *Post* had to follow. After Woodward persistently called Rosenfeld asking for a job, Rosenfeld hired him a little more than a year after his failed tryout.

First assigned to the night police beat, Woodward overcame police officers' cultural resistance to fresh-faced young reporters with his almost obsequious deference and polite persistence, which would open doors and create sources for him over his entire career. He took police officers out for drinks or meals and listened intently as they talked about themselves and their work. The information he picked up led to his first investigative stories about malfeasance in the department. On his own time during the day, with little sleep, Woodward made the rounds of other city agencies. He flattered workers with the undivided attention of a *Washington Post* reporter and unearthed more investigative stories.

In May 1972, Alabama governor and presidential candidate George Wallace was shot and seriously wounded in an assassination attempt in a suburban Maryland shopping center. Woodward volunteered to work on the story. He called Mark Felt several times for leads about the FBI's investigation of the gunman, Arthur Bremer. As an unnamed source, Felt helped Woodward produce several front-page stories in the *Post*. Woodward was able to write in one of them that "at least 200 FBI agents were still following leads across the country and have found no indication of a conspiracy in the Wallace shooting."

In the nine months that Woodward worked at the *Post* before the Watergate burglary, he had more bylines on front-page stories than any of the other sixty Metro reporters. Ben Bradlee took notice of his work. One day he made a show of sitting down next to the rookie reporter's desk in the newsroom to chat with him about a story.

Woodward's one limitation was the wooden quality of his writing, which also was sometimes hard to understand. He required extensive editing and often rewriting by editors, including me, throughout his years at the *Post*. But he never seemed to mind. His passion was discovering what no other journalist could find and then figuring out what it meant.

Bernstein, on the other hand, was well known in the newsroom for his skill as a writer, in addition to his own instinctive resourcefulness as a reporter. His stories were easy and appealing to read. I had been impressed by his talent and fascinated by his personality before I went on fellowship leave. Although he could be brash and arrogant, Bernstein exuded a boyish charm that could ingratiate him to anyone, including news sources. It was almost impossible to break off a conversation with him, even over the telephone. But Bernstein could also be strikingly selfish and irresponsible in his work habits, his handling of money, and his relationships with women.

In the newsroom, Bernstein was frequently emotional and opinionated, sometimes jumping to premature conclusions from his reporting. He was wary of acceding to editors when he believed they were trying to water down his stories. He ignored most of the newsroom's few expectations about hours, expenses, and following editors' directions. Before

Watergate, Rosenfeld had sent Bernstein to the Virginia news staff as the last opportunity for him to keep his job.

Woodward was politely inscrutable, making him something of a mystery to me even after I had known and worked with him for decades. He cultivated an image of conservative habits, carefulness, and reliability. Woodward was cautious about reaching conclusions from his reporting, even later when writing best-selling books on his own. He helped Bernstein become more patient, while Bernstein taught Woodward ways to manage a big, ongoing story.

Woodward dressed conservatively in suits and ties, like a young lawyer, with his long dark hair slightly overlapping his shirt collar in back. He kept a toothbrush and toothpaste in his desk drawer for use after every meal. Bernstein frequently wore jeans, let his unruly hair grow much longer, and kept new shirts in his desk drawers for late-night or early-morning changes when he did not make it home.

In short, they were an odd couple. But they almost perfectly complemented each other for the most demanding investigative reporting assignment imaginable. From the beginning, even before Mark Felt's assistance to Woodward in their underground garage meetings, the two reporters followed the money chain linking Nixon campaign contributions, the Nixon reelection committee, the Nixon White House, and those paid to carry out nefarious activities like the Watergate burglary. They sought sources among FBI agents, prosecutors, defense lawyers, White House officials, and, especially, employees of the Committee for the Re-Election of the President, which came to be known by the acronym CREEP.

Woodward and Bernstein devised techniques that would become basic for investigative reporters long afterward, even into the digital age. With the help of another newsroom employee, they obtained a printed list of all the CREEP employees, whom they methodically began to contact. "The thing to do is to work from the bottom up, finding secretaries, clerks, and middle-level aides," Bernstein told me in an interview for my 1976 book, *The New Muckrakers*. "They're the people without the vested interests of their bosses, and very often you will get a much better version of the truth from them than you would get from superiors or the target you're after."

That meant spending nights and weekends knocking on doors. "Like magazine salesmen, for every sale, you had fifty rejects," Bernstein said to me. "People can come to perceive you as a friend if you come to see them at their homes. It really involves a different kind of relationship. If you think there is a chance of their agreeing to let you in by prearrangement, you call first. Otherwise, you just go and knock on the door. We went back to several places several times, were thrown out again and again, and then maybe on the fourth time, they will say, 'Okay, we'll talk to you.'"

Woodward has used this technique throughout his career. Even when reporting for his many books, long after he had become famous, he would just show up in the evening at the door of a government official. "Your inclination is to see somebody in their office," he told me. "But you usually do twice as well if you can get to see them in their homes. Even in the White House, people have names and addresses, and they go home at night. No phone calls. No appointments. If you ever take one of those interviews and graph it to plot the useful information against the amount of time you spend in someone's home, you'll find the useful information comes at the end of a long interview."

The secretaries and other CREEP employees who would talk to Bernstein and Woodward often could or would tell them only fragments of what they thought might be going on, and they described being frightened about saying anything. Sometimes what they would say depended on how much the two reporters appeared already to know, making it seem less like revealing a secret that could identify them as a source.

"The idea is that you want to triangulate information," Bernstein told me. "You want to find out how many different versions of a particular set of facts there are, and you want to reconcile them and find out exactly where the truth lies."

Bernstein's instinct for what the truth appeared to be at each stage of their reporting was at the heart of many disagreements between him and Woodward about what each story should say. They repeatedly rewrote each other's drafts—Bernstein to smooth out the prose and underscore the story's meaning, and Woodward to try to eliminate any overreaching of the facts they had at the time. It was often left to Sussman—and later to me—to referee the disputes and put together the final story.

The tireless drive and limitless curiosity of Bernstein, Woodward, and Sussman had given them a huge head start on the rest of a seemingly disinterested and skeptical Washington press corps. Although a *New York Times* correspondent had found the Dahlberg check in Miami shortly before Bernstein did in late July, he did not connect it to the Nixon reelection committee. Two weeks later, over lunch in Washington, the then acting FBI director, L. Patrick Gray, told *New York Times* Washington bureau reporter Robert M. Smith about certain evidence the FBI had that the Nixon White House could be involved in the Watergate burglary. But Smith was leaving the *Times* the very next day for law school. He passed along the tip, including a tape recording of the luncheon conversation, to a *Times* Washington bureau editor, Robert H. Phelps. Phelps then left for a month-long trip to Alaska, and the information disappeared.

Even after publication of the Pentagon Papers, the growing opposition to the Vietnam War, and the counterculture movement that began in the 1960s, many national news reporters, especially in Washington, hung onto their old habits while covering government and politics. They knew that presidents sometimes lied or hid scandalous behavior in their private lives, but reporters at the time often did not see that as relevant to the nation's business.

Too many national news reporters gave too much deference to what they were told by their sources in government and politics, whom they talked to every day and came to know well. They regarded the "dirty tricks" they came across in political campaigns as relatively insignificant and outside the lines of the game they covered, as though it were a sport, like baseball. For too many long months, Watergate appeared to many of them to be well outside the lines.

Woodward and Bernstein and the other Metro reporters and editors working on Watergate were not constrained by that culture. Even as the story's national implications steadily grew, we worked to keep it with Metro, away from skeptics on the *Post*'s own national news staff. This would eventually grow into a tense rivalry between the underdog Metro staff and a seemingly entitled national staff in Ben's highly competitive newsroom. Although I had unsuccessfully sought a national staff reporting job when I was finishing my fellowship in London, I was becoming committed to Metro.

On September 15, 1972, Hunt, Liddy, and the five burglars—McCord and Miami residents Bernard Barker, Frank Sturgis, Vir-
gilio Gonzalez, and Eugenio Martinez—were indicted in federal court
on multiple charges of conspiring to break into the Democratic National
Headquarters in the Watergate. A spokesman for the Justice Department
said the indictments ended its investigation because "we have no evidence to indicate that any others should be charged."

But Bernstein had tracked down the CREEP bookkeeper, Judy Hoback, at her Washington home. In a series of visits by Bernstein and
Woodward, the bookkeeper told them about large cash payments made
from a secret fund at CREEP to senior campaign officials and Liddy.
Bernstein next showed up at the home of Hugh Sloan, the former trea-
surer of CREEP, who had resigned after the Watergate burglary because of
his suspicions of CREEP involvement. Reluctantly, because he respected
President Nixon, Sloan shared those suspicions with Bernstein and told
him that CREEP officials had destroyed records after the arrests. The new
information was confirmed in telephone conversations Bernstein had
with Justice Department and FBI sources and others that Woodward had
with a reluctant Mark Felt, who had access to reports from the FBI investigation of the Watergate burglary. As they pieced it together, Woodward
and Bernstein reported all of this in front-page stories in the September
17, 18, and 20 editions of the *Post*.

On September 28, Bernstein returned with Woodward to Sloan's
house. During a two-hour conversation in which he was still cautious
about how much he would reveal, Sloan filled in more information about
CREEP's secret fund and some of the names of the five people who controlled its disbursements, led by former Nixon campaign manager and
former Attorney General John Mitchell. Woodward later called a source
involved in the federal investigation of Watergate, who confirmed everything, saying that Sloan and Hoback, the bookkeeper, had already
disclosed it all to investigators. Woodward and Bernstein then met with
Sussman, Rosenfeld, and Simons in Ben's office. After they assured Ben
that they were certain about Mitchell, he told them to write it right away.
By early evening, their story was approved by all four of those editors and
set into type for the next day's newspaper.

"John N. Mitchell, while serving as U.S. Attorney General, personally controlled a secret Republican fund that was used to gather information about the Democrats, according to sources involved in the Watergate investigation," the story began. "Beginning in the spring of 1971, almost a year before he left the Justice Department to become President Nixon's campaign manager on March 1, Mitchell personally approved withdrawals from the fund, several reliable sources have told *The Washington Post*."

After the others went home, Bernstein stayed in the newsroom, calling CREEP officials for comment. He was still at his desk when he received a CREEP statement at 11 p.m. that dodged the story's main points. At 11:30, Bernstein reached Mitchell in a room at the Essex House Hotel in New York. In a telephone conversation that became part of Watergate lore, Mitchell responded to Bernstein's reading of the story's first three paragraphs by saying, "All that crap, you're putting it in the paper? It's all been denied. Katie Graham's gonna get her tit caught in a big fat wringer if that's published. . . . You fellows got a great ball game going. As soon as you're through paying Ed Williams and the rest of those fellows, we're going to do a story on all of you."

Edward Bennett Williams, a close friend of Ben Bradlee, was the *Post*'s lead outside lawyer at his firm of Williams, Connolly and Califano. Mitchell's rambling reaction sounded like a threat from the former attorney general, which went beyond the usual White House and reelection campaign denials in reaction to previous Watergate stories. It turned out to be a preview of escalating White House and Republican attacks on the *Post*.

While he was in the newsroom that night, Bernstein got an unsolicited call from a government lawyer who told him that the Watergate burglary might have been part of efforts by Republican operatives to disrupt the campaigns of Democratic presidential candidates. The caller said a lawyer friend of his had been approached by old army buddy named Donald Segretti, who offered him a paid opportunity to participate. Bernstein found the lawyer, who described how Segretti tried unsuccessfully to recruit him on behalf of the Nixon reelection campaign to spy on and sabotage the campaigns of Nixon's prospective Democratic opponents. When a *Post* freelance contributor was sent to interview Segretti at his home in Los Angeles, he refused to comment. But Bernstein found others who had been approached by Segretti, as well as a Justice Department source who confirmed that its investigation had turned up political campaign sabotage associated with Segretti.

When Woodward returned from a weekend trip to New York, he telephoned Mark Felt to arrange their first clandestine meeting in an underground garage in suburban Rosslyn, Virginia, just across the Potomac River from Washington. Felt was now associate director of the FBI, the number two job. At Felt's insistence, Woodward kept his identity secret from everyone at the Post except Bernstein. Woodward had established a "deep background" arrangement with Felt, in which Woodward could use information from him in his reporting without ever identifying or quoting him. With this in mind, Simons christened Woodward's confidential source "Deep Throat," in a joking reference to a pornographic movie popular at the time.

Woodward and Bernstein promised all their many confidential sources that their identities would be kept secret from everyone except a few Post editors, including me, until the sources died or released the reporters from their promise of confidentiality. This was essential to their reporting. Without that protection, most of their sources would never have talked to the reporters, for fear of losing their jobs in government or the Nixon reelection campaign. After Watergate, such confidential sources would play important roles in greatly increased investigative reporting by American journalists.

Woodward and Bernstein wrote memos recording their interviews, with the confidential sources' names at the top, to share with each other and their editors. I remember how valuable the memos were for us, and how much they helped us trust their reporting. These were not "anonymous sources." They were people to whom Woodward and Bernstein had promised confidentiality but whose identities were known to several Post editors, including me. The sole exception was Deep Throat, and nothing was published for which he was the only source.

An "x" appeared at the top of Woodward's memos of his conversations with Felt, except once when he wrote "M.F." at the top—which he said meant "my friend." I had completely forgotten that when, many years later, I was trying to guess Deep Throat's identity.

Following Felt's directions for their underground garage meetings, Woodward took two different taxis and walked the rest of the way to the garage and down to its bottom floor. Woodward's notes later filled two-and-a-half single-spaced typewritten pages about what was his longest and perhaps most important conversation with Deep Throat.

Felt wouldn't talk specifically about Segretti. But he confirmed a list of clandestine political disruption tactics employed by the Nixon White House and reelection committee, including eavesdropping, investigating leaks to the press, following families of Democratic politicians, planting false news stories, and disrupting Democratic candidates' campaign events. Felt told Woodward that "you can safely say more than 50" operatives like Segretti were engaged in intelligence-gathering and sabotage against the campaigns of Democratic presidential campaigns.

"It's all in the files" of the FBI's investigation of the many leads that grew out of its inquiry into the Watergate burglary, Felt told Woodward. "Justice and the Bureau know about it, even though it wasn't followed up" because the Justice Department's federal grand jury inquiry had been limited to the burglary.

Under an unusually large headline, "FBI Finds Nixon Aides Sabotaged Democrats," at the top of the *Post*'s front page on October 10, 1972, Woodward and Bernstein wrote: "FBI agents have established that the Watergate bugging incident stemmed from a massive campaign of political spying and sabotage conducted on behalf of President Nixon's reelection and directed by officials of the White House and the Committee for the Reelection of the President.

"The activities, according to information in FBI and Department of Justice files, were aimed at all the major Democratic presidential contenders and—since 1971—represented a basic strategy of the Nixon reelection effort," the story said. "During their Watergate investigation federal agents established that hundreds of thousands of dollars in Nixon campaign contributions had been set aside to pay for an extensive campaign aimed at discrediting individual Democratic presidential candidates and disrupting their campaigns."

Sussman, Rosenfeld, Simons, and even Ben Bradlee worked unusually closely with Woodward and Bernstein as their stories greatly expanded the Watergate scandal beyond the burglary of the Democrats' Watergate headquarters. They also were among the first Watergate stories that I reviewed regularly in my role as Rosenfeld's deputy. I steadily became more involved, but I did so mostly in the background during the months before early 1973—the months recounted in the *All the President's Men* book and movie. The character who was doing my job at the time was portrayed in the movie as boring the other senior editors in the daily front-page conference by offering mundane local news stories while they were focused on Watergate.

Woodward and Bernstein reported in stories over the weekend of October 15 and 16 that Segretti had been hired by Nixon's White House appointments secretary, Dwight Chapin, and paid by Nixon's personal attorney, Herbert Kalmbach, for his campaign sabotage activities. This pushed the scandal more deeply into the White House.

At the October 16 White House press briefing, Nixon's press secretary, Ron Ziegler, responded by accusing the *Post* of publishing stories "based on hearsay, innuendo, guilt by association." That afternoon, in a speech at a Republican gathering in Washington, Republican National Committee chairman Bob Dole accused the *Post* of being "a partner in mud-slinging" with the campaign of Democratic presidential candidate George McGovern. At a specially called 5 p.m. news conference at CREEP headquarters, the reelection committee's new chairman, Clark MacGregor, said that the *Post* "has maliciously sought to give the appearance of a direct connection between the White House and Watergate—a charge the *Post* knows and half a dozen investigations have found to be false."

Ben reacted by writing a rare statement of his own for the news media, saying that "not a single fact contained in the investigative reporting by this newspaper about these activities has been successfully challenged."

But reporters on the *Post*'s own national staff remained skeptical about Metro's Watergate stories. They were hearing from their government sources that Woodward and Bernstein and the rest of us in the Watergate gang on Metro were in over our heads and risked embarrassing the newspaper. They thought that we did not really know what we were doing.

The national news editor, Richard Harwood, who had been one of Ben's early star hires, made the first of repeated attempts to convince Ben that the national news staff should take over the story, since it now involved the White House and national politics. Rosenfeld reminded Ben that the national reporters were unlikely to match Woodward and Bernstein's hunger, open-mindedness, and propensity to work long hours.

"There really wasn't any choice," Ben said later. "The boys had started with it and had done all the work. It was their story, and there never was a time when we seriously considered taking it away from them."

WOODWARD AND BERNSTEIN WERE DETERMINED TO IDENTIFY the senior White House official whom Sloan had said was the fifth person who controlled CREEP's secret fund. Several middle-level White House aides had told them that Nixon's chief of staff, H. R. "Bob" Haldeman, must have approved the Segretti-Chapin campaign sabotage operation because Dwight Chapin and Herbert Kalmbach primarily reported to him. The crew-cut, square-jawed Haldeman was the most powerful and feared man in the White House besides Nixon.

When Woodward met Mark Felt on the night of October 20 in the underground garage, he came away feeling that Felt, even though he was the number two official in the FBI, must have feared Haldeman's power. No matter how many ways Woodward asked the question, Felt refused to confirm that Haldeman was the fifth person controlling the secret fund. "You've got to do it on your own," he told Woodward.

Woodward and Bernstein decided to go back to Hugh Sloan's home on October 23. Sloan, who earlier had worked for Haldeman in the White House, was more skittish than ever when they asked about Haldeman and the secret fund. "Let me put it this way," he told them, "I have no problems if you write a story like that." He also said that he had testified accurately to the federal grand jury investigating Watergate. Woodward and Bernstein came away believing that they had a big story about Sloan telling the grand jury that Haldeman was the fifth person controlling the CREEP secret fund that financed the burglary and political sabotage.

After Sussman, Rosenfeld, Simons, and Bradlee questioned them more closely than ever about their sourcing for the story, Bernstein telephoned an extremely reluctant Justice Department source. When the source refused to help him, Bernstein said he would count to ten, and, if the story was accurate, the source would stay on the line. After Bernstein counted to ten, the source was still on the line and asked, "You've got it straight now?"

"Testimony Ties Top Nixon Aide to Secret Fund," announced the big headline at the top of the *Post*'s front page on Wednesday, October 25. "The *Post* has been told," the story said, that Haldeman and the other four men who controlled the secret fund, including John Mitchell, had been named by Sloan in his grand jury testimony.

Bernstein did not stay in the newsroom that Tuesday evening, "making one more call" about the Haldeman story, as he often did. Instead, he and Woodward were up all night writing an outline for a book about Watergate, for which they would receive a $55,000 advance.

Barry Sussman, who had practically been the third coauthor of many of their stories, was not with them that night. He was not invited to join them on the book project, which he resented. By the summer of 1973, when Woodward and Bernstein finally had time to finish writing what became *All the President's Men*, Sussman had already taken a leave from the *Post* to research and write his own book on Watergate.

When Woodward and Bernstein arrived in the newsroom late Wednesday morning, they saw, on television, Sloan and his lawyer, James Stoner, being briefly interviewed on a downtown Washington sidewalk by Daniel Schorr of CBS News. "Mr. Sloan did not implicate Mr. Haldeman in that testimony at all," Stoner told Schorr. At the White House, Ron Ziegler flatly denied the Haldeman story and robustly attacked the *Post* and Ben Bradlee for "character assassination" and "a political effort . . . to discredit this administration and individuals in it."

Woodward and Bernstein kept their luncheon appointment at a nearby hotel with their book publisher, Dick Snyder of Simon and Schuster, before returning to the newsroom to try to find out what had gone wrong. Woodward telephoned Stoner, who said, "Your story is wrong. Wrong on the grand jury." Sloan's lawyer explained that "the denial is specifically related to your story. No, he has not said it to the FBI. No, he has not said it to any federal investigators." In response to a series of follow-up questions in which Woodward asked if that meant the story was nevertheless right about Haldeman and the secret fund, Stoner repeatedly responded, "No comment."

Ben surprised the two reporters and their editors at a meeting in his office that afternoon by reacting calmly when they told him they were virtually certain that the story was right about Haldeman but wrong about Sloan's grand jury testimony. Rosenfeld told them to go back to all their sources before writing anything more. Ben turned to his typewriter and, after several drafts, wrote a statement for the news media that said simply, "We stand by our story." Another *Post* reporter, Peter Osnos, was assigned to include it in a story about Stoner's denial and Ziegler's diatribe.

Sussman spent much of that day going back over Watergate stories and the denials and attacks from White House and CREEP officials. He was in his element, carefully sifting through it all to determine what he thought was true. He then wrote a memo about his research, addressed to "Rosenfeld/Simons/Bradlee/Bernstein/Woodward/Downie."

"My conclusions are that we appear to have made one definite error and perhaps a second: a) Sloan did not name Haldeman to the FBI, b) Haldeman was not interviewed by the FBI," Sussman wrote. "Beyond that I feel there is no indication from what Ziegler, MacGregor and Dole said that we have made any other mistakes. That is, I feel at this point that we are right on Haldeman."

That evening, Bernstein got through to Sloan by telephone from the newsroom. I was listening in on an extension phone, my first opportunity to hear how he dealt with a key but reluctant confidential source. It was a different kind of investigative reporting than my past searches of court and land transaction files and on-the-record interviews with public officials, fraud victims, and perpetrators. Bernstein tried out on Sloan what the reporters thought had happened: Haldeman had indeed controlled the secret fund, but Sloan had not testified about it to the grand jury.

"Bob Haldeman's name has never come up in my interviews with the grand jury," Sloan said carefully. "Our denial is strictly limited to your story. It just isn't factually true. I never said it before the grand jury. I was never asked." In answer to Bernstein's seemingly never-ending, imaginatively rephrased questions about what that meant, Sloan would only say things like: "I'm not trying to influence your pursuit of the story. The denial was strictly low-key, purposely low-key."

I again listened on an extension when Bernstein telephoned the Justice Department source with whom he had played the ten-second confirmation game. The source said that he had thought that Bernstein had instructed him to stay on the line for all ten seconds *if the story was wrong*. I was being pulled deeper into the Watergate story.

A few days later, on October 29, CREEP chairman MacGregor confirmed the existence of the cash fund in a television interview in which he denied that it was "secret" or was used for any illicit activities. That morning, Woodward moved a flower pot containing a small red flag from the front to the back of his apartment's balcony, the signal that he wanted to meet with Mark Felt. It was 3 the next morning when he found Felt in the underground garage.

"Well, Haldeman slipped away from you," Felt scolded Woodward. "I'm probably not telling you anything you don't know, but your essential facts are right. From top to bottom, this whole business is a Haldeman operation. He ran the money. Insulated himself through these functionaries around him."

When Woodward and Bernstein told Bradlee and Simons what Sloan and Deep Throat had said, the editors still weren't ready to risk another uncertain story while the *Post* was under so much scrutiny. But then Democratic candidate George McGovern, in a Sunday television interview, cited the entire Haldeman story as fact. In contrast, on a competing Sunday morning show, Vice President Spiro Agnew, who had become an increasingly strident foe of the press, called it "a contrived story constructed out of two untruths attempting to tie this to the President."

After seeing this at home, Simons telephoned Rosenfeld to say the *Post* needed a story from Woodward and Bernstein after all, clarifying what they now knew. They wrote that their sources said the *Post* was incorrect about Sloan's grand jury testimony, but the sources "confirmed once more that Haldeman was authorized to make payments from the fund."

One source went so far as to say, "'this is a Haldeman operation,'" the story stated, "and that Haldeman had 'insulated' himself, dealing with the fund through an intermediary." Deep Throat was still being used only as corroboration of what had come from other sources, but his own words had not previously been quoted and would not be again.

"I had very bad feelings about quoting Felt so directly," Woodward wrote decades later in *The Secret Man*, a book about his relationship with

Felt. "It really was contrary to the rules we had established of deep background. But I was frantic to get a story in the paper correcting our mistake."

After that mistake, as the November 7 national election approached, Woodward and Bernstein found their sources drying up. Although there had been occasional incremental stories in the *New York Times*, the *Los Angeles Times* and *Time* magazine, the *Post* had been mostly alone on Watergate for months. Between June 17 and December 31, 1972, the *Post* published two hundred Watergate stories—most of them on the front page. That was twice as many as the nearest competitor, the *New York Times*, which had far fewer Watergate stories on its front page.

It is hard to describe how isolated those of us working on Watergate often felt at the time. We were a relatively small number of young Metro reporters and editors without experience in federal investigations, national politics, or the workings of the White House. Our work was still being questioned by others in our own newsroom and largely ignored by the much of the rest of the news media. People were telling Katharine Graham that we would ruin her newspaper, which was under constant attack from the White House and Republican Party leaders.

As she later wrote in her memoir, *Personal History*, Mrs. Graham was feeling beleaguered. "During these months, the pressures on the *Post* to cease and desist were intense and uncomfortable, to say the least," she wrote. Most of her friends and business colleagues, as well as many readers who wrote to her, expressed concerns about the *Post*'s reporting. And she worried about why so little of it had been picked up by other newspapers and the television networks. "I sometimes privately thought," she wrote, "if this is such a hell of a story, then where is everybody else."

Then, on October 27 and 28, *CBS Evening News* anchor Walter Cronkite devoted unprecedented amounts of time at the beginning of his broadcasts to introduce his huge national television audience to the Watergate story. Cronkite's producer, Gordon Manning, had asked Ben, an old friend from their *Newsweek* days, for Watergate documents. But Ben told him the *Post* didn't have any. Instead, Cronkite displayed big blowups of *Post* front pages to illustrate a tutorial on Watergate that consumed the first fourteen of the twenty-two noncommercial minutes of his October 27 *CBS Evening News* broadcast and another eight minutes the next night. Watching in the *Post* newsroom, our little Watergate gang on Metro was euphoric.

Nevertheless, Nixon was reelected on November 7 in one of the largest landslides in American history. He won more than 60 percent of the popular vote and every state except Massachusetts and the District of Columbia. The Nixon administration's attacks on the *Post* escalated, and it doled out exclusive interviews and scoops to our competitors. The *Post*'s Style reporters were banned from covering White House social activities. Friends of Nixon in Florida challenged the licenses of *Post*-owned television and radio stations there.

Meanwhile, Woodward and Bernstein were having difficulty regaining traction in their reporting. Beginning at the end of November, with the reluctant approval of Ben, who knew that it could be illegal, they tried to contact members of the federal grand jury investigating Watergate. They wanted to determine whether the grand jury had somehow been prevented from investigating criminal involvement in Watergate beyond the seven men indicted on September 15. Woodward memorized the names of the twenty-three grand jurors from records in the federal court clerk's office. He and Bernstein then went from house to house to try to interview them. None of them volunteered any useable information, and several reported the approach to the federal judge in charge of the case, John J. Sirica. After being persuaded by *Post* lawyers not to cite and jail Woodward and Bernstein for contempt, Sirica lectured them in open court instead.

EARLY IN THE FEDERAL TRIAL OF HOWARD HUNT, G. GORDON Liddy, and the five Watergate burglars in Judge Sirica's courtroom on Monday, January 8, 1973, Hunt surprised everyone by pleading guilty to six counts of burglary and illegal eavesdropping. As he left the courtroom, he denied to waiting reporters that any "higher ups" were involved "to my personal knowledge."

On Friday, after court recessed for the weekend, Bernstein followed one of the accused burglars from Miami onto an airplane and charmed the man into revealing that Hunt had urged all of them to plead guilty and reassured them that they and their families would be cared for financially. After Bernstein returned to Washington on Saturday, Hunt's lawyer denied it all in a telephone interview. When *Post* lawyers warned Simons that publishing a story about the matter might prompt Sirica to accuse Bernstein of obstructing justice and to try to force him to identify his source, Simons and the reporters decided to wait another day.

But in Sunday's *New York Times*, reporter Seymour Hersh wrote that the four Miami men and their families were being paid to keep quiet and that one of them, Frank Sturgis, told Hersh that John Mitchell was being kept informed about their activities. *Time* magazine then issued a press release on Sunday, saying it would report that the Miami men had been promised $1,000 for each month they spent in jail. Woodward and Bernstein's story was then published in Monday's *Post*. Later, in court on Monday, the four Miami men pleaded guilty and evaded all the questions that a skeptical Judge Sirica asked them about their motivation and the source of the money they were carrying when they were arrested inside the Watergate.

It was perhaps the only time in my long career at the *Post* that I wasn't that unhappy about being beaten on a story. Finally, we were not going to be so alone. Sy Hersh, as he has always been known, was on the case.

Hersh, a notably aggressive investigative reporter, had been assigned to the Watergate story by *Times* editors in December, on orders from *Times* managing editor Abe Rosenthal. As a freelancer in 1969, Hersh had uncovered the My Lai massacre of more than one hundred civilians by American troops during the Vietnam War, a story Ben Bradlee had bought and published in the *Post*. Hersh soon developed his own sources among Watergate investigators, prosecutors, and defense lawyers, occasionally beating Woodward and Bernstein to new developments.

"There was a vacuum after the election when Carl and I weren't really concentrating," Woodward later said in an interview with me for *The New Muckrakers*. "We had taken some time off, and we were working on our book and traveling around making speeches. Hersh moved right into that vacuum."

When I interviewed Hersh about it for *The New Muckrakers*, he characteristically boasted: "If you ask me whether I think I could have cracked Watergate myself if I had been on it from the beginning like Woodward and Bernstein were, I'd have to say 'yes.'"

Hersh and Woodward became sparring friends. They played tennis at an indoor court in suburban Virginia, ate pizza afterward, and gossiped about Watergate. "We'd share anecdotes and humor of the situation we were in the middle of, but we never traded information," Woodward said. "Sometimes, without actually asking, Hersh would try to steer the conversation in a way that might get me to reveal some of our sources, but I wouldn't play. He tried to milk me in a manipulative but good-natured way. It was tricky sometimes, but fun—absolute fun."

The jury convicted Liddy and McCord of conspiracy, burglary, and bugging in Judge Sirica's federal courtroom on January 31. There was no indication that the Justice Department was going to pursue the investigation further, although the grand jury had not been disbanded.

National editor Richard Harwood sent a memo to senior editors saying Watergate was now behind us. In it, he said he would outline coverage of the political fallout to be done by the national news staff. That would not affect our determination on Metro to continue our investigative reporting, but the memo was an insulting assumption that it would come to naught. Rosenfeld, Sussman, and I ignored Harwood's memo. And we never heard anything about it from Ben.

The news on March 7, 1973, was not a revelation for *Post* readers, but it won what much of the rest of the news media called "vindication" for the newspaper. Acting FBI director L. Patrick Gray released to Congress an FBI interview in which Nixon lawyer Herbert Kalmbach admitted he had paid Daniel Segretti, on instructions from Dwight Chapin in the White House, for the surveillance and sabotage of Democratic presidential candidates. That was exactly what Woodward and Bernstein had first reported five months earlier in the *Post*. In their March 8 story, they reminded readers about all the White House denials, now rendered false. A jubilant Ben Bradlee gave the story overwhelming display on the front page with oversized photos of Kalmbach, Chapin, and Segretti.

Bernstein and Woodward did not break the next big Watergate story. Judge Sirica did.

McCord and Liddy had been convicted after Hunt and the four burglars from Miami had pleaded guilty. On March 23, Sirica sentenced Liddy, Hunt, and the four Miami men to prison terms. But he surprised everyone by making public a letter that McCord had sent him through the probation officer doing his presentencing investigation. Without naming names, McCord said in the letter that the defendants were pressured to plead guilty and remain silent, that some witnesses committed perjury, and that there were others involved in the Watergate operation who were not identified during the trial, though some of the witnesses could have done so.

McCord's letter changed everything. Judge Sirica postponed sentencing McCord, while he gave information to the Senate committee now investigating Watergate. The Senate had created the Select Committee on Presidential Campaign Activities—better known as the Senate Watergate Committee—by a unanimous vote on February 7. At the same time, the Justice Department had kept the Watergate grand jury in session, and it was hearing from new witnesses.

Thanks to Sirica and McCord, Watergate had finally become the number one story for the national news media. Reporters working on it had more potential sources than ever, including among the Watergate Committee senators, their staff, and the lawyers for its witnesses. Newspapers and news magazines competed over scraps of new information, although they seldom broke new ground. *Time* and *Newsweek* put Watergate on their covers and devoted multipage spreads to it inside. Television networks staked out the homes of White House officials. The chairman of the Senate Watergate Committee, Sam Ervin, a rotund seventy-six-year-old North Carolina Democrat with a jowly face and a deceptively folksy Southern manner, announced that its hearings would begin May 17 and be nationally televised.

On the afternoon of April 17, President Nixon announced in the White House press room that he was taking charge of a White House Watergate investigation. "On March 21, as a result of serious charges which came to my attention, some of which were publicly reported, I began new inquiries into this matter," Nixon said. "I can report today that there have been major developments in the case concerning which it would be improper to be more specific now, except that to say that real progress has been made in finding the truth."

After the president left the press room, press secretary Ron Ziegler was badgered by reporters about the contradictions between the president's statement and what Nixon and Ziegler had said in the past. "This is the operative statement," Ziegler famously responded. "The others are inoperative."

We wondered what was going on.

Woodward met with a source at CREEP who said that Jeb Magruder, the deputy campaign director and a former aide to Haldeman in the White House, had told the Watergate prosecutors that John Mitchell and White House counsel John Dean had been involved in the Watergate burglary and the payments to keep the burglars from talking. Back in the newsroom, Woodward called White House and Justice Department officials who confirmed all the details. While Woodward was writing the story, Ben came over, looked at what he was doing and started typing himself on a typewriter at a desk behind Woodward's. Ben rewrote the first three paragraphs of the story, which covered the entire top third of the *Post*'s April 19 front page:

> Former Attorney General John N. Mitchell and White House Counsel John W. Dean III approved and helped plan the Watergate bugging operation, according to President Nixon's former special assistant, Jeb Stuart Magruder.
>
> Mitchell and Dean later arranged to buy the silence of the seven convicted Watergate conspirators, Magruder also has said.
>
> Magruder, the deputy campaign manager for the President, made these statements to federal prosecutors Saturday, according to three sources in the White House and the Committee for the Reelection of the President.

That morning, John Dean issued a statement saying he would not "become a scapegoat in the Watergate case." Bernstein found "an associate" of Dean's who said he was willing to tell him, without being identified, Dean's side of the story. Dean had been at a meeting at which the Watergate bugging was discussed, the associate said, but had made clear that he wouldn't have anything to do with it. It was Dean who told the president on March 21 that there was a cover-up, according to the associate, and others close to Nixon had decided to make him a scapegoat.

Bernstein called another associate of Dean's, and Woodward went back to his source at CREEP. They both said that Dean had told them the same things. Woodward's source added that there was virtually nothing about the cover-up that Haldeman had not approved. Bernstein and Woodward's April 20 front-page story said that "Dean is prepared to tell a federal grand jury all that he knows about the Watergate bugging and that he will also allege that there was a cover-up by White House officials, including H. R. Haldeman, President Nixon's principal assistant."

Even with all the belated competition, the *Post* owned the story. More sources were becoming more helpful to Woodward and Bernstein by the day, settling scores, and trying to protect themselves, friends, and legal clients, so long as they would not be identified in the published stories.

As I became increasingly involved in editing them, Woodward and Bernstein produced one front-page story after another with new information from their sources. I was becoming experienced and adept at supervising their use of confidential sources, making certain that all important information was corroborated by multiple knowledgeable sources. I knew their stories were more important than ever.

On April 22, Woodward and Bernstein reported that money from the president's reelection campaign had been set aside to buy the silence of the Watergate burglars. On April 23, they reported that Nixon had been warned that some of his aides were involved in the burglary and cover-up. On April 27, they reported that acting FBI director L. Patrick Gray had destroyed documents from Howard Hunt's White House safe after being told by Dean and John Ehrlichman, assistant to the president for domestic policy, that the documents should "never see the light of day"; Gray resigned that day. On April 29, Bernstein and Woodward reported that Dean would testify that Haldeman and Ehrlichman were supervising the Watergate cover-up. And on April 30, they reported that Charles Colson, special counsel to the president, had approved the Watergate bugging.

Meanwhile, in Los Angeles on April 27, where Daniel Ellsberg was being tried under the Espionage Act for his release of the Pentagon Papers, the federal judge in that case, Matthew Byrne, announced that the Watergate prosecutors had informed him that Hunt and Liddy had supervised a burglary of Ellsberg's psychiatrist in 1971. The burglary was part of the White House "Plumbers" unit's illegal surveillance to combat Nixon's "enemies" and use wiretaps to plug leaks to the media, which

Woodward and Bernstein had touched on in earlier stories. On May 11, Byrne would dismiss all the charges against Ellsberg because of government misconduct.

The next big move was President Nixon's. On Wednesday, April 30, he announced on national television that Haldeman and Ehrlichman had resigned and Dean had been fired. Nixon said he accepted responsibility for actions they took in "an effort to conceal the facts from the public, from you, and from me," without specifying what the facts were. He also replaced the attorney general, Richard G. Kleindienst, with Defense Secretary Elliot Richardson. Nixon said he gave Richardson the responsibility for "uncovering the whole truth" about the Watergate scandal. The next day, in a grudging answer to a reporter's question at his press briefing, Ron Ziegler said, "I would apologize to the *Post*, and I would apologize to Mr. Woodward and Mr. Bernstein."

THREE OF THE FOUR WATERGATE NEWS STORIES ON THE FRONT page of the *Post* on May 1, including the main story on the removal of the three top Nixon aides, were reported and written by national news staff reporters who covered the White House and politics. With the Senate Watergate Committee hearings approaching, national news editor Richard Harwood walked over to the Metro staff side of the newsroom one afternoon to seek my support for also assigning his reporters to cover the Senate hearings.

"It's time for grown-ups," Harwood, a gruff, sometimes bullying ex-Marine, told me. He was a distinguished journalist, much older and more experienced than me, but this was too much.

"It's Metro's story," I responded angrily, loud enough for everyone around us to hear. "It's staying in Metro."

It did not end there. Bradlee and Simons sent a memo on May 8 to Rosenfeld, Sussman, Harwood, and star national reporter Haynes Johnson, saying they had decided to set up a national–Metro task force with Haynes Johnson in charge. "All Watergate matters will clear through this desk," the memo said.

Rosenfeld strongly opposed this in "a most confidential memo" to Bradlee and Simons on May 10. "Furthermore," he added, "Len Downie has developed a background into the story and brings to it also his experience as an investigative reporter."

At the time, I did not know about these memos, which I found, while researching this book, in the Ben Bradlee archive at the Harry Ransom Center at the University of Texas at Austin. Without my asking, Rosenfeld had gone to bat for me.

Bradlee and Simons then reversed themselves in what misleadingly seemed like a Solomonic decision. Metro reporters would cover the Senate hearings, and I would edit all their stories. A Watergate central office would be created for Harwood, Rosenfeld, and Sussman to monitor the hearings on television and make suggestions, which I could disregard. I also would continue to edit Bernstein and Woodward's stories, as well as assign and edit additional Watergate investigative stories by other Metro reporters.

Metro's reporting was still the heart of the Watergate story, and I had become its primary editor. We would be better able than late-coming national reporters and editors to determine how information from testimony at the hearings fit with what Woodward and Bernstein had uncovered on their own—and what its meaning was for the investigation and, ultimately, for the president's fate. There would be plenty of opportunity for the national staff to weigh in on the governmental and political impact.

I realized later that this responsibility and how I handled it was an important step in my nascent development as a newsroom leader. But at the time, my focus was on the story and the awesome responsibility I felt for its implications for the country, as well as for the newspaper.

On May 16, the night before the Senate Watergate Committee hearings began, Woodward again met Mark Felt in the underground garage. Felt warned him that everyone's lives were in danger and that they should be wary of electronic surveillance. Woodward and Bernstein told Bradlee about this in a late-night conversation outside his Georgetown home. A subsequent sweep of *Post* phone lines turned up nothing, and everyone eventually concluded that it was all a false alarm. But Felt also had given Woodward details about Dean's discussions with Nixon about the Watergate cover-up, including the need to raise $1 million to pay off everyone. More reporting confirmed that.

Meanwhile, Bernstein was told that Justice Department prosecutors and the Watergate grand jury had stepped up their investigation, targeting Haldeman and Ehrlichman even before the president fired them. On May 18, the second day of the Senate Watergate hearings, the new attorney general, Elliot Richardson, appointed Archibald Cox, former U.S. solicitor general under President Kennedy, as special prosecutor in charge of the Watergate investigation. They were both sworn in on May 25.

The Senate hearings quickly became a national obsession. Replacing regular daytime television programming, including soap operas, from mid-May until early August 1973, they were watched by tens of millions of viewers in homes, schools, and workplaces across the country. Everyone wanted to know, as the Senate committee's ranking Republican, Howard Baker, frequently asked witnesses, "What did the President know, and when did he know it?"

I wanted *Post* readers to be able to turn to the newspaper each morning to better understand what they had seen and heard on television the day before. Rosenfeld and I chose a Metro court reporter, Larry Meyer, who had become a Watergate expert while covering the burglary trial, to be the lead writer about the hearings. Woodward and Bernstein would continue their investigative reporting.

Meyer was in Room 318 of the Old Senate Office Building from the time when each day's hearing began until about 4 p.m., when he had to return to the newsroom to start writing. When testimony continued past 4, I sent other reporters to stay until the end. Peter Osnos watched the hearings in Harry Rosenfeld's office and wrote the bottom half of each day's story from what he saw and heard. On some days, other reporters were needed for additional stories about the testimony and documents the committee released.

In those days before desktop computers in the newsroom, we had usually been able to work on Watergate in relative isolation on Metro's side of the newsroom until we showed typed and pencil-edited story drafts to Ben and Howard. During the Senate Watergate hearings, however, other editors and reporters came over to Meyer's desk and read over his shoulder as he worked at his typewriter. They had their own ideas about that day's testimony and what his story should say. I welcomed all suggestions, but the final decision was mine.

When Meyer's sometimes hot temper boiled over under the pressure, I calmed him down. From my perspective watching the hearings on television, I also helped him by pointing out what I saw as the drama, revelations, and meaning in the verbal jousting between committee senators and witnesses who were still trying to avoid responsibility for their actions.

I edited all those stories, along with the extensive excerpts of the thousands of pages of hearing transcripts that filled page after page of the *Post* each day. Our work took so long that, on some days, we had only some of the stories and transcript text finished for the evening printing of the first edition of the newspaper. We then stayed into the night to make additions, revisions, and corrections for later editions.

One day, Meyer received a postcard in the newsroom from his wife. "Having a wonderful time," she wrote. "Wish you were here." She had sent it from their home.

I was so caught up in the completely engrossing work that I did not notice whether Gerry Rebach, my second wife of just two years, was bothered by my long hours in the newsroom. She never complained at the time, but my preoccupation with the *Post* would become a serious problem years later, after we had children.

Bernstein and Woodward worked to find out what the most important witnesses were likely to say before they appeared in front of the Senate committee. In one instance, they were able to report on the June 9 *Post* front page, several weeks before his public testimony, that Dean "has told Senate investigators and federal prosecutors that he had discussed aspects of the Watergate cover-up with President Nixon on at least 35 occasions" between January and April.

Dean testified about all that and much more during five dramatic days of the Senate Watergate hearings, beginning June 25. In addition to previous conversations with the president about the cover-up, he testified that he told Nixon in the Oval Office on March 21 that "there was a cancer growing on the presidency" and that he, Haldeman, Ehrlichman, and others in the White House had been involved in the Watergate burglary and cover-up, including perjury. When he later discussed with Nixon the demand by the convicted Watergate defendants for $1 million to remain silent, Dean testified, the president told him and Haldeman "that that was no problem."

The next bombshell was the surprise testimony by White House aide Alexander Butterfield. He revealed the extensive taping system that had recorded everything said in the Oval Office and on the president's White House telephone calls since the spring of 1971. Butterfield's testimony, Larry Meyer wrote, "indicates that the White House may have in its possession the means to prove that President Nixon knew nothing about the cover-up of the Watergate affair until March 21, 1973, as he has maintained, or that former White House counsel John W. Dean III was correct in testifying that President Nixon knew about the cover-up well before March 21." The revelation prompted months of legal struggles over requests and subpoenas from the Watergate special prosecutor, the Senate committee, and the House Judiciary Committee to obtain from the White House some or all of the tapes for their investigations.

MEANWHILE, MARK FELT, WHO RETIRED FROM THE FBI ON JUNE 22, told Woodward that the bureau's files contained an allegation that Vice President Agnew had received a bribe, $2,500 in cash, that he had put into his office desk drawer. In fact, as governor of Maryland, Agnew had been taking bribes from government contractors for years, and the pattern continued after he became vice president.

Working under the Maryland news editor and me, Metro reporter Richard Cohen had been investigating rumors about Agnew's corruption, with help from Carl Bernstein. As it happened, so was *Wall Street Journal* reporter Jerry Landauer. They both hit pay dirt. In almost identical stories published August 8, Cohen and Bernstein in the *Post*, and Landauer in the *Journal*, reported that Agnew had been secretly informed by federal prosecutors in Baltimore that he was under investigation for bribery, conspiracy, and tax evasion.

Fortunately for my workload, the Senate Watergate hearings had just recessed, and Bernstein and Woodward were taking time off to write their book, *All the President's Men*. However, Rosenfeld spent most of August on vacation in England and Wales, so I was left to direct all of Metro's news coverage, including the breaking Agnew investigation and any Watergate stories.

On August 15, Cohen reported in the *Post* that several Maryland engineering contractors had testified to a federal grand jury that they made cash payments to Agnew to receive choice state contracts. There also were allegations that he had received payments while vice president for influencing a federal government contract.

Although many of the other news media outlets joined in pursuit of the Agnew story, the *Post*'s own editorial page and its senior political writer condemned the confidential sources who gave Cohen information from a secret grand jury investigation, even though he obtained it legally. I thought, to the contrary, that the sources were performing a public service. I've never understood the condemnation of "leaks" of information that the American public should know.

By September, the national news staff was working with us on Agnew. A September 22 front-page story by Cohen and the *Post*'s lead White House reporter, Lou Cannon, revealed that the vice president's lawyers and Justice Department officials had been "engaged in what was described yesterday as delicate negotiations concerning a possible Agnew resignation coupled with a guilty plea to a relatively minor offense."

That is exactly what happened on October 10, 1973. In a surprise appearance in federal court in Baltimore, Agnew resigned as vice president, pleaded guilty to a single count of tax evasion, and was sentenced to three years' probation and a $10,000 fine.

The subject of that court hearing had been scheduled to be a subpoena from Agnew's lawyers of the notes of several reporters, including Cohen, to determine the sources of their stories. Katharine Graham had thrilled us by taking legal ownership of Cohen's notes so that a judge would have to jail her for contempt if she refused to turn them over. Ben Bradlee memorably called it "the Gray-haired Widow Defense." Agnew's plea made it all moot.

President Nixon appointed House Minority Leader Gerald Ford to replace Agnew as vice president, and Ford was confirmed by the Senate in December.

Special Watergate prosecutor Archibald Cox had been trying for months to obtain the White House tapes. On August 29, Judge

Sirica, still presiding over the Watergate grand jury, ordered the White House to produce nine tapes of presidential conversations and meetings that Cox had sought. The president appealed, but the U.S. Court of Appeals backed Sirica on October 12. Nixon's lawyers then offered summaries of "relevant portions" in a compromise. But Cox and Attorney General Elliot Richardson refused it.

I was at home on Saturday night, October 20, when I got a call from the newsroom. At the direction of the president, his new chief of staff, General Alexander Haig, had ordered Attorney General Elliot Richardson to fire Cox. Richardson refused and resigned. Haig then ordered Deputy Attorney General William Ruckelshaus to fire Cox, and he refused and resigned. Finally, Solicitor General Robert Bork did the deed. This was a national staff story, but I needed to hurry to the newsroom to see what Metro could do. I remember telling Gerry that I wondered whether there would be tanks on the streets downtown.

What came to be called the "Saturday Night Massacre" turned out to be a big mistake for Nixon. The political and public backlash forced Haig to find a new special prosecutor, Houston lawyer Leon Jaworski. The House Judiciary Committee took preliminary steps toward considering impeachment of the president. A month later, the White House told Judge Sirica that there was a gap of eighteen-and-a-half minutes in a still unreleased recording of a conversation between Nixon and Haldeman three days after the Watergate burglary—an erasure that was never plausibly explained.

By late February 1974, John Dean, Donald Segretti, and a half dozen White House and CREEP officials had pleaded guilty in the expanded criminal investigation of Watergate. On March 1, the Watergate grand jury indicted Haldeman, Ehrlichman, Mitchell, and four other former White House aides for conspiracy and false statements. In addition to the indictment, Jaworski sent a briefcase containing a sealed grand jury report, along with accompanying evidence of a case against the president, to Judge Sirica, with the recommendation that it be forwarded to the House Judiciary Committee.

The Watergate grand jury also named Nixon as an unindicted co-conspirator in the indictment. But Jaworski kept that information a secret when the indictment was made public on March 4. The naming of

Nixon would not be revealed until June 8 when an investigative story by Woodward and Bernstein appeared in the *Post* and a story by Ron Ostrow appeared in the *Los Angeles Times*.

Woodward and Bernstein also discovered that the grand jury had voted 19–0 that it had accumulated enough evidence to indict Nixon for conspiracy to obstruct justice. "The unofficial 'straw vote' was taken at the request of one of the grand jurors," they wrote, "after it was determined by the grand jury that the Constitution precluded indictment of an incumbent president" before being impeached and removed from office. I have a copy of my handwritten editing of that story.

Considerable negotiation often was involved in my editing of Bernstein and Woodward. They sometimes wrote competing versions of a story, and I wound up rewriting the opening paragraphs after determining what they should say. Bernstein sometimes stayed late rereading the first edited version and trying to revise it more to his liking. I was always worried that he would try to insert what amounted to a "Nixon is guilty" paragraph. Once, I was called at home late at night by a copy editor asking if I had approved changes Bernstein had made after I left. I had not, so I left my wife and our already late dinner to return to the newsroom to fix things.

All the President's Men was published June 15, and Woodward and Bernstein squeezed out time to promote it. Not that much promotion was necessary, because the book quickly became a big best seller. They somehow continued to produce revealing *Post* stories, from sources who reached all the way up to Chief of Staff Alexander Haig, about chaos in the White House in the dying days of the Nixon administration. That laid the foundation for their next best-selling book, *The Final Days*.

On July 24, after months of legal struggles over the White House tapes, the U.S. Supreme Court ruled unanimously that Nixon had to turn them over to the Watergate special prosecutor and the House Judiciary Committee. Days later, before the tapes were turned over, the House Judiciary Committee approved three articles of impeachment against the president: obstructing justice, violating the constitutional rights of American citizens, and defying subpoenas. Then came the revelation of a previously unknown Oval Office conversation on June 23, 1972—days after the Watergate burglary. In it, the president and Haldeman discussed using the CIA to persuade the FBI to limit the burglary investigation, beginning the cover-up. What became known as the "smoking gun" tape was Metro's last significant Watergate story.

By the night of August 8, 1974, the national news staff had been given responsibility for covering what remained of the special prosecutor investigation and the impeachment process. When President Nixon announced on television from the Oval Office that he would resign at noon the next day, Woodward, Bernstein, and I watched in stunned silence. After wandering the newsroom looking dazed, the two reporters typed out some background notes for the national reporters before they disappeared. I no longer remember what I did the rest of the evening. The next day, I watched Nixon leave the White House and Ford become president, before I returned full-time to local news coverage.

WE COULDN'T ANTICIPATE IT THEN, BUT OUR WORK ON WATERgate—and the *All the President's Men* book and movie—would spark a sweeping change in American journalism. Investigative reporting would become a priority for the news media, continuing into the digital age. Newspapers, television networks and stations, and digital news organizations would create investigative teams and showcase their work. Generations of young people would enter journalism schools, aspiring to be investigative reporters.

Investigative reporting would expand to every aspect of American society—from government, politics, business, and finance to law enforcement, education, social welfare, religion, culture, and sports. It would smash past taboos by aggressively challenging government secrecy and probing the private behavior of politicians and other public figures. The tradition of aggressive investigative reporting has in recent years manifested in revelations about the administration of President Donald Trump, the victimization of women in the workplace, and the sexual crimes of Catholic priests.

Right after Watergate, in 1975, I was among a half dozen investigative journalists who founded Investigative Reporters and Editors, a group to promote the mission, values, and best practices for investigative reporting and to provide training in its techniques. Membership in the IRE and attendance at its annual training conferences would grow over the decades to many thousands of journalists around the country and the world, helping each other and their news organizations to produce more accountability journalism.

IN 1975, AFTER I SUCCEEDED HARRY ROSENFELD AS METRO EDITOR, I was ending a meeting in my office when I noticed someone sitting on the floor in a back corner. It was Dustin Hoffman.

He spent nearly four months in the *Post* newsroom, preparing to portray Carl Bernstein in the movie version of *All the President's Men*. He became part of the landscape of the newsroom, which allowed him to watch and absorb how we worked. He roamed the newsroom relatively unobtrusively, sat in on meetings, watched and interviewed reporters, and even listened in on their telephone conversations. He also spent hours with Bernstein outside the newsroom and celebrated a Passover Seder with him at his parents' home in suburban Maryland.

Robert Redford's occasional presence in the newsroom was more disruptive because of the attention he unintentionally attracted. He was both preparing to portray Woodward and envisioning the movie that had been his idea, even before Woodward and Bernstein's book had been written and published. Redford wanted to make a movie that would honestly portray investigative journalism and its role in American democracy. After Woodward and Bernstein came to trust him, they and their publisher signed a deal for the movie in September 1974.

Redford found a director, Alan Pakula, who shared his vision. Pakula also spent time at the *Post*, making notes and interviewing Woodward, Bernstein, Ben Bradlee, and Katharine Graham. He found supporting actors—Jason Robards as Ben, Jack Warden as Harry Rosenfeld, and Martin Balsam as Howard Simons—who also visited the newsroom.

Pakula and Redford eventually decided not to portray Katharine Graham in the movie, which disappointed her. Pakula said at the time that he would like to make another movie about her pioneering role as a woman publisher during the Pentagon Papers and Watergate, but he never did. He would die in a tragic auto accident in 1998. In 2018, Stephen Spielberg would make a movie, *The Post*, about Mrs. Graham's momentous decision to publish the Pentagon Papers, and I would be one of the script and onset consultants.

Pakula's production manager and his assistants spent even more time in the newsroom, taking 1,000 photographs and making meticulous notes. They obtained the construction blueprints and measured everything. On a huge soundstage in Burbank, California, they reproduced the main newsroom in almost the same size with the same bright fluorescent overhead lighting, brightly colored furnishings, and glass-walled offices along its perimeter. Copies of the same works of art hung in the soundstage newsroom, along with 1972 calendars displaying the correct date for each scene.

The movie newsroom contained the same two hundred desks, plus the same wastebaskets, Teletype, Telex, fax and photo machines, typewriters, telephones and other equipment, and even books. The phones had the correct extension numbers on them, and 1972 phone directories were on the desks. All the equipment and technology worked. Unseen actors played the appropriate people on the other end of the line for Woodward and Bernstein's telephone calls.

The *Post* sent packing crates of used paper, unopened mail, old galley proofs, and other trash from our newsroom to scatter on the desks on the movie set. It also reprinted the front pages of seventeen different editions of the *Post* for placement on the desks on days depicted in the movie. The production manager put a photograph of each desk in our newsroom into the drawer of the comparable desk in the movie newsroom so the set decorator could recreate it.

After much rewriting of the script, overseen by Redford and Pakula, the movie closely followed the book. In scenes involving important interviews of sources, Pakula made sure that the words were those that Woodward and Bernstein had reported. One of his assistants had spent weeks in the *Post* newsroom to chart what went on there each hour and day of the week so that the actors playing reporters and editors in the background would be doing the appropriate thing in every scene.

At the premiere of the movie on April 4, 1976, before an audience of 1,100 at the Kennedy Center, I had a difficult time following the narrative because I was so distracted by the fact that the newsroom in the movie was identical to the one where I worked. At the beginning of each scene, I could tell the hour of the day and the day of the week by what was happening in the background. At the end of the row of desks in which Redford as Woodward was often seen talking on the telephone, I could see my own office with the actor in it depicting me doing just what I would have been doing at that time.

The portrayals of Woodward, Bernstein, and Bradlee were strikingly accurate and made them lifelong celebrities. However, managing editor Howard Simons was not happy about how he was portrayed in the movie: completely overshadowed by Ben, even though he had played a key role in the crucial early weeks and months of the Watergate investigation. It and other disagreements turned what had been a close relationship between the two men into an increasingly acrimonious estrangement until Simons left the *Post*. Barry Sussman was not portrayed in the movie at all.

Woodward returned to the *Post* from a book leave in the autumn of 1975, while Bernstein remained on a leave from which he never really returned. Woodward sat back down at his old desk in Metro and began contacting sources until he found new investigative stories for the *Post's* front page. He reported Howard Hunt's abortive plan to drug or poison muckraking columnist Jack Anderson. He uncovered the National Security Agency's electronic eavesdropping on long-distance telephone calls and cables of American antiwar leaders, decades before news media exposure of the NSA's similar secret antiterrorism surveillance after the September 11 attacks on the United States.

Alan Pakula went on to direct the 1993 movie *The Pelican Brief*, based on the John Grisham novel about a *Washington Post* reporter who helps a young law student unravel a murderous conspiracy involving government officials. By that time, I was the executive editor of the *Post*. Pakula, who also wrote the screenplay, telephoned me one day to ask if one of the newspaper's editors could serve as a consultant for the newsroom scenes that would be filmed in a downtown Washington office building. When he realized that I was expecting the fictional newspaper still to be called the *Post*, Pakula corrected me: "I would never make a fictional movie about the *Washington Post*."

That seemed right to me.

7

The Legend of Deep Throat

AFTER WATERGATE, NOTHING WAS THE SAME. The movie *All the President's Men* had made Ben Bradlee, Bob Woodward, and Carl Bernstein celebrities; most of the rest of us felt somehow privileged to be working in the newsroom glorified by the film. Before the movie was released, Ben put Harry Rosenfeld in charge of national news, and, on Rosenfeld's recommendation, I succeeded him as Metro editor in the autumn of 1974.

In the three decades that followed, as I would move from Metro editor to London correspondent, national news editor, managing editor, and executive editor, one loose end from Watergate loomed ever larger: who was Deep Throat? Woodward's "deep background" source became mythologized after his portrayal by the actor Hal Holbrook in the shadows of the Arlington, Virginia, underground garage in the movie.

In the world of journalism, Deep Throat was an iconic symbol of the importance of confidential sources and journalists' promises not to identify them unless released from their confidentiality agreements. At various times, journalists were even willing to go to jail if a court ordered them to break their promise and reveal a source—and some did so.

Because that principle is so vital to journalism—and to investigative reporting in particular—I'm pausing in the chronicle of my *Post* career to tell the story of Woodward's decades-long fidelity to his confidential source relationship with Deep Throat. It became something of a legend.

Woodward did not even tell Ben Bradlee that Deep Throat was Mark Felt until 1976, when Ben asked, after publication of Bob and Carl's second book, *The Final Days*. During Watergate, Ben knew Woodward's confidential source as an unnamed Justice Department official. The only other people who knew Deep Throat's identity at the time were Woodward's wife, Elsa Walsh, and Bernstein.

The mystery spawned a cottage industry of speculation, in the news media, books, and even college classrooms, about who Deep Throat might be—or whether he existed at all. Some people, including David Obst, Woodward and Bernstein's agent for *All the President's Men*, insisted that Deep Throat must be a composite invented by Woodward to hide the identities of other confidential sources and make the narrative more dramatic. Felt himself cleverly told the *Wall Street Journal* in June 1974 that he thought Deep Throat was a "composite," when he was asked whether he fit the description in *All the President's Men*.

John Dean had made several wrong guesses. In his 1982 book, *Lost Honor*, he fingered Alexander Haig, who was deputy national security adviser during the early stages of Watergate and the White House chief of staff by the time Nixon resigned. Dean later took that back, although other authors also erroneously named Haig. In his 2002 book, *Unmasking Deep Throat*, Dean stated his new belief that the source did not work for the FBI. In early 2005, Dean wrote in the *Los Angeles Times* that he had "little doubt that one of my former Nixon White House colleagues is history's best-known anonymous source."

Journalists Taylor Branch (in *Esquire* magazine in 1976) and Michael Kelly (in the *New York Times Magazine* in 1993) guessed that Deep Throat was David Gergen, the journalist, television commentator, and perennial White House aide. Gergen was a Nixon White House speechwriter who later worked in various capacities for presidents Gerald Ford, Ronald Reagan, and Bill Clinton. Former acting White House counsel Leonard Garment, who had himself been the target of speculation, erroneously theorized in his 2000 book, *In Search of Deep Throat*, that it was former Nixon political strategist John P. Sears. Others mentioned at various times included former acting FBI director L. Patrick Gray, former assistant attorney general Henry Peterson, and even Henry Kissinger.

The most ambitious, although ultimately misguided, attempt at identifying Deep Throat was a four-year investigation, begun in 1999, by sixty University of Illinois journalism students and their professor, former *Chicago Tribune* investigative reporter Bill Gaines. They exhaustively analyzed thousands of pages of declassified FBI reports on the Watergate investigation, a computer spreadsheet of Woodward and Bernstein's stories, and even archived drafts of the *All the President's Men* book manuscript, with the authors' notes in the margins. They compared travel records of Nixon administration officials with dates of Deep Throat's meetings with Woodward. They checked death records to eliminate suspects who were no longer alive, as Woodward had stated that he and Bernstein would reveal Deep Throat's identity upon his death.

The students and Gaines came up with seven likely candidates: David Gergen, Nixon aide Patrick Buchanan, Nixon speechwriter Raymond Price, deputy press secretary Gerald Warren, Nixon aide Stephen Bull, White House lawyer Jonathan Rose, and deputy White House counsel Fred Fielding, who was later White House counsel for presidents Reagan and George W. Bush. They finally settled on Fielding. He was a smoker and drinker, as was Deep Throat, and, as John Dean's deputy, had access to White House and FBI materials related to Watergate. He also had been an army captain who worked at the Pentagon at the same time that Woodward did when he was a navy lieutenant in the mid-1960s.

Not all the speculation was wrong. The Nixon White House tapes revealed many years later that Nixon's chief of staff, H. R. Haldeman, told the president in the Oval Office on October 19, 1972—just three months after the Watergate burglary—that a source had informed him that Mark Felt was one of Woodward's confidential sources. Haldeman successfully urged Nixon not to do anything about it. "If we move on him," Haldeman was later heard telling Nixon on tape, "he'll go out and unload every-thing. He knows everything that's to be known in the FBI. He has access to absolutely everything."

In 1976, Assistant Attorney General Stanley Pottinger was questioning Felt before a federal grand jury investigating the 1972 and 1973 FBI bur-glaries of the homes of the Weathermen, a left-wing radical organization, when a grand juror, out of the blue, asked Felt if he was Deep Throat.

"I saw Felt look stunned and go white," Pottinger recalled in an e-mail to Woodward, Bernstein, and Ben Bradlee on June 2, 2005, two days after Deep Throat's identity was publicly revealed. "I told the stenographer to stop taking notes, went over to Felt and whispered: 'You're under oath, so if you answer this question, you have to answer it truthfully. On the other hand, I consider the question to be outside the bounds of our official investigation, so, if you prefer, I'll withdraw the question.'

"Flushed, he said very fast, 'Withdraw the question,'" Pottinger re-called. "And I did."

Woodward telephoned Pottinger later that day to say Felt had called from a pay phone outside the courthouse to tell him what had happened. At a subsequent off-the-record lunch, Pottinger told Woodward that he now assumed Felt was Deep Throat, but he would not reveal it.

In 1980, Felt was convicted, with another FBI official, Edward Miller, for being responsible for the FBI's break-ins of suspects' homes during its investigation of the Weathermen domestic terrorism group. Felt and Miller were later pardoned by President Reagan.

Journalist and author Jim Mann, who had worked on some of the Wa-tergate stories on the *Post*'s Metro staff before leaving the paper in Sep-tember 1972, wrote in the *Atlantic Monthly* in May 1992 that Felt was one of three Watergate-era FBI officials who could have been Deep Throat. He noted that Felt had been passed over as FBI director after J. Edgar Hoover's death in the spring of 1973 and again when L. Patrick Gray resigned as acting director. "Felt was known in Washington as a person willing to talk to the press," Mann wrote. He added that Felt had denied being Deep Throat in Felt's 1979 book, *The FBI Pyramid*.

Over the years, Felt periodically denied speculation in other publi-cations that he was Deep Throat. "I can tell you that it was not I and it is not I," he told the popular *Washingtonian* magazine in 1974. "No, it's not me," he told the *Hartford Courant* newspaper in 1999. "I would have done better. I would have been more effective. Deep Throat didn't exactly bring the White House crashing down, did he?"

SOMETIME AFTER I BECAME EXECUTIVE EDITOR OF THE *POST* IN 1991, I decided to join the guessing game myself. After all, I had a big advantage. I knew the names of the many confidential sources of Woodward and Bernstein who were not Deep Throat—because they had been identified at the top of the typed notes of their interviews. Alexander Haig, for instance, was one of them.

My first guess was Elliot Richardson. He had not been one of those named confidential sources. He was the attorney general fired by Nixon in the Saturday Night Massacre. And years later, he had tipped me to a story about a multimillion-dollar procurement problem at the Justice Department. I told Woodward my guess. Not until after Richardson died, on December 31, 1999, did Woodward tell me I was wrong.

Next, I guessed L. Patrick Gray, who had resigned as acting FBI director during the Watergate investigation. He also was not among the named confidential sources in Woodward and Bernstein's interview notes. Woodward told me years later that it wasn't Gray, although he was then still alive.

With the advantage I had, I thought I should get only three strikes in this game. Because of my detailed knowledge of what Deep Throat had told Woodward, I thought really hard. I knew it had to be someone senior at Justice or the FBI during Watergate. Who was left? I thought about the investigative reporting I had done decades earlier. I remembered a telephone conversation I'd had with Mark Felt several years before Watergate, when he was number three at the FBI. I had been impressed by his willingness to help. Then I remembered the "M.F." at the top of the first page of one of Woodward's typed memos from an interview with Deep Throat, which he had said at the time meant "my friend"—the way he had often referred to Deep Throat. How had I missed that?

In November 2002, I wrote Felt's name on a piece of paper, with an explanation, sealed it in an envelope, and gave it to Woodward to open when Deep Throat died.

IN EARLY 2005, WOODWARD SAID IN A TELEVISION INTERVIEW that Deep Throat was getting quite old. I heard that Woodward had begun saying the same thing in his answers to the usual questions about Deep Throat during his public speaking appearances. I knew that Woodward always thought carefully about what he was saying. Did this mean that Deep Throat might be near death? If so, the *Washington Post* was not prepared for that. I summoned Woodward to my office.

By that time, Woodward was an accomplished, famous, and wealthy author. After the Watergate books with Bernstein, he researched and wrote a dozen best-selling books about the administrations of Bill Clinton and George W. Bush, the Iraq War, the CIA, the Pentagon, the Supreme Court, the Federal Reserve, and the overdose death of television comedian John Belushi. He also maintained a relationship with the *Post*. With the title of assistant managing editor, he had, for a time, led the *Post*'s investigative reporting unit.

We published advance excerpts from his books in the *Post*, and the newspaper benefited from individual stories and tips that he found in his research. In times of journalistic crisis, such as the September 11, 2001, terrorist attacks, Woodward showed up in the newsroom and went to work. He never forgot the support he had gotten from Ben Bradlee, Katharine Graham, Don Graham, and me during and long after Watergate.

We were not social friends, but Woodward and I always had a meaningful professional relationship. I read some of his book manuscripts in advance and selected excerpts for *Post* editors to adapt for the newspaper. I worked with him on individual stories he produced for the paper. He often was cagey about the content of books he was working on until they were quite far along, or until he surfaced something that he and I thought should go into the newspaper right away. When he was being secretive about what he was working on, our conversations could be somewhat stilted. That was the case when I began talking to him about Deep Throat that day.

I told Woodward that we had to start preparing for Deep Throat's death. We would need to publish stories right afterward about who he was, his relationship with Woodward, his role in the Watergate investigation, the significance of his remaining an unnamed confidential source for more than three decades, and more. Woodward didn't seem to engage right away. He wondered aloud whether we would have to identify Deep Throat immediately after he died, as no one else would yet know that that person was Deep Throat. Couldn't we wait to prepare everything? he asked.

I could usually tell in such conversations when Woodward was holding something back from me. I also knew that he would be forthcoming if I insisted. It was a Midwestern sense of duty that we shared. In the *Washington Post* newsroom, which we both loved, he still treated me as his boss. "You're the editor," he often told me.

"Bob," I asked him, "what aren't you telling me?"

"Well," he responded somewhat sheepishly, "I've written this book about me and Deep Throat."

He wanted to publish it a few weeks after Deep Throat died, with a prepublication excerpt just before that in the *Post* that would break the news.

"The book is fine with me," I told him. "But when he dies, we have to report it right away. And I want to publish whatever our readers should see from your book right away. In fact, I want to read the manuscript as soon as possible."

It turned out that the book grew out of a conversation, years earlier, between Woodward and Ben Bradlee. Ben suggested that Woodward write a first-person account of his relationship with Deep Throat that would appear along with a news story in the *Post* the day after he died. Characteristically, Woodward turned that idea into a manuscript for a book, which Ben read in an early draft. Ben recalled later that he had also told Woodward "that he needed to bring the current executive editor, Len Downie, into the loop." I wonder when Woodward would have done that if I hadn't made the first move.

After more discussion over the next few weeks, I arrived at Woodward's house at 9 a.m. on Thursday, March 3, 2005. He took me into his dining room, where the table was set for two for brunch. He brought out the 50,000-word manuscript for *The Secret Man*. I quickly saw that Mark Felt was indeed Deep Throat.

"You were right!" Woodward announced, smiling. He had already opened the envelope that I had given him twenty-seven months earlier. I had not remembered that the note inside said: "Mark Felt, who has been at the top of my list since 1972, long before Jim Mann's excellent *Atlantic* article, or the U. of Illinois' naïve study. Len"

Woodward then told me about his conversations with Felt in recent years, beginning with a telephone call to him in January 2000. He was surprised to find that Felt was unable to remember his own age, details about Watergate, or even his own 1980 criminal trial. At the end of February, while on a trip for a speech, Woodward decided to visit Felt, who now lived with his daughter, Joan, in Santa Rosa, California. Woodward introduced himself to Joan Felt as an old friend of her father from Washington. He took Felt to lunch and then returned to Felt's apartment over the garage for more conversation. Felt recognized Woodward as a friend. But he could not recall anything about being a source of Woodward's during Watergate, or much of anything else from his years in Washington.

In late April 2002, Woodward was contacted separately by Felt's fifty-five-year-old son and the family's lawyer, John D. O'Connor, who both said that Felt had told them he was Deep Throat. But when Woodward got Felt on the phone, Felt once again could not remember anything about it. When Woodward occasionally called Joan to check on her father, she told him that she and the rest of the family wanted to have her father recognized as Deep Throat before he died, if in fact it was true. Woodward told me he still did not acknowledge to her that her dad was Deep Throat.

In the manuscript for his book, Woodward wrote: "It is critical that confidential sources feel they would be protected for life. There needed to be a model out there where people could come forward or speak when contacted, knowing they would be protected. It was a matter of my work, a matter of honor."

I could not have agreed more. Deep Throat had indeed become that model.

In Woodward's dining room, we discussed how to proceed. He tried once more to persuade me to delay the *Post*'s revelation of Mark Felt as Deep Throat until his book could be published weeks after Felt's death. I asked him how we could report the death of such a prominent person without revealing that secret, which would be big news. I reminded him, "You have always said that the identity of Deep Throat would be disclosed on his death."

We finally agreed that, when Felt died, the *Post* would immediately publish, at minimum, a news story written by another *Post* reporter, a profile of Felt, and reaction stories. On the second day, we would publish about 5,000 words from Woodward's manuscript detailing their relationship. He could publish the book as soon after that as possible.

I then went through the manuscript with Woodward, as though I were his book editor, because he wanted to keep it secret from everyone else at the *Post*, his publisher, and his agent. The next day, Woodward sent me an e-mail thanking me for my "ideas, concepts and fixes." He found what we did together "very creative and collaborative. I miss those times, and it is good to recapture that."

TWO MONTHS LATER, ON MAY 31, 2005, I WAS WITH MY SENIOR editors and Don Graham, who was then the *Post*'s CEO, at our annual retreat. It was held that year at the Chesapeake Bay waterside resort of St. Michael's, Maryland, eighty miles east of Washington. I was leading a discussion of changes we were making at the newspaper when my mobile phone started ringing. I ignored it and continued talking.

When my phone rang again, I turned if off. Moments later, a conference center employee quietly entered the room and put phone messages on the table in front of me. I pushed them aside.

But when Don Graham's phone rang, he decided to step outside onto a stone patio and answer it. Don was a methodical man; if someone was trying to interrupt him during a meeting, it must be important. Through a large window on the opposite side of the conference room, I could see Don point a finger at me and signal emphatically that I should come out and join him immediately.

Bob Woodward was calling about Deep Throat.

Woodward told me from his Georgetown home in Washington that earlier that morning *Vanity Fair* magazine had posted an article in which Mark Felt's family and their lawyer, John O'Connor, identified Felt as Deep Throat. Woodward insisted that this did not mean that Felt himself was releasing Woodward from his confidential source agreement. He reminded me that he had concluded that the ninety-one-year-old Felt, who apparently suffered from dementia, was no longer competent to make that decision.

Woodward told me that Bernstein, who was in New York, agreed with him after reading the *Vanity Fair* story. Bernstein even wrote a statement for the news media in which he and Woodward reaffirmed the confidentiality agreement with Deep Throat.

I telephoned Ben Bradlee, who then had an office in retirement in the *Post* building two floors above the newsroom. Ben said that he had already told Woodward that the Felt family had effectively released the *Post* from the confidentiality agreement. Woodward had not passed that on to me.

I would have to decide what to do. I called Woodward back and told him that we would talk as soon as we both arrived in the newsroom. I said I was initially inclined to go ahead and confirm that Felt was Deep Throat, but I would hear Woodward out first. I telephoned the newsroom and directed that preparation begin on a package of stories about the identification, pending my final decision.

I ended the meeting, quickly packed my car, and drove back across the Chesapeake Bay Bridge to Washington at speeds that risked arrest.

WHEN I ARRIVED BACK AT THE *POST* AROUND 2:15 P.M., PHOTOGraphers and television cameramen were already gathered outside the main entrance. Inside, the fifth-floor newsroom felt on edge. It turned out that everyone had read the *Vanity Fair* article online, saw the first news reports about it, and were wondering what I would do. As I had decided weeks earlier, as a contingency, one of the *Post*'s best writers, David Von Drehle, was already at work on a news story that would be ready for the revelation of Deep Throat's identity. I now told Von Drehle that it would name Mark Felt.

I read the eight-page *Vanity Fair* article, written by O'Connor with the cooperation of Felt's family, in which O'Connor said of Felt, "On several occasions he confided in me, 'I'm the guy they used to call Deep Throat.'" He also cited Woodward's conversations with Mark and Joan Felt as evidence. "Joan and I spoke to Woodward on a half-dozen occasions over a period of months about whether to make a joint revelation," O'Connor wrote, but Woodward had demurred without acknowledging that Felt was Deep Throat.

I spoke on the phone again with Ben, who said he still figured "this was the end" of the confidentiality agreement with Felt.

Woodward arrived in the newsroom about 2:30 and joined me in my office. It was the same office, with different furnishings, in which he and Bernstein had so often met with Ben and other editors to discuss Watergate stories more than thirty years earlier.

"I'm more convinced that this is truly it," I told Woodward, adding that Ben and Don Graham agreed with me. Felt's family had ended the confidential source agreement. We didn't have much time. The *Vanity Fair* story was all over the internet. Our website editors were pressing me for a decision.

Woodward was very uncomfortable. He usually made sure he was in control of situations like this, but he had been taken by surprise. He again made the devil's advocate argument about whether Felt had really given his consent to the *Vanity Fair* article, and whether that meant the end of the newspaper's confidentiality agreement with him. I told Woodward that I'd concluded that Felt either knew what he was doing in revealing himself or, if he was not in a position to know, his daughter and lawyer were acting on his behalf.

Woodward asked whether we should allow them to force our decision.

"They already have," I told him. "Bob, it's over."

Woodward went to his newsroom office and telephoned Bernstein, whose shuttle flight to Washington was still on the tarmac in New York. Bernstein told him that the first statement confirming that Mark Felt was Deep Throat should come from them.

Within a couple of hours, Woodward and I met Bernstein with hugs when he got off the elevator on the fifth floor. I carried Bernstein's overnight bag to my office, where we quickly reviewed the day's discussions. I had made my decision, but I wanted them to be in agreement, however reluctantly.

Ben then came into the newsroom, and we greeted him with more hugs. Reporters and editors gawked as *Post* photographers took pictures of the historic scene.

It was time. At 5:12 p.m., this news alert was posted on the *Post*'s website:

WOODWARD CONFIRMS IDENTITY OF "DEEP THROAT"

"Former FBI official W. Mark Felt was the source for leaked secrets about Nixon's Watergate cover-up, The Washington Post confirms after Felt's admission."

"W. Mark Felt was 'Deep Throat' and helped immeasurably in our Watergate coverage," Woodward and Bernstein said in their statement, which also was posted. "However, as the record shows, many other sources and officials assisted us and other reporters for the hundreds of stories that were written in The Washington Post about Watergate."

A full news story followed seventeen minutes later. A longer version and additional stories filled six pages in the June 1, 2005, *Washington Post*. The next day, a lengthy excerpt from Woodward's forthcoming book about his relationship with Mark Felt was spread across the top of the front page and filled another three pages inside.

I was quoted in the news story as saying that "the newspaper decided that the newspaper had been released from its obligation by Mark Felt's family and by his lawyer. They revealed him as the source. We confirmed it."

I praised Woodward in my statement for keeping his promise even during the months when he knew that the Felt family and their lawyer were considering their revelation. "This demonstrates clearly the lengths to which Bob and this newspaper will go," I said, "to protect sources and confidential relationships."

Long afterward, I often was asked publicly how it felt to be "scooped" by *Vanity Fair* on the *Post*'s own story. As uncomfortable as it was at the time, I explained, it could not have worked out better for the newspaper. Whenever a source was promised confidentiality by the *Washington Post*, the reporter could point to the faithfulness of Woodward and the *Post* in honoring his agreement with Mark Felt for so many years, even at the risk of losing control over it.

8

Encountering Terror

T HE FIRST SKETCHY REPORTS CAME INTO THE newsroom around noon on Wednesday, March 9, 1977, after I had left for a luncheon appointment I can no longer remember. Violent men with guns were seen invading the eight-story national headquarters of B'nai B'rith, the national Jewish service organization, just three blocks northwest of the *Post* in downtown Washington.

It was nearly a quarter century before the September 11, 2001, terrorist attacks on the United States. There were no TSA checkpoints at airports, no barricades around government buildings in Washington and other cities, no lockdowns at schools or workplaces because of the threat of "active shooters." Despite a spate of relatively small-scale bombings by left-wing underground extremist groups in a few American cities during the 1970s, domestic terrorism would not be considered a serious national threat until the 1995 truck bombing by Timothy McVeigh that killed 168 people in the Alfred P. Murrah Federal Building in Oklahoma City.

There was no precedent for what I would confront in my second year as the *Post*'s Metro news editor. Terrorists had never before invaded buildings in Washington, violently taken scores of hostages, and threatened mass killings if their demands were not met. I had not previously directed coverage of a big, breaking story about which my decisions could affect people's lives. For the first time, I would have to consider requests from public officials about what they did or did not want the *Post* to report.

I had already put strong editors in place under me, including my deputy, Tom Wilkinson, and the *Post*'s first African American city editor, Herb Denton. While I was at lunch, Wilkinson sent a reporter to B'nai B'rith on Rhode Island Avenue NW, where he saw police sealing off the building and setting up a perimeter around it. Then Wilkinson assigned another reporter to find the B'nai B'rith listing in the District of Columbia telephone directory and to start calling their offices. It was standard procedure on the Metro staff to phone people living or working near a newsworthy happening to ask what they knew while reporters hurried to the scene.

The *Post* reporter making the call into B'nai B'rith was able to reach some employees and a few men working on a renovation of the building. They had barricaded themselves in rooms on the lower floors. Hours before any reliable information was available from police, they told our reporter that the invaders were black men waving rifles and machetes and yelling anti-Semitic curses. They said the men had grabbed and beaten people and taken them upstairs in the building's elevators.

Around 1 p.m. came word that a second building had been invaded. Gunmen were seen taking hostages inside the imposing blue-and-white Washington Mosque and Islamic Center along Embassy Row on Massachusetts Avenue NW. It was about two miles northwest of B'nai B'rith. A *Post* reporter's telephone call to the Islamic Center was answered by a man who identified himself as one of three American Muslims who he said had taken hostages in the center's offices. He said their takeover was connected to the occupation of the B'nai B'rith building. He added that further information would have to await announcements later in the day: "You'll know soon enough."

When I returned to the newsroom, I worked with my editors to deploy reporters and tentatively assign stories. I relied on what I had learned as a reporter and city desk editor during the 1968 riots and the anti–Vietnam War demonstrations in Washington. I realized that I would have to make decisions about how our reporting could affect the safety of the people taken hostage inside those buildings.

I decided that we should inform the police about what we knew from our reporters' telephone conversations, including the possibility that something more might happen. I knew that we had a policy of providing information to authorities in those rare instances when we determined that there was a clear and present danger to public safety and that doing so would not compromise our independence from law enforcement.

About 2:20 p.m., the *Post*'s city government reporter, Milton Coleman, was returning to his beat from lunch when he saw police officers with guns drawn running into a side entrance of the District Building—the six-story Classical Revival city hall on Pennsylvania Avenue NW, near the White House grounds in Washington, D.C. As more police officers arrived and blocked access to the building, Coleman found a public telephone and called *Post* city editor Herb Denton, who told him that self-identified Muslims had already taken over the B'nai B'rith headquarters and the Islamic Center, and that the three incidents were probably connected.

I assigned reporters in the newsroom to call into the District Building to try to find out what had happened to the mayor and members of the city council. People who were hiding in the city council's fifth-floor offices told *Post* reporters that two gunmen had invaded the building, gone upstairs, shot several people, and taken hostages into a city council member's office. The people reached on the telephone said that Mayor Walter Washington was hiding in his office suite at the opposite end of the fifth floor.

The District Building was just three blocks east of the White House, the B'nai B'rith building was six blocks north of it, and the Islamic Center was surrounded by foreign embassies on Massachusetts Avenue. The invasions, violence, and hostage taking at the three buildings appeared to be a coordinated terrorist attack in the heart of the capital city.

Hundreds of police officers and dozens of FBI agents soon surrounded each of the three buildings and blocked access to the surrounding streets.

All police reserves were called up. Other city buildings and courts, as well as office buildings within the cordoned-off areas, were cleared and shut down. Numerous city officials and some members of Congress were put under police protection. Federal monuments were ordered closed.

I stationed *Post* reporters and photographers with walkie-talkies and radio cars among the gathering crowds of news media and onlookers, including relatives of hostages, on the three siege perimeters. I assigned reporters in the newsroom to call and maintain contact with the FBI, Secret Service, Pentagon, and State Department. I established a chain of command through Wilkinson and Denton to try to ensure that our journalists on the street and on telephones would not interfere with the authorities or endanger the hostages while gathering as much information as they could.

I told Ben Bradlee and Howard Simons what was going on and how I was handling it. They left the decision making to me. It became a crash course for me in crisis news coverage and newsroom management.

By 2:45 p.m., the District of Columbia emergency command center, first used during the 1968 riots, was fully activated at police headquarters. It was a corridor of offices, including the police chief's, with sophisticated communications equipment that could connect it directly to other public safety agencies, the White House, and the Pentagon. I could confer with officials and our reporters there to confirm information from our street reporting and our contacts with the hostage takers.

I decided to continue those contacts through telephones inside the besieged buildings. We kept our telephone calls as infrequent and brief as possible, despite the many calls being made by other news media and even members of the public. We tried not to interfere with calls being made by the police. We made no attempt to negotiate with the hostage takers or to reveal to them information we had, especially what we knew about the movements or plans of the police.

IT WAS MID-AFTERNOON WHEN MAX ROBINSON, THE AFRICAN American news anchor at Washington, D.C., television station WTOP, received a telephone call from Abdul Aziz, the thirty-five-year-old son-in-law of Hamaas Abdul Khaalis, leader of the local Hanafi Movement, a group of American Muslims. Khaalis had broken with the Nation of Islam, also known as the Black Muslims, and befriended basketball star Kareem Abdul Jabbar, who had converted to Hanafi Islam. Khaalis had established a Hanafi Muslim residence and headquarters in a stone mansion purchased in 1971 by Abdul Jabbar for the Hanafis on upper 16th Street NW, about six miles directly north of the White House.

The Hanafis and Black Muslims became bitter rivals. In December 1972, Khaalis sent letters to all fifty-seven Nation of Islam mosques calling its then leader, Elijah Muhammad, "a lying deceiver," guilty of "fooling and deceiving people." On January 18, 1973, while Khaalis was out shopping, seven Black Muslims from Philadelphia attacked the 16th Street house in retaliation. They murdered two adults and five children in Khaalis's family. His daughter, Amina, was shot three times but survived.

Five of the attackers were later convicted of the murders and imprisoned for life. Another was acquitted when one of the others refused to testify against him. The seventh defendant was granted a new trial when Amina Khaalis refused to be cross-examined by the defense. Hamaas Abdul Khaalis himself was fined $750 when the judge in the cases, Leonard Braman, held him in contempt for shouting at the defendants during the first trial, "You killed my babies. You killed my babies and shot my women!"

Abdul Aziz, Amina Khaalis's husband, who met Max Robinson at the time of the 1973 murders, told him in a telephone call that his father-in-law was the leader of the takeovers of the three Washington buildings. With the assistance of Aziz, Robinson then talked by phone with Hamaas Abdul Khaalis, who was inside the B'nai B'rith building. Khaalis angrily threatened to kill scores of hostages that he and his men had under guard on the eighth floor, unless his demands were met.

Khaalis demanded an end to any showings of a commercial movie, *Mohammed, Messenger of God,* scheduled to premiere that day in New York and Los Angeles. Starring Anthony Quinn and financed largely by Middle Eastern investors, it did not depict the prophet Mohammed in person, which is generally forbidden by Muslims. But Khaalis told Robinson, "It's misrepresenting the Muslim faith." In addition, he wanted the imprisoned killers of his family members brought to him for "retribution." And he wanted the $750 he was fined "by the Jewish judge" to be returned to him.

When Robinson's conversation with Khaalis was subsequently broadcast, I decided that the *Post* should also attempt to contact Khaalis. "We have told this government to get busy and get the murderers that came into our house on January 18 and murdered our babies. And shot up our women," Khaalis told a *Post* reporter in a telephone conversation. "Tell them the payday is here. We gonna pull the cover off of them. No more games."

This was indeed terrorism—intended to force authorities to bend to the will of the Hanafi gunmen, to coerce the media to spread their message of grievance and anger, and to have their B'nai B'rith hostages feel the brunt of their anti-Semitism.

By then, the police had managed to occupy the lower floors of the B'nai B'rith building, freeing people who had hidden there. Led by Metropolitan Police chief Maurice Cullinane, the police began their own telephone conversations with Khaalis to assure him that they would not push past barricaded stairways and storm the upper floors, so long as he did not harm anyone else and he maintained communication with the police.

About forty people either escaped the building or were freed by Khaalis, without explanation. Eleven of them had been beaten or stabbed, and others complained of chest pains. The freed hostages estimated that Khaalis and his men still held more than one hundred hostages—B'nai B'rith employees and construction workers—in a large eighth-floor conference area that was being renovated and had been stripped down to a concrete floor. I stopped our phone calls to Khaalis after he made clear to our reporter and to other news media callers that he did not like the *Washington Post* because of how we had covered the Hanafi Muslims in the past.

One of our reporters did continue to talk periodically to one of the three men who had taken over the Islamic Center. He sounded much calmer than Khaalis, although every bit as threatening. The twelve people taken hostage at the Islamic Center included its director, Mohammed Abdul Rauf, who telephoned the Egyptian consul general's office in New York during the afternoon, asking that someone intercede to stop the showings of the movie *Mohammed, Messenger of God*. By that evening, audiences were turned away, the premieres were cancelled, and the film was withdrawn by its distributors.

POST REPORTERS WERE UNABLE TO CONTACT THE TWO GUNMEN holding hostages in the District Building, but they continued to talk to some of the estimated seventeen people hiding in council offices, as well as those who had made it out of the building. They said the gunmen came up the stairs to the fifth floor, apparently in search of the mayor. But they turned the wrong way—left rather than right—and wound up in the complex of city council offices, behind double glass doors. They began herding seven hostages into the offices of the city council chairman, who was not there.

At the door to the council complex, one of the gunmen fired his shotgun at a building guard who was opening the door from the hallway. The security guard, Mack Cantrell, was shot in the head and later died at George Washington University Hospital. Next to him, a twenty-four-year-old WHUR radio reporter, Maurice Williams, who happened to be walking toward the council offices from an elevator, was hit in the chest and fell dead. Then council member Marion Barry, who stepped into the corridor when he heard a commotion there, was struck by a stray shotgun pellet in his chest, just missing his heart. Barry managed to stumble into a vacant council office.

Heavily armed police with bulletproof vests and shields moved upstairs in the District Building, to the fifth floor, in sight of the gunmen holding hostages. As *Post* reporter Milton Coleman watched from across the street, police and firemen brought to the District Building vehicles and equipment, including hook-and-ladder fire trucks that could not be seen by the hostage takers. Officials at the emergency command center at D.C. police headquarters asked the news media not to report their precise locations or to speculate why they might be there. Although I would have agreed anyway, it was an easy decision because we would not start printing the early edition of the next day's newspaper until after 10 p.m.

The command center officials also asked us to report misinformation, such as that the police had been unable to get far inside the B'nai B'rith building, which I refused to do. I had to balance what I thought the public should know with what I thought could endanger the hostages.

Late in the afternoon, Coleman saw a fire ladder extended up to a fifth-floor window on one side of the District Building. Firemen took a stretcher up the ladder and carefully brought down Marion Barry. He would recover from his wound at nearby George Washington University Hospital, and two years later be elected Washington's mayor.

Behind the District Building, another hook-and-ladder truck, not visible to Coleman, was used after nightfall to gradually rescue some of the people who had been hiding in other city council offices. At 6:15 p.m., in sight of the gunmen, a phalanx of heavily armed police brought Mayor Washington out of his fifth-floor office and took him downstairs and out of the building to the command center about ten blocks away.

THE THURSDAY, MARCH 10, EDITIONS OF THE *WASHINGTON POST* were filled with stories about the Hanafi sieges. As had been the case with the Senate Watergate hearings four years earlier, I wanted the *Post* to help its hundreds of thousands of readers to understand and learn more about what they had been seeing and hearing on television and radio.

Unknown to us for many hours, the ambassadors from Egypt and Pakistan and Chief Cullinane had begun negotiations with Khaalis on Wednesday night. Eventually, Khaalis offered that he and the others would free all the hostages and put down their weapons if, after being arrested, he could be released without bail pending his trial. Cullinane called local prosecutors, who contacted U.S. attorney general Griffin Bell. When he agreed to the deal, they called Harold Greene, chief judge of the D.C. Superior Court, at 1:15 a.m., and he reluctantly agreed to release Khaalis without bail four hours later in his courtroom.

The three gunmen holding hostages at the Islamic Center and the two at the District Building surrendered to police. Khaalis and the six gunmen at B'nai B'rith walked out unarmed and gave themselves up without even informing the 105 hostages they left on the eighth floor, who didn't know they were safe and free until police appeared. All 134 freed hostages were taken to George Washington University Hospital for examination and treatment. Forty of them, mostly men, had major or minor bruises from being hit and tied up. Khaalis and the other gunmen would later be tried, convicted, and sentenced to long terms in prison, where Khaalis would die in 2003.

We managed to get news of the negotiations and the hostages' release into the final editions of the Friday, March 11 newspaper. The Saturday paper featured, among other stories, a reconstruction of the siege, details of the negotiations that ended it, interviews with the hostages, and news about the hostage takers' arraignment in court. My goal was to cover every possible angle of the story. In the years ahead, as managing editor and executive editor, I would become known, if not notorious, in the *Post* newsroom for this kind of blanket coverage of major news events.

The Hanafis' siege, which lasted just over thirty-eight hours, has been largely forgotten. Yet directing the coverage and making the critical decisions involved was one of my formative experiences as an editor. I learned how to get the best out of a large staff of strong-willed professionals on daily deadlines, challenging them without dictating. I worked through the editors under me while maintaining enough contact with their reporters to get directly involved in their most important stories. I made sure that the editors and reporters knew I also was open to feedback and disagreements—ready to change my mind whenever I was shown a better way.

The experience impressed on me the responsibility of a newspaper to inform everyone as fully and accurately as possible in a time of crisis, without endangering lives, regardless of what other news media might be doing. I did not know then, of course, but it would be an even greater responsibility and more difficult to fulfill in the media cacophony of the future digital age.

BEN BRADLEE, WHO HAD EVEN LESS INTEREST IN LOCAL NEWS after Watergate, gave me great freedom to manage Metro in my own way. During my four years as Metro editor, I expanded the staff and its mission. I became identified in the newsroom with local news.

So it came as a surprise when Ben summoned me to his office in the autumn of 1978 and asked if I would be interested in becoming the *Post*'s London bureau chief.

London? I knew it was considered the *Post*'s most desirable foreign assignment. At that time, being a foreign correspondent was especially attractive, with generous financial support from the newspaper, independence from the daily whims of editors back home, and virtually unlimited travel. Yet I had never really thought about becoming a foreign correspondent, in part because I had a terrible ear for any language I would have to learn for a posting other than London.

Ben told me that the incumbent correspondent, Bernard Nossiter, was refusing to leave. Nossiter had been in London for nearly eight years, twice the usual length of a foreign posting, and had become a somewhat revered, comfortable, expense account–dependent Anglophile who regularly appeared on British television. "Maybe if I sent an assistant managing editor to replace him," I remember Ben telling me, referring to my formal newsroom title, "he might get the message."

I wondered if Ben was just joking about a vexing problem that he wanted to share with me. He could have ordered Nossiter home himself in no uncertain terms. But he was avoiding confrontation with the veteran correspondent, who, in previous postings, had worked for the newspaper in Paris and New Delhi. In case Ben *was* serious, I told him I would think about it.

I first talked to Gerry. Even though she was several months pregnant with our first child, she was ready to live abroad again, as we had during my fellowship. The more flexible schedule of a foreign correspondent could be an improvement over the relentlessly long hours of my work on Watergate and management of the Metro news staff. It could also be an opportunity to improve my still developing writing skills and to grow journalistically in new ways.

I then consulted Herb Denton. He was close to Don Graham, with whom he had served in the U.S. Army in Vietnam, after both graduated from Harvard. Herb was a very private person who never let on whether he talked to Don about me. But he told me that the experience of being a foreign correspondent could help prepare me for more senior roles in the newsroom.

Just as I would six years later, when the managing editor's job opened up, I went back to Ben. I made a determined pitch for London. Whatever his reasons, Ben eventually gave me the job.

I stepped down as assistant managing editor for metropolitan news in October 1978, and Gerry and I began preparing for my new assignment. We had to decide, with the assistance of the *Post*'s relocation company, what to pack and what to store. I signed an agreement with the newspaper for housing, cost of living, and tax equalization allowances. I began reading books on British history, government, and politics. I expected to study about Ireland, Denmark, Norway, Sweden, and Finland, which I knew were also part of the London bureau's responsibilities. I scheduled appointments at their embassies.

What I did not know while doing all of this was that I would become a foreign correspondent much sooner than I expected, in a very different country, with no preparation at all.

9

Tragedy in Jonestown

$\mathfrak{I}$T WAS SOMETIME AFTER 11 ON SATURDAY night, November 18, 1978, when *Washington Post* managing editor Howard Simons telephoned me at home. He got my attention when he said that *Post* correspondent Charles Krause might have been killed. Simons told me that Krause was with a group of Americans traveling with California congressman Leo J. Ryan when gunmen had attacked them that evening on a remote jungle landing strip in the South American country of Guyana. Ryan and several journalists were reported to have died. No one at the newspaper had heard from Krause, and Simons feared the worst.

He wanted me, foreign correspondent Karen DeYoung, and photographer Frank Johnston to fly to Guyana as soon as possible. A plane was being chartered for us at Washington National Airport. DeYoung and Johnston were to start covering the story when we got to Guyana. As a senior editor of the paper, preparing to be a foreign correspondent, I was to find out what happened to Krause and to make the necessary arrangements if he had been killed. Simons told me to wear a suit. I agreed to leave right away.

I had never been to South America. I knew nothing about Guyana. I did not know why a U.S. congressman and a group of reporters would have gone there, or why they would have been attacked. I didn't know exactly what I would be doing there, or when I might be back.

Assistant foreign editor Rick Weintraub called DeYoung. She was the *Post* correspondent for the northern tier of South American countries, which included Guyana. She was home in Washington for Thanksgiving, having begged off going on the trip with Congressman Ryan. She knew that he and a group of journalists and "concerned relatives" were going to Guyana to inspect the remote jungle commune where hundreds of American followers of a messianic San Francisco cult leader, the Rev. Jim Jones, were living with him. DeYoung was worried about Krause. She agreed to pick me up so we could leave immediately.

Weintraub also telephoned foreign editor Peter Osnos at home. Osnos had made the decision to send Krause, the *Post*'s other South America correspondent, who was covering an election in Caracas, Venezuela, to join Ryan on the trip to Guyana in DeYoung's place. Osnos was intrigued by the supposedly utopian settlement, known as Jonestown, that Jones and some of his followers had constructed in a remote northeastern corner of Guyana. San Francisco news media and an organized group of relatives had accused Jones of intimidation, brutality, sleep deprivation, and brainwashing of the commune's nearly 1,000 racially diverse residents, who ranged from families with young children to the elderly. In the summer of 1977, Jones had persuaded most of his followers to leave his San Francisco Peoples Temple church and resettle in Jonestown to escape scrutiny. Ryan, a northern California congressman, was going to investigate conditions there.

Krause had met up with Ryan's group in Trinidad, from where they flew to the Guyana capital of Georgetown. The group included Ryan, Jackie Speier, who was his chief aide, a diplomat from the U.S. Embassy in Guyana, two lawyers who represented Jones, eight other newspaper and television journalists, and four of the concerned relatives hoping to persuade their loved ones to leave Jonestown. On Friday afternoon, November 17, they traveled 160 miles on a chartered twin-engine Havilland from Georgetown airport to the air strip at Port Kaituma. After negotiating on the air strip with a group of Jones's representatives who had opposed their visit, the group was finally driven that evening, in the back of a dump truck, the eight miles along a dirt road to Jonestown.

To their surprise, they were welcomed in the settlement's main pavilion with dinner, music, and dancing by scores of residents, whose outwardly ecstatic behavior seemed stilted to some of the visitors. As Jones watched closely, residents in and around the pavilion talked about how happy they were living in Jonestown. But the journalists were confined to the pavilion for the evening, and Jones reacted irritably to their questions about the reports of ill-treatment at Jonestown. After an inspection tour was negotiated for the next day, Ryan and Speier spent the night in bunk beds in one of the many neat wooden structures dotting the settlement. Krause, the other journalists, and the concerned relatives were taken to Port Kaituma village, where they slept on the floor of an open-air discotheque.

When they returned to Jonestown on Saturday, they found an increasingly tense atmosphere. The journalists had to overcome resistance from Jones and his lieutenants to look around the compound and into buildings, including one that was startlingly overcrowded with elderly black people. Some residents told NBC News reporter Don Harris that they wanted to leave Jonestown with Ryan's group because they were not happy there and feared Jones. Ryan and Speier collected names, as defecting residents began gathering around them. Jones became visibly upset, especially when Harris asked him on camera why the defectors did not want to stay.

By 3 p.m., more than a dozen residents had gotten their belongings and joined the visitors as they walked out on a dirt track to the dump truck to go to the Port Kaituma air strip. Ryan, who had stayed a little longer, continuing conversations, was suddenly attacked by a Jones lieutenant wielding a knife. Other people intervened and prevented Ryan from being hurt, while Jones watched impassively some distance away. When Ryan emerged from the compound to join the others on the truck, his clothes were matted with blood from a cut on the assailant's hand.

Although an NBC News crew had filmed much of this, none of it was yet known in the outside world. Nor what was to happen next.

Ryan's group and the defecting Jonestown residents arrived at the air strip late Saturday afternoon to fly back before dark to Georgetown on two planes. While they were beginning to board, they were attacked by gunmen who arrived from Jonestown on a truck and a tractor-pulled trailer. Vague Guyanese government reports of numerous deaths and injuries in the attack emerged in the news media hours later. Osnos remembered telling his wife, as he was leaving home Saturday night to go to the newspaper, "I killed Krause"—by sending him with Ryan to Guyana.

DEYOUNG AND I MET JOHNSTON AT A VIRTUALLY DESERTED National Airport well after midnight. We found the pilot of the small, propeller-driven airplane the *Post* had chartered. All the available private jets had been quickly scooped up by the television networks, which, at a time before satellite transmissions, needed them to ferry film back and forth from Guyana. The three of us helped push our plane onto the runway. It was nearly 2 a.m. Sunday when we finally took off.

As we flew south through the early morning sky, DeYoung took charge, which was fine with me. I had never done anything like this. She was an experienced, self-confident foreign correspondent. She had been a lone freelancer in West Africa before coming to the *Post*, and she had already done reporting in many places in Latin America. I watched her and learned.

DeYoung grew increasingly impatient with the slow progress of our little prop plane. After a few hours, she used the plane's radio telephone to call the *Post*'s foreign staff administrative assistant at home to demand that he find us a jet plane to which we could transfer when we finally made it to Miami. He succeeded in reserving the last available small private jet at the Miami airport.

It was daylight when we landed in Miami and located our jet. Lined up next to it was a group of other journalists hoping to catch a ride. A *New York Times* reporter was first in line. DeYoung, Johnston, and I looked at each other. We turned him down. The *Times*, after all, was our competitor. Instead, as I remember, we took an Associated Press reporter and another photographer. We were relieved when the plane climbed swiftly into the sky.

As fast as the jet flew, we still had to endure an unexpected, tense delay when our pilot stopped to refuel on the Dutch Caribbean island of Aruba. Our plane was met by military officers on the tarmac. Without visas or other official notice of who we were or why we had landed there, we were ushered into the military's airport offices. The plane and our luggage were searched, presumably for illicit drugs. Over what I remember as my feeble objection, DeYoung was taken into an inner office for questioning. Her passport was full of Latin American entry stamps, including some from Cuba. Somehow, she convinced the senior military officer about the truth of our emergency journey to Guyana, and we were finally allowed to proceed.

It was already dark again when we finally landed early Sunday evening at the airport outside Georgetown. Guyana was a racially heterogeneous former British plantation colony of less than a million people on the northeast Atlantic coast of South America. Its economy was based on bauxite mining and sugar and rice agriculture. At that time, it had a single-party, quasi-socialist government. We soon found that its officials expected to be addressed as "comrades."

The airport was filled with jets, some of which bore crude signs designating the television networks and other news organizations that had chartered them. Among the few people at the airport was Bernard Shaw, then the Latin America correspondent for ABC News, and his crew, filming a standup report to be flown back to New York.

With no taxis in sight, DeYoung managed to get us, with our luggage, onto a passing bus, already crowded with people and animals, for the long, winding ride into Georgetown. We had reservations at the Tower Hotel on Main Street, where Krause was registered. When we got off the bus, still a walk away from the hotel, DeYoung called from the nearest pay phone and asked for Krause's room. When she was told the room's extension was busy, the three of us relaxed a bit. If Krause was on the phone, he was alive.

After checking in at the hotel, where much of the rest of a burgeoning press corps was staying, we went straight to Krause's room and knocked on the door. It was about 6:30 p.m. To our great relief, he answered, wearing only a towel around his waist. He was talking on a telephone, the cord of which he stretched to the doorway, while holding a notebook. He was dictating to someone at the *Post* a story he had written in longhand.

"Are you okay?" we blurted out. "What happened? Were you shot?"

Without answering, Krause lifted part of the towel to show us a wound where a bullet had passed through the flesh of his left hip.

He later told us that he had been hit and played dead when gunmen from Jonestown opened fire on Ryan's group at the Port Kaituma air strip on Saturday night. Before the gunmen disappeared back into the jungle, Ryan, NBC News reporter Don Harris and cameraman Robert Brown, *San Francisco Examiner* photographer Greg Robinson, and defecting Jonestown resident Patricia Parks were all killed. Ten others were wounded, many of them, including Jackie Speier, much more seriously than Krause. Most of the Jonestown defectors had run off and hidden in the jungle.

Krause and the remaining survivors were evacuated by the Guyana military, after waiting overnight for planes to take them out on Sunday. The seriously wounded spent the night in a military tent on the air strip. Krause stayed mostly awake with other survivors under police guard in a nearby Port Kaituma bar. He interviewed the remaining defectors, who described concentration camp–like conditions behind the façade of a socialist paradise at Jonestown. They said that the paranoid Jones frequently woke everyone for "white nights" mass suicide drills, in case the settlement was threatened by the American or Guyanese governments. One of the defectors was able to identify some of the air strip attackers. Krause wrote it all down in his notebook, along with a first-person account of the attack and his survival.

After being evacuated to the Georgetown airport, Krause was treated for his wound on an American military hospital plane sent by President Jimmy Carter. The other wounded were flown back to the United States, where they all eventually recovered. Jackie Speier, who nearly lost an arm and a leg to severe bullet wounds, would be elected to Congress from Ryan's old district thirty years later.

Krause got off the plane before it left for the United States and stayed in Georgetown to work on the story. After giving a witness statement to the Guyanese police, he finally got back to his room in the Tower Hotel on Sunday afternoon while the three of us were still in the air.

After showering, Krause had the hotel send his editors at the *Post* a Telex message informing them for the first time that he was okay. Neither they nor Krause yet knew what had happened in Jonestown after the attack on the air strip. He had only heard speculation overnight in Port Kaituma that Jones might force his followers to kill themselves in the aftermath of the defections and the air strip attack.

By the time we reached his room, Krause had contacted the *Post* by telephone through the hotel's single phone operator. He gave a writer in the newsroom everything in his notes for a news story about the air strip shooting and the visits to Jonestown. We heard Krause then dictating the first-person story he had written in his notebook on Saturday night in the Port Kaituma bar:

> When the Jonestown truck and tractor suddenly pulled to the side of the small landing strip here, those who knew Peoples Temple best, the 16 disaffected former members, said there was going to be trouble. . . . Suddenly, at least three men from the Jonestown vehicles began coming toward us. . . . Then, the shooting began. It seemed to be coming from the left side of the aircraft I was standing near, a Guyana Airways Twin Otter. I ran around the other side and dove behind a wheel, thinking it would protect me.
>
> Others, I couldn't exactly see whom, were already there and at least two people jumped on top of me as the shooting intensified. I lay there still, hoping they would think I was dead. Shots were being fired very close by. I felt the dirt spraying over me as the bullets came. . . . Suddenly, my left hip burned and I knew that I had been hit.

Congressman Ryan lay dead a foot and a half away from Krause, on the other side of the plane's wheel.

BY MONDAY MORNING, NEARLY ONE HUNDRED MEMBERS OF THE world's news media had descended on Georgetown. They converged in the cramped auditorium of Guyana's Ministry of Information. Earlier in the morning, the ministry had made the shocking announcement that hundreds of people in Jonestown, including Jim Jones, had been found dead there by government investigators on Sunday. Guyanese authorities had been alerted late Saturday night by a Jonestown resident who had escaped what he described as a Jones-directed mass suicide and walked through the jungle to a police outpost.

At the packed news conference, the minister of information, Comrade Shirley Field-Ridley, told us that Guyanese police investigators had counted 408 bodies lying out in the open under a hot sun in Jonestown. She said the Guyanese military was searching the rainforest around Jonestown for hundreds more people thought to be missing. She informed the assembled journalists that they would be unable to go to Jonestown because of the ongoing investigation, the rapidly deteriorating dead bodies, and the remoteness of the site. Only one pool reporter and photographer could be taken by plane to Port Kaituma and then flown by helicopter to Jonestown. They could share what they saw and photographed there with the rest of the press corps when they returned to Georgetown.

Bedlam broke out while the stately Field-Ridley watched helplessly. Without thinking, I jumped up from my seat a few rows away from her and shouted above the din that only one reporter in the room had been wounded and had survived the shooting at the Port Kaituma air strip. I said that reporter was Charles Krause of the *Washington Post*, and I pointed to him in the front row. "Why don't you let Krause go?" I asked Field-Ridley. "He deserves it!" Surprisingly, there was a murmur of agreement.

Meanwhile, the news photographers, as they were accustomed to doing, met quietly in a corner to decide among themselves who would be their best representative for the pool assignment. They chose Frank Johnston of the *Washington Post*.

As Krause and Johnston left, Field-Ridley asked me belatedly if the pool reporter and photographer should both be from the same news organization. I said that Krause was a special case, that Johnston had been chosen by his peers, and that they both could be trusted to cooperate fully with the rest of the news media when they returned. She smiled when I added, "Besides, I think they're already on their way to the airport."

Field-Ridley and nearly all the journalists there did not yet know that I also worked for the *Post*. But as everyone filed out of the auditorium, someone I didn't recognize came up beside me and asked, "Aren't you Len Downie?" I admitted that I was. He responded, "You son of a bitch!"

I was pleased.

With Krause alive and on his way to Jonestown to report and write another first-person story, my role changed dramatically. DeYoung was going back to Washington for Thanksgiving, before resuming her responsibilities elsewhere in South America. My job now was to be the lead news writer about something about which I had known nothing just twenty-four hours earlier. Literally overnight, I had become a foreign correspondent, covering a very big story in competition with the rest of the world's news media. I felt nervous and a bit disoriented. Now, I would have to learn on my own.

So I went back to basics. I interviewed Guyanese government and American embassy officials, and I asked questions at news conferences held by Guyanese officials and by the two lawyers for Jim Jones, Mark Lane and Charles Garry. Lane and Garry, who were well-known, self-promoting lawyers, had stayed in Jonestown after Ryan's group left for the Port Kaituma air strip. As it became clear to them that a very disturbed Jones and his gun-carrying lieutenants were gathering up Jonestown's residents for what could be a mass murder-suicide, the two lawyers talked their way out of the settlement, fled into the jungle, and eventually made it back to Georgetown.

I also interviewed Lane separately to pin down details, and I wrote the news media's most detailed story about what had happened in Jonestown before the mass deaths. I had not written a story for the *Post* in nearly eight years. To my relief, it was not that difficult. All those years of editing had greatly improved my story conceptualization and writing, even on deadline.

The editor in me knew, however, that Krause was the man of the hour. When he and Frank Johnston returned from Jonestown that Monday night, Krause wrote a memorable first-person account about what he found there. It was displayed above my news story at the top of the front page of the *Post* the next day:

> Jonestown, Guyana. When the Rev. Jim Jones learned Saturday that Rep. Ryan had been killed but that some members of his party had survived, Jones called his followers

together and told them the time had come to commit the mass suicide they had rehearsed several times before.

"They started with the babies," administering a potion of Kool-Aid mixed with cyanide, Odell Rhodes recalled yesterday when I revisited Jonestown to view the horrifying sight of 409 bodies—men, women, and children, most of them grouped around the altar where Jones himself lay dead.

Rhodes is the only known survivor of Jonestown who witnessed a part of the suicide rite before managing to escape. He was helping Guyanese authorities identify the dead yesterday.

Guyanese police officials who were investigating the crime scene told Krause that Jones and two others had been shot rather than poisoned. They said that investigators found large amounts of cash, checks, jewelry, and gold, along with more than eight hundred American passports hidden in trunks in a Jonestown building. That left the question of what had happened to at least four hundred more Jonestown residents.

FOR THE NEXT SEVERAL DAYS, MY REPORTING FOCUSED ON THE mystery of the missing Jonestown residents, the slow removal of the disintegrating bodies of the dead by the American military, and their transport by air to the United States. A handful of residents who had fled the mass murder-suicide emerged from the jungle to tell reporters about how Jones had essentially kept everyone in Jonestown prisoner, with heavily armed guards and severe punishments for anyone who tried to escape.

On Wednesday, November 21, *Post* executive editor Ben Bradlee telephoned Krause in Georgetown. After Krause told him that he was feeling fine, Ben said, "Okay, kid. Can you get back to Washington tomorrow? You're going to write a book."

The *Post* had signed a contract with Berkley Books to write, by the following Monday, the finished manuscript for a paperback book that would go on sale within days. It would be the first of what would become, in the years ahead, a trend of instant books produced by the *Post*, the *New York Times*, and other news media about big, breaking news events.

Krause was given a ride to New York by ABC's Bernard Shaw on the network's charter plane, and he was back in the *Post* newsroom on Thanksgiving Thursday. With help from editors and writers on the *Post*'s national news staff, Krause met the deadline for what became *Guyana Massacre: The Eyewitness Account.*

Finally, at the end of the week in Guyana, U.S. troops methodically removing bodies from Jonestown realized that they had counted many more than expected—775 by Friday, a final total of 909 by Saturday. "We simply began to discover more and more bodies," a U.S. Air Force spokesmen told those of us still covering the story in Georgetown. "Under adults we found smaller adults and children, and more small babies than anticipated."

Another *Post* reporter, Fred Barbash, arrived to replace me, and he began writing the main news story on Saturday. My last story from Georgetown, based on reporting all week by myself and Krause, was a long reconstruction of what had happened at Jonestown from its inception to the mass murder-suicide. It included what had emerged about the relationship Jones had established with the Guyanese government, which allowed him to lease the land for Jonestown and avoid any meaningful government oversight of it, or of the large number of illegal guns kept there.

This was a kind of journalism I had not previously done. Working remotely out of a hotel room in a place where I had never been before, I had to quickly cultivate new sources and extensively report and write breaking major news stories on daily deadlines. It was what I would very soon be expected to do regularly as the London bureau chief.

10

Foreign Correspondent

𝕴 WAS ENGAGED IN VERBAL COMBAT WITH BRIT-ish prime minister Margaret Thatcher in the most memorable and meaningful interview of my forty months as a foreign correspondent. It was on the afternoon of June 3, 1982, and we were sitting in chairs facing each other, alone in her small study on the second floor of 10 Downing Street.

Thatcher had agreed to the interview to send an unmistakable message about the ongoing Falkland Islands War to presidents Ronald Reagan of the United States and Leopoldo Galtieri of Argentina. She wanted to make clear that she would accept nothing less than the unconditional surrender of Argentine forces that had been occupying the British colony off the coast of Argentina for the past two months. The Reagan administration was trying to negotiate a settlement of the dispute between the two American allies. Thatcher was now making her position clear in her first interview with the news media since British forces had landed in the Falklands twelve days earlier.

It was quite warm and humid in the three-century-old, black brick townhouse on Downing Street, the traditional home and offices for British prime ministers in governmental London. It had no air conditioning at the time, and we were both perspiring. As I expected, Thatcher argued with the premises of some of my questions. When I asked her whether she was seeking to humiliate Argentina by insisting on its unconditional surrender, for example, she shot back, "Do you want Britain humiliated?"

But Thatcher invariably answered forthrightly and seemed to relish the back and forth. What was scheduled as a half-hour formal interview stretched into a seventy-minute animated conversation, which I thoroughly enjoyed. Seizing the opportunity, I asked about her uncompromising determination to dismantle Britain's postwar welfare state. Thatcher leaned forward from the edge of her chair and looked directly into my eyes. "The reason I am in politics," she said firmly, "is because I believe in certain things and try to put them in place."

I asked whether she was trying to turn the clock back to Victorian times with her emphasis on the values of industry, duty, self-reliance, and private charity, rather than government welfare. Thatcher declared, "I would be proud to be called a Victorian lady. Look at the enormous increase in industry and commerce in this country during Victorian times, which brought with it a consciousness of duty to others. They built the hospitals. They built the schools. They built the prisons. They built the industries. They built the town halls."

I saved one question for last—just in case it ignited Thatcher's well-known temper. I asked why she had not done more for women in politics after becoming Britain's first woman prime minister. "I earned it," Thatcher told me emphatically; "they can earn it."

Several good stories came out of that interview, thanks to my deep immersion in my foreign assignment for three and a half years. It was only a few weeks before I would be leaving London to become national news editor of the *Post*. The Thatcher revolution had dominated a good deal of my time there, and the Falklands War capped it off. But as London bureau chief, I found much more to report and write about, not only in Britain, but in Ireland, Scandinavia, and other parts of Europe. I wrote nearly 650 stories from a dozen countries in those forty months, about everything from British and European politics, economics, and people to international crises and terrorism.

I covered some of the worst of the violent sectarian "troubles" in British-ruled Northern Ireland, along with Irish Republican Army bombings in Britain. I shadowed NATO and European Economic Community diplomats in London, Brussels, Luxembourg, and Rome as they argued over how to respond to the Soviet invasion of Afghanistan and the taking of American hostages in Iran. I witnessed the emotional return of those hostages to freedom at the U.S. air base in Frankfurt, West Germany.

I recorded history being made during the months of British-led negotiations in 1979 that created the black majority African country of Zimbabwe out of the war-torn former British plantation colony of Rhodesia. For that, I spent many hours at majestic Lancaster House, near Buckingham Palace, where the talks were held. I interviewed, among other participants, Robert Mugabe, the imposing leader of Rhodesia's largest African nationalist force, who would become Zimbabwe's strong-man president.

The experience as London bureau chief gave me what amounted to a crash course in world affairs. It also required me to rise to the challenge of a different and demanding kind of journalism, working mostly on my own across an ocean from the *Post* newsroom. I learned how to see the United States through foreign eyes, and how to report meaningfully for an American audience about people and events in other nations. I gained perspective on American foreign policy, politics, and society from the similarities and contrasts I found in the UK and in the European countries I covered.

I discovered that being an American journalist abroad could be an asset in ways I had not expected. My nationality and accent essentially exempted me from what I found to be the surprisingly persistent British class system and the tribal hatreds of Northern Ireland. My American approach to reporting, grounded in the First Amendment, freed me from insidious government restrictions on and complicity by the press in Britain, where a leading editor told me it would have been impossible to pursue a story like Watergate.

In fact, the *Post*'s reputation for Watergate helped to open doors for me everywhere I went. I became comfortable dealing with national leaders, government officials, politicians, and diplomats of many countries. It was initially a heady experience for "Land Grant Len" to be a welcomed personage at the highest levels in European capitals. In time, I realized it also was a serious responsibility, reporting and writing stories that I knew were being closely read in those capitals and in Washington.

Although I did not know it then, the work was preparing me for even greater responsibilities that lay ahead. I mostly assigned and edited myself, increasing my self-confidence. I significantly sharpened my source-making, reporting, and writing skills, which later would make me a much better editor.

It also was a memorable personal experience. I had a spacious London bureau office on the top floor of a Georgian townhouse in the fashionable Mayfair neighborhood, a few blocks from Grosvenor Square. Gerry and I lived much of the time a mile or two away in Chelsea, and I often walked to and from my office across the imposing grassy expanse of Hyde Park in good weather.

Gerry and I took full advantage of London's charm and culture, and we enjoyed exploring Britain, even while driving on the left side the road. Our two children, Joshua and Sarah, were born in historic Queen Charlotte's Hospital in west London, making them dual American and British citizens. With the children, we met English families through National Health Service play groups.

I grew accustomed to being interviewed on British television and radio. When John Lennon was shot to death outside his apartment house in New York, I was asked to explain the proliferation of guns and the frequency of gun violence in the United States, in contrast to strict gun laws and rare shootings in Britain. I explained to British viewers why I thought the American melodrama *Dallas* had become the most popular television show in Britain. When Robin Day, a leading BBC Television broadcaster, asked me, on his late evening program, what I noticed most about living in London, I caused a small sensation by saying it was the absence of showers in most homes, including ours. It probably was not the only time that I appeared to be an awkward Yankee lacking appreciation for quainter aspects of British life.

I became a member of the Royal Automobile Club, where I could take my most important sources to lunch in the elegant dining rooms of its imposing building on Pall Mall. When traveling on assignment, I frequented fine hotels and restaurants throughout Europe. In London, I lacked the cars and drivers that were at the disposal of competing correspondents for the *New York Times* and *Time* and *Newsweek* magazines, but I had an on-call office account for the always dependable London black cabs. More important, unlike the several correspondents in each of those London bureaus, I was on my own. I had the freedom to write about anything and everything.

I HAD MOVED TO LONDON WITH GERRY IN FEBRUARY 1979 AND started working there right away. Late in the evening of Wednesday, March 28, I was sitting alone in the foreign correspondents' gallery, high above the Speaker's chair, in the House of Commons, when the Labour Party government of British prime minister James Callahan was brought down by a single vote, 311–310, on a motion of no confidence. It was the first time in fifty-five years that a government had been voted out of power in the House of Commons, and it was so unexpected that no other American correspondents were there. I had come to the Commons that afternoon to educate myself by listening to what became six hours of parliamentary debate about Britain's economic and labor problems, initiated by the leader of the opposition Conservative Party, Margaret Thatcher.

As the members filed out, I stood up and stared down at the emptying chamber. I was stunned by what had happened and the realization that I had only a few hours to pull together a major story about it for the front page of the *Washington Post*. Robin Day, whom I had not yet met, happened to turn around in the broadcasters' gallery below me and noticed my unease. After we introduced ourselves, he explained as much as he could before he rushed off to the BBC.

I relied on research I had already done and on the parliamentary debate. Thatcher had argued that the five-year-old Labour government had "centralized too much power in the state," had forced too much redistribution of income with high taxes and extensive welfare programs, and had allowed labor unions to disrupt the country with frequent long strikes. She advocated substantial cuts in taxes and government spending. It was a preview of what she would tell British voters during the traditional month-long campaign for a national parliamentary election that would take place in just five and a half weeks.

The Conservative Party mounted an American presidential-style campaign built around Thatcher's strong personality and straightforward, rather un-English speaking style. She was a middle-class outsider in the aristocratic party, who was able to become its leader in part because she had been underestimated as a woman. The campaign was an ideal way for me to immerse myself in British politics and the issues roiling the country. I followed Thatcher and Callahan around the country to report on their daily rallies and press conferences and to talk to voters and some of the candidates for Parliament. My editors told me that interest in the election, and especially Thatcher, was high in Washington.

I believe one of my stories in particular stoked that interest. At a rally I covered in Birmingham on April 21, Thatcher said that, after she had warned about "the growing danger of Soviet expansion, the Russians said I was an Iron Lady." As her audience roared its approval, she declared, "They were right. Britain needs an Iron Lady." That was in the top of my story on the front page of the next day's *Post*, under the headline, "'Iron Lady's' Tough Politics: Thatcher Seeks to Lead Britain to the Right." It indelibly labeled her as the Iron Lady for admiring American conservatives.

The Conservative Party won a big parliamentary majority in the May 3, 1979, election, and Thatcher became prime minister on May 5. In a story on the *Post*'s May 6 front page, I wrote about the essence of Thatcher and the philosophy she would try to impose on Britain, playing off Thatcher's own words.

Just before entering 10 Downing Street for the first time as prime minister, she was asked by someone in a crowd of journalists outside: "With whom would you want to share this historic moment?"

Thatcher responded, "Well, of course I owe just about everything to my father," a grocer and strict Methodist in the town of Grantham in northeastern England. "He brought me up to believe in all the things I believe, and they're just the values on which I've fought this election."

"Those values," I wrote in the *Post*,

> the worth of hard work, the importance of thrift, the opportunity for self-improvement, honesty and a deep

religious belief in right and wrong, are the heart and soul
of Thatcher's conservative philosophy. It is a simple, personal fundamentalist conservatism rather than the doc-
trinaire ideology of the intellectuals and politicians of
the right who have been her strongest supporters on the
road to Downing Street. She has a strong, unswerving
belief in the rightness of her course.

With the encouragement of my editors, I made a priority of being the
most authoritative American news media chronicler of Thatcherism, as
her crusade to remake Britain came to be called. I talked regularly to cabinet members, other government officials, and members of Parliament,
outside the British "lobby" system, in which British reporters covering
the prime minister, cabinet departments, and Parliament were briefed
off the record by cabinet ministers and spokesmen in so-called lobby
groups, producing groupthink stories without attribution.

I met weekly at Downing Street with Thatcher's press secretary, Bernard Ingham, a burly man with big bushy eyebrows that rose and fell
with his facial expressions. Although a civil servant in the British system,
he became Thatcher's alter ego. I found that what he told me was often
what Thatcher was thinking, saying or doing behind the scenes. I also
established reporting relationships with Conservative members of her
cabinet and Parliament who became increasingly, if not publicly, skeptical about Thatcher's policies and her leadership of the country.

Even in the face of a sharp recession, price inflation, and rising unemployment, Thatcher persisted in keeping interest rates high, cutting
income taxes, and shrinking government spending on welfare programs.
She told me and other American correspondents gathered in a Downing
Street dining room at the end of June in 1980 that the resulting layoffs,
factory closings, and business failures amounted to a needed restructuring of the British economy—evidence that her policies were beginning
to work.

But economic turmoil persisted in Britain during most of my time in
London. I wrote extensively about how much Thatcher's policies divided
the country and even her own party. In the summer of 1981, I covered ten
days of rioting in racially mixed, high-unemployment neighborhoods in
cities from London to Manchester to Birmingham, something I never ex-

pected to see in Britain. Thatcher's standing and that of the Conservative Party plunged in opinion polls. What no one could anticipate was the jingoistic 1982 Falklands War, which would unite much of the country behind Thatcher.

ROSALEEN SANDS, THE FIFTY-SIX-YEAR-OLD MOTHER OF PROVIsional Irish Republican Army member Bobby Sands, faced reporters gathered outside the maximum-security Maze prison near Belfast in Northern Ireland on April 30, 1981. She told us that her twenty-seven-year-old son was near death after refusing food for sixty-one days in the prison cell where he was serving a fourteen-year sentence for weapons possession after a shootout with Northern Ireland police.

Mrs. Sands said she would obey her son's instructions not to authorize intravenous feeding if he fell into a coma. "He asked me not to, and I promised not to," she told us in a quiet, resigned voice. "It's a sad thing to say. I love my son just like any other mother."

Sands was the leader of hundreds of Provisional IRA members incarcerated in the Maze for terrorist acts in British-ruled Northern Ireland. He was the first of four Maze prisoners who went on a hunger strike to try to force the British government to give them special status as political prisoners, rather than common criminals. Prime Minister Thatcher had responded by declaring, "There can be no special status for convicted criminals."

As he neared death, Sands became a symbol of resistance for Northern Ireland's Catholic minority against deeply felt discrimination by the Protestant majority and the British government—and harassment and brutality by Northern Ireland's Royal Ulster Constabulary police and Protestant paramilitary militias. Sands had even been elected twenty-one days earlier to a vacant seat in the British Parliament from a constituency with a narrow Catholic majority near the border with the Republic of Ireland.

Sands fell into a coma on May 4 and died early the next morning. His death prompted a resumption of the violent rioting that had periodically convulsed Belfast since the late 1960s. Mostly young Irish Catholics in roving bands pelted police with milk-bottle firebombs, bricks, and stones.

The predominantly Protestant police responded with repeated volleys of rubber bullets. British military armored vehicles roamed the streets and formed roadblocks to protect Protestant neighborhoods. It was the first time I had seen this violence, which had long been commonplace there.

While I was in Belfast, Britain sent 600 troops to augment the 11,100 already occupying Northern Ireland to back up the police. On May 7, they formed a cordon around an Irish Catholic section of the city where Bobby Sands's requiem service, funeral procession on foot, and burial took place. I watched as his body was escorted from his family's parish church by masked IRA men in paramilitary uniforms along three miles of streets, thickly lined with tens of thousands of people of all ages, to an IRA cemetery plot. At one point along the way, IRA members fired volleys of rifle shots over the casket. I had never seen anything like it before.

The hunger strike grew over the next several months. Nine more Maze prisoners died before it ended, when the British government finally allowed IRA prisoners to wear their own clothes and gain more freedom of movement within the Maze prison. Each death had been accompanied by more violence in the streets of Belfast and more attention in Washington.

The hunger strikes were part of what made Northern Ireland an unexpectedly big story and learning experience for me. In addition, shortly after I arrived in London, the IRA had significantly stepped up its terrorist campaign to force Britain out of Northern Ireland, with notably violent attacks there and elsewhere.

On March 22, 1979, thirty-one IRA bombs damaged dozens of banks, shops, and government offices in seventeen Northern Ireland communities. The next day, the British ambassador to the Netherlands, Sir Richard Sykes, was shot to death by two IRA gunmen just outside his residence in The Hague. Sykes had written a report a few years earlier recommending increased security for British diplomats abroad.

A week later, the IRA assassinated a senior Conservative member of Parliament, Airey Neave, when a bomb destroyed his car as he drove up the exit ramp of the House of Commons underground garage. Neave was an outspoken supporter of strong anti-IRA security measures in Northern Ireland.

Although there had been many other IRA bombings in Britain before I arrived at the London bureau, the killing of Neave made a deep impression me. I had walked along that driveway when going into the House of Commons beneath Big Ben. At the time, I couldn't imagine anything similar occurring on Capitol Hill in Washington. The imminent threat of political violence was a new reality for me.

Months later, the IRA made headlines worldwide with two coordinated attacks. On August 27, Lord Louis Mountbatten, the elder statesman of Britain's royal family, was assassinated when a bomb blew apart his yacht off the northwest coast of Ireland, about fifteen miles from the Northern Ireland border. Five hours later, two massive roadside explosions killed eighteen British soldiers on the eastern coast of Northern Ireland, just across the border from the Republic. Mountbatten, a decorated World War II naval commander and the last viceroy of India, was a second cousin of Queen Elizabeth II and a mentor to her son, Prince Charles. I wrote about it all from London.

In mid-October, I covered two more IRA attacks in London. On October 10, a nail bomb hidden in a parked laundry truck exploded outside the British Army's Chelsea Barracks, within walking distance of where I lived. Forty soldiers and residents in the surrounding neighborhood were injured, and a woman passing by was killed. A week later, British Army Lt. Gen. Steuart Pringle lost a leg when a bomb tore his car apart as he was driving away from his home in a leafy south London suburb.

Earlier, I had decided to do extensive reporting to educate myself and Washington *Post* readers about the then apparently intractable conflict between Irish Catholics, who made up a third of Northern Ireland's population, and Protestants, who constituted the two-thirds majority. I knew from reader reaction that my coverage was closely followed, especially by Irish Americans.

First, I had history to learn. The Protestants were the descendants of English and Scottish settlers who began moving to the northern part of the British-ruled Irish island in the seventeenth century. When Ireland was given independence in 1921, Britain retained the six counties of Northern Ireland. Catholic Irish nationalists wanted British rule there to end, and Northern Ireland to be unified with the neighboring Republic. Protestants feared what would happen to them if that occurred.

Sporadic sectarian violence exploded into the violent troubles in the late 1960s, with frequent bombings, shootings, paramilitary and gang warfare, and rioting by both Catholics and Protestants. Belfast, a red-brick, nineteenth-century industrial town, was considered one of the most dangerous cities in the world in the 1970s. Adjacent Protestant and Catholic working-class neighborhoods in West Belfast, just outside the commercial center, became completely segregated. They physically separated themselves with numerous steel barriers, brick walls, and bricked up abandoned buildings that resembled crude Berlin walls scattered through West Belfast.

I first went to Northern Ireland in mid-March 1980 to join a dozen British and Irish reporters and photographers on a British government-arranged tour of the Maze prison, seven miles southwest of Belfast. At the time, two years before the hunger strikes began, nearly four hundred Provisional IRA prisoners were carrying out a "dirty protest" of their treatment as criminals rather than prisoners of war.

They had smashed out their cell windows, destroyed their furniture, and refused to dress, wash themselves, use toilets, or clean their cells. Instead, they smeared excrement on the cell walls. This caused great controversy at a time when a British inquiry found that Northern Ireland police had systematically abused IRA terrorist suspects while questioning them. British and Irish news media demanded to inspect conditions inside the H-shaped Maze prison blocks housing the protesting IRA prisoners, and I decided to go with them.

We went through the unnerving experience of being locked inside the prison. Then we were taken into one wing of an H-block, where we inspected dirty protest cells from which IRA prisoners had been temporarily removed minutes before our arrival. We were not allowed to interview any of them.

"Excrement covers the concrete walls of the prison cells like an uneven coat of paint. Cold air pours in through the smashed-out windows, moderating the stench," I wrote. "On the floor are two bare foam mattresses with clumps of dark woolen blankets on them. In one corner is a pile of more excrement, shredded toilet paper, broken egg shells and other garbage. In another is an open chamber pot full of urine. Besides two orange plastic mugs and a water pitcher on the window ledge, the only other object in the cell is a black-beaded rosary, somehow immaculate and shiny, hanging from a light switch against the excrement on the wall."

We saw another wing of H-block cells receiving periodic cleaning while the prisoners were shifted elsewhere. Workmen in plastic sanitation suits used high-pressure steam to clean excrement off the walls and urine off the floors. We walked past occupied cells where we heard prisoners shouting IRA slogans and banging their plastic mugs on the green metal cell doors. Although I had done investigative reporting inside the local jail and prison in Washington, this was much more disturbing.

I returned to Northern Ireland several times, which helped me understand the kind of tribal and religious conflict and terrorism that would surface in other forms around the world during my career as an editor. It was the nearest I would come to being a correspondent in a war zone.

Flying to Belfast from London, I encountered strict security at Heathrow Airport that rivaled El Al flights I had taken to Israel. At the isolated passenger gate, all our baggage was opened and inspected for weapons or bombs and then sealed in clear plastic bags. All of us had to submit to thorough body searches. Then we were looked up and down by plainclothes officers of the Special Branch, roughly Britain's equivalent of the FBI and Secret Service. Some travelers were stopped, as I once was, for questioning about identification and reasons for traveling to Northern Ireland. Those who did not give satisfactory answers could be detained for a week or more under 1970s prevention of terrorism laws.

In Belfast, I found the city center shopping district enclosed by metal security barriers and barbed wire. Everyone had to enter through checkpoints, where all bags and briefcases were inspected, and some people were questioned. I had to pass through additional military security to enter the Europa Hotel, where most visiting journalists stayed. After the Europa opened in 1971, it was bombed two dozen times before its security was sufficiently tightened.

I began by interviewing members of the British Parliament from rival Protestant and Irish Catholic parties. I talked to British officials in their offices in the imposing Stormont Castle in Belfast. I had an unsettling encounter in an IRA-guarded house in the heart of Irish Catholic Belfast with Gerry Adams, the militant leader of the so-called political arm of the IRA, who was thought to be behind much of the IRA's violence. They all stuck to talking points and party rhetoric.

Much more important, though, I roamed the hardscrabble, self-segregated Catholic and Protestant neighborhoods of cramped Victorian houses and public housing projects of inner-city West Belfast. It felt like occupied territory with police and British Army posts fortified with corrugated metal stockades topped by barbed wire. There were frequent roadblocks manned by armed British soldiers in the openings of the graffiti-covered walls separating the sectarian neighborhoods. Driving in those neighborhoods meant charting a course through mazes of closed streets and enduring stops and questioning at security checkpoints in the roadblocks. Northern Ireland police and British military patrolled the Catholic neighborhoods in armored vehicles, which attracted bottle- and stone-throwing children.

With introductions, I was welcomed by families on both sides of the sectarian divide into the small parlors of their modest homes. They were eager to educate me about both historical and current grievances. Irish Catholics complained about job discrimination, the violence of Protestant gangs, and harassment by the police and military. Protestants living just on the other side of the dividing walls blamed Catholic gangs and the IRA for incessant rioting, robberies, terrorist attacks, and murders. They said they would be victims of discrimination or worse if the British allowed Northern Ireland, which they had always called Ulster, to be united with the Republic, in which they would become the minority.

Outside these neighborhoods, I found mostly Protestant middle-class people and business leaders who insisted that the news media were painting a misleading picture of Northern Ireland. They pointed to Belfast's comfortable country club suburbs and Northern Ireland's improving economy, rich farmland, quaint towns, and scenic countryside, full of lakes, rivers, and streams. They cited opinion polls indicating that sizeable numbers of both Catholics and Protestants might welcome some form of reconciliation.

I reported all this and more in numerous stories, focusing on whether there could ever be a political solution in Northern Ireland. I personally doubted it because I had found the sectarian strife be so intractable.

I did not foresee that Britain and Ireland would eventually sign an agreement on Good Friday, April 10, 1998, that would end direct British rule—although not sovereignty. It would establish a measure of home rule in Northern Ireland, open its border with Ireland within the European Community, and leave the question of unification to the future. Belfast would eventually become a safe, modernizing city, although with remaining segregated sectarian inner-city neighborhoods divided by still-standing "peace walls."

WHILE THERE WAS AN OVERFLOW OF NEWS FOR ME TO COVER during my time as London bureau chief, I also was able to take advantage of occasional once-in-a-lifetime journalistic opportunities.

Just a month after the assassination of Lord Mountbatten in 1979, I took time away from Northern Ireland's troubles to cover Pope John Paul II's visit to the Republic, the first papal visit to Ireland in history. It was the pope's initial stop on a nine-day tour that later took him to six American cities, including Boston, New York, Chicago, and Washington, D.C. A year earlier, Cardinal Karol Wojtyła from Poland had been elected pope, the first non-Italian pope in more than four hundred years.

I was amazed by what I saw. More than half the people living in Ireland and Northern Ireland walked long distances and endured hours-long traffic jams to see and hear the pope at outdoor masses over three days throughout the country. On the first day, the pope celebrated Mass for 1.2 million people packed into Dublin's vast, verdant Phoenix Park— and then for another half million people in a natural amphitheater in the hills around the village of Kilineer outside Drogheda, thirty miles from the Northern Ireland border. For hours after each service, John Paul II rode slowly through the huge crowds in his open popemobile, reaching out to touch as many hands as he could. I had never seen such an outpouring of people or witnessed such unalloyed joy.

In the moment, it did not matter that I doubted that the pope's visit could lead to a revival of the steadily receding Catholic Church in Ireland, given its overwhelmingly young population, robust economic expansion, and increasing exposure to the outside world. Before his arrival in the country, I wrote about the growing number of young Irish people who were skipping Mass and turning away from religious vocations. Irish secularization would continue into the twenty-first century with successful referenda allowing same-sex marriage and abortion. The exposure of widespread sexual abuse by Catholic clergy in Ireland and many other countries, including the United States, hastened the process.

JUST BEFORE DAWN ON A BITTERLY COLD MORNING AT THE U.S. Rhein-Main Air Base in Frankfurt, West Germany, on January 21, 1981, I experienced the most emotional moment of my time as a foreign correspondent. Under a bright full moon, about 10,000 American diplomats, dignitaries, and servicemen and their families, including small children, had gathered on the tarmac of the base opposite Frankfurt's busy commercial airport.

As soon as the Americans saw the distant lights of the first of two U.S. Air Force C9 Nightingale hospital planes approaching the runway, they began shouting, applauding, and waving homemade welcome signs and thousands of small American flags. The gleaming gray-and-white aircraft, with UNITED STATES OF AMERICA emblazoned on each side, were carrying the fifty-two Americans who had been held hostage for 444 days in Iran after the takeover of the U.S. Embassy there.

Tears came to my eyes. The planes taxied alongside the tumultuous crowd in the glare of television floodlights. I could see many of the freed Americans waving from the windows to the cheering people outside in a movie-like tableau. The former hostages emerged from the planes one by one, bundled in gray-fleeced Air Force parkas that covered the warm-weather clothes television viewers had seen them wearing when they changed planes in Algiers. They were led to two waiting blue U.S. Air Force buses while the crowd sang "God Bless America."

Within fifteen minutes, the buses were loaded and driven away. West German police brought rush hour traffic to a halt on the network of high-speed autobahns radiating from the Frankfurt airport while the buses made their way to the U.S. military hospital in Wiesbaden, thirty miles to the west. At first, reporters and photographers were kept literally in the cold outside the sixteen-acre hospital grounds. The freed hostages were free to stroll outside the grounds to talk briefly to journalists, as some did, during breaks from medical testing and any necessary treatment.

Over the next several days, in interviews and press conferences, I and Bradley Graham, the *Post*'s Bonn correspondent, heard from some of them, and from hospital doctors and U.S. officials, about their condition and their treatment in Iran. Many of the former hostages were surprisingly fit and enjoyed meals of lobster and then steak on their last evenings in the Wiesbaden hospital. Others were reported to be suffering from depression and posttraumatic stress.

On Friday morning, January 25, they all boarded planes to reach Newburgh, New York, in time to watch the Super Bowl on television. They then went to nearby West Point to be reunited with their families.

MY LAST TWO AND A HALF MONTHS IN LONDON WERE UNEXPECT-edly consumed by the Falklands War. On April 2, 1982, Argentina invaded and took military control of the neighboring Falkland Islands. Although the Falklands had been a British colony for 150 years, Argentina had long claimed sovereignty over what it called the Malvinas, and its military junta hoped to gain popular support at a time of economic crisis by reasserting control. Margaret Thatcher responded that the 1,800 Falklanders were "of British tradition and stock." She immediately ordered formation of an expeditionary force of 28,000 troops and more than one hundred ships to retake the islands 8,000 miles away near the tip of South America. The British armada arrived at the Falklands in late April and created a two-hundred-mile military exclusionary zone around them.

Skirmishes at sea ensued, even as negotiations between the two American allies, brokered by the Reagan administration, dragged on, with neither side backing down. On May 2, the British nuclear-powered submarine HMS *Conqueror* torpedoed and sank the Argentine warship *General Belgrano* just outside the exclusionary zone, killing 368 of the more than 1,100 troops aboard. On May 4, Argentina retaliated. An Exocet anti-ship missile fired from one of its aircraft hit the British destroyer HMS *Sheffield*, setting it on fire, killing twenty of its crew when it sank.

Perhaps because of the Reagan administration's involvement, the remote war had become a big story in Washington, often dominating the *Post*'s front page. But covering it was challenging. Only selected British journalists could travel with the expeditionary force, and their dispatches were closely censored by Defense Ministry officials at sea and in London. For our readers, it was left to me, in London, and the *Post*'s South American correspondent, Jackson Diehl, in Buenos Aires, to cope with the government propaganda in the two capitals in sometimes conflicting stories.

In London, the Defense Ministry used closed, off-the-record, lobby system briefings for British defense writers to spread misinformation about the British military's progress, invasion plans, losses in the field, and knowledge of the enemy's activities—all to mislead Argentina through the news media. The defense reporter for a leading British newspaper was so appalled by this that she regularly told me what went on in the briefings. Since I was not bound by the lobby system rules, I was able to write about the deception.

I also took advantage of my relationships with other government sources. A member of Thatcher's war cabinet, Foreign Secretary Francis Pym, told me on deep background about the cabinet's deliberations when Thatcher ordered the attack on the *Belgrano*, even though it was sailing away from, rather than toward, the exclusionary zone. I had spent a day with Pym while he was campaigning for his parliamentary seat outside Cambridge in April 1979, and he became a helpful source for me under American ground rules.

After my war cabinet story, I appeared on Robin Day's BBC show, *Question Time*, to discuss the differences in government-press relationships in Britain and the United States. The leading political correspondent for a respected British Sunday newspaper told Day that he would never contact anyone in the war cabinet to avoid "doing anything that might endanger our boys."

That epitomized for me the position of the press in Britain, a country without First Amendment freedoms. The government could and did issue secret Defence Notices (or D-Notices) to the news media to stop all reporting about anything it unilaterally decided could threaten national security. Broad contempt powers enabled judges to tightly control what could be published in Britain about court cases in progress. Strict libel laws made it possible for anyone with a good lawyer to silence press criticism or investigations into their affairs. Combined with my earlier involvement in Watergate stories, my experience in Britain would significantly shape my approach to journalism about national security and the activities of public figures when I would later have to make decisions about those issues in the *Post* newsroom.

By the beginning of June, British forces had landed on the main island of East Falkland and were closing in on Stanleyville, the capital. Thatcher then used my June 3 interview to emphasize that she would settle only for an unconditional Argentine surrender and complete withdrawal from the Falklands. Support for her Conservative Party had by then escalated to 51 percent of British voters from 38 percent just four weeks earlier in a respected opinion poll. I asked Thatcher to explain why she had so much support for a costly war on behalf of the 1,800 Falkland Islands residents—and why she believed it was so important for the kind of Britain she wanted to lead.

"I think what we are seeing now is something quite fundamental in the drawing together of the British people once liberty and justice are challenged once again," she said, summoning memories of the embattled island nation's experience during World War II. "If you ask a person here what he would associate with Britain, it's not talk about the welfare state or any sort of benefits. He would say, 'We are a free country.'"

British forces captured Stanleyville, and the Argentine commander there surrendered his thousands of troops on June 15. The Iron Lady had won decisively—both militarily against Argentina in the Falklands, and diplomatically against the United States, which had been seeking a settlement that Thatcher opposed as a defeat.

Later, as managing editor and then executive editor of the *Post*, I would talk twice more with Thatcher. In a 1988 Downing Street interview with me and *Post* London correspondent Karen DeYoung, the prime minister emphasized her support for the changes Mikhail Gorbachev was making in the Soviet Union. In 1992, after she had left office, I had an unusually candid conversation with then Baroness Thatcher. She told me and *Post* London correspondent Gene Robinson that her successor, Prime Minister John Major, whom she had nominated, had responded too weakly to several domestic and foreign affairs challenges. "I had thought he was a man," Thatcher told us, tellingly. "If only he were a man."

11

Charles and Diana

 AN OBLIGATORY BUT ENJOYABLE DUTY OF ANY London bureau chief was writing about members of the royal family. American readers never seemed to tire of stories about the monarchy that had been left behind in 1776. During my time in London, the biggest story about the royals was the relationship and marriage of Prince Charles and Lady Diana Spencer.

On July 29, 1981, I watched the "wedding of the century" from a gallery in the north transept of St. Paul's Cathedral, high above the raised, red-carpeted platform at the front of the nave. The ceremony under the great dome of St. Paul's—accompanied by soaring music from trumpets, organ, orchestra, and choirs—was the centerpiece of a day-long showcase of British pageantry that Charles had promised when I hosted him at a dinner with American correspondents in London nearly four months earlier.

Among the 2,500 people who filled the cathedral were the many members of the British royal family, most of Europe's remaining royalty, various heads of state, and Nancy Reagan, representing the U.S. president. Prime

Minister Margaret Thatcher and members of her cabinet were relegated to the twelfth row. As the Archbishop of Canterbury performed the ceremony, I watched from my perch everything the bride and groom did, including touching displays of public affection that were rare for the royal family.

In the moment, it appeared to be the culmination of a fairy-tale love story that British and American media had been chronicling breathlessly since the previous autumn. But after I left London, their romance would become a mismatch, leading to adultery, divorce, and Diana's tragic death, sixteen years after the royal wedding watched on television by 750 million people. It is only as I write this that I realize how my role in reporting on Charles and Diana as London correspondent was part of an evolution in journalism about the private lives of public people that often preoccupied me as executive editor years later.

I began my royal chronicles by writing about the over-the-top British press coverage of speculation about Prince Charles's rumored relationship with Lady Diana Spencer on the occasion of his thirty-second birthday in November 1980. Nineteen-year-old Diana had previously been seen in Charles's company at polo matches, horse races, and dinner parties. British journalists, who were camped outside the royal family's vast Sandringham estate in Norfolk, England, pieced together sightings of her at the celebration of the prince's birthday party held there. The story dominated the front pages of Britain's most popular newspapers. My account of it from London was displayed on the front of the *Post*'s Style section.

A few months later, when Charles and Diana announced their engagement, on February 24, 1981, I wrote a long story that filled much of the Style section. I described Lady Diana Spencer as a strikingly attractive, tall, slim young woman with large blue-gray eyes and short blond hair. She was born into one of Britain's oldest noble families, raised on a baronial estate, and often visited Sandringham. Members of her family had served the royal family in various capacities since the eighteenth century. Diana was working as a nanny and nursery school teacher while living with several other young women in a London apartment bought by her father, the eighth Earl Spencer.

When I first went to London as the *Post*'s correspondent, I knew that I would be writing about the royal family. I went to a knighting ceremony to see the queen touch a sword lightly on each shoulder of the recipient of a knighthood. I got to know the press secretaries to the queen and Prince Charles. Like Bernard Ingham, Thatcher's press secretary, they were civil servants who became helpful sources for me. Long before Lady Diana came into the picture, I had arranged with the prince's press secretary for Charles to come to dinner with the Association of American Correspondents in London in 1981, when I was its president. The dinner happened to take place at the stately Brown's Hotel only weeks after his engagement to Diana.

Charles struck me that evening as someone uncomfortable in the role he was destined to play most of his life, waiting to become king. He was just under six feet tall, and trim in his plainly tailored suit. His face was a flushed pink, his ears protruded from under relatively close-cropped dark hair, and his arresting blue eyes drew attention from a prominent nose once broken in a schoolboy rugby game. I thought that the almost constant movement of his hands—one jamming into his coat pocket, the other fingering his breast pocket handkerchief; or one grasping the other behind his back, or the right hand turning the small gold signet ring on his left little finger—betrayed a protective shyness hidden by his practiced ease of conversation with strangers.

At a reception with us before dinner, Charles said at one point that he especially enjoyed meeting Americans because they were usually comfortable talking to him. None of us, except for ABC television correspondent Peter Jennings, a proud Canadian, called him "Your Royal Highness" or even "Sir," as we had been instructed by a palace aide. Sitting next to me at dinner, Charles said that when he met British people, "you have to get through a certain amount of anxiety or nervousness to start with" on their part. "After 20 minutes or so, people are beginning to realize that you are vaguely human, that you actually talk reasonably and are not totally from a different world. Then you have to go."

Time and again during the dinner conversation with us, from which Charles could not be quoted at the time under palace ground rules, his answers to questions from the American journalists made it clear that, in fact, he *was* from a different world. Why did he play polo? Because his friends did, and it was the only sport at which he excelled. What was his job? Representing the royal family to the British people and Britain to the world—in addition to using his public appearances, speeches, and writings to try to influence British architecture, job training, and race relations, although he had no real authority in those or any other areas. Pressed about this, he said, "I work bloody hard right now."

When would he become king? Charles described how, when he was young, Lord Mountbatten, his favorite uncle and mentor, took him aside to answer that very question. He said that the British royal family was not like the less grand "bicycle kings and queens of Europe," as Mountbatten called them, who mixed informally with their subjects and retired when they got older. Mountbatten told Charles that his mother, Elizabeth II, would be queen so long as she lived.

Asked more about what he could accomplish during what could amount to a lifetime as crown prince, Charles talked about modest steps, such as bringing a person of color from the Commonwealth onto his staff. Another decade would pass before he would start Duchy of Cornwall organic foods, which were produced in a 100,000-acre agricultural estate that was part of his holdings as heir to the throne.

Charles described living much of the time in a three-room apartment in vast Buckingham Palace, often eating dinner alone from a tray in front of the television. At some point in the evening, he said, one corgi would appear, then another and another, eventually followed by "my mother." They would exchange pleasantries about their day's activities, and then the Queen and the corgis would disappear.

When asked about the upcoming royal wedding, Charles brightened and detailed plans for its grand music and pageantry, "one of the things that Britain has always done best." I cannot remember him saying much about Lady Diana, except for her role in the wedding planning.

Diana was even more of an enigma before their marriage. She was coy with the reporters and photographers who followed her everywhere when she was out and about in London, but she never seemed to be upset with the attention. Her "shy Di" image in the British tabloid press contrasted with her charismatic presence on camera in palace-sanctioned television interviews with her fiancé.

Among the numerous celebratory events preceding the wedding were a series of garden parties that the queen and Prince Phillip hosted at Buckingham Palace. I went to one in the formal "morning dress"—top hat, waistcoat, and tails—that I also would wear for the ceremony in St. Paul's Cathedral. Charles and Diana surprised and delighted the 6,000 invited guests by emerging from the palace with the queen and Prince Phillip. As the royals made their way through the throng, Diana was surrounded by more people than the queen. She impressed garden party veterans with the ease with which she smilingly approached and chatted with many of the guests.

As I later strolled through the vast palace gardens with the queen's press secretary, Michael Shea, ABC television's Barbara Walters approached us. She asked Shea if she could interview Prince Charles about the wedding. When he said only BBC television would be doing that, she tried again. In his best British diplomat's voice, Shea then responded firmly, "Miss Walters, that is just not on. Good day."

For the British people, the royal wedding was the occasion for a boisterous patriotic celebration and revival of pride in the monarchy at a time of national economic crisis, social unrest in England, and sectarian violence in Northern Ireland. On July 29, a million people lined the two-mile route for the colorful royal processions. Mounted troops in ceremonial dress paraded, along with horse-drawn, gold-encrusted state carriages, through historic central London from Buckingham Palace to St. Paul's Cathedral and back again. Loudspeakers along the way broadcast to the crowds the sounds of the wedding ceremony. When my day's work was done, well after midnight, I walked from my Mayfair office to my home in Chelsea. The streets, from which traffic had been banned for the day, were still filled with partying people.

I NEXT SAW PRINCE CHARLES AND PRINCESS DIANA IN PERSON IN November 1985, after I became managing editor of the *Post*. They had come to Washington to appear at a "Best in Britain" promotion at a J. C. Penney department store in the Virginia suburbs. I attended a small late morning reception for them at the British embassy, where I met and conversed with Diana. I was somewhat surprised when she wanted to discuss what she thought was relatively serious coverage of the royal family in the American news media, compared with the gossipy popular tabloid press in Britain. She also asked about the access American journalists had to U.S. politicians, compared with what I had experienced in Britain, and how often President Reagan held press conferences. It was not the kind of small talk for which I had prepared.

I did not know that the storybook royal marriage was already fraying. In a year's time, Charles would resume a long-ago affair with Camilla Parker Bowles, and Diana would soon take a lover of her own. In September 1996 when, as executive editor of the *Post*, I talked very briefly with Diana for the next and last time, she had just been divorced after a long separation from Charles and years of open conflict with the royal family.

By then, of course, she was celebrated worldwide for her charity work, fashion sense, and popularity with the British people. She had agreed to a request by Katharine Graham, who had become a consoling older friend, to be the guest of honor at a major fundraising gala that Mrs. Graham held in Washington for breast cancer research. It was in honor of the late *Post* fashion writer Nina Hyde, who had died of breast cancer. Diana looked so beautiful and, I thought, vulnerable, when Mrs. Graham introduced us, that I was not able to muster much to say.

A little less than a year later, on the night of August 30, 1997, I was in Minneapolis attending a wedding dinner for the oldest son of a *Post* editor. Word spread that Diana had been killed in a horrific auto accident hours earlier in Paris. I called the newsroom to begin directing the coverage and took the first plane back to Washington the next morning.

Not surprisingly, I pushed for voluminous coverage of the accident; the investigations of its possible causes; Diana's relationship with playboy Dodi Fayed, who died in the crash with her; the role of the tabloid photographers who had been chasing their car; the outpouring of grief by the British people; the controversially restrained reaction of the royal family; Diana's funeral in Westminster Abbey and burial on her family's ancestral estate; her legacy as "the people's princess"; and the relationship with the media that helped make her so popular. The *Post* published nearly eighty stories about it all during the three weeks after Diana's death.

Relentless pursuit of Diana by British reporters and photographers was controversial after her death. But I had no difficulty with what I published about Diana's exceptionally compelling, very public, and ultimately tragic life story. Before her death, she had revealed so much about her private life, her relationships with Charles, and the royal family, in interviews with print and broadcast journalists and authors. By that time, I had already had to make more difficult decisions about the private lives of public figures, and I would have to make even more in the time to come.

12

Public Lives, Private Lives

EVERYTHING CHANGED WITH GARY HART.

When the forty-six-year-old Democratic U.S. senator from Colorado announced that he was running for president in February 1983, he was little known nationally. At age thirty-six, Hart had managed the 1972 presidential campaign of Senator George McGovern, who lost in a historic landslide to President Richard Nixon. Hart was then elected to the Senate from Colorado in 1974 and reelected in 1980. I was aware of him because he had visited me in my London office when I was the *Post*'s correspondent there. Hart seemed quite self-absorbed, as he told me about creating an international network of rising young leaders like himself. I did not write a story.

I had to learn more about Hart when I directed the *Post*'s coverage of the 1984 presidential election campaign as the newspaper's relatively new national news editor. Ben Bradlee had brought me back to the newsroom from London less than a year earlier to gain national news experience under the guidance of assistant managing editor Peter Silberman. I focused especially on political coverage because it was so important for the *Post* and its readers.

The relatively exalted status of national reporters in the newsroom also created a good leadership test for me. I had to demonstrate that I could become knowledgeable about what they covered, and that I could motivate them while respecting their accomplishments. In my two years as national editor, I learned lessons and built trust from which I would benefit for years.

Hart was good-looking, ambitious, and aloof. He presented himself as a new generation presidential candidate, crusading for what he offered as new ideas for the economy, the environment, national defense, and foreign policy. He surprised the political world by beating former vice president Walter Mondale in the New Hampshire presidential primary in February 1984, becoming Mondale's main challenger for the Democratic nomination to run against President Ronald Reagan.

However, *Post* stories by one of my national reporters, George Lardner Jr., in February and March, raised questions about Hart's age and change of name. The Congressional Directory, Hart's campaign literature, and his Colorado driver's license, among other records, had listed his birthdate as November 28, 1937. But his Kansas birth certificate showed that he was born Gary Hartpence on November 28, 1936. Hart continued to insist in two interviews with Lardner that he was born in 1937, until the reporter confronted him with the birth certificate. "It's no big deal," Hart then told Lardner. "It's whatever the records say."

Hart also told Lardner that his late parents wanted to change the family name to Hart because Hartpence sounded too Germanic. But his surviving uncles and a sister said that Hart, in 1961, talked his parents into changing their last name along with him, because he was going into politics and wanted to make it easier to spell. When other reporters then asked Hart about these discrepancies after the *Post* stories appeared, he sounded increasingly defensive and irritated as he gave varying and unconvincing explanations for his differing birthdates and name change.

His responses raised questions for me and for our political reporters about Hart's lack of veracity and evasiveness, which would linger. The investigative journalist in me wondered what else we would find that Hart was hiding.

Hart won a majority of the 1984 Democratic primaries and caucuses before being narrowly beaten by Mondale in the final delegate count at the Democratic nominating convention. After Mondale lost the ensuing election to Reagan, Hart became the presumed frontrunner for the 1988 Democratic presidential nomination.

Silberman said years later that Ben had told him he was pleased with our 1984 election coverage. I had established a good working relationship with many of the national staff's journalists. Some of them were among those in the newsroom who recommended me when Don Graham asked them about who should succeed Howard Simons as managing editor in 1984.

When Gary Hart formally announced, on April 13, 1987, his candidacy for president, I had been managing editor for nearly three years. Even before Hart's announcement, reporters covering him had heard rumors from competing campaigns about Hart and women other than his wife, Lee. Questions about his marriage had circulated in political circles since 1972, when Hart was McGovern's campaign manager, but journalists had not pursued them. He and Lee had been separated twice, once in 1979 and again in 1982.

Post reporter Paul Taylor, who was covering Hart in 1987, urged *Post* editors to consider what he and the newspaper should do about the new rumors he kept hearing from his political sources. We had a meeting in Ben Bradlee's office with Taylor, the national news editors, and political columnist David Broder. As Taylor later wrote in his book, *See How They Run*, we discussed the obvious questions about what would amount to unprecedented reporting about a presidential candidate's private life.

"If a candidate for President is believed to be a womanizer, but there's no suggestion that his sexual activities have ever interfered with his public duties, is it even worth investigating, much less publishing?" Taylor recalled us debating. "Is a series of one-night stands more reportable than a single long-term extramarital affair? Does it matter if a candidate has an open marriage understanding with his spouse?"

Broder, then the recognized dean of American political journalists, with whom I had worked closely during the 1984 campaign, suggested a way forward, which Ben and I adopted. We would assign someone to re-search an in-depth character profile of Hart to determine the relevance, to his fitness for the presidency, of any extramarital sexual activities and questions about his honesty, dating back to the 1984 campaign. Reporter David Maraniss was assigned to begin the project in early May of 1987.

Thus, in the *Post* newsroom, the "character issue" for presidential candidates was born.

FOR MORE THAN HALF OF THE TWENTIETH CENTURY, WHAT RE-porters knew about politicians' private lives, especially their sex lives, was mostly kept out of news coverage. As recently as the 1960s, journalists and news organizations turned a blind eye to the compulsive sexual escapades of presidents John F. Kennedy and Lyndon B. Johnson while they were in the White House, along with similar behavior by untold members of Congress.

It was Senator Edward Kennedy's behavior that became news in 1969, when he drove off a bridge connecting Chappaquiddick Island and Martha's Vineyard, killing his passenger, twenty-eight-year-old Mary Jo Kopechne. After trying and failing to find and rescue her from the water, Kennedy did not report the accident to police for ten hours. The scandal may have prevented him from being president, but Kennedy still became a revered elder statesman in the Senate.

In September 1972, when I was metropolitan news editor, I supervised reporting by the *Post*'s local news staff on a story about Speaker of the House of Representatives Carl Albert crashing his car into parked vehi-cles while apparently drunk. He had just come out of the Zebra Room, a well-known bar and lounge in the genteel Cleveland Park neighborhood of Washington. The damage to the other cars was minor, and police did not investigate further. Congressional reporters did not follow up, despite their knowledge of Albert's drinking, and nothing more came of it. I was not surprised by the lack of further reporting, and I was not then in charge of the *Post*'s congressional coverage.

I reacted more aggressively in October 1974 to the alcoholism and bi-zarre behavior of Rep. Wilbur Mills. As chairman of the House Ways and Means Committee, which effectively controlled federal taxation, Mills was considered the most powerful man in Congress at the time. After President Nixon resigned in August because of Watergate, and I had become the *Post*'s metropolitan news editor, I had few misgivings about pursuing what, once again, began as a local police story.

Police stopped the car Mills was driving, with its headlights out, near the Tidal Basin at 2 a.m. on October 7. They found the congressman intoxicated and his face bleeding. He had broken his glasses trying to stop a woman from jumping out of the car and into the Tidal Basin when police pulled him over. The woman was helped by the police out of the relatively shallow water. She turned out to be a stripper, Annabell Battistella, who performed in a local burlesque club under the stage name Fanne Fox, the "Argentine Firecracker." Mills issued a statement claiming that he and his wife were close friends of Battistella and her husband, and that she had taken ill before she decided to get out of his car.

I asked two of my reporters, Stephen Green and Margot Hornblower, to investigate. They pieced together the real story of Mills's boozy year-long affair with Battistella. She and Mills had met at the Silver Slipper strip club in downtown Washington, where they often were seen drinking heavily and quarreling loudly. Although our story attracted national attention, Mills was reelected from his Arkansas district a month later. But on November 30, Mills, now being shadowed by the media, turned up intoxicated at the Pilgrim Theater burlesque house in Boston, where Battistella was performing. Mills held a bizarre impromptu press conference with Battistella when reporters showed up outside her dressing room. Facing national disgrace and a potential congressional investigation, Mills joined Alcoholics Anonymous, entered rehab, relinquished his House committee chairmanship, and retired from Congress in 1976.

Two reporters on the *Post*'s Style staff took the next step in May 1976. "For nearly two years, Ohio Congressman Wayne Hayes, powerful chairman of the House Administration Committee, has kept a woman on his staff who says she is paid $14,000 a year in public money to serve as his mistress," began the May 23 front-page story by Marion Clark and Rudy Maxa.

"I can't type. I can't file. I can't even answer the phone," thirty-three-year-old Elizabeth Ray said in a quote that became infamous. Clark and Maxa confirmed that Ray did no work for her $14,000 salary in her otherwise empty office in the Longworth House Building on Capitol Hill. Ray told her story to the two reporters after Hays divorced his first wife and married his secretary from his Ohio congressional office, rather than Ray. She said Hays wanted to continue his arrangement with her. Tipped off by Ray, the reporters observed the dinner portions of two of her dates with Hays at restaurants near her apartment in suburban Arlington, Virginia.

The *Post* was criticized for keeping follow-up stories on its front page for more than a week. But Hays eventually apologized publicly for his behavior and resigned from Congress on September 1, 1976.

It had been eleven years since the Wayne Hays story when the *Post* assigned David Maraniss to determine the veracity and relevance of the persistent rumors in political circles that presidential candidate Gary Hart was involved in extramarital sexual relationships. Before Maraniss could begin, however, the *Miami Herald* reported, in a front-page story on Sunday, May 3, 1987, that an attractive young woman had spent Friday night and most of Saturday with Hart in his Capitol Hill townhouse in Washington. His wife, Lee, was at their home in Colorado.

Acting on a tip, *Herald* editors and reporters had staked out the townhouse and watched the comings and goings of Hart and the woman, whom the paper did not initially identify. The reporters and Hart wound up confronting each other outside his townhouse on Saturday night, with the woman inside. Hart denied that anyone had spent the previous night there. He said that the woman was "a friend of friend" who was staying with other friends nearby, and that he was "not involved in any relationship." When the reporters told him that they knew the woman had previously made telephone calls to him from places around the country, Hart said the calls were "casual, political."

Coincidentally, that day's *New York Times* Sunday magazine featured a profile of Hart. In response to questions from the writer, E. J. Dionne, about the womanizing rumors, Hart had told him, "Follow me around. . . . I'm serious. If anybody wants to put a tail on me, go ahead. They'd be very bored." His words took on new relevance after the *Herald* had done just that.

On Monday morning, *Post* reporter Paul Taylor called Hart's campaign manager, Bill Dixon, about the *Herald* story. Dixon repeated Hart's denial. He identified the woman as Donna Rice, whom, Dixon said, Hart had met at a fundraising party on a boat docked in the Turnberry Isle resort just north of Miami.

That same morning, Rice, a model, bit-part actress, and part-time pharmaceuticals salesperson, held a press conference in a lawyer's office in Miami. She also repeated Hart's account of the weekend, and said of him, "We're just pals." But she surprised reporters by adding that Hart had invited her in April to join him and another man and woman on a day trip in a chartered yacht from Florida to Bimini in the Bahamas. She said it had unexpectedly turned into an overnight stay when the island's customs office closed before the scheduled return trip. She said that she spent the night apart from Hart.

Tom Edsall, who wrote the *Post* story about the Rice press conference, then received an envelope from a source who did not want to be identified. Edsall gave it to Ben Bradlee. The envelope contained a private detective's report of Hart spending Saturday night, December 20, 1986, at the home of another woman in Washington. The detective had been following Hart for an unnamed client who suspected the politician was involved with his wife. But this woman was unmarried. The detective photographed Hart entering her house at 8:45 p.m. Saturday and leaving at 7:48 a.m. Sunday. There also was a photo of the woman picking up a newspaper from her neighbor's house at 6:55 a.m.

Ben and other people in the *Post* newsroom immediately recognized the woman as someone they knew—a Washington lobbyist who had previously worked on Capitol Hill. Bradlee decided to contact her to ask about the detective's report and the nature of her relationship with Hart. The *Post*'s national politics editor told Paul Taylor about these events by telephone on Tuesday night, May 5, and sent him the detective's report. Taylor was out of town covering Hart in the aftermath of the Donna Rice stories. He had just watched Hart talk that day to an American Newspaper Publishers Association audience in New York about his morality and high standard of public and private conduct.

"The nakedness of his deceit," Taylor later wrote in his book, "had put me in an uncharitable frame of mind."

On Wednesday, at a crowded press conference at the Hanover Inn on the Dartmouth University campus in New Hampshire, Taylor asked Hart a series of questions about what he had told the newspaper publishers.

"When you said that you did nothing immoral, did you mean that you had no sexual relationship with Donna Rice last weekend or at any other time you were with her?" Taylor asked.

"That's correct," Hart answered.

"Do you believe that adultery is immoral?"

"Yes."

"Have you ever committed adultery?" Taylor asked.

Hart argued with the question, which Taylor repeated, as their dialogue continued, but he never answered yes or no.

The dam burst. Other reporters at the press conference followed up aggressively. Was Hart's relationship with his wife monogamous? He said he didn't have an answer to that. Would he submit to a polygraph test? "Gimme a break," he responded.

After writing and transmitting his story from his laptop computer to the *Post*, Taylor talked on the telephone with Ben. The Washington lobbyist had confirmed to Ben that Hart was with her that Saturday night in December and that they had a long relationship. She said Hart had told her he would leave Lee to marry her. She was furious about Donna Rice and worried that her career would be ruined if she was named in a story about the detective's report. Ben assured her that the *Post* would not name her, a decision with which I agreed.

Taylor next talked to me and Bob Kaiser, then the assistant managing editor for national news. Taylor said he opposed any negotiation with Hart or his people about whether the story would be published. We totally agreed. Our decision making would not be affected by what Hart decided to do. We instructed Taylor to tell that to Hart. We were just seeking his response to what was in the detective's report.

Shortly before 11 p.m., Taylor found Hart campaign press secretary Kevin Sweeney at the Eastgate Motel in Littleton, New Hampshire, where Hart's traveling campaign workers were staying. Taylor read him the detective's report from his computer and asked to talk to Hart about it. Sweeney told other senior aides, who contacted Hart, who was staying with Lee twenty miles away in at the Colonnade Hotel in Lyndon-ville, Vermont.

Eventually, Hart himself called Sweeney and asked if he thought it was a story that would be published. "Yes, it's a story," Sweeney told him.

"This thing is never going to end, is it?" Hart said to Sweeney. "Look, let's go home."

Taylor reported in a front-page story on Friday, May 8, that Hart had decided to drop out of the presidential race "hours after The Washington Post presented a top campaign aide with documented evidence of a recent liaison between Hart and a woman with whom he has had a long-term relationship."

The story made clear that the *Post* had not negotiated with Hart about withholding that fact if he withdrew. "There were no ultimatums, no negotiations," Ben was quoted as saying. "We simply asked to talk to Hart about the information we had gathered."

On June 2, the *National Enquirer* published a photograph of Donna Rice sitting on Hart's lap on a Florida boat dock. Hart was wearing a tee shirt with the name of a boat called *Monkey Business* emblazoned on it. The photo was published after Hart had dropped out, but it would always define him nevertheless.

Hart rejoined the Democratic presidential primary race six months later, on December 15, 1987, running against the news media as much as the rest of the field. After finishing dead last in the February 8, 1988, Iowa caucuses, with less than 1 percent of the vote, he dropped out for good in March.

The rules had changed. Adultery would never again be off limits in decisions about how to report on politicians—from the White House to statehouses to city halls. Veracity, trust, judgment, and all the other elements of, yes, character, would also come into play. Hand-wringing and arguments about this change, much bemoaned by many journalists in the wake of the Hart affair, continued for years.

I had no such qualms. For me, from then on, decision making about such stories would mean determining whether questionable personal conduct was true and not just rumor, whether the newspaper could confirm it was true, and if it was relevant to the politician's public responsibility. Applying my rule would present many challenges in the years ahead.

MY POLICY ABOUT REPORTING ON POLITICIANS' PERSONAL CON-duct came into play again after Vice President George H. W. Bush chose Indiana senator Dan Quayle to be his vice presidential running mate when Bush ran for president in 1988. Media coverage of Quayle, a surprise choice, questioned his experience, academic record, and whether his well-to-do family had exerted undue influence in his joining the National Guard to avoid the Vietnam War draft. Quayle told me years later, when writing his memoir, that he thought the *Post* and the rest of the news media had been too hard on him. I thought most of the coverage had been a legitimate examination of the man who would be a proverbial heartbeat away from the presidency.

The challenge for me came when a convict named Brett Kimberlin called several news organizations to say he had frequently sold marijuana to Quayle when Quayle was in law school and afterward. Kimberlin was serving a fifty-year sentence in federal prison for drug smuggling and a 1978 series of bombings in Speedway, Indiana. *Post* reporters interviewed Kimberlin and found that none of the dates and places he cited checked out. It was an easy call. I concluded that his story was not true.

In a very different situation, there was not much for me to decide in January 1989 when newly elected President Bush selected four-term senator John Tower of Texas to be his secretary of defense. Decades before the #MeToo movement, Tower was well known on Capitol Hill for his habitual physical and sexual harassment of women who worked there. He had a reputation as a senator with whom no woman under the age of ninety could safely share a Senate elevator.

Yet the news media had largely ignored both that behavior and his admittedly heavy drinking, until Tower, after retiring from the Senate, was nominated by Bush. By then, it was clear that the rules had changed.

Tower's reputation for sexual harassment and alcoholism filled news accounts in the *Post* and other media of what became a heated political debate over his nomination, although few specific examples were cited. Tower's heavy drinking was such that Senate Armed Services Committee

Chairman Sam Nunn publicly questioned whether Tower could "carry out his military command responsibilities 24 hours a day." Tower himself pledged on television to abstain from alcohol if he were to be confirmed.

It was generally accepted by other politicians and the news media that the accusations about Tower's conduct were true, and that his conduct had affected his performance in office. In March 1989, the Democratic-controlled Senate voted against confirming Tower.

BY THAT TIME, I HAD SPENT MANY YEARS OVERSEEING WASHINGton *Post* investigations of suspected drug use by Washington mayor Marion Barry. My decision making about Barry's conduct was complicated by his extraordinary political success, his enduring charismatic appeal among much of the city's black community, and his public complaints of racial bias in the *Post*'s coverage of him. I also had known Barry since I first wrote about him in 1966.

After serving as president of the D.C. School Board and then as a member of the city council, Barry became Washington's second elected mayor in 1978. He was endorsed by the *Post* editorial page as a promising leader for the city's relatively new home rule government. Barry initially improved the city's finances and public services, created a summer jobs program that employed tens of thousands of local young people, and replaced many white city employees from the city's pre–home rule era with African Americans. Later, he facilitated redevelopment of the city's commercial downtown. Endorsed for the second time by the *Post*'s editorial page, Barry won reelection in 1982, with 80 percent of the vote.

His private behavior became a public issue after the *Post* reported in 1983 that police had long been investigating allegations that Barry was at a December 22, 1981, party at the This Is It strip club downtown while cocaine was being used. In response to the story, Barry acknowledged being at the party, but he denied that he had seen or used cocaine.

In June 1984, a former D.C. government employee, Karen Johnson, was convicted of selling cocaine after a federal grand jury investigation in which she refused to answer questions about possible drug use by other city employees, including the mayor. Johnson spent an additional eight months in jail for contempt for her refusal to testify. After the grand jury questioned Barry about Johnson, he acknowledged publicly that he had occasionally visited Johnson at her apartment, but he denied that he had used cocaine.

Various sources told *Post* reporters and editors that Barry—who was married to his popular, elegant, third wife, Effie—had numerous clandestine relationships with women with whom he used cocaine. As managing editor, I decided that we should investigate as aggressively as we could, including shadowing the mayor. Our reporters followed his Lincoln Town Car to various places around town, but they were never able to determine with certainty who he was visiting.

We closely covered the continuing federal investigation, and we exposed increasing favoritism in the awarding of city jobs and contracts to friends of Barry, including women friends. Nevertheless, the *Post* editorial page again endorsed Barry when he ran for a third term in 1986. A senior editorial page editor approached me in the newsroom to ask why our coverage of Barry was so negative when the newspaper was endorsing him. I reminded him of the *Post*'s separation between news gathering and editorial opinion, and I told him not to interfere with our work.

In May 1987, a local television station reported that Karen Johnson had recently told a federal grand jury that she had used cocaine with the mayor. The *Post* then reported that Johnson testified that she sold and used cocaine with the mayor on twenty to thirty occasions in 1980 and 1981.

Barry denied it all. He accused federal investigators and the news media, particularly the *Post*, of unfairly targeting him.

On Thanksgiving weekend in 1987, as rumors persisted about the mayor and women and drugs, we decided to send a reporter Barry did not know to shadow him on vacation in the Bahamas. Traveling without his wife, Barry stayed at a beachfront casino resort in Nassau with city employee Bettye Smith, a young woman named Theresa Southerland, three male friends, and Barry's seven-year-old son, Christopher. After watching the group for several days in the hotel's public areas, including the casino and the swimming pool, the reporter introduced himself to the mayor and asked some questions.

Barry telephoned Milton Coleman, my assistant managing editor for Metro news, to warn that he would turn the city's black community against the *Post* if it published a story. Coleman, who had covered the mayor as a city hall reporter and knew him well, told Barry that the *Post* was going ahead. The story quoted the mayor saying that Smith was someone he often visited at her home, but that their relationship was not romantic. He referred to her as Christopher Barry's "Aunt Bettye," who was babysitting him.

It was not a very revealing story, but our decision to follow Barry to the Bahamas was not wrong. Several years later, during Barry's sensational 1990 federal trial on charges of cocaine possession and perjury, Theresa Southerland and others on the trip testified that Barry used cocaine and had sex with Southerland in a hotel room at the Nassau resort. Southerland told the jury that she and the mayor frequently used cocaine while she was one of his girlfriends between November 1987 and November 1989. Bettye Smith also testified at the 1990 trial that she had used drugs with Barry in her Washington home since 1983.

On the night of December 22, 1988, we heard that police detectives had been called back from investigating a suspected cocaine dealer, Virgin Islands resident Charles Lewis, at a downtown Ramada Inn, because the mayor was visiting the man in his hotel room. We sent reporters to the hotel, police headquarters, and the Virgin Islands. By 2 a.m., we were able to publish a story in the late editions of the December 23 *Post*. It created a sensation in the rest of the news media.

Later that day, in an interview with *Post* reporters for a December 24 front-page story, Barry acknowledged visiting Lewis in his hotel room at Lewis's request, but denied seeing any cocaine. He described Lewis as a former city employee and friend whom he had visited at hotels when Lewis was in Washington.

Reacting to Barry's denials, Police Chief Maurice Turner told a *Post* reporter in a series of background interviews over the next several days that the mayor had visited Lewis at the Ramada Inn at least six times over five days in December. Turner told the reporter that he had suspected for a long time that Barry had a drug problem, but had been unable to prove it. He said he suspected that the mayor used cocaine in homes around Washington and on boats docked on the Potomac River. Taking advantage of this guidance, the *Post* published several more stories about the investigation of Barry, which Turner formally referred to the U.S. Attorney.

At an emotional news conference on December 29, Barry vowed to "fight for my character, fight for my integrity and fight for my commitment" to the city. He added, "I have been tried, convicted, sentenced and doing time by some members of the media and the community."

The next day, Barry went on local television to apologize to the city and the nation for using "bad judgment" in visiting Lewis at the Ramada Inn. Referring vaguely to reports of his friendships with women who were not his wife, he said that he could understand that people might be embarrassed by his behavior, even though he had done nothing illegal.

One winter afternoon, Barry called and asked to meet me in a secluded bar of the fashionable Madison Hotel, across the street from the *Post* building. He had often talked to me on the telephone about *Post* coverage of him. We were the only people in the bar, and we did not order anything to drink. Barry began the conversation by reminding me about how far we had both come since I first met him in 1966.

Then, in response to my questions, without admitting or denying that he used drugs, he asked me why his private behavior mattered if he was doing a good job for the city. I said that cocaine possession, use, and sale were illegal, and he was the mayor, with authority over the police, who should be enforcing the law. But why, he persisted, even as we were getting up to leave, did his personal behavior matter?

It seems corny, as I recall it while writing this. But as we emerged from the hotel, I noticed the big, white sign on our building across the street that said: THE WASHINGTON POST. It was glowing brightly in the frosty twilight, like something out of the movies.

"Look at that," I said to Barry, as I pointed to the sign before he stepped into his waiting Town Car. "I may not be the mayor, whose behavior reflects on the whole city," I told him. "But if I was running around or doing drugs, it would reflect badly on that important institution over there and its credibility."

"Great to see you, Len," Barry responded, reaching out his hand. "Let's stay in touch."

In the spring of 1989, Charles Lewis was arrested in the Virgin Islands and convicted of selling cocaine to an undercover officer. What we did not know at the time was that he agreed to cooperate with investigators in exchange for leniency. He told them that he used cocaine with Barry at the Ramada Inn in Washington and in the Virgin Islands over the past three years.

Most important, as it turned out, he told them that a former model and city contractor, Rasheeda Moore, had smoked cocaine with Barry in the Virgin Islands in 1986. Federal prosecutors found Moore in Los Angeles and brought her to Washington. Moore, who had been one of Barry's girlfriends for five years, became jealous of his other women and decided to cooperate with prosecutors to avoid being prosecuted herself.

The world met Rasheeda Moore on a shadowy videotape showing Barry smoking crack cocaine in a room in the Vista Hotel, a block away from the *Washington Post*, on the night of January 18, 1990. In a sting arranged by police and the FBI, Moore had lured Barry there and offered him cocaine that was delivered to the room by another woman. After he smoked some of it in a pipe, put the pipe down, and got ready to leave, the mayor was arrested.

"Bitch set me up," Barry was memorably heard to say on the videotape. "I shouldn't have come up here . . . Goddamn bitch."

Barry abandoned his intended campaign for a fourth term as mayor after he was charged with twelve counts of cocaine possession and perjury in earlier grand jury testimony. A parade of former girlfriends and other witnesses, including Charles Lewis, testified during Barry's trial about dozens of times that the mayor had used cocaine with them. Barry's lawyer conceded that his client had sometimes used cocaine, but he argued that the prosecution had not proved Barry's possession of the drug in the specific instances with which he was charged. He argued that Barry had been entrapped at the Vista Hotel.

In the end, Barry was convicted on one count of possession, based on the testimony of a woman named Doris Crenshaw, who told the jury that they had used cocaine in a room at the storied Mayflower Hotel in Washington in November 1989. He was acquitted on one charge, and the jury was unable to reach a unanimous verdict on the other ten, including the charge based on the sting at the Vista Hotel.

After serving six months in prison, Barry returned to forgiveness and political support from much of Washington's black community. He was elected to the city council from the low-income Ward 8, in which he lived. Then he won a fourth term as mayor in 1994. "I'm in recovery," he proclaimed, "and so is my city."

Neither statement turned out to be true. Washington suffered from a crack cocaine epidemic, record murder rates, mismanagement of many city departments, and a severe government financial crisis. President Clinton and Congress transferred control of most city departments from the mayor to a temporary financial control board.

Barry still won two more elections as the Ward 8 council member. But his drug use continued, his health deteriorated, and he pleaded guilty to misdemeanor charges for failing to file federal income tax returns for many years. Barry died of cardiac arrest at the age of seventy-eight in 2014.

Before I retired as executive editor of the *Post* in 2008, Barry, in some of his darkest days, suggested in phone calls to me that he and I organize a reunion for all the local journalists who had reported on him over the decades. I always put him off.

DECISIONS ABOUT REPORTING ON THE PRIVATE LIVES OF PUBLIC figures could sometimes be beyond my control in the increasingly crowded and competitive multichannel news media world that was emerging in the 1990s.

That is what happened on January 23, 1992, when Gennifer Flowers, a forty-two-year-old Arkansas state government employee, alleged in the supermarket tabloid *Star* that she had had a twelve-year affair with Governor Bill Clinton, who was running for president. The *Star* said that Flowers provided details of the affair and tapes of numerous telephone conversations with Clinton. Our reporters had heard rumors about Clinton and women, but had not verified any of them. As executive editor for less than a year, I was only briefly uncertain about the *Star* story, which I decided to report in a *Post* story. The rest of the news media, led by television, jumped on it.

Bill and Hillary Clinton then appeared on the CBS News show *60 Minutes* on Sunday, January 26, immediately after the network's broadcast of the Super Bowl, to respond to questions about the story from correspondent Steve Kroft. The Clintons said that Flowers was an acquaintance who had told Bill Clinton about being pressured, along with other Arkansas women, to tell tales about the governor.

"When this woman first got caught up in these charges, I felt as I've felt about all these women, that they had just been minding their own business and they got hit by a meteor," Hillary Clinton told Kroft. "I felt terrible about what was happening to them. Bill talked to this woman every time she called, saying her life was going to be ruined."

"It was only when the money came out," Bill Clinton chimed in, "when the tabloid went down there offering people money to say they had been involved with me, that she changed her story. There's a recession on."

When Kroft said he was assuming from their answers that the governor was "categorically denying" that he ever had an affair with Flowers, Bill Clinton responded, "I've said that before. And so has she."

When Kroft asked if, when Clinton said there had been problems in his marriage, did he mean adultery, Clinton said, "I think the American people, at least people that have been married for a long time, know what it means and know the whole range of things it can mean."

Later in the interview, Bill Clinton added, "You go back and listen to what I've said. You know I have acknowledged wrongdoing. I have acknowledged causing pain in my marriage. I have said things to you tonight and to the American people from the beginning that no American politician has.

"I can remember a time when a divorced person couldn't run for president, and that time, thank goodness, has passed. Nobody's prejudiced against anybody because they are divorced. Are we going to take the reverse position now that if people have problems in their marriage and there are things in their past which they don't want to discuss which are painful to them, that they can't run?"

Flowers then held a press conference to describe an affair with Clinton. She played some of the tapes of telephone conversations with the governor, which the Clintons had acknowledged in their *60 Minutes* interview. The nature of her relationship with him, other than very friendly, was not clear from the tapes, which Flowers had sold with her story to the *Star* for $150,000.

I did not approve of that kind of tabloid journalism. The *Post* never paid for news. But the *60 Minutes* interview sounded to me like damage control. Bill Clinton, with Hillary's approval, was saying that whatever he had done in his private life and marriage was not relevant to his candidacy for president. He later won a majority of the 1992 primaries and caucuses, and was easily nominated to run against the incumbent, President George H. W. Bush.

Bush never directly touched on Clinton's private life during the 1992 campaign. But political reporters heard rumors that Bush himself had had an affair with his longtime close aide, Jennifer Fitzgerald. I asked our extraordinarily well-sourced White House reporter, Ann Devroy, about the rumors. She said she had spent two months looking into them in the early 1980s when Bush was Ronald Reagan's vice president, and had never found any evidence of an affair. She said that Fitzgerald, who had worked as Bush's closest assistant ever since he was a special envoy to China in 1974, had a reputation for strictly guarding access to him, which generated gossip. We did not initially write about it.

But the *New York Post* published a story on August 10, 1992, headlined "The Bush Affair." It reported on a footnote in a new book referring to Bush and Fitzgerald staying alone together in a guest house in Geneva during arms control talks in Switzerland in 1984 while Bush's wife, Barbara, was on a book tour in the United States. Bush was asked about the story the next day by a CNN television reporter at a press conference and by an NBC television reporter in an interview at the White House.

Bush angrily told CNN correspondent Mary Tillotson that the *New York Post* story was "a lie." Tillotson told him that she was asking "because you've said that family values and character are likely to be important in the presidential campaign." Bush responded, "I'm not going to take any sleazy questions like that from CNN." He told *Dateline NBC* correspondent Stone Phillips later in the day, "You're perpetuating the sleaze by even asking the question, to say nothing of asking in the Oval Office."

Bill Clinton publicly castigated the *New York Post* for publishing the story about Bush. "I felt for him," he told reporters. "I like him on a personal level. I like his wife. I just don't think it should be part of the campaign."

I published a story by our news media reporter, Howard Kurtz, about these exchanges. Kurtz wrote that "several news organizations, including the *Washington Post* and the *Los Angeles Times*, have investigated the rumor but found no evidence to substantiate it."

Neither presidential candidate's private life became an issue in the campaign. The economy was generally considered to be the most significant issue as Clinton won the presidency in November 1992.

WEEKS BEFORE THE ELECTION, IN SEPTEMBER 1992, A FREELANCE journalist, Florence Graves, contacted the *Post* about evidence she was gathering of habitual sexual harassment by sixty-year-old Republican U.S. senator Bob Packwood of Oregon. Packwood was known nationally as an advocate for women's rights and for hiring and promoting women on his congressional staff. At the same time, he had a reputation among former employees, Capitol Hill staffers, and journalists for making unwanted advances on women.

Graves had identified and talked to women who said they were victims of sexual harassment by Packwood at various times since his election to the Senate in 1969 through 1989. Packwood was married from 1964 until he and his wife divorced in 1991. But the women whom Graves had contacted were reluctant to talk for publication.

After reviewing what she had found and checking her credentials, I put Graves on a contract with the *Post* and partnered her with a staff reporter, Charles Shepard. I asked them to report the story from scratch, including persuading as many of the women as possible to be identified and speak on the record. It was a painstaking process. As the reporters worked, Packwood campaigned to keep his seat in the upcoming November 3 election, with support from several national women's rights groups.

Graves and Shepard initially found nine women who worked for or with Packwood who, independently of each other, gave specific accounts for publication of unwanted kissing, grabbing, groping, and attempts at undressing by Packwood, when most of them were in their twenties. They soon left their jobs with Packwood but were afraid to do anything more about his behavior toward them. Several former Packwood employees told Graves and Shepard that more experienced women staffers told young women in his office to avoid working alone with him after hours.

When Graves and Shepard first contacted Packwood's office in October to discuss the allegations, his chief of staff, Elaine Franklin, accused the reporters of conducting a "witch hunt," politically motivated by Democrats supporting his election opponent, Oregon congressman Les AuCoin. However, AuCoin's campaign knew nothing about the *Post*'s reporting, and news media in Oregon had failed for years to follow up on tips about Packwood's behavior.

By late October, the reporting by Graves and Shepard had progressed enough for them to question Packwood himself about the accusations of sexual harassment by six women who agreed to be named in the reporters' interviews with Packwood. The reporters asked to interview Packwood on October 23, but he did not agree to do so until October 29, five days before the election.

Meanwhile, Packwood telephoned Katharine Graham at the *Post*. He told her what the reporters were working on, denied any impropriety, and asked to meet with the editor who would decide about publishing the story. Packwood then sent a rather chatty October 22 letter to Mrs. Graham, repeating his request to meet with the editor "for some length of time if *The Washington Post* is considering a story." Mrs. Graham told Packwood that I was the editor in question. She informed me of his phone call and letter, leaving the decision to me, as always.

A few hours before the October 29 interview, Packwood telephoned me to ask that I meet with him. I agreed to do so as soon as possible. He wrote me a letter that same afternoon, saying that he would be campaigning in Oregon. He wanted time after that to find "records or other materials to disprove any allegations" and to meet with me in Washington "before you consider running any story."

In the interview with Graves and Shepard that evening in Oregon, monitored by Packwood's chief of staff, Elaine Franklin, and Portland lawyer Jack Faust, Packwood denied making any sexual advances toward the women the reporters named, or anyone else. He asked for time to gather any information that might "tend to detract from the credibility" of the women who had accused him.

On October 31, three days before the election, Graves, Shepard, their editors, and I reviewed their progress.

Did we have enough women on the record, with their stories sufficiently corroborated? What was Packwood going to tell us about his accusers? Did we owe it to Oregon voters to publish something before the election? Or was it too late to be certain that the story would be sufficiently accurate, full, and fair, with so little time for Packwood to respond, or for us to correct any errors?

We all concluded that there was still too much more reporting and editing to do. We realized Packwood had been stalling us, but we also knew that our work was not yet done. The reporters informed Packwood that a story would not be ready before the election, but that we were going to continue our reporting and publish as soon as possible afterward.

I never doubted that the story, when finished, would meet my criteria. The accusations were true. The reporters were proving them to be true. Packwood's nonconsensual sexual behavior with women who worked for him was relevant to his public position as a United States senator. I just wanted more information.

Packwood then faxed me eight statements from people who knew three of his named accusers. None of the statements dealt directly with the accusations the women had made. Instead, the statements suggested that the women may have been attracted to Packwood, may have invited his advances, or were untruthful. Several included potentially embarrassing allegations about the women's sexual histories and personal lives.

On election day, Packwood won a slim victory over AuCoin. Over the next three weeks, Graves and Shepard were able to gather much more information in dozens more interviews, including several with Packwood. They found a tenth woman who told them about being sexually harassed by Packwood. They were able to further corroborate the accounts of all ten women with people they talked to after the incidents occurred.

Graves and Shepard also interviewed former aides of Packwood who were upset by the statements he had sent to me smearing the reputations of his accusers. Faust, the Portland lawyer, told the reporters that he and other friends of Packwood advised him to acknowledge his behavior and move on. All of this went into the story, along with the women's detailed accounts of the physical harassment they suffered and the people they told about it at the time.

Graves and Shepard informed Packwood of the story's progress and told him that it would be published on Sunday, November 22. Instead of contacting me for the face-to-face meeting he had once requested, the newly reelected senator sent, on Friday, November 20, a brief written statement.

"I will not make an issue of any specific allegation," Packwood's statement said. "If any of my comments or actions have indeed been unwelcome or if I have conducted myself in any way that caused any individual discomfort or embarrassment, for that I am sincerely sorry. My intentions were never to pressure, to offend, nor to make anyone feel uncomfortable, and I truly regret if that has occurred with anyone either on or off my staff."

Reporting and editing continued throughout Saturday. The story appeared at the top of the front page of the *Post*'s Sunday editions. We could not have finished any sooner.

Nevertheless, some readers asked why it was not published before the election, when it could have affected the outcome. I wrote an explanation that appeared in the *Post* on the following Sunday, November 29. "The answer is that on election day we still needed to do much more reporting, writing and editing before we had a story sufficiently full, accurate and fair to publish," I wrote. "As it turned out, our work could not be completed until three weeks after the election."

Under public pressure, the Senate Ethics Committee conducted a drawn-out investigation, including public hearings, of Packwood's behavior. Out of more than forty women who eventually told Graves of unwanted sexual advances by Packwood, about half cooperated formally with Senate investigators. The accounts of seventeen of the women were included in the Senate Ethics Committee's bill of particulars against Packwood. Although Packwood was still in the Senate, his power and influence in the chamber vanished as he fought for his political life.

Finally, in 1995, the Senate Ethics Committee unanimously recommended that Packwood be expelled from the Senate for ethical misconduct. Before the entire Senate could vote on the recommendation, Packwood resigned and left the Senate on September 7, three years after Florence Graves brought her reporting to the *Post*. In end, we had made a difference.

I HAD A MUCH MORE DIFFICULT DECISION TO MAKE AFTER Republican U.S. senator Bob Dole of Kansas was nominated to challenge President Bill Clinton in the 1996 presidential election. By that time, it was becoming routine for the *Post* to examine both the private and public lives of candidates for high public office, especially the presidency.

Over the past several years, we and much of the rest of the news media had been investigating reports that Clinton had engaged in extramarital sex with women besides Gennifer Flowers while he was governor of Arkansas, sometimes with the assistance of his state troopers. Hanging over the 1996 campaign was the question of whether Dole would make this an issue. His Republican supporters had portrayed Dole, a war hero and respected senator, as an honorable alternative to Clinton. But Dole himself had steered clear of Clinton's private life.

In August, as part of our biographical profiling of Dole, we published a long front-page story by reporter Kevin Merida about Dole's unusual 1972 divorce from his first wife, Phyllis Holden. He had married Holden, an occupational therapist, in 1948, after she helped him cope with a permanent disability from World War II combat wounds that severely limited his use of his arms and made handwriting difficult. Holden helped Dole get through college and law school by writing notes and exams for him from his dictation.

Merida reported that Dole, as a congressman and then as a senator beginning in 1969, had worked increasingly long hours and spent more and more time away from his family home in suburban Virginia. Dole completely surprised Holden in 1971 by telling her that he wanted a divorce. He began sleeping in the basement when he was home.

With nominal participation from a bewildered Holden, the divorce was rushed through a Kansas court by lawyers and judges who were friends of Dole. In 1975, Dole married Elizabeth Hanford, a federal trade commissioner who would later become a cabinet member and a U.S. senator herself. As we later wrote in our 2002 book, *The News About the News*, my managing editor, Robert Kaiser, and I decided that how Dole handled his first marriage and the divorce, leaving both his wife and daughter, Robin, in the dark, was revealing about the character of a man seeking to become president.

What we did not expect was that Merida would be contacted by several readers who told him that he missed part of the story. They said Dole had had an affair with a Washington woman for several years before asking his wife for a divorce.

Bob Woodward and another *Post* reporter, Charles Babcock, interviewed the woman in question, who eventually agreed to confirm her relationship with Dole. She showed the reporters datebooks that noted when she and Dole got together, mostly at her apartment, in 1968. Woodward and Babcock found friends and neighbors who remembered Dole coming to visit her. After a few more meetings during the next two years and only telephone contact in 1971 and 1972, the woman said she ended the relationship when Dole's divorce did not bring them together. Dole's campaign refused to answer questions or to make Dole available to the reporters.

It was clear to me that the story was true, and the reporting had confirmed it. That met two parts of my test. But was it relevant to Dole's candidacy for president?

Woodward and Babcock drafted several versions of the story for Kaiser and me to read. Kaiser thought all along that it should be published, citing a passage in Dole's acceptance speech at the Republican National Convention: "One must never compromise in regard to God, and family, and honor, and duty, and country."

But I had doubts about the relationship's relevance beyond what we had already published about Dole's deteriorating first marriage and divorce. I engaged other editors and reporters in conversations, meetings, and memos, on the question of publishing the story.

Most of my senior editors argued in favor of publication. Citing my own previous public position, Karen DeYoung, then the assistant managing editor for national news, reminded me in her memo that "the *Post* tradition [is] fully and carefully reporting all pertinent aspects of a presidential candidate's life."

Woodward wrote a 2,500-word memo to me, urging publication because "the *Post* has taken an aggressive position on Clinton and his sex life," although that involved his official role as governor of Arkansas. "The presumption is in favor of publication of the truth. Not everyone has to agree on relevance," Woodward wrote to me. "Any decision not to publish a story we know is true and many believe potentially relevant is rooted in subjectivity that goes beyond an editor's normal role."

That stiffened my spine to make what I thought was the right decision, regardless of the pressure on me. I strongly believed that it *was* my role as executive editor to decide what should and should not be published in the *Washington Post*, and that readers expected nothing less from me. I had and would continue to exercise that responsibility so long as I had the job.

In his memo to Kaiser and me, David Broder, then still the dean of American political journalists, explained why he was unconvinced by his colleagues' arguments for publishing the story. "I know of no instance," he wrote, "in which we have reached back almost three decades and made a news story of a consensual, extramarital affair involving someone in public life." In one of our meetings, Broder pointed to Dole's unblemished long marriage to Elizabeth Dole and suggested that some kind of statute of limitations should apply to Dole's consensual affair before that.

Kaiser sent me his own memo on October 14, arguing that deciding not to publish the story could impact the presidential campaign just as much as publishing would. He said that Dole may have already altered his strategy because of his knowledge of our reporting, and our readers didn't know it. Kaiser also was worried that it would look as though we had tried to influence the course of the campaign if it became known later that we had withheld the story.

I believed that such decisions should not be based on the anticipated impact of publishing or not publishing, unless a human life or the nation's security was clearly at risk. I did not believe that the newspaper should be used to achieve a desired outcome, one way or the other. And I did not worry about being publicly second-guessed about my decision.

Meanwhile, Dole emissaries met with us to argue against publication. Elizabeth Dole telephoned publisher Don Graham with the same request. Following the precedent set by his mother, Don told Elizabeth Dole that he would only relay her message to me. As usual, Graham told me that the decision was mine to make, although he added that he would not publish the story if it was up to him.

I did want Don's opinion about whether I had a conflict of interest in making the decision. I had separated from my wife, Gerry, after twenty-five years of marriage, and I was in a relationship with someone else. Everybody already knew about it because I had instructed the *Post*'s Style section to publish the fact of my separation in its gossip column. Don said that eliminated any conflict for me. The newspaper also would later report that I remarried in 1997. I believed that some aspects of my private life were fair game because of my influential public role at the *Post*.

In the end, I saw no clear relevance in Dole's long-ago consensual affair to his qualifications or campaign for president. It was a close call, but I decided not to publish the story.

A week later, the weekly supermarket tabloid *National Enquirer* published a strikingly accurate version of the story based on its own interviews with the woman and some of her friends. The *New York Daily News* matched the *Enquirer*'s story, and Dole was asked about it at an October 25 press conference. "You're worse than they are," he told the questioner, referring to the *Daily News* and the *Enquirer*.

Since that exchange had occurred publicly in a campaign press conference, I decided it should be reported well down in our daily campaign story, with an explanation that the *Post* had earlier confirmed the affair but decided not to publish a story about it. I was quoted in the story, saying, "I decided that the information we had about this personal relationship twenty-eight years ago was not relevant to Robert J. Dole's current candidacy for president and did not meet our standards for the publication of information about the private lives of public officials."

There were *Post* reporters and editors who still did not agree with my decision about the original Dole story. They complained to each other, although not to me, about so much work going into the story, only to have the information published elsewhere. Only the *New York Post*, *Newsday*, the *Boston Globe*, *Newsweek*, and CNN briefly mentioned the story. Most other news media—including the *New York Times*, *Los Angeles Times*, *Wall Street Journal*, *USA Today*, NBC News, CBS News, and ABC News— ignored it.

I believed that I had upheld the newspaper's standards and mine, and many other news media executives apparently agreed with me. There was no evidence that it was an issue for voters. No one accused me or the *Post* of trying to influence the election.

President Clinton defeated Dole and a surprisingly strong third-party candidate, billionaire businessman Ross Perot, to win a second term in November 1996. By then, Independent Counsel Kenneth Starr had already spent two years investigating Bill and Hillary Clinton's dealings with a Little Rock financial institution while Bill was governor of Arkansas. The *Post* had been conducting its own investigations of that and of allegations about Bill Clinton and women, which earned me the enmity of both Clintons.

13

Confronting
the Clintons

JIRST LADY HILLARY CLINTON WAS NOT HAPPY. She wanted to know why the *Washington Post* was "going after the president." She was not satisfied with my explanation that we were just pursuing significant questions about the relationships the Clintons had with the failed Madison Guaranty Savings and Loan Association in Little Rock, Arkansas, when Bill was governor.

Those relationships included a land investment, known as Whitewater, in which the Clintons were partners with Madison Guaranty's owners, Jim and Susan McDougal. Mrs. Clinton also had been one of the lawyers for Madison Guaranty while working for the Rose Law Firm in Little Rock. All of that had become the subject of a federal investigation.

We were meeting on a cold morning in January 1994, a year after President Clinton's inauguration, in the Map Room on the ground floor of the White House. We faced each other in red high-back armchairs, not far from a blazing fireplace. Mrs. Clinton's press secretary, Liz Caputo, sat nearby but never joined the conversation, which I had agreed was not for publication in the *Post*.

The only light moment came at the beginning of our hour-long conversation. When neither of us started to speak at first, we realized that we had each been told, by senior White House counselor David Gergen, that the other person requested the meeting. Typical Gergen, we agreed, smiling briefly.

Mrs. Clinton knew that Gergen also had arranged and attended a meeting in my office at the *Post* a month earlier. He and other White House aides discussed with me and other *Post* journalists our requests for documents about Whitewater, Madison Guaranty, and Mrs. Clinton's legal work for the savings and loan. I knew that Mrs. Clinton was angry about that meeting. And I knew that she had overruled Gergen's recommendation to the president (and assurance to me) that the documents should be given to us.

She began our White House conversation by telling me that the Clintons had endured a hostile press in Arkansas, and they had expected things to be different in Washington. Instead, she felt the *Post* was unfairly hounding them with our Whitewater stories and our requests for information and records.

I told her that the newspaper had to report on the ongoing federal investigation of Madison Guaranty and the question of whether the Clintons had been involved in any conflicts of interest with the savings and loan and the McDougals while her husband was governor. I explained that one of the *Post*'s most important roles was holding presidents, Republican or Democrat, accountable to voters. I spent some time reviewing the questions we had about Madison Guaranty, Whitewater, and the Rose Law Firm. Mrs. Clinton said these questions were not relevant because she and Bill had done nothing wrong.

"Then just let us see the documents," I told her, referring to Madison Guaranty and Rose Law Firm documents that she had, which we had been seeking. "If there is nothing there, then there is no more story."

Mrs. Clinton said she had not read most of the documents and did not even know where many of them were. She blamed Jim McDougal for anything that had gone wrong at Madison Guaranty and for the failure of the Whitewater real estate investment. "He got us into this deal," she said, "and he left us holding the bag. We made no money in this deal. We lost money."

As for her legal work for the savings and loan, Mrs. Clinton added, without any further explanation, that she might not have spent enough time on it or done a good enough job.

"I probably made a mistake in the way I handled it," she told me, "but Bill had nothing to do with it. He wasn't involved at all."

She said the documents in question might affect her reputation as an outstanding lawyer. I suggested that any short-term embarrassment could be offset by ending speculation about Whitewater and the Clintons, if the records did not reveal any wrongdoing.

Mrs. Clinton then changed the subject. To my surprise, she brought up the rumors and press reports about her husband and other women. She began by describing him, while he was governor, as having been too kindhearted to refuse telephone calls from Gennifer Flowers, whom Mrs. Clinton said was an unhappy state employee appealing for assistance.

Next, without my asking, she brought up recently published stories elsewhere, in which several Arkansas state troopers alleged that they had assisted Bill Clinton in clandestine liaisons with women while he was governor. She told me that some of the troopers were drunks and malcontents, and that she had urged her husband to fire them for incompetence. In an early iteration of what would be her often-stated belief that the Clintons were victims of "a vast right-wing conspiracy," she said that their conservative enemies had raised money to support troopers who fed these stories to the press.

Finally, Mrs. Clinton asked me for advice on how to deal with the press in Washington. I explained that I could not give that kind of advice in my role as executive editor of the *Post*. I added, however, that I would always be ready to respond to any problems she had with the *Post*'s coverage of her or the president. I said that she or Liz Caputo could call me at any time. I explained that I could not assure her that she would always like our coverage, but I wanted the *Post* to be accurate and fair. We stood and shook hands, and I left the White House.

I knew that it had not been a warm meeting. I thought that Mrs. Clinton, in a lawyerly way, had talked around the truth. But I hoped that our conversation might have cleared the air somewhat.

Hours later, I got a call in my office at the *Post* from Ann Devroy, our extraordinarily well-sourced White House correspondent.

"What the hell did you say to Hillary?" Devroy demanded in her direct way.

"Why?"

"Because she's going around the White House saying that you thought she was lying to you and that you hate her."

I would later hear from Devroy that Mrs. Clinton was telling everyone that I was jealous of Ben Bradlee and his Watergate fame, and that I was trying to use Whitewater to destroy President Clinton.

I FIRST MET BILL CLINTON AT A DINNER AT THE 1988 DEMO-cratic National Convention in Atlanta. It was one of several such get-togethers with politicians that *Washington Post* editors and reporters held at both parties' nominating conventions every four years. Clinton, then the relatively little-known, if long-serving, Arkansas governor, was scheduled to give the presidential nominating speech for Massachusetts governor Michael Dukakis later that evening. Since there were several higher-profile guests than Clinton at that dinner, and I was then still only the *Post*'s managing editor, we were seated together at one end of the long table.

We chatted amiably, although Clinton was nervously preoccupied with delivering his first nationally televised speech on such a big stage. He was worried about whether he would be able to hold the attention of the typically unruly convention hall audience. He excused himself and left the dinner early to get ready. Clinton's concern was justified. His thirty-two-minute speech seemed to drone on forever. The biggest applause line, as he later wrote in his memoir, came when he said, "In closing . . ."

Television commentators at the convention and late-night talk show hosts made fun of Clinton, which turned out to be a blessing in disguise.

When Johnny Carson later invited him onto NBC's *Tonight Show*, Clinton became a hit by deftly trading amusing one-liners with Carson about his convention performance and by playing his saxophone with the *Tonight Show* band. I did not pay much more attention to him until he emerged as a strong candidate for the Democratic nomination at the beginning of the 1992 presidential campaign, and the story broke about Clinton's affair with Gennifer Flowers.

When I next met Clinton, he was president-elect and I was the *Post*'s executive editor. He was the guest of honor at a grand dinner that Katharine Graham staged for Washington politicians, journalists, and other notables at her Georgetown home before Clinton's inauguration in January 1993. In responding to Mrs. Graham's toast welcoming him to town, Clinton said that he found Washington to be "a better place than most Americans think it is." But he also made clear, as he did in his inaugural address, that he thought Washington should be more responsive to the needs of the American people.

I was impressed. But I also remembered Jimmy Carter, a Southern state governor who came to Washington as a post-Watergate reformer. He and the people he brought with him from Georgia clashed with the power structure in the capital as they struggled with unexpected challenges. Press coverage of the Carter administration was skeptical almost from the beginning of what turned out to be a one-term presidency.

Despite some early legislative accomplishments, the Clinton administration also got off to a rocky start. After the president's pledge to allow gays to serve openly in the military ran into strong opposition from military and congressional leaders, it was watered down to the "Don't Ask, Don't Tell" policy that forced gay military men and women to hide their sexual identities. A cabinet nomination was derailed when it came to light that the nominee for attorney general had illegally hired undocumented immigrants as nannies and had failed to pay Social Security taxes for them. A touchy-feely weekend retreat that the Clintons held at Camp David for cabinet members and White House staff, with professional facilitators, was compared by Ann Devroy in the *Post* with a similar retreat Carter held at a low point of his presidency.

Four months into the new administration, the seven employees of the White House travel office were fired for alleged mismanagement and financial irregularities. This especially interested reporters because the office handled charter airplane and hotel arrangements for press travel with the president, the cost of which was paid by their news organizations. White House justifications for the firings were soon overtaken by *Washington Post* reporting that Hollywood friends of the Clintons were seeking to seize control of the travel office and the charter business. Intensive press coverage of what became known as "Travelgate" led to the rehiring of the office's former employees in other positions, the removal of the Clintons' friends from any role in White House travel, and questions in the media about Hillary Clinton's denial about being personally involved.

Ten days after the travel office firings, the Clintons brought David Gergen into the White House as counselor to the president. He was tasked with helping to smooth its operation and to improve the Clintons' relationships with the press and the Washington establishment. Gergen had previously worked in various White House roles for presidents Nixon, Ford, and Reagan. He also had been a magazine editor and television pundit. He knew everybody who mattered in Washington.

In June, at Gergen's suggestion, the Clintons hosted a half dozen White House dinners of forty people each for Washington journalists and celebrities. My wife, Gerry, and I attended one of the dinners on June 29. We each sat at one of the four round tables for ten in the Green Room on the first floor of the White House. Hillary Clinton sat across from me at our table, with cellist Yo-Yo Ma on her left. I noticed that she never looked at me during dinner. I guessed that she was unhappy about our coverage of the young administration, especially the travel office firings.

Characteristically, President Clinton could not have been friendlier, regardless of what he was really thinking about me or the *Post*. After dinner, I was among the guests taken upstairs to mingle with him and the senior White House staff in the Yellow Oval Room on the second floor. On this pleasant summer evening, we also were invited outside onto the Truman Balcony overlooking the South Lawn and the Ellipse. President Clinton made a point of chatting with each of us in his engaging way, as though no one else was around. He and I talked about books we had been reading. The *Post*'s coverage of the Clintons never came up. He then took a small group of us on a tour of the second floor, including the Lincoln Bedroom.

The dinners received mixed reviews in the press because of their obvious attempt to curry favor, and they soon were dropped. But I found it useful to observe how President Clinton worked the room and side-stepped an opportunity to bring up the *Post*'s coverage with me.

Four months after that White House dinner, I put on the *Post*'s Sunday, October 31, front page a story revealing that the U.S. Resolution Trust Corporation had formally asked federal prosecutors to investigate whether the 1989 failure of Madison Guaranty in Arkansas involved fraud or other violations of the law. The relationships between the savings and loan's owners and the Clintons were among the issues under investigation. The RTC had been set up by the Treasury Department to shut down and recover as much money as possible from 747 federally insured savings and loans that failed in the 1980s, costing taxpayers billions in deposit insurance. Madison Guaranty's failure had cost taxpayers an estimated $47 million.

When the RTC found evidence of wrongdoing, it made formal criminal referrals for further investigation and possible prosecution to the Justice Department. In Madison Guaranty's collapse, the RTC had found evidence of questionable insider dealing by the McDougals and Arkansas political figures. The October 31 *Post* story, by reporter Susan Schmidt, revealed that the RTC had pointed, in its Madison Guaranty referral, to checks deposited in then Governor Clinton's reelection campaign and to the McDougals' involvement with the Clintons in the Whitewater Development Corporation. "As part of the investigation, the RTC went to extraordinary lengths to trace real estate transactions involving Whitewater Development Corp., a land company Bill and Hillary Clinton jointly owned with [the McDougals]," Schmidt wrote.

Schmidt was a strong-willed, resourceful reporter. She was covering the fallout from the savings and loan scandal back on March 8, 1992, when the *New York Times* first reported the partnership of the Clintons and McDougals in the ill-fated Whitewater real estate investment. The two couples had bought two hundred acres in the Ozark Mountains in

Arkansas, which they unsuccessfully tried to develop as vacation prop-erties. Jim and Susan McDougal later took control of Madison Guaranty, which was regulated by the state of Arkansas, while Clinton was gov-ernor. That 1992 story, by *Times* reporter Jeff Gerth, also reported that Hillary Clinton and her law firm actively represented Madison Guaranty and McDougal, and that she had proposed to state regulators ways to try to keep the savings and loan afloat before it was closed down.

"It raises questions," Gerth wrote, "of whether a governor should be involved in a business deal with the owner of a business regulated by the state and whether, having done so, the governor's wife through her law firm should be receiving legal fees for work done for the business."

"Many questions about the enterprise cannot be fully answered" without the Whitewater venture's records, Gerth wrote, adding, "The Clintons said many of them have disappeared."

Most of the rest of the news media gave the story scant attention as the 1992 presidential campaign heated up. But with my encouragement, Schmidt periodically pursued it and requested more information and records about the Clintons' Whitewater investment. In a meeting with *Post* editors and reporters in August 1992, Hillary Clinton told us that she would not turn over anything more than had already been released, which was very little.

"I think we've given you all we're going to give you," she said, "and I feel that's good advice I've received, and I'm going to stick with it."

The investigative reporter in me wondered why.

Schmidt went on maternity leave from March 1993 until that autumn. While she was gone, the White House travel scandal erupted, and deputy White House counsel Vincent Foster, who had been diagnosed as suffer-ing from depression, committed suicide. He had blamed himself for the some of the administration's early stumbles, including the travel office controversy. He, too, had been a partner at the Rose Law Firm and had worked on some of the Clintons' financial records, which would later raise questions about what happened to them after his death.

When Schmidt returned to the newsroom, she and another aggres-sive *Post* reporter, Michael Isikoff, went back to work on Whitewater and found out about the RTC investigation of Madison Guaranty and its criminal referral to the Justice Department. They were in competition with Gerth and other reporters, who also had been tipped to the referral. When Schmidt and Isikoff interviewed Bruce Lindsey, the White House aide closest to both Clintons, he deflected most of their questions about the referral, falsely claiming he had not known about it. But Schmidt was able to get a key confirmation from a Justice Department source.

Her October 31 story was the first to reveal the existence of the criminal referral and some of its content. As Mrs. Clinton later wrote in her memoir, *Living History*, "The *Post*'s Halloween article and a similar *New York Times* article that soon followed" were cause for concern. The Clintons soon hired David Kendall, of the prominent Washington law firm Williams and Connolly, to be their private attorney for Whitewater.

For me, Schmidt's story and Bruce Lindsey's lack of cooperation raised questions about the behavior of the Clintons during their years in Arkansas and whether the federal investigations might affect his presidency. But few of the national staff editors and reporters saw the same significance as I did in Madison Guaranty, Whitewater, the Rose law Firm, and the Clintons, all of which felt to them like an election campaign leftover. They could not understand what some of them considered an obsession of mine.

Nevertheless, I formed a Whitewater investigative task force and held frequent meetings in my office with its members, including Schmidt and Isikoff. They produced several stories in early November with more details about the investigations into Madison Guaranty and Whitewater, including the fact that Vincent Foster had worked with Hillary Clinton on Whitewater legal matters. They also sent a letter to Bruce Lindsey at the White House with a list of questions and document requests about Whitewater and Madison Guaranty, to which there was no response.

During the first week of December, my managing editor, Bob Kaiser, called the White House to talk to David Gergen, whom he had known at Yale as a fellow student journalist on the *Yale Daily News* in the early 1960s. Kaiser told Gergen that two weeks had passed with no answer to the *Post*'s letter to Bruce Lindsey. Gergen said that he did not know about the letter and that he would look into it.

After conferring with others in the White House, Gergen got back to Kaiser and arranged an early evening meeting in my office at the *Post* on Monday, December 6, to listen to our requests. He brought with him

Bruce Lindsey and Mark Gearan, the new White House director of communications. They and *Post* reporters and editors working on Whitewater filled the chairs and couches facing my desk. Gergen and Gearan sat the farthest away at the back of the office. But a slight, grim-looking Lindsey took a chair right in front of my desk. He appeared ready for a fight.

At Gergen's urging, I expounded at length on the questions to which we were seeking answers, as well as the documents we had now been seeking for well over a year. I recited our efforts going back to the 1992 campaign to obtain documents and other information about Whitewater and Madison Guaranty's relationship with the Clintons and with Bill Clinton's gubernatorial campaigns.

"First, you tell us what story you want to write," Lindsey interjected.

I explained that we didn't work that way. We would not know what stories to write until we could review the documents.

Lindsey said the documents in the possession of the White House were incomplete and could be misinterpreted. Then he complained about the *Post*'s reporting on Whitewater and other issues involving the Clintons, which he argued had been unfair and typical of the national news media's "gotcha" journalism.

"Why should we give you any of this?" he demanded, sitting a few feet in front of me. "You'll just use them to write more stories. Then you would want something else."

Nevertheless, Gergen indicated that he thought I had made a good case for cooperation. He promised in front of everyone that he would give me an answer within a week.

Sue Schmidt and other reporters at the meeting talked afterward about how hostile Lindsey had been, which they thought had embarrassed Gergen and Gearan, who had come to negotiate. Schmidt said it felt as though Lindsey and the Clintons were hiding something, which was also what I was thinking.

As Gergen later recounted, he returned to the White House to convince senior officials and the president that they should turn documents over to the *Post*. Gergen, who had been President Nixon's chief White House speechwriter during Watergate, warned Clinton that it would be risky to stonewall the *Post*. Clinton agreed, but he said the first lady would have a say, too. As Gergen waited for that, he called me to say he would need more time.

According to Devroy—and the accounts of Clinton White House officials years later—Mrs. Clinton was furious that Gergen had arranged the meeting at the *Post*, and that he had virtually promised to give me documents. She and Bruce Lindsey were adamantly opposed to giving us anything. Finally, more than two weeks after the meeting in my office, I received a terse letter from Lindsey.

"As you know, in March, 1992, the Clinton Campaign released a report by an independent accounting firm which established that the Clintons lost at least $68,900 on Whitewater Development Corporation," the letter stated. "They received no gain of any kind on their investment. The Clintons were not involved in the management or operation of the company, nor did they keep its records. We see no need to supplement the March, 1992 CPA report or to provide further documentation."

I called Gergen at the White House after receiving the letter on a Monday morning. "I just want to tell you that this is a serious mistake," I told him. "We're not going to drop this. We will go full bore on this investigation."

Trying again, Gergen arranged my early January meeting with Hillary Clinton in the White House. Her evasion at that meeting of any meaningful discussion of Whitewater issues and her refusal to let the *Post* see any of the records only left me with more questions, as did her unprompted refutation of stories and rumors about her husband and other women.

From November 1993 through early February 1994, we published sixty-two stories about various aspects of the Whitewater and Madison Guaranty investigations, sixteen of which appeared on the front page. Other news media stepped up their coverage, and the White House was inundated with reporters' questions. Republicans began calling for congressional investigations and hearings.

In mid-January, the Clintons decided to instruct David Kendall to turn over to the Justice Department records that the lawyer had been collecting about Whitewater, while invoking the Clintons' privacy rights to keep them out of public view. The president also decided to ask Attorney General Janet Reno to appoint a special counsel to take over the federal investigations. On January 20, Reno announced that respected New York lawyer Robert B. Fiske Jr. would serve as a Justice Department special counsel to investigate the Clintons' relationships with Whitewater and Madison Guaranty, as well as any violations of criminal or civil law by anyone "arising out of that investigation."

While I aggressively pushed *Post* reporters to find answers to the questions about Whitewater, I moved more cautiously on reports and rumors of Bill Clinton's extramarital activities with women. I did not know whether they could meet my criteria of being true, provable, and relevant to his presidency.

After the Gennifer Flowers stories early in 1992, rumors had persisted throughout the presidential campaign about Clinton and other women, none of which could be substantiated. On July 26, just after the Democratic National Convention in New York, we published a story by Michael Isikoff about the Clinton campaign's efforts to discredit the rumors. In a remarkable interview, Betsy Wright, the senior Clinton aide overseeing that campaign, told Isikoff that the campaign was paying a lawyer and private investigator to tamp down what she called "bimbo eruptions"—potential allegations about Clinton and more than two dozen women. Her phrase would enter the political lexicon and dog Clinton for years.

In mid-December 1993—a month before my White House meeting with Hillary Clinton—the conservative magazine *American Spectator* circulated copies of a story in its upcoming January issue, in which several Arkansas state troopers said they helped Clinton engage in surreptitious sexual encounters while he was governor. The troopers said they recruited women for him, transported him in state vehicles to rendezvous with the women in motels and other places in Little Rock, and lied to Mrs. Clinton to cover for him. A few days later, the *Los Angeles Times* published a similar story on its front page. An Arkansas lawyer and political enemy of Clinton, Cliff Jackson, had put the troopers together with journalists from both publications.

Jackson also introduced Isikoff to Paula Jones, a former low-level Arkansas state employee. On February 11, 1994, after her first name had appeared in the *American Spectator* article, Jones and her lawyer said at a press conference in Washington that Clinton had made unwanted advances when a state trooper took her to meet Clinton in a Little Rock hotel suite on May 8, 1991. Their account was so sketchy that I decided not to publish a brief story like those that appeared on inside pages of some other newspapers. Instead, I directed Isikoff to find out more.

Isikoff, a wiry, somewhat disheveled reporter who alternated between being confrontational and empathetic in his interviews, then talked to Jones. She told him in detail that Clinton had exposed himself to her and asked her to perform oral sex, which she refused to do. In separate on-the-record interviews, five of Jones's friends and family members told Isikoff that Jones had described the encounter to them shortly after it happened. One of the friends, a state government coworker, said the two of them were working at the registration desk at a state-run economic conference when she saw Clinton staring at Jones. She said that a state trooper then came by to invite Jones to talk to the governor in a hotel suite. After fifteen minutes, she told Isikoff, Jones came back, shaking and upset, and told her what had happened.

As Isikoff continued his reporting, the White House was busy discouraging reporters from pursuing the Arkansas state troopers' allegations. Among those reporters was Ann Devroy, who told close Clinton aide George Stephanopoulos that I thought Paula Jones's story should be pursued to determine whether it was part of continuing compulsive sexual behavior by Clinton. Stephanopoulos then invited me to lunch on February 17 at the historic Jefferson Hotel near the *Post*. His purpose was, in the friendliest way possible, to talk me out of publishing the Paula Jones story.

Stephanopoulos questioned Jones's credibility and motives, implying that she was seeking money for her story. He told me that he believed Clinton's insistence to him that he did not remember even meeting Jones. He pointed out the conflict between Jones's account of sexual harassment and what one of the troopers had told the *American Spectator* was a consensual encounter that a "Paula" had with Clinton at the hotel in 1991. Neither that nor Clinton's denial, I thought, was exculpatory.

As Stephanopoulos later recalled in a memoir, I said little, taking notes as I heard him out. I was there to listen. I knew how devoted Stephanopoulos was to Clinton at the time, and I wondered if he really believed what he was being told. The conversation had little impact on my deliberation about the story.

By the end of February, Isikoff had finished a draft he thought was ready to publish. "You have to put this on the front page," he told me excitedly. But his national staff editors had doubts. The Arkansas state trooper who took Jones in to see Clinton in the hotel room would not talk, even after Isikoff went to his house. White House lawyers insisted that Jones's story was not true and that it was concocted by Clinton haters like Cliff Jackson.

I still was not ready to publish the story, which understandably irritated Isikoff, who blamed his editors. But I did not kill it. Instead, I assigned other reporters and editors to work with him to try to expand the inquiry to other women alleged to have had affairs with Clinton, to determine whether we could establish a pattern.

As time went on, and no pattern was found, Isikoff became increasingly frustrated. He proposed a novel way of telling the Paula Jones story as a journalistic dilemma about sex and the president. That inadvertently led to an angry argument between him and one of his editors, Fred Barbash, in which Isikoff became so vituperative that I suspended him for two weeks. When that leaked out, right-wing journalists and activists produced newspaper articles and advertisements accusing the *Post* of suppressing a story about sexual harassment by Clinton.

After Isikoff returned to work, he collaborated with two reporters on still another, somewhat more ambiguous version of the story, which even he worried would leave readers in doubt about whether to believe Paula Jones. Managing editor Kaiser reviewed the story and concluded in a memo that it had not made a strong enough case against Clinton, despite all the effort that had gone into the reporting. I agreed with his judgment about that story draft, but not his stated belief that we could never produce a publishable story.

Meanwhile, it became known that lawyers for Paula Jones were planning to sue Clinton for sexual harassment before the three-year statute of limitations expired on May 8, 1994. On May 3, the conservative *Washington Times* newspaper reported that Clinton was hiring a top criminal defense lawyer, Robert Bennett, to defend him if the suit was filed.

Those developments changed everything. A legal battle between Paula Jones and the president of the United States over her allegation of sexual harassment, no matter what the truth would prove to be, was an important story. Thanks to Isikoff, we knew much more about it than the rest of the news media. I asked Isikoff and the reporters working with him to get their story ready for the next day's paper.

I put it on the front page of the *Post*'s May 4 editions. It was the first story extensively detailing Paula Jones's account, corroborated by friends and family, of what happened three years earlier at the Excelsior Hotel in Little Rock. She had described to Isikoff how Clinton unexpectedly tried to kiss her, put his hand on her upper leg under her culotte, pulled down his trousers and underwear, sat down next to her on a couch, and asked her to perform oral sex. She said she had not talked about it publicly during the 1992 campaign because she still worked for the state of Arkansas and did not think anyone outside her immediate circle would believe her.

When Jones's lawyers filed her sexual harassment lawsuit against Clinton in the federal courthouse in Little Rock on May 6, many in the crowd of reporters there carried copies of Isikoff's story in the *Post*, with passages underlined. I considered it a case of workplace sexual harassment, rather than the consensual extramarital sex that Gennifer Flowers and the Arkansas state troopers had told about.

In his story about the lawsuit, Isikoff presciently pointed out that federal court rules could give Jones's lawyers the opportunity to take sworn depositions from witnesses, including the Arkansas state troopers in Governor Clinton's security detail. He could not imagine that might also include President Clinton, as it eventually would.

Isikoff also could not foresee the significant role he would play much later, in competition with the *Post*, in reporting on the events leading to Clinton's impeachment. Within a few weeks of the filing of the Jones lawsuit, Isikoff left the *Post*, with my blessing, for *Newsweek* magazine, then also owned by The Washington Post Company.

IN AUGUST 1994, CONGRESS REVIVED THE EXPIRED INDEPENDENT counsel law and Clinton signed it, as he had earlier promised to do. Chief Justice William Rehnquist of the U.S. Supreme Court appointed a three-judge Special Division of the U.S. Court of Appeals for the District of Columbia to oversee the independent counsel process. In turn, those judges, considered by our reporters to be legally and politically conservative, removed Robert Fiske, they said, because he had been appointed by Clinton's attorney general. They replaced him with Kenneth Starr, a Republican former appeals court judge and U.S. solicitor general in the George H. W. Bush administration. Starr had been a public proponent of the Paula Jones lawsuit against Clinton.

Three months later, in the 1994 mid-term elections, the Democrats lost control of both houses of Congress to the Republicans. In July 1995, the Republicans set up a Senate Special Whitewater Committee, which would conduct eleven months of inconclusive hearings. In August 1995, a federal grand jury convened by independent counsel Starr indicted James and Susan McDougal and Bill Clinton's successor as Arkansas governor, Jim Guy Tucker. They were charged with being involved in fraudulent loans and fictitious land sales that enabled them to illegally profit from a failed rural Arkansas land investment improbably called Castle Grande. The money lost by Madison Guaranty in the fraudulent land deal cost taxpayers about $4 million when the savings and loan collapsed.

Madison Guaranty was one of about a thousand savings and loans that failed in the 1980s after becoming overextended with uncollectible mortgage loans, many because of fraud. It cost taxpayers $160 billion to reimburse the savings and loans' depositors. That was the context I had in mind while we were investigating what had happened at Madison Guaranty and any role the Clintons had in its conduct and demise.

Castle Grande came up again on January 4, 1996, when the Whitewater investigation took a surprising turn. Hillary Clinton's close personal aide Carolyn Huber said that when she was moving things in her office to make room for new bookshelves, she had found Mrs. Clinton's long-sought Rose Law Firm billing records in a box under a table. She said she had not noticed what the records were when she moved them to her office in the summer of 1995 with other items from a table in the White House Book Room. Mrs. Clinton had long said that she had not known where the records were since at least 1992.

The records showed that Mrs. Clinton had billed Madison Guaranty for about sixty hours of work, half of it for the Castle Grande project, identified in the records as "IDC." She had previously told investigators that she had not done any work on Castle Grande. After the records were found, she said she did not realize that IDC was that project.

The billing records were turned over to the independent counsel's office, which summoned Mrs. Clinton before the Whitewater grand jury. She testified that what happened to the records between 1992 and their discovery by Huber was a mystery to her. After she finished testifying, she repeated the message to the reporters, microphones, and cameras amassed outside the federal courthouse in downtown Washington.

Most of the news media were now covering the twists and turns of the Whitewater saga. But Sue Schmidt's determined digging and my front-page display of many of her stories particularly angered Hillary Clinton. In early 1996, she asked White House lawyers to prepare a report analyzing the accuracy and fairness of Schmidt's coverage, which was to be presented formally to me and then made public.

By all accounts of the episode, the draft report, written by one of the White House lawyers, focused mostly on the tone, headlines, and front-page display of Schmidt's stories in the *Post*, compared with stories in the *New York Times, Wall Street Journal*, and *Los Angeles Times*. White House press secretary Mike McCurry, who opposed a public attack on the *Post's* coverage, decided to ditch the report altogether. He collected all the copies of the draft, and they disappeared. Schmidt heard about it from one of the *Post's* White House reporters. No one at the White House contacted me.

In May 1996, the independent counsel's office won its first major Whitewater investigation convictions. The McDougals and Arkansas governor Jim Guy Tucker were found guilty of fraud related to their Madison Guaranty and Castle Grande dealings. Kenneth Starr's team of prosecutors was still investigating Hillary Clinton's work as a lawyer on Castle Grande and other Madison Guaranty matters, including whether she had been truthful about it in her Whitewater grand jury testimony.

In an unusually long story that we published on June 2, Sue Schmidt and reporter David Maraniss, one of the *Post's* best writers, explored the still unanswered questions about that work and Mrs. Clinton's lack of candor. It filled four pages in the *Post*. For the next year, as the Starr investigation dragged on, it appeared from our reporting to be focused mostly on those and other questions about Mrs. Clinton's conduct.

In the meantime, President Clinton was elected to a second term by a landslide over Bob Dole in the November 5, 1996, elections. However, the Republicans kept control of both the House and the Senate, which would matter later.

BY THIS TIME, EVERYONE AT THE *POST* SENSED THAT MY MARRIAGE to Gerry had not been a happy one for years. I think Gerry and I grew apart because of differing interests, my consuming devotion to the *Post*, the long hours I spent there, and the disproportionate burden on her of caring for our two children.

Over time, I became attracted to a divorced friend of Gerry's and mine. Our children all attended the same private school. Our friend Janice Glick was a sales director at a Washington hotel, and she occasionally volunteered as the hotel advance person for Vice President Al Gore when he traveled on government business. We realized during the 1996 Democratic National Convention in Chicago, where I was supervising the *Post*'s coverage and Janice was handling arrangements for Gore, that we were interested in the same things, including politics and each other.

Gerry and I divorced, and Janice and I were married in the chambers of a federal judge in Washington in September 1997. Katharine Graham generously held a party for us in her Georgetown home.

To avoid a conflict of interest for me, Janice gave up her volunteer work for Gore, whom I had known since he was a young congressman. She was strongly supportive of my work at the *Post*, and she was much more outgoing and popular than I was in our social life with newsroom staff and people in federal Washington. As was the custom at Washington dinners, Janice was usually seated at a different table than I was, between politicians and other influential men. She invariably brought me back tips she'd gathered from them.

AT THE END OF MAY 1997, I TELEPHONED THE WHITE HOUSE about a completely different subject than the independent counsel's investigation.

President Clinton and I had each been chosen to speak at the senior class graduations of his daughter, Chelsea, and my son, Joshua. They attended rival private high schools in Washington. I knew that most of the parents of the graduating seniors at Joshua's rather progressive school, Georgetown Day, would rather have had Clinton as their speaker.

I called Mike McCurry to tell him about this problem, and to ask a favor. I said I would like to tell the Georgetown Day graduates and their families the same opening joke that the president would be telling the Sidwell Friends School graduates and their families. McCurry said that was a great idea, and he would get back to me.

Days went by. I wrote most of my speech. Yet there was no word from the White House. I called McCurry again on the morning of May 3, a few days before the two graduations. He told me the problem was that Clinton had decided to write his speech entirely himself, rather than using a speechwriter. No one else in the White House knew what was in it. I said that I completely understood. I would just have to try something else.

To my surprise, President Clinton called me at the *Post* that afternoon. The conversation was as pleasant as it could be. We shared our pride in our children, our nervousness about speaking at their graduations, and the fact that each of us had been admonished by our children not to embarrass them. Clinton told me that, even though he had spoken to millions of people over the years, "I'm scared to death about this speech." He said the best advice he had gotten was to repeat the admonition King Henry VIII had given to each of his wives: "I'm going to keep this short."

That was the joke I used in my speech, along with a brief version of my conversation with the president, which delighted my audience.

The president and I also agreed to exchange speeches. His arrived with a short note written at the top of the first page: "To Len Downie. Thanks for your good advice and insight on this. Bill Clinton."

With mine, I attached a two-page handwritten note in which I suggested that we talk about the *Post*'s coverage. "I was surprised, after our good conversation," I wrote, "to hear from Ann Devroy that, when you talked to her on the telephone, you expressed the belief that I don't like you and that the *Post* is out to get you." He was echoing, of course, his wife's view.

I explained in my note, as I had to Mrs. Clinton in person more than four years earlier, that I believed that my role and that of the *Post* was simply to hold all presidents accountable to our readers and other citizens. I pointed out that I tried to keep such an open mind that I stopped voting when I became the *Post*'s managing editor in 1984. I said I would be happy to talk to him about this.

A week passed with no response. I telephoned Mike McCurry once again.

"You have to understand," McCurry told me. "When the president uses your name, he's usually screaming at me."

"I'm sorry about that," I said. "But it would be okay if he screamed at me in person. I can take it."

I told McCurry that I had had plenty of tough conversations over the years with national and corporate leaders. It was part of the job. I just wanted to hear the president's concerns about our coverage.

That afternoon, Clinton again called me at the *Post*. I got the impression that McCurry might be holding the phone up to his ear to make sure he talked to me, if only briefly. We complimented each other on our speech texts.

"But what about the note I sent with mine?" I had to ask.

"Oh, I got your letter, Len. I didn't really say anything like that to Ann. The *Post*'s coverage has been basically fair and well-balanced, except maybe one or two instances when there seemed to be a party line."

I explained the separation between our news coverage and the opinions of the editorial page, which had been tough on the Clintons.

"Oh, I know that, Len," he responded. "Anyway, just wanted to thank you."

No confrontation. No engagement. I did not try again.

QUESTIONS ABOUT CLINTON AND WOMEN HAD LARGELY FADED into the background of news media coverage of Kenneth Starr's Whitewater investigations until a May 27, 1997, U.S. Supreme Court ruling in the Paula Jones case. In a surprise, the court ruled unanimously that a sitting president did not have legal immunity from allegations involving his personal conduct. Justices Ruth Bader Ginsburg and Stephen Breyer, both appointed to the court by Clinton, joined in the decision, which allowed Jones's lawsuit to proceed in federal court. Lawyers for Jones could start deposing witnesses under oath.

Meanwhile, Bob Woodward had been interviewing Arkansas state troopers. Two of them told him on the record that independent counsel prosecutors and FBI agents had questioned them extensively about their knowledge and involvement in Clinton's extramarital relationships while he was governor. The troopers said they had been asked about twelve to fifteen women by name, including Paula Jones. Sue Schmidt confirmed it all with sources in the independent counsel's office, and I put their story on the front page of the *Post* on June 25. I wondered why the independent counsel was investigating the president's sex life.

What we did not yet know at the *Post* was that Michael Isikoff, at *Newsweek*, had found Linda Tripp, a former White House aide who was working in a Department of Defense public affairs division at the Pentagon. Over time, she told Isikoff about a young woman she knew at the White House, who was telling Tripp about an affair she was having with the president. Tripp eventually told Isikoff that she taped telephone conversations with the young woman about the relationship, at the suggestion of New York literary agent Lucianne Goldberg.

Isikoff eventually identified the young woman as Monica Lewinsky. He kept reporting, while also working on other stories for *Newsweek*. He found that Lewinsky's name had somehow come up in the Paula Jones case. He met with Tripp and Goldberg to discuss the tapes. He later was told that independent counsel prosecutors and FBI agents were investigating Clinton's relationship with Lewinsky, and whether Clinton's close friend, Washington lawyer and business executive Vernon Jordan, had been asked by Clinton to find Lewinsky a job outside the government.

On Friday night, January 16, Sue Schmidt got a telephone call from a reporter at *Time* magazine who asked if she knew anything about *Newsweek* working on a big story about a new witness in the independent counsel's investigation. Schmidt called one of Starr's prosecutors, who said Isikoff had been hounding him about it, but he couldn't talk yet to either Isikoff or Schmidt about what was going on. Schmidt initially guessed that it might have something to do with Starr's various Whitewater investigations. With the Martin Luther King Jr. holiday coming on Monday, she began a long weekend of trying to find out.

On Saturday, as he later recounted in his book *Uncovering Clinton*, Isikoff thought that he had enough for an explosive story. He went to *Newsweek*'s Washington bureau to offer it to *Newsweek* editors and senior writers there and, by telephone, in its headquarters in New York. The deadline for the next week's magazine, to be printed on Sunday, was that evening. After seven hours of debate, the news magazine's editors decided there were still too many unresolved questions. They decided to hold the story.

For six hours on that same day, January 17, President Clinton was questioned under oath in a deposition by Paula Jones's lawyers in the Washington offices of Clinton's attorney, Robert Bennett. Jones was there, and federal judge Susan Webber Wright presided. It was the first time that a sitting president had ever been interrogated as a defendant in a court case. White House reporter Peter Baker's front-page story in the *Post* on Sunday described the drama but not the content of the closed-door deposition. Baker did not know what answers the president gave to questions he was asked about Jones and other women who had testified about Clinton in sealed depositions in the case.

At 2:32 a.m. on Sunday, less than eight hours after the *Newsweek* meeting had ended, Matt Drudge's gadfly internet website, the Drudge Report, posted a "world exclusive." Its headline was: "*Newsweek* Kills Story on White House Intern Blockbuster Report: 23-Year-Old, Former White House Intern, Sex Relationship with President."

"The Drudge Report has learned that reporter Michael Isikoff developed the story of his career, only to have it spiked by top *Newsweek* editors hours before publication," the item said. "A young woman, 23, sexually involved with the love of her life, the President of the United States, since she was a 21-year-old intern at the White House. She was a frequent visitor to a small study just off the Oval Office where she claims to have indulged the president's sexual preferences."

But Drudge's item did not mention Lewinsky's name or the independent counsel's investigation. It was not until midnight Sunday that a second Drudge Report item said only that "former White House intern Monica Lewinsky, twenty-three, has been subpoenaed to give a deposition in the Paula Jones case."

Schmidt, who never saw Drudge's items, heard about them and Lewinsky's name on Monday. A *Post* newsroom researcher found that Lewinsky was then working in the legislative affairs press office at the Pentagon. Schmidt knew that Linda Tripp had been a witness in Starr's investigation of the White House travel office firings, and that Tripp did not like Clinton. She also knew that Tripp had been moved from the White House to a press office in the Pentagon, as Lewinsky was. She guessed that they might somehow be connected.

After a *Post* editor found Tripp's address in a Maryland suburb, Schmidt drove to her house. When she knocked on the front door, someone turned off all the lights in the house and never came to the door. Schmidt knew she was on the right track. She contacted her source in Starr's office, who told her that Starr was investigating the president's relationship with Lewinsky, and that Tripp had given the prosecutors tapes of telephone conversations about it with Lewinsky.

On Tuesday, I telephoned Don Graham under our "no surprises" rule, an agreement that Ben Bradlee had established with Katharine Graham, and that I, as executive editor, continued with Don. While leaving the decision making to the editor, the owner of the newspaper should know when we were about to publish something that could become controversial. I told Don that we were closing in on a story about Kenneth Starr investigating the president and Monica Lewinsky. He told me that the editor of *Newsweek* had already briefed him about a similar story, on which Isikoff was working. Given the intense newsgathering competition between the *Post* and *Newsweek*, Graham would not tell either of us anything more.

Peter Baker then located and telephoned Lewinsky's lawyer, William Ginsberg. He confirmed on the record that Starr was investigating her involvement with Clinton. Without commenting on whether Lewinsky had a sexual relationship with the president, Ginsberg said that he had been negotiating with Starr's prosecutors, whom he accused of badgering her.

"If the president of the United States did this—and I'm not saying that he did—with this young lady, I think he's a misogynist," Ginsberg told Baker. "If he didn't, then I think Ken Starr and his crew have ravaged the life of a youngster."

Ginsberg said that a young person like Lewinsky could be devastated "if you're not terribly sophisticated and you're misled by the people at the center of the political system, and that includes the president and his staff and the special prosecutor."

All evening, I had been standing out in the newsroom, hovering over the harried national news editors, talking directly with their reporters, and reading the story as it developed. Bob Kaiser, in his last year as my managing editor, was working with me. Although we were very close to having a story we could publish, we could tell that it would not be done in time for the relatively small early edition of the Wednesday newspaper for distribution to outlying areas. I still hoped that the story would be ready for the later editions for delivery to 800,000 Washington area homes and offices.

Our federal court reporter, Toni Locy, made the final breakthrough. A Justice Department source told her that the three-judge panel supervising Starr had authorized him to expand his investigation after Attorney General Janet Reno forwarded Starr's urgent request to them. I asked Baker, who had been talking to White House officials all day, to call them about what we had. One of Clinton's lawyers, Lanny Davis, confirmed that the independent counsel had been given the authority to investigate the Clinton-Lewinsky relationship. We had multiple sources for the story's main points.

By 10:30, I could tell that the story would be finished in time for the later editions. I ordered that the front page be changed to put a four-column headline at the top for the 1,608-word story. For the first time since the launch of our website less than two years earlier, I also decided to put the story online as soon as it was ready, before the printed newspapers started coming off the presses at 12:34 a.m.

As reported on washingtonpost.com under the bylines of Susan Schmidt, Peter Baker, and Toni Locy, the story began:

> Independent counsel Kenneth W. Starr has expanded his investigation of President Clinton to examine whether Clinton and his close friend Vernon Jordan encouraged a 24-year-old former White House intern to lie to lawyers for Paula Jones about whether the intern had an affair with the president, sources close to the investigation said yesterday.

> A three-judge appeals court panel on Friday authorized Starr to examine allegations of suborning perjury, false statements and obstruction of justice involving the president, the sources said. The former intern, Monica Lewinsky, began work in the White House in 1995 at age 21 and later moved to a political job at the Pentagon, where she worked with Linda R. Tripp, who had moved there from an administrative job at the White House.
>
> Sources said Tripp provided Starr with audiotapes of more than 10 conversations she had with Lewinsky over recent months in which Lewinsky graphically recounted details of a year-and-a-half-long affair she had with Clinton. In some of the conversations—including one in recent days—Lewinsky described Clinton and Jordan directing her to testify falsely in the Paula Jones sexual harassment case against the president, according to sources.
>
> Lewinsky gave a sworn affidavit in connection with the Jones case Jan. 7, and sources who have seen her affidavit said she denied having an affair with Clinton.

The story said that Lewinsky, an unpaid intern at the White House in the summer of 1995, volunteered to answer telephones there during a government shutdown later that year. She was then hired as a legislative affairs staff assistant in 1995, and she occasionally delivered correspondence to the Oval Office, where she came into contact with the president.

ABC News and the *Los Angeles Times*, which also had been pursuing the story, broadcast and published their own, less detailed versions early Wednesday. Most of the other media outlets—from the *New York Times, USA Today*, and the *Chicago Tribune* to CBS, NBC, and CNN—were taken by surprise. They had to play catch-up on television and the internet on Wednesday and in newspapers on Thursday.

At 7 p.m. on Wednesday, *Newsweek* posted on its website a 10,000-word story, "Diary of a Scandal," with abundant details from Isikoff's months of dogged reporting about Lewinsky, Tripp, and the tapes, which no one else had. It described a sting in which Linda Tripp, wearing a wire, lured Lewinsky to the Ritz-Carlton Hotel in suburban Virginia, where Starr's prosecutors confronted her. Threatening her with prosecution, based on Tripp's recorded conversations with her, they tried (unsuccessfully) to persuade Lewinsky to become a wire-wearing informant against Clinton.

DURING THE ENSUING YEAR, THE *POST* WOULD PUBLISH ABOUT 1,300 stories about the independent counsel investigation and the Paula Jones case, the responses of the White House and the Clintons, profiles of the many people involved, the news media's role, the public's reaction, and the politics of impeachment. It became the first twenty-four-hour media frenzy in the developing cable and internet era. We often were able to stay a step ahead of our competitors, in part because of our reporters' many well-informed sources among Starr's prosecutors, other lawyers, and White House officials.

Long before Clinton's impeachment, the sheer number of our stories, their dependence on unidentified confidential sources, and their focus on the sex life of the president drew criticism from some Democrats, media critics, and readers. Clinton remained a popular president in public opinion polls, even though growing majorities believed that he had had extramarital affairs and lied about them. What was significant for me, besides the developing legal questions of perjury and obstruction of justice, was the question of whether the president of the United States engaged in sexual activities with a young subordinate employee in the White House, their workplace, regardless of how willing a partner Lewinsky might have been.

On February 6, 1998, we put on the front page a story by Peter Baker and Sue Schmidt revealing that Linda Tripp had given Paula Jones's lawyers a sworn statement summarizing what Lewinsky had told her about the affair with Clinton. The reporters had obtained a copy of the one-page document that Tripp signed on January 21, the same day that we had reported the expansion of the Starr investigation to include the Clinton-Lewinsky relationship. Tripp gave it to the Jones lawyers in lieu of her taped conversations with Lewinsky, which she already had given to Starr's prosecutors nine days earlier.

The statement was the first document to support what various confidential sources had been telling reporters about Clinton and Lewinsky. In it, Tripp stated that Lewinsky "revealed to me in detailed conversations on innumerable occasions that she has had a sexual relationship with President Clinton since November 15, 1995. She played for me at least three tapes containing the president's voice and showed me gifts they exchanged."

A month later, Peter Baker reported in an exclusive front-page story in the *Post* on March 5 that the president denied having sexual relations with Lewinsky in his January 17 deposition in the Paula Jones case. Clinton testified under oath that he saw her at the White House only about five times. The story's only attribution was: "according to a detailed account of his sealed deposition."

The story said that Clinton acknowledged in the deposition that he talked to Vernon Jordan about efforts to find a new job for Lewinsky. But he testified that his personal secretary, Betty Currie, initiated the job hunt. He also acknowledged exchanging gifts with Lewinsky, as well as personal messages after she was transferred from the White House to the Pentagon.

Under questioning about other women, the story said, Clinton testified that he had sexual relations once with Gennifer Flowers in 1977. It was the first time he had admitted any intimate contact with the Arkansas state employee, who had repeatedly alleged since 1992 that she had had a twelve-year affair with him.

No one disputed the accuracy of our story after its publication. Instead, the White House and Clinton's lawyers blamed Jones's lawyers for what the president called the "illegal" disclosure of the deposition. In turn, Jones's lawyers accused the White House of disclosing it to make Clinton's versions of events public.

The president's press secretary, Mike McCurry, scolded the *Post*. "As a matter of journalistic principle, most news organizations take seriously the responsibility to alert readers to the identity and motive of anonymous sources," he said. "The *Post* chose not to do this in this case, and you have to ask them why."

I told the *Post*'s media reporter, Howard Kurtz, for a story we published the next day, that, sometimes, "our agreements with sources are such that we're not able to go beyond what a carefully written and edited story says, but we are satisfied with the accuracy and contents of the story.

There are occasions when this is only way we can publish something that is really important."

The accuracy of our March 5 story was validated about a week later when the transcript of Clinton's deposition was made public in federal court, as part of seven hundred pages of documents collected in the Jones case. Included were depositions from Flowers and a woman named Dolly Kyle Browning, who each described long affairs with Clinton in Arkansas. In a deposition by former White House aide Kathleen Willey, she said Clinton groped her unexpectedly before she broke away in a private hallway leading to the Oval Office. There was also testimony from several Arkansas state troopers repeating what they had told reporters years earlier about facilitating Clinton's clandestine liaisons with women in Arkansas.

In late July, we were able to report from multiple confidential sources that Starr and Lewinsky had reached an agreement giving her full immunity from prosecution in exchange for testimony about her sexual relationship with the president and their discussions about ways to keep it secret. On August 6, Lewinsky testified before the federal jury, which had already listened to the tape recordings made by Linda Tripp.

President Clinton testified to the grand jury on August 17, via closed-circuit television from the Map Room in the White House. Afterward, in a live five-minute television address to the American people from the same room, the president admitted to having "a relationship with Miss Lewinsky that was not appropriate." That contradicted his deposition in the Paula Jones case and his declaration on television seven months earlier: "I did not have sexual relations with that woman, Miss Lewinsky."

On September 9, independent counsel Starr submitted his report, recommending impeachment of President Clinton, to the U.S. House of Representatives. Starr cited eleven possible grounds for impeachment, including perjury, witness tampering, and obstruction of justice. The House released the extraordinary 453-page report to the news media and the public on September 11. It described in graphic detail ten occasions in the White House, over eighteen months, when Clinton and Lewinsky engaged in a variety of specific sexual acts other than intercourse. It stated that Lewinsky performed oral sex on Clinton while he talked on the telephone with members of Congress. It also confirmed that the president's DNA was found on a navy blue dress that Lewinsky wore during one of their sexual encounters.

The eleven counts of possible impeachable offenses included lying in Clinton's January 17 deposition in the Paula Jones case and in his August 17 grand jury testimony about the nature of his relationship with Lewinsky. They included alleged attempts to influence potential witnesses, including Lewinsky and Betty Currie, and lies to White House aides, expecting that they would repeat his lies to the grand jury.

After consulting with Kaiser, other senior editors, and Don Graham, I decided to publish the full report in a twenty-five-page special section of the Saturday, September 12, *Post* and on our website, washingtonpost .com. Both contained warnings about the sexually explicit language in the report. I did it despite my reputation for being rather prudish about the language I allowed into the newspaper. After all, the printed *Post* was invited as a guest into the homes of hundreds of thousands of Washington area families.

However, for better or worse, this was the independent counsel's official report, which would be used by Congress to decide whether to remove the president of the United States from office. I concluded that our readers should have the opportunity to see all the evidence Congress would be considering. Some other newspapers, including the *New York Times*, also published the full report. In addition, the *Post* contracted with the book publishing company PublicAffairs to publish the report on October 6 in a paperback book, with analysis from *Post* journalists.

On September 21, the House released a videotape of all four hours of the president's August 17 federal grand jury testimony, along with 3,183 pages of evidence from the independent counsel's investigation. About 900 pages consisted of Lewinsky's account of her relationship with Clinton. The president's entire videotaped testimony to the grand jury was broadcast unedited by most of the television networks, including ABC, CBS, NBC, and CNN.

There was still a behind-the-scenes story to tell. We published in the Sunday, October 11, *Post* an exceptionally long story by Sue Schmidt that took our readers inside the informal network of conservative lawyers and others who helped Paula Jones and her lawyers in her lawsuit against Clinton. These lawyers also worked with Linda Tripp and Lucianne Goldberg on Tripp's exposure of Monica Lewinsky's relationship with the president. Among the group were some people who would become better known years later, including conservative lawyer, author, and commentator Ann Coulter and New York lawyer George Conway, husband of President Trump's close White House aide Kellyanne Conway, who himself would become an outspoken critic of Trump.

President Clinton reached an out-of-court settlement of Paula Jones's lawsuit on November 14, 1998. He agreed to pay her $850,000, without acknowledging any wrongdoing or offering an apology. His lie in his deposition in the Jones case about his relationship with Lewinsky was one of the counts in Starr's recommendation for Clinton's impeachment.

Finally, on Saturday, October 19, the Republican-controlled House of Representatives impeached the president of the United States for only the second time in history. It charged Clinton with "high crimes and misdemeanors" for lying under oath and obstructing justice to cover up his affair with Lewinsky. In close votes, after weeks of debate, the House voted in favor of those two of four proposed articles of impeachment.

In the Senate trial, two thirds, or sixty-seven, of the senator-jurors would have to vote for conviction to remove the president from office. At the time, there were fifty-five Republicans and forty-five Democrats in the Senate. Richard Nixon had resigned in 1974 before the House could vote to impeach him. Andrew Johnson was acquitted by the Senate after being impeached by the House in 1868.

As we covered the Senate impeachment trial, there was little more original reporting to do. Polls showed that a majority of Americans opposed Clinton's impeachment. After the November 1998 elections, the Democrats gained five seats in the House, only the second time since the Civil War that the party of the president picked up House seats in the sixth year of his presidency. But there was no change in the party makeup of the Senate.

Shortly after noon on Saturday, February 13, 1999, the Senate acquitted Clinton in dramatic but unsurprising votes. The first article, on perjury, received only forty-five votes for conviction and fifty-five for acquittal. The second, on obstruction of justice, failed on a 50–50 tie.

Conviction required the votes of two-thirds, or sixty-seven, of the one hundred senators. It was thirteen months to the day after Linda Tripp had told Starr's prosecutors about the tapes of her conversations with Lewinsky.

In his last full day in office, January 19, 2001, President Clinton agreed to a deal with Robert Ray, Starr's successor as independent counsel, to avoid criminal prosecution in private life for perjury in his deposition in the Paula Jones lawsuit. For the first time, Clinton acknowledged in writing that "certain of my responses to questions about Ms. Lewinsky were false." He agreed to pay $25,000 in fines and accept a five-year suspension of his bar license in Arkansas. He also agreed not to seek reimbursement from the government for millions of dollars he owed in legal fees to his private lawyers.

In the end, Whitewater, Madison Guaranty, and all the other flotsam and jetsam of the Clintons' Arkansas and White House years played no role in the president's impeachment or his final agreement with the independent counsel's office. Ray closed out all the other investigations with no further action.

However, during the 2016 presidential race between Hillary Clinton and Donald Trump, eight years after I retired from the newspaper, the *Post* obtained interesting independent counsel records from the National Archives through the Freedom of Information Act. They showed that a draft indictment of Hillary Clinton was seriously considered by Starr and his prosecutors in April 1998. They deliberated over indicting her for obstruction of justice for covering up illegal activity at Madison Guaranty when she was one of its lawyers at the Rose Law Firm. One of the prosecutors, Paul Rosenzweig, told the *Post* that he had concluded that a conviction of Hillary Clinton was unlikely. The proposed indictment was shelved so that the prosecutors could focus their attention on Bill Clinton and Monica Lewinsky.

FOR THE SECOND TIME IN MY CAREER AT THE *POST*, I WAS INstrumental in journalism that confronted a president with impeachment. Critics of our coverage of the Clintons contended then, and for years afterward, that whatever happened with Madison Guaranty and the Rose

Law Firm was too parochial to follow the Clintons into the White House. They questioned how relevant our extensive reporting on the allegations about Bill Clinton's sex life was to his performance as president. They saw vindication in his acquittal in the Senate and his popularity at the end of his term. They concluded that the news media, led by the *Washington Post*, had gone way too far.

I strongly believe that we did what we should have done in holding the Clintons accountable for their behavior. Even as I write this, I believe that there remain significant unresolved questions about the veracity of both Clintons, about Hillary Clinton's conduct as a lawyer for a corrupt savings and loan, and, most important, about Bill Clinton's treatment of women during his two decades as a state governor and president of the United States.

I also now see our investigation of Bill Clinton in the light of recent news media exposure of the mistreatment of many women by many powerful men that has given rise to the #MeToo movement—in addition to numerous revelations about Donald Trump's veracity, treatment of women, financial manipulations, and presidential conflicts of interest. This is the role of the press—always striving to hold the powerful accountable—to which I devoted my career.

14

The Resort Hotel Bunker

 EN BRADLEE OFTEN SAID THAT THE SECRET
to becoming a great editor was for your newspaper to have the right owner. For Ben, of course, that was Katharine Graham. Their relationship, through the Pentagon Papers and Watergate, was legendary.

For me, that right owner was her son, Don Graham, the *Post*'s CEO during all my seventeen years as executive editor. Don was always there for consultation, but he left all final decisions about the news and the newsroom to me, even when he disagreed with me at the time. He supported my mission for the Graham family's newspaper, and he trusted me to carry it out.

Less than a year after I succeeded Ben, my relationship with Don was put to a little test. In May 1992, I faced a decision about an unusual story. The Speaker of the U.S. House, Tom Foley, asked me not to reveal the existence of a vast, elaborately outfitted congressional bunker hidden underneath the historic Greenbrier resort hotel in White Sulphur Springs, West Virginia, 250 miles southwest of Washington.

For thirty years, the bunker had been kept perpetually ready to house the entire U.S. Congress in the event nuclear war broke out, so that representatives and senators could safely carry on business for as long as possible. In a meeting with me and Bob Kaiser, in Foley's office in the U.S. Capitol, the veteran Washington state Democrat threatened to shut down the long-secret facility if we published a planned story about it in the *Washington Post Magazine*.

I informed Don, under our "no surprises" rule. If he were me, he said, he would not publish the story. He could not see a good reason to make the *Post* responsible for the congressional bunker's demise. But the decision would be mine.

Don and I met over breakfast every Tuesday in a hotel near the *Post*. Building on our increasingly close professional relationship over the years, we could talk freely and frankly, although we did not always agree. Don questioned some of my intended newsroom personnel decisions, which I made anyway. We sparred over the size of the steadily growing newsroom budget each year, but Don was indulgent when I overspent.

Don was protective of the newspaper's notably strong local circulation and lucrative advertising base. He worried whenever our use of language, length of stories, or their subjects might alienate the less educated among our longtime readers. But Don strongly supported my emphasis on investigative reporting. And he always made clear to complaining public officials or advertisers that I made the final decisions about news coverage, independently of the CEO. We were never the closest of social friends, but we shared essential values, understood each other well, and had deep respect for each other.

In the end, I did not find the decision about the Greenbrier story difficult to make. But I remember it as a significant early step in our relationship as editor and owner.

I HAD BEEN TO THE GREENBRIER AT LEAST ONCE, FOR A CONFERence, and I never guessed that a congressional doomsday bunker could be hidden under the West Virginia Wing of the hotel. Beginning in 1959, that wing and the bunker beneath it were built together with secret federal financing to conceal the existence of the bunker. Its government code name was "Project Greek Island."

The 112,544-square-foot bunker was constructed of steel-reinforced concrete. Its concrete roof, where it extended underground beyond the hotel's West Virginia Wing, was covered with dirt twenty feet deep. Its four hidden steel-and-concrete doors could withstand a nuclear blast and seal off the bunker from contaminated air. It had its own huge underground water storage tanks, electrical generators, heaters, and air-purification system.

Members of Congress entering in the event of a nuclear war were expected to be cleansed in decontamination chambers. They would sleep, along with selected congressional staff aides, in eighteen dormitories resembling those in military barracks, with bunk beds for 1,100 people. Each bed had a nameplate for its current designated occupant.

There were numerous bathrooms and group shower rooms (both mostly for men), lounge areas with televisions, a cafeteria that would serve stored, prepared meals three times daily, a well-equipped medical facility with operating rooms and an intensive care unit, and a crematorium for anyone who died while the bunker was sealed off from the outside world. Sophisticated telecommunications facilities, including a television studio, were connected by cables running up through the ground to hidden antennas, all maintained by the Army Signal Corps.

The bunker contained one auditorium with 470 upholstered seats for meetings of the House of Representatives and another with 130 seats for Senate sessions. Adjacent to them was a grand hall, with massive pillars, for joint sessions of Congress. The Greenbrier used it as an exhibit hall, along with the auditoriums, for business conferences for unsuspecting guests.

Most hotel employees knew nothing about the rooms' potential dual use or the hidden blast door or the existence of the rest of the bunker. Only a few hotel officials did know, along with security-cleared employees and contractors who secretly maintained it. Townspeople heard rumors. They all kept the secret from outsiders for three decades until enterprising *Post* reporter Ted Gup began investigating.

Over time, Gup interviewed current and former hotel employees, contractors, and government officials. He located photos, drawings, and even blueprints. He pieced together a remarkably detailed description of the innards of the bunker complex from sources who had been inside it. He even was able to tell about painted outdoor scenes that were mounted in frames resembling windows on the walls of the dining area.

Just once, during the Cuban missile crisis in 1962, the Greenbrier bunker was put on high alert and prepared for imminent occupation by members of Congress. But it was never used then, or later, although its readiness was constantly maintained at a hidden cost to taxpayers of millions of dollars each year.

Gup's reporting raised questions about the bunker's continued usefulness. The Greenbrier was well over four hours away from Capitol Hill by train or car. Although the landing strip at the small airport nearby had been lengthened for commercial airlines, lawmakers would have to go to National Airport outside Washington and find enough planes to fly them there. While there would have been hours of warning time for bombers carrying nuclear weapons from Russia when the bunker was opened in 1962, missiles could strike within minutes by 1992.

Perhaps most important, members of Congress would not be able to bring their families with them. "When they told me my wife would not be going with me," former House Speaker Tip O'Neill told Gup in an interview, he lost interest in the relocation bunker. "I said, 'Jesus, you don't think I'm going to run away and leave my wife? That's the craziest thing I heard of.'"

Gup wrote a richly detailed story about the bunker's construction, contents, and operation—and the intrigue surrounding it all. We planned to publish it in the May 31, 1995, edition of the *Washington Post Magazine*, inside Sunday editions of the newspaper.

IN HIS CAPITOL HILL OFFICE, SPEAKER FOLEY, WHO WAS RESPONsible for the operation of the bunker, made his strongest possible pitch to me and Kaiser for not publishing Gup's story. He responded to our questions about its viability three decades after its construction by emphasizing it was all that Congress had as refuge from an attack on Washington.

He said individual members of Congress would have to decide for themselves whether they would go there without their families.

Foley was on the spot. He risked being the House Speaker who "lost" the Greenbrier bunker, without any plan to replace it. Adverse publicity could make him more vulnerable in his increasingly competitive congressional constituency in the state of Washington.

At one point, Bob Dole, majority leader of the Republican-controlled Senate, joined the meeting. However, he did not seem very interested in the subject, and he stayed for only a few minutes. Before leaving, Dole made what seemed to be a half-hearted effort to persuade us not to run the story. He added that Foley, as House Speaker, was in charge of the bunker, and we should listen to him.

Kaiser and I left the Capitol agreeing that nothing we heard had persuaded us not to publish the story. The bunker was obsolete and had been for years. I informed Don and decided to go ahead.

Within a week of the story's publication, Congress and the Department of Defense decided to close the bunker. It was gradually powered down and then officially decommissioned. The Greenbrier decided to give its hotel guests exclusive tours of the bunker, beginning in 1995. Two years later, it added paid public tours twice a week. The complex was closed for renovations in 2004 and reopened for tours by hotel guests and the public in 2006, with museum-like exhibits and a video about the Cold War and the history of the bunker. Admission for the public in 2019 was $39 for adults.

Some years ago, Don Graham took the tour as a guest while attending a conference at the Greenbrier. The tour guide, who did not know who he was, castigated the *Post* for publishing the story that ended the bunker's use for Congress and deprived the surrounding community of its not-so-secret source of patriotic pride. When others on the tour who knew Don asked about that, he later told me, "I spoke up about why we did it."

15

The Unabomber's Ultimatum

THE PACKAGE WAS DISCOVERED IN THE *POST*'S mail room on Wednesday night, June 28, 1995. It measured eight and a half by eleven and a half inches and was a half inch thick. It was wrapped in taped brown paper, on which there were eight 32-cent Old Glory stamps, two San Francisco postmarks, and the words "FIRST CLASS" in bold letters. It was addressed to Michael Getler, the *Post*'s deputy managing editor. The return address was: Boon Long Hoe, 3609 Reinoso Ct., San Jose, CA 95136.

Earlier that day, FBI director Louis Freeh's chief of staff, Robert Bucknam, had telephoned Don Graham to tell him that he had reason to believe a package may have been sent to the *Post*. The *New York Times* had received a package the previous day, Bucknam said, addressed to its deputy managing editor, Warren Hoge. It had been sent by the person the FBI called the Unabomber.

The contents of the packages turned out to be mostly identical: a carbon copy of a fifty-six-page, typewritten, single-spaced manuscript; ten more pages of typed footnotes and corrections to be inserted into the manuscript; and copies of letters to the *Times* and to Robert Guccione, publisher of *Penthouse* magazine. Our package also contained a typewritten, four-paragraph letter to "Washington Post" from "FC"—the Unabomber's signature, which stood for "Freedom Club."

The Unabomber had been terrorizing the country. Over seventeen years, beginning in 1978, he had mailed or planted sixteen well-disguised homemade explosive devices around the country, killing three people and injuring twenty-three others, many severely. The Unabomber had sent the most recent mail bomb two months earlier to the California Forestry Association in Sacramento, killing its president when he opened it.

After we notified the FBI that our package had arrived, agents came quickly. They took it to be opened and its contents photocopied at FBI headquarters a dozen blocks away. One copy was returned to the *Post*. As I write this, it is sitting next to me on my desk at home.

The 35,000-word manuscript was a densely argued anarchist manifesto titled "Industrial Society and Its Future." It advocated worldwide revolution against modern society's "industrial-technological system" because "its consequences have been a disaster for the human race." It castigated both "leftists" for trying to "oversocialize" everyone and "conservatives" for supporting "technological progress and economic growth."

In the note to the *Post* and the letter to the *Times*, the Unabomber offered "to desist terrorism" if either newspaper, or both simultaneously, published the entire manifesto. If neither "respectable" publication did so, *Penthouse* magazine could, as Guccione had publicly offered to do.

However, in the letter to Guccione, the Unabomber speculated that the *Times* and the *Post* "may just say, 'What the heck, let *Penthouse* publish it and that will stop the bombings.'" If that happened, the Unabomber warned Guccione, "we reserve the right to plant one (and only one) bomb, intended to kill, AFTER our manuscript has been published" by *Penthouse*.

The Unabomber gave the *Post* and the *Times* three months to decide. This was one decision that Don and I would make together. It would not be easy. Lives could literally be in the balance.

Don called the publisher of the *Times*, Arthur Ochs Sulzberger Jr., whom he knew well. After Don told Sulzberger that they should not let the Unabomber play one newspaper against the other, they agreed to coordinate the decision making. They asked me and the executive editor of the *Times*, Joe Lelyveld, if we thought there was any journalistic reason to publish the entire manifesto. Not surprisingly, we both said there was not.

I assigned reporters to write stories about the manifesto and the Unabomber's ultimatum. We soon reported that the FBI had sent copies of the manifesto, which was filled with academic jargon and references to scientific history, to dozens of university professors to determine whether the author appeared to be a former student or colleague. The *Post* and the *Times* then each published 3,000 words of representative excerpts from the manifesto so that our readers could see some of what the FBI, the academic community, and the *Post* and the *Times* were studying.

THE UNABOMBER'S FIRST ATTACKS WERE NOT IMMEDIATELY CONnected to each other by investigators. Bombs that exploded a year apart at Northwestern University damaged a professor's office in June 1978 and injured a student in June 1979. A bomb that exploded in November 1979, in the cargo hold of an American Airlines plane flying from Chicago to Washington, caused fire and smoke that injured twelve people before the plane made an emergency landing at Dulles International Airport.

A pattern was found only after the CEO of United Airlines, Percy Wood, was severely injured by a bomb hidden in a book mailed to his home in a Chicago suburb. The ensuing investigation by the FBI, the Postal Inspection Service, and the Bureau of Alcohol, Tobacco and Firearms linked that attack to the three previous unsolved bombings. The agencies determined from the remains of the devices that they likely were made by the same person. They formed an FBI-led task force they called UNABOM because the four bombs had targeted universities (UN) and airlines (A).

In 1981, after a similar bomb failed to detonate in a University of Utah classroom, another one injured a professor's secretary, Janet Smith, when she opened a package in the mail at Vanderbilt University in May 1982. A small metal tag on that device was imprinted with the letters "FC," leading investigators to believe that the bomber was seeking attention.

They also concluded that the mailing label was typed on a 1920s-era Smith-Corona typewriter, which, along with the FC marking, would be used for all future bombs.

Following a three-year pause, four bombs turned up in 1985. In May, an explosive disguised as a three-ring binder was placed in a classroom building at the University of California at Berkeley. It exploded when a graduate student, John Hauser, opened it, blowing four fingers off his right hand. A package with a hidden bomb sent in June to the Boeing Fabrication Division in Auburn, Washington, failed to detonate when its batteries died after the package was left on a shelf. It was later discovered and safely disarmed. In November, a package bomb mailed to a University of Michigan psychology professor injured his research assistant when it exploded as he was opening it.

The first death occurred in December 1985, when Hugh Scutton, the owner of a computer store in Sacramento, saw what appeared to be dangerous debris—two pieces of wood attached by protruding nails—in the store's parking lot. It exploded when he bent over to pick it up. In February 1987, Gary Wright, the owner of another computer store, in Salt Lake City, was seriously injured by a similar bomb in that store's parking lot. Earlier, another employee had seen, through a window, a man putting something wooden on the ground near her car. Her description produced an artist's depiction, which was widely published and broadcast, of the Unabomber as a man in a hooded sweatshirt wearing dark aviator sunglasses.

Six years passed. On June 22, 1993, University of California geneticist Charles Epstein lost three of his fingers when he opened a disguised bomb mailed to his Tiburon, California, home. Two days later, Yale computer science professor David Gelernter lost his right hand and suffered severe burns and shrapnel wounds when he opened a similar package mailed to his university office.

At about the same time, the *New York Times* received a letter mailed by the Unabomber to deputy managing editor Hoge, whose name could be found on the "masthead" list of senior editors inside the paper. The letter had been typed on the same Smith-Corona typewriter as the mailing labels on the package bombs. "I'm back," the Unabomber wrote. "And I'm going to begin my campaign of terrorism again."

A federal interagency task force was expanded and headquartered in San Francisco. For the first time, the FBI put information about the case on the internet. It held numerous press conferences to appeal for the public's help. It created an 800 number that attracted tens of thousands of telephoned tips. FBI director Freeh announced a $1 million reward for information leading to the identification and arrest of the Unabomber. UNABOM had become the largest, longest, and most expensive active investigation in FBI history.

It would get worse. On December 10, 1994, Thomas Mosser, a Burson Marsteller advertising executive and avid golfer, was killed when he opened a shoebox-sized package mailed to his New Jersey home with the return address of a golf equipment company. On April 24, 1995, timber industry lobbyist Gilbert Murray was killed when he opened a mailed package addressed to his predecessor as president of the California Forestry Association in Sacramento. Both packages were wrapped in brown paper, with numerous postage stamps and mailing labels typed on the same Smith-Corona typewriter.

The investigative task force kept expanding, driven by an increasing sense of urgency. But its hundreds of interviews and investigations of more than 2,400 possible suspects led nowhere. In May 1995, the Unabomber even sent the FBI taunting letters, before mailing the manifesto to the *Post*, the *Times*, and Bob Guccione, as well as the FBI and *Scientific American* magazine, in late June.

Don and I deliberated about what to do. Should we let a murderous terrorist dictate what we would publish in the *Post*? Would the Unabomber really stop if we published the manifesto—or keep killing if we did not?

Don called Robert Bucknam, FBI Director Freeh's chief of staff, for advice. The FBI was undecided about how best to proceed until it analyzed the Unabomber's writings and reviewed its other information. Don and I discussed what to do with Bo Jones, who had become the *Post*'s president, in charge of its business operations and legal affairs. We did not think we would set a precedent for dealing with terrorism if we published the manifesto, but we would have to have a very compelling public safety reason.

We met Sulzberger and Lelyveld at FBI headquarters in downtown Washington to be briefed on the UNABOM task force's investigation. We heard from its profiler that the FBI thought the Unabomber was a white man in his forties from Chicago who lived somewhere in the San Francisco Bay area. The task force had found that most of the bombs had been constructed from various scrap materials, including random pieces of wood fashioned into attractive-looking boxes in which some of the explosives had been hidden. Agents showed us remarkably compact boxes that task force technicians had constructed from similar materials to show us what the bombs probably looked like.

At our second meeting in the large headquarters conference room, we were joined by FBI director Freeh and the head of the UNABOM task force, who had come to Washington from San Francisco. He shared much more information from the investigation. He said he could not advise us about publishing the manifesto. Task force members had been divided over whether it was wise to give in to a terrorist. But he said he thought the Unabomber would keep his word about what he would do depending on whether the manifesto was published.

That set the stage for a climactic, crowded meeting with Attorney General Janet Reno, Freeh, the five of us from the *Post* and the *Times*, and many members of the UNABOM task force, on Wednesday, September 13, 1995. The Unabomber's deadline was drawing near.

"We'd like your recommendation," Don remembered telling Reno. "We're absolutely not public safety experts, and we'd like to know what you think best. Then we'll decide and get back to you."

Seated at the middle of a very long conference table, Reno said that she and the task force had two options to recommend to us.

One was to have the newspapers print the manifesto in a pamphlet to be distributed to bookstores and newsstands around the country. Don and I did not think that was feasible because it would be too difficult to distribute a pamphlet reliably that way. Don also was wary of getting into an ongoing publishing relationship with the Unabomber, who, like other authors, Don said, could argue that his writing had not been given enough attention.

The second option Reno recommended was for us to publish the entire manifesto in one or both newspapers. The FBI theorized that if copies of the newspapers containing the manifesto could be put on sale in the San Francisco area, agents could watch who bought them and perhaps catch the Unabomber. I remember thinking that was somewhat far-fetched. But it was possible that someone somewhere reading the manifesto might recognize who its author could be.

Don remembered Sulzberger and Lelyveld being quite cooperative during our discussions. Yet it appeared to me during the meeting with Reno that they sounded reluctant to publish the manifesto in the *Times*, even though it already distributed newspapers in the San Francisco area, whereas the *Post* did not.

Afterward, the five of us went to a nearby coffee shop, where Don presented an idea with which I had agreed. The *Post* could print the manifesto in a small-type stand-alone tabloid to be inserted along with the advertising circulars in a weekday edition of the paper. The *Times* would pay half of the approximately $30,000 cost. Sulzberger and Lelyveld immediately agreed.

That is what happened. Tucked inside the Thursday, September 19, 1995, editions of the *Post* was an eight-page, stand-alone insert containing the entire Unabomber manifesto. It did not look anything like the newspaper itself, which differentiated it from the news pages.

"After weighing the question for nearly three months," began a news story about it on the *Post*'s front page, "The *Washington Post* and the *New York Times* have agreed to publish in today's *Washington Post* a 35,000-word manuscript submitted by the Unabomber, the serial mail bomber who has promised to stop his deadly attacks if either newspaper ran his lengthy critique of industrial society."

The story quoted from a joint statement by Don and Sulzberger, stating that the manifesto was published "for public safety reasons" on the recommendation of Reno and Freeh. "If we failed to do so," the two publishers said, "the author of this document threatened to send a bomb to an unspecified destination 'with intent to kill.'" They added that the manifesto was appearing only in the *Post* "because it has the mechanical ability to distribute such a section in all copies of its daily paper."

Some in the news media and university journalism schools were critical of the *Post* for acceding to the Unabomber's threat and publishing the manifesto. But most members of the public calling the *Post* were asking for extra copies, which we had decided not to print. The FBI was flooded with tips, which, however, did not pan out. Agents did detain but then released a man who bought a copy of the newspaper in a store outside San Francisco. There were no more bombings, but also no real leads to the Unabomber.

Nevertheless, I was comfortable with our decision. We had explained it publicly. So far, it appeared that we had saved lives. Neither the Unabomber nor any other terrorist ever again demanded that we publish anything else.

WHAT NEITHER WE NOR THE FBI KNEW WAS THAT, IN SCHENEC-tady, New York, the wife of a man named David Kaczynski was urging her husband to find and read a copy of the Unabomber's manifesto. Linda Patrik told her husband that what she had already read in news coverage of the manifesto about the Unabomber's opposition to modern technology sounded like what she knew about his estranged older brother, Ted Kaczynski, a mathematics prodigy and, briefly, university professor who had long ago moved to a remote cabin without electricity or running water on land the brothers bought in rural Montana. After sending his family what Linda later called "extremely negative, insulting and violent-sounding letters," Ted had broken off communication with his family.

"It was Linda who strongly encouraged me to pick up a copy of the *Post* the day the manifesto was published," David remembered. "She even called around to several news vendors to discover where we might find a copy. It turned out only a few sold the *Post*, and, when I visited those that did, the issues had all sold out."

They later tried two local libraries. One had not yet received that copy of the paper. The manifesto insert was missing from the copy at the other library. At Union College, where Linda was a professor, a colleague downloaded the manifesto from the internet for her. Don and I did not remember posting it on our fledgling internet site, then called Digital Ink, but someone must have done so when it was published in the paper.

In the ensuing weeks, the couple read the manifesto over and over, comparing it with letters that Ted had sent long before from his Montana cabin. In his memoir, *Every Last Tie: The Story of the Unabomber and His Family*, David later described how he agonized over the possibility that the Unabomber was his brother and, if so, what he would do about it.

The couple eventually contacted Linda's friend, Susan Swanson, a private investigator in Chicago. They asked her to obtain a language comparison analysis of the manifesto and typed copies of Ted's writings. An expert engaged by Swanson estimated that there was a 40 percent to 60 percent chance they were written by the same person. Linda and David then asked a lawyer friend of Swanson's to approach the FBI, hoping to keep secret David Kaczynski's involvement in turning in his brother. After some false starts, the UNABOM task force concluded from the writings that Ted Kaczynski must be the Unabomber.

Agents staked out his Montana cabin for three months before arresting him on April 3, 1996. They searched the cabin and found a live bomb, various bomb components, the Smith-Corona typewriter, the original manifesto manuscript, and thousands of pages of handwritten journal entries in which the Unabomber's crimes were detailed. Somehow, CBS News had found out about the impending arrest, and anchor Dan Rather reported on the *Evening News* that David Kaczynski had "fingered his brother."

David decided to take advantage of his media interviews to try to save his brother from execution. Ted Kaczynski ultimately avoided the death penalty by pleading guilty to all the charges of carrying out the bombings and murdering three people. He was sentenced to life in prison.

On September 13, 2016, twenty years after Don and I had decided to publish the Unabomber's manifesto in the *Post*, Don and his wife, journalist Amanda Bennett, hosted me; Bo Jones and his wife, Bebe; and David Kaczynski and Linda Patrik at his Washington home. My wife, Janice, was unable to be there. Don, Jones, and I had left the *Post* by then. David had just published his memoir.

We wanted to hear more about how David and Linda made it through all those months of coping with the possibility that David's brother was the Unabomber. They wanted to hear more about how we made the decision to publish the manifesto. I was moved and impressed by this modest couple who had performed an immeasurable service for their country under the most difficult circumstances imaginable.

It was a rare opportunity for me to feel some emotion about what the newspaper had done, even though "the story" had not involved original journalism. It added to my appreciation for all the years in which Don and Bo Jones had supported me and the newsroom—and all the stories that had made a difference.

16

The Buck Stops Here

𝕴T WAS JUST AFTER 2:30 A.M. ON NOVEMBER 8, 2000, when we realized that the historically close presidential election was not over. I was standing next to the nearly deserted national news desk with Steve Coll, who had become my managing editor two years earlier. We were trying to decide what to do about the new front-page plates that had just been put on the printing presses five floors below us. Should the front page of the final edition of the next morning's *Washington Post* report that Texas governor George W. Bush had won?

Our incomparable lead political reporter, Dan Balz, had written three alternative lead paragraphs for his election story. One had Vice President Al Gore winning, as the television networks had projected much earlier in the night. Another had Bush winning, as the television networks had projected just after 2:15 a.m. Balz's third version had the election still undecided. I had sent the Bush-winning story to our production department for the front page of the final edition. Sources told Balz that Gore was about to concede the election.

But now, in the final few minutes before the presses would start to print the final edition, Coll and I had doubts. Bush's lead in the decisive state of Florida was shrinking. I had chosen Coll to be Bob Kaiser's successor as managing editor when Kaiser stepped down to write books and stories for the *Post* because he, like Kaiser, was smarter than I was. Coll, a trim man with a boyish face, tousled hair, and schoolboy glasses, scribbled numbers on a sheet of scrap paper.

We compared Bush's dwindling lead in Florida to the number of votes still to be counted. We realized that Gore still had a mathematical chance of overtaking him. At the very least, the narrow margin of victory for either man in the state would be subject to a mandatory recount.

I called the night production manager and ordered that the front-page plates be taken off the presses immediately. Within minutes, the alternative top of Balz's story was sent through the computer system and engraved onto new printing plates. I soon felt the building vibrate as the huge presses started printing newspapers with a new front-page headline: "Presidential Cliffhanger Awaits Florida Recount."

At about 4 a.m., a Bush aide told reporters that an hour earlier Gore had called Bush to concede the election, but had just called again to retract his concession. There would be a recount in Florida to decide who would become president.

We updated all our stories for an Election Extra edition of the newspaper that was finished for street sale in the afternoon. For the first time in a presidential election, we also updated our website, washingtonpost.com, hour by hour, for what became a record-breaking audience on the internet.

Disaster averted. It would not have been quite as bad as the "Dewey Defeats Truman" banner headline on the front page of the *Chicago Daily Tribune* in 1948. Bush would finally be declared the winner on December 13, after a controversial split decision by the U.S. Supreme Court aborted a hotly contested Florida recount. But I would not have wanted a wrong election night front page to embarrass the *Post*.

Nearly twenty other major newspapers erroneously had Bush winning in big headlines at the top of the front pages of their November 8 final editions, including the *Miami Herald, New York Times, USA Today, Boston Globe, Chicago Tribune, Philadelphia Inquirer,* and *Dallas Morn-*

ing News. The television networks projected the wrong winner twice. But who was counting?

NEWSROOMS ARE NOT DEMOCRACIES. SOMEONE MUST MAKE FINAL decisions about what goes into the newspaper, on the air, or online. I made countless such decisions during my quarter century as managing editor and executive editor of the *Post*. What stories should be displayed on the front page? When was a potentially controversial story ready for publication? Was it accurate and fair? Were there potential libel issues? When might a story's language or photographs offend readers?

I delegated many decisions to the smart, talented editors working under me. But I was an unusually involved top editor, constantly asking questions, making suggestions, reading story drafts, and engaging editors and reporters in decision-making discussions. While the stories came from those reporters and editors, I saw myself as a catalyst that made their best work possible. But I always believed that the buck stopped with me, and I enjoyed the challenge and adrenaline rush of that ultimate responsibility.

With almost no formal training in managing a newsroom that grew to nine hundred people, I learned by doing. As executive editor, I established a relationship with each of my managing editors, beginning with Bob Kaiser, of complete candor with one another, especially when we disagreed. I asked Tom Wilkinson, my closest personal adviser, who had become a senior editor for newsroom personnel, to bring me all the bad news that no else would tell me.

Each year, Wilkinson also was tasked with asking a representative sample of journalists throughout the newsroom to anonymously evaluate me. I was both praised for being an activist editor and criticized for sometimes being too "intrusive in the coverage and editing of stories." Staff members found me to be open, direct, and willing to change my mind, yet too often ready to say what I thought before listening to them. I learned that I played a disproportionately important role in their professional lives. As hard as I tried to discourage it, what "Len says" too often ruled the day, even when I was not around.

I made mistakes, the most important of which I detail in chapters that follow. I also made story decisions with which members of the newsroom staff or readers strongly disagreed, such as the stories about the private lives of politicians, including the Clintons.

Sometimes, I got caught up in the media competition on a big breaking story without putting it in better perspective for *Post* readers. Like much of the rest of the news media, for example, the *Post* covered the 1995 murder trial of O. J. Simpson too much like a legal soap opera. I was stunned by African Americans, including those in our newsroom, loudly cheering for a not-guilty verdict. I realized that it reflected their deep resentment of racism, particularly what they saw as racist law enforcement in Los Angeles, something we had not adequately reported.

For African Americans, the Simpson case was all about race. And race had long been an issue in the *Post* newsroom, especially because of the large African American population in the Washington area. Although the *Post* had long ago been among the first major American newspapers to hire black journalists, their numbers had grown slowly. Women also were underrepresented in the newsroom when I became executive editor.

While I was still managing editor, with Don Graham's backing, I set up and oversaw a new, generously funded newsroom merit pay system. I designed it to rationally reward performance, while shrinking unreasonable salary discrepancies between white men and women and minorities. To do so, I regularly reviewed with senior editors the performance and pay of every *Post* journalist, which enabled me to monitor more closely the work of the entire staff.

As executive editor, one of my priorities was increasing the number of women and minority journalists in the newsroom, as well as their opportunities for good assignments and supervisory positions. I frequently put race and gender issues on the agendas of staff meetings and the annual off-site retreats for senior editors. I created newsroom diversity task forces and acted on their recommendations to improve recruiting, hiring, training, and career development.

It was a slow process, with setbacks along with progress. But it steadily increased the number and success of women and minorities in the newsroom. During the twenty-four years I was managing editor and executive editor, the proportion of women in the *Post* newsroom increased from 34 percent to 45 percent, and the number of journalists of color doubled from 12 percent to 25 percent. Women and journalists of color became a majority of the top forty editors in the newsroom.

This was not only the right thing to do—and good for newsroom morale. It was essential to have a diversity of backgrounds among our journalists to most effectively and fairly report on a wide variety of people, places, and subjects.

As Ben had, I insisted on complete nonpartisanship in the *Post*'s news coverage and noninvolvement of *Post* journalists in political activity or advocacy of any kind. The newsroom's Standards and Ethics policy, which I strictly enforced, required our journalists to "avoid active involvement in any partisan causes—politics, community affairs, social action, demonstrations—that could compromise our ability to report and edit fairly." That meant that members of the news staff could not contribute money to candidates, parties, or causes, sign petitions, or participate in any of the many protest marches in Washington.

I stopped voting when I became managing editor in 1984, although I did not require other *Post* journalists to do the same. As the final decision maker on the *Post*'s news coverage, I did not want to decide, even privately, who should be president or hold any other public office, or what position to take on policy issues. I wanted my mind to remain open to all sides and possibilities.

I know it sounds unlikely or naïve, but I really can see all sides and possibilities in most issues, so much so that it often frustrates my much more opinionated wife, Janice. I believe that my open mind made it easier for me to pursue and direct aggressive reporting that held all kinds of officials and institutions accountable.

In 1989, when I was still managing editor, some *Post* journalists wanted to participate in a huge march for abortion rights in Washington. I visited the various newsroom staffs to remind them that it would be a violation of our ethics policy. A few marched anyway. Ben Bradlee and I did not discipline them, but we forbade "those who forgot about this on Sunday" from violating the policy again. Some of the journalists were unhappy, but it was the last time the policy was knowingly violated. I periodically explained in memos to and meetings with the staff how important it was to not compromise the independence and credibility of our news reporting.

At the *New York Times*, U.S. Supreme Court reporter Linda Greenhouse had participated in the 1989 abortion rights march, in violation of the *Times*'s similar policy, even though she covered abortion issues at the court. Decades later, in her memoir, *Just a Journalist*, Greenhouse insisted she had a right to march as a private citizen, separate from her role as a journalist. She also acknowledged making monthly donations to Planned Parenthood. I believe that should have disqualified her from continuing to report on the court, although the *Times* left her on the beat.

In her memoir, Greenhouse strongly disagreed with the policies at both the *Times* and the *Post*. She wrote that it was wrong of me to have stated publicly, "I didn't just stop voting. I stopped having even private opinions about politicians or issues so that I would have a completely open mind in supervising our coverage."

"I regard it as troubling, even frightening to impose on journalists a sense of isolation from the civic life around them, from the very essence of citizenship," Greenhouse wrote about what I had said.

But I believe that the journalist's role as a singular kind of citizen is to inform other citizens as truthfully and impartially as possible about what they need to know to participate effectively in civic life. Today, especially, with all the accusations of news media bias, it is more important than ever for truth-seeking journalists to avoid all appearances of bias and to let their work speak for itself. It needs to be all about the story.

In late October 2000, two weeks before the presidential election, I had written an editor's column reminding readers of the strict separation at the *Post* between news coverage, which I directed, and editorials, opinion columns, and candidate endorsements, supervised separately by the editor of the editorial page. I explained that the editorial page's endorsement of Al Gore for president did not affect our coverage of the campaign, and that the camps of both presidential candidates had complained at times about coverage they did not like.

"If we have a bias," I wrote, "it is our love of a good story. And there can be no better story than a hard-fought election that appears to be going down to the wire. We have been trying to make sure that our fascination with the race does not interfere with our responsibility to give voters as much information as possible about the candidates themselves, the issues, what is on voters' minds, and how the campaign is being conducted.

"This mission is more deeply felt by our staff than readers may realize," I added. "If we do our job well, the voters can best determine where the story goes from here."

AS IT TURNED OUT, OUR JOB BECAME TRYING TO DETERMINE JUST what the voters *had* determined in the 2000 presidential election.

We sent a dozen reporters to places in Florida where ballots were being recounted, while hordes of lawyers for Gore and Bush argued with each other, with state election officials, and in court over how the recount should be done. Dozens more *Post* journalists worked on it in the newsroom. A *Post* precinct-by-precinct analysis of voting patterns in Florida showed that significant numbers of presidential votes were never counted in some places, including predominantly African American neighborhoods, because of outmoded voting machines and confusion over how to mark ballots. Bob Woodward and legal reporter Charles Lane wrote about Justice Antonin Scalia's key role in the U.S. Supreme Court's 5–4 decision that stopped a statewide hand recount that had been ordered by the Florida Supreme Court.

Before those rulings were made, Gore called me at home from the vice president's house on Observatory Circle in Washington, where he was personally directing his camp's efforts to win the court battles and the Florida recount. He tried to persuade me to report and publish a story that he thought might cast doubt on the fairness of the U.S. Supreme Court's deliberations. The facts in such a story had already been reported in the *Post* much earlier, so I told him there would be no reason to publish another version, unless it was to try to influence the outcome of the case. I turned him down.

At one point during the recount, Bush's margin over Gore in Florida had shrunk to about a hundred votes. Gore was still a few hundred votes behind Bush when the recount was stopped. As a result, he lost the presidential election by three electoral votes while winning the popular vote nationwide—only the fourth time that had happened in American history.

I decided that the *Post* should join seven other news organizations—including the Associated Press, *New York Times*, CNN, and the Tribune Company, which then owned the *Los Angeles Times, Chicago Tribune*, and *Baltimore Sun*—in a consortium that spent nearly $1 million on our own recount. NORC, a nonprofit research firm affiliated with the University of Chicago, hired trained investigators to examine 175,100 Florida ballots that Gore wanted recounted. There were problems obtaining the relatively small number of ballots they sought. But, based on those they reviewed, Bush still would have won narrowly in Florida.

A similar study conducted by the *Miami Herald, USA Today*, and the Knight Ridder newspaper chain came to a similar conclusion. Bush "would have won a hand recount of all disputed ballots in Florida's presidential election if the most widely accepted standard for judging votes had been applied," *USA Today* reported.

The *Post* published more than two hundred stories about the long count in November and December of 2000, plus a book that was released in 2001, *Deadlock: The Inside Story of America's Closest Election*. We also covered the story continuously on washingtonpost.com, attracting growing record audiences on the internet and making the *Post* more of an around-the-clock news organization.

I HAD FIRST MET GEORGE W. BUSH DURING THE 2000 PRESIDEN-tial campaign. I arranged a ride on his plane to talk to him during a flight from one campaign stop to another. He steered the conversation away from issues to basic politics, which he clearly enjoyed discussing in detail. What impressed me most was his interest in people, including the *Post* reporters who were covering him. He gave them nicknames, and shrewdly noted their working styles. He struck me as personable and politically astute, if not intellectually impressive.

Bush was quite friendly when I introduced Janice to him at a grand dinner party that Katharine Graham staged at her Georgetown mansion in February 2001, a month after his inauguration. It was a festive evening, with Bill Gates, Warren Buffett, Henry Kissinger, Ethel Kennedy, Barbara Walters, and Diane Sawyer among the guests, along with Washington media folks. Bush, with his folksy manner, seemed quite comfortable.

Unlike Bill Clinton, Bush had not come to Washington as a complete outsider, despite his deep Texas roots. He had quietly spent considerable time studying the presidency of his father, George H. W. Bush, during visits to the White House. And he surrounded himself with Washington veterans at the top of his own new administration. Vice President Dick Cheney had been secretary of defense, a congressman, and White House chief of staff. Secretary of State Colin Powell had been chairman of the Joint Chiefs of Staff and White House national security adviser. Secretary of Defense Donald Rumsfeld had been defense secretary once before and White House chief of staff. Bush's chief of staff, Andrew Card, had served in the White House and cabinet of George H. W. Bush. They all were well known to *Post* journalists.

After all the turmoil of Clinton's second term and the demanding drama of the 2000 long count, 2001 promised to be a quieter time for the *Post* newsroom.

17

9/11

MY CELL PHONE RANG A FEW MINUTES BE-fore 9 a.m. on September 11, 2001, while I was walking into the lobby of the *Washington Post* with publisher Bo Jones. My executive assistant, Pat O'Shea, was calling me from her apartment. While watching television as she dressed, she saw a news report that a plane had crashed into one of the World Trade Center towers in New York City. She thought it must have been a horrific accident.

I was coming from my weekly breakfast with Jones. Instead of accompanying him to the seventh floor for our Tuesday morning senior staff meeting, I rushed off the elevator at the fifth-floor newsroom. As usual at that hour, it was nearly empty, with televisions on overhead.

As I looked up, I saw a second plane fly directly into the second World Trade Center tower. I knew then that it must be a terrorist attack. Eight years earlier, Islamic terrorists had detonated a car bomb beneath the World Trade Center's North Tower in an unsuccessful attempt to send it crashing into the South Tower. More than 1,000 people had been injured, six fatally.

I hurried across the newsroom to the national news desk where an editorial assistant was trying unsuccessfully to get through on the telephone to our reporters in New York. I called the national news editor, Liz Spayd, who had paused on the way out of her house to try calling New York, also with no luck. I was able to get through to our washingtonpost.com editors, located on the eleventh floor of an office building in nearby Arlington, Virginia. They were putting the first wire service bulletins online.

At 9:40 a.m., another editorial assistant, driving to the *Post* from suburban Virginia, called the newsroom from her car, her voice shaking. She had just seen a plane crash into the Pentagon in Arlington. Photographer Craig Cola called the website from the George Washington Parkway to tell his editor, Chet Rhodes, that he should turn the site's rooftop webcam toward the Pentagon, because it was on fire.

American Airlines Flight 77, scheduled from Washington Dulles Airport to Los Angeles, with sixty-four people aboard, had crashed into the Pentagon at 9:40 a.m. It opened a burning hole, five stories high and two hundred feet wide, deep into the northwest side of the familiar five-sided building.

In New York, American Flight 11, scheduled from Boston to Los Angeles, with ninety-two people aboard, had flown into the North Tower of the World Trade Center, between the 93rd and 99th floors, at 8:45 a.m. United Airlines Flight 175, also scheduled from Boston to Los Angeles, with sixty-five people aboard, flew into the South Tower, between the 77th and 85th floors, at 9:05 a.m.

Later, United Flight 93, scheduled from Newark to San Francisco, with forty-four people aboard, crashed in a rural field in Stony Creek Township near Shanksville, Pennsylvania, at 10:10 a.m.

Nobody yet knew why all this was happening.

All air traffic was immediately grounded. Planes in the air throughout the country were ordered to land at the nearest airports. Overseas flights bound for the United States turned back. Too late, U.S. Air Force fighters started patrolling the skies.

On television, billowing smoke from the Pentagon appeared to be coming from buildings in downtown Washington, D.C., leading to false reports of explosions at the White House, the Capitol, and the State

Department. President George W. Bush was in Sarasota, Florida, reading to students in an elementary school. In his absence, Vice President Cheney and key senior officials were taken down into the Presidential Emergency Operations Shelter under the East Wing of the White House.

Everyone else in the White House, and in the Capitol, at the other end of Pennsylvania Avenue, spilled outside in confusion on a bright, sunny, late summer morning, as emergency sirens sounded. All other government buildings were soon evacuated, including CIA headquarters in suburban Virginia. Private businesses shut down. Panicked workers trying to go home clogged the city's streets and highways in an unprecedented traffic jam.

Post reporters and photographers attempting to get to the Pentagon across the Potomac River had to abandon their cars and walk. Reporters Arthur Santana and David Cho and photographer Jim Parcell still managed to reach the Pentagon in time to slip inside the security cordon being formed by police and the military. Photographer Juana Arias left her car on a nearby freeway, climbed two fences, and sneaked past the security lines. Photographer Rich Lipski convinced residents of a high-rise apartment building in Arlington with a clear view of the burning Pentagon that his job depended on being able to shoot pictures from the roof.

I called my wife, Janice, who never watched morning television, to tell her what was happening. I said that I did not know when I would be home or even have time to talk to her on the telephone again.

In the pressure of the moment, I also did not really have time to react emotionally to the enormity of the terrorist attacks. My increasingly intense focus was on what I and the newspaper had to do. I could feel adrenaline rising inside me, while I stayed outwardly calm, knowing from years of experience what to do.

Even on relatively quiet days, leading a newsroom resembles crisis management. I sometimes thought of it as being a smaller-scale equivalent of designing, manufacturing, and distributing a different model car every single day, 365 days each year. It was enormously rewarding, day after day, working with the extraordinarily talented and dedicated news staff that Ben Bradlee and I had built over the years. Often, it felt like an extended family.

On that day, the newsroom rapidly filled with reporters, editors, photographers, artists, and other staff members who had somehow made their way through the gridlock outside. Those who were not scheduled to work that day came in anyway. Others returned from vacations and sick leave. The chief of the Metro copy editing desk, Marcia Kramer, showed up and insisted on taking over for the duration, even though she had been told by her doctor to stay home with a severely broken left arm. Bob Woodward and other star reporters—David Maraniss, Dana Priest, and David Von Drehle—interrupted book projects to come in and work for the duration.

The mood was somber, but purposeful. It was one of those times when I felt down to my bones that this was why I was a newspaper journalist. Television would broadcast the story twenty-four hours a day. But the *Post* and its website would give our readers so much more to help them make some sense of the horrifying visual images and disjointed interviews and commentary.

The four reporters in our New York bureau—plus fashion columnist Robin Givhan and sports columnist Sally Jenkins, who both lived there—headed toward southern Manhattan on their own, before we could contact them. The South Tower of the World Trade Center collapsed at 9:59 a.m., and the North Tower fell at 10:28 a.m., trapping and killing a then unknown number of people. New York bureau chief Bart Gellman commandeered a limousine, hitched a ride on a motorcycle, and walked the rest of the way to get within a dozen blocks of Ground Zero. He stood in ashes and debris from the fallen towers to interview survivors and eyewitnesses. Some of them told him that they had seen people leaping to their deaths from the Twin Towers before they collapsed.

I hurried upstairs to Bo Jones's meeting long enough to get agreement from him and the production and circulation vice presidents to publish an "Extra" edition of the newspaper as soon as possible that afternoon. I asked managing editor Steve Coll to put together a team of editors and reporters to replace the first twenty pages of that morning's final edition with stories and photographs of the attacks in Washington and New York. With the front-page banner headline "Terror Strikes Pentagon, World Trade Center" in the biggest, boldest type possible, the edition was finished at 1 p.m. and sold out by late afternoon.

Other reporters in the newsroom were assigned to feed information in story form through the newsroom's relatively new web editor, Tracy Grant, to washingtonpost.com. Its editor, Doug Feaver, cleared everything else off our five-year-old website, while his staff refreshed and expanded the terrorist attack coverage continuously. The website requested, received, and posted hundreds of e-mails from readers reacting to the day's shocking events. Washingtonpost.com attracted thirty million page views on September 11 alone, by far the most traffic for our news site at the time.

I organized the bulk of the newspaper's staff to fill every section of the Wednesday, September 12, editions with the most complete coverage possible of the terrorist attacks. At the same time, Coll and I set our goals going forward. We wanted stories every day that revealed important news about the attacks and their aftermath that our readers would not find elsewhere. We wanted detailed narratives that accurately reconstructed what happened with engaging storytelling. We wanted investigative reporting that dug into how it happened. And we wanted to profile everyone who lost their lives at the Pentagon, in addition to a representative sample of those who died in New York.

We assembled ad hoc teams for these tasks. Reporters and editors throughout the newsroom were borrowed from their usual assignments to work on the teams. We sent additional reporters, photographers, and editors to New York.

Steve Coll and I complemented each other well. My strengths were hard news, breaking stories, investigative reporting, and the overall direction of the newspaper. Coll focused on narrative journalism that had typically been identified more with magazines and books, as well as foreign and national news. He was a mentor to many of the newsroom's best writers, and he saw himself as their representative among senior editors and as their advocate for front-page display.

In fifteen years at the *Post*, Coll had written for the Style section, won a Pulitzer Prize for explanatory journalism as a business correspondent in New York, worked as a foreign correspondent in South Asia and London, and revamped and edited our Sunday magazine, all before becoming managing editor. He also had written four books about Wall Street and South Asia. He spoke and wrote with precision. With his boyish face, glasses, sandy hair, open-necked dress shirts, and thoughtful demeanor, he appeared to be more like an academic than a newspaperman.

For someone visiting the newsroom during those first hours and days after the terrorist attacks, it would have looked like mass confusion. Only on national election nights was the newsroom as full of people working that frantically on deadline. During that first week, those people temporarily overwhelmed the computer system with messages, reporting notes, and stories.

The Wednesday, September 12, edition of the *Washington Post*, produced on Tuesday by scores of *Post* journalists, was filled with sixty-six stories about the attacks and their impact on the two cities and the rest of the country. One front-page story was the first to report that the government had convincing evidence that Islamic terrorists who hijacked and crashed the planes were connected to al Qaeda leader Osama bin Laden. Another story described how hijackers had used knives and box cutters as weapons to force passengers, the crew, and the pilot to the back of the plane before American Flight 77 was flown into the Pentagon. That story was pieced together from relatives' accounts of cell phone conversations with doomed passengers on the plane.

On Thursday, September 13, a similar revelatory story appeared on the front page, based on relatives' accounts of phone conversations with passengers on United Flight 93. Passengers had called relatives to tell them about the hijacking of that plane. The relatives told the passengers about the suicide attacks by other planes on the World Trade Center. Then some passengers told their relatives that they had decided to storm the hijackers in the cockpit. The hijackers had turned around the San Francisco–bound aircraft and, investigators would later conclude, intended to fly it into the Capitol. As the passengers apparently fought the hijackers for control in the cockpit, it crashed into the Pennsylvania field instead.

On Wednesday, Bart Gellman worked his way past police and National Guard lines all the way to Ground Zero. He described in Thursday's paper the devastation from up close and interviewed firefighters about their futile search for survivors.

At the Pentagon, Arthur Santana stayed so long inside the security cordon that he was pressed into duty, with my permission, as a rescue volunteer, after identifying himself as a *Post* reporter. He turned a diary of what he saw and did over two days there into another front-page story on Thursday.

A team of two dozen national and Metro staff reporters produced the most complete account anywhere of who the nineteen hijackers were and how they were organized, led, and trained, including those who became licensed pilots in the United States. Bob Woodward revealed that five pages of handwritten instructions had been found in one of the hijackers' checked bags, which had not made it onto the plane he helped fly into the World Trade Center. The instructions included Islamic prayers and reminders to bring "knives, your will, IDs, your passport," and "make sure that nobody is following you."

We soon began publishing our first investigative stories. They exposed shortcomings in airport and aircraft security that had long been recognized but not remedied, holes in the U.S. military's air defense system, and the FBI's failure to detect the hijackers entering and living in the country and taking flying lessons.

Bob Woodward, Bart Gellman, and Pentagon reporters Tom Ricks and Vernon Loeb uncovered numerous failed secret efforts to capture or kill bin Laden in an ongoing covert CIA operation authorized in 1998 to stop al Qaeda terrorist operations aimed at the United States. Woodward reported that the CIA concluded that bin Laden, a wealthy Saudi exile, had paid an estimated $100 million since 1996 to buy protection from the ruling Islamic fundamentalist Taliban regime in Afghanistan for al Qaeda headquarters, residential communities, and training camps there. The CIA believed that bin Laden was involved in planning and paying for the 1998 terrorist bombings of U.S. embassies in Africa and the 1999 suicide bomb attack on the USS *Cole* in port in Aden, Yemen.

DAVID MARANISS CAME TO ME WITH AN IDEA. HE WAS ONE OF the paper's most thorough reporters, best interviewers, and most evocative writers. He was a seemingly shy, slightly shambling bear of man with unruly hair and a nervous laugh. He hid his intensity and intellect, letting his work speak for itself. At the *Post*, Maraniss had won the Pulitzer Prize for national reporting for revelatory biographical stories about Bill Clinton during the 1992 presidential campaign. He also had written books about Clinton, House Speaker Newt Gingrich, and Green Bay Packers head coach Vince Lombardi.

Maraniss wanted to reconstruct what happened on September 11 in human detail, in the way that *New Yorker* magazine writer John Hersey had famously done, decades earlier, in his book-length article about the people in Hiroshima, Japan, on the day it was destroyed by an atomic bomb at the end of World War II. I immediately agreed and offered him all the resources he would need.

"I wanted to write something that would have both immediacy and permanence, that would be of value to readers not just then but years later," Maraniss recalled almost a decade later in a collection of his newspaper, magazine, and book journalism. "I wanted to capture the prosaic poetry of everyday life and the moment when it is changed forever. . . . I wanted to make readers feel what it was like for victims and survivors."

With the help of fifteen reporters in Washington and New York, Maraniss interwove the poignant stories of ordinary people—doomed passengers on the four planes, people who survived and those who died at the World Trade Center and the Pentagon, their relatives, and first responders—into a moving narrative of what happened to them on what had begun as an ordinary day. Huddled in a small newsroom office, he researched and wrote the story in less than five days of nearly around-the-clock work. He interviewed survivors, relatives of victims, and other people on the telephone. He used detailed memos from the fifteen reporters, who also worked on other stories. I stopped in occasionally to look over his shoulder, but I realized there was little he needed from me.

Out of all the horror and sadness of 9/11, Maraniss created a moving masterpiece of journalism. The headline at the top of the *Post*'s front page on Sunday, September 16, in big, bold type, was simply: "September 11, 2001." Under it, in somewhat smaller italics: "Steve Miller Ate a Scone, Sheila Moody Did Paperwork, Edmund Glazer Boarded a Plane: Portrait of a Day That Began in Routine and Ended in Ashes."

"Real people, not characters in a movie," Maraniss wrote in the story, "yet all of them soon to be caught up in surreal scenes of dread and death and horror organized by perpetrators who seemed to understand perfectly the symbols and theatrics of American culture. People surviving or dying in ways at once shudderingly alien and hauntingly familiar, if only on celluloid. People rendered speechless by what they witnessed. People making selfless choices, some leading to death. People allowed only the choice of how to die, reduced to a hand or a limbless corpse on the street. People in their own isolated hells yet somehow connected to one another and to the entire world by spectacular technology that could spread their voices and their images and do everything but save the doomed among them."

The story filled four pages inside the paper. It still moves me when I reread it. Two weeks later, Maraniss and two other reporters described the incalculable emotional impact of the attacks in the days afterward on the lives of surviving victims and the widows and children of some of those who perished.

In all, the 9/11 attacks killed 2,996 people, including the 19 hijackers on the four planes, and injured 6,000 others. Among the dead in New York were 343 firefighters and 72 law enforcement officers. In Washington, the dead included 115 employees and 10 contractors at the Pentagon, and 64 passengers, crew, and hijackers on American Flight 77.

For days, downtown Washington streets were patrolled by the D.C. National Guard. For months, military vehicles monitored the highways around the Pentagon. Many Washington institutions, businesses, and families made emergency plans in case of another terrorist attack. At the *Post*, we decided that our building, located just four blocks from the White House, would be sealed if necessary, while we continued to work. I told Janice that if there was an attack of any kind while I was in the newsroom, she should expect me to stay there. I wanted her to have her own plan for escaping the city.

IN A TELEVISION ADDRESS TO THE NATION ON THE NIGHT OF September 11, President Bush declared his determination to hunt down those responsible for the terrorist attacks, along with anyone who harbored them. As we reported in the ensuing days, that meant Osama bin

Laden, al Qaeda, and Afghanistan's Islamic fundamentalist Taliban regime, which had provided a safe haven for them.

On Monday, September 17, Bush signed two secret presidential memoranda. One empowered the CIA to carry out a worldwide covert campaign against al Qaeda and other terrorist organizations, including putting its own paramilitary teams into Afghanistan. The other memorandum authorized the first steps in an unconventional war against al Qaeda and the Taliban in Afghanistan. Bob Woodward reported important aspects of the CIA's role, while a team of *Post* national staff reporters revealed that hundreds of suspected terrorists were being secretly detained worldwide to disrupt any plans for more attacks.

Congress unanimously passed resolutions authorizing all necessary and appropriate force to fight al Qaeda and the Taliban in what was dubbed Operation Enduring Freedom. NATO allies promised assistance, as the alliance invoked Article 5 of the NATO treaty for the first time.

The CIA's first paramilitary team secretly entered northern Afghanistan on September 26 to support leaders of anti-Taliban tribal forces, known as the Northern Alliance. On Sunday, October 7, Bush went on national television from the White House to announce the first American and British bombing strikes against al Qaeda and Taliban targets in Afghanistan. The bombing would grow in intensity and continue for weeks. More CIA teams, plus U.S. Army Green Beret Special Forces and 10th Mountain Division troops, infiltrated the country to closely assist the Northern Alliance fighters, often traveling with them on horseback. By early November, the Northern Alliance was engaged in heavy fighting with the Taliban and closing in on the capital of Kabul.

Informing our readers about what was happening in this mostly secret war, without much cooperation from the CIA or the U.S. military, was challenging. Yet *Post* national staff reporters, with help from around the newsroom, consistently penetrated the secrecy in Washington, forcing the Bush administration to subsequently acknowledge, release, and explain vital information to the public. Bob Woodward mined sources in the administration, intelligence services, and the military, both for the *Post* and what became his eleventh book, *Bush at War*. It was a familiar dual role for Woodward, which I monitored and believed to be, on balance, beneficial to the newspaper.

Reporting from the battlefield was much more difficult. Initially, to maintain operational secrecy, neither the CIA nor the U.S. military allowed anyone in the news media access to their operatives and troops in Afghanistan. This was not the CIA covert operation that would later raise questions about how it was treating suspected terrorists that it captured around the world. Nevertheless, it was important to report on what was happening in Afghanistan. So we sent several reporters, including the intrepid Bill Branigin, a veteran *Post* foreign correspondent who knew the region well, and Peter Baker, the *Post*'s Moscow correspondent. They each found ways to be driven into northern Afghanistan in September and travel with the rag-tag Northern Alliance forces.

Keith Richburg, an equally resourceful veteran reporter, had a much more arduous journey to join them in October. News always seemed to find Richburg and vice versa. He had been the *Post* correspondent in Haiti when Baby Doc Duvalier was ousted, in Africa when the Rwandan genocide occurred, in Indonesia when Suharto was deposed, and in Hong Kong when Britain turned over its former colony to China. He had just become the *Post*'s bureau chief in Paris when he volunteered to go to Afghanistan.

Richburg flew to Moscow and then Tajikistan, where he was driven to the Afghan border. A night trip by boat across the Panj River took him to a Northern Alliance base camp. He then hitched a ride in a Russian-made jeep with two photographers and an Afghan physician taking medical supplies to the Northern Alliance front lines. But their vehicles were stranded by the season's first snowstorm in the middle of nowhere in the rugged Hindu Kush mountains. The only way to continue was on horseback through treacherous high mountain passes. Richburg and other travelers on twelve horses with Afghan guides survived two blinding, frigid blizzards during the day-long trek.

"Cold and dangerous," Richburg later wrote about the ordeal. "There was the danger of simply falling off the horse from exhaustion and being stranded at 14,000 feet in freezing conditions. There was the danger that the horse might miss a step in the blinding sleet and snow and send himself and his rider hurtling down a half-mile drop. And then there were the wolves baying in the distance."

Finally, they made it to safety in a small village at the edge of the Panjshir Valley in Northern Alliance–held territory. An Afghan taxi took Richburg to the Northern Alliance forces advancing toward Kabul from the north, as the Taliban retreated to the hills in southeastern Afghanistan. On November 14, Bill Branigin reported from Kabul that Northern Alliance soldiers and police officers had taken control of the capital, where they were welcomed with flowers and confetti.

On November 22, Richburg wrote a particularly significant story from there about finding al Qaeda "books, handwritten notes, leaflets, identity cards and notations scrawled on scraps of paper" in houses scattered around Kabul where numerous al Qaeda foreign volunteer fighters had lived, studied, and trained. Stockpiles of grenades, antitank missiles, and bomb components were found in the basements of some of the houses, which had been hastily evacuated during the retreat of the Taliban and al Qaeda.

"The disarray of some of the houses also showed the hurried state of the foreign fighters' exit as Taliban defenders left the city the night of November 12 and the early morning hours of November 13," Richburg wrote. "Clothes and papers were strewn about. Food was left on plates. In at least two houses were piles of black hair that looked as if it came from beards, suggesting some of the militants cropped their facial hair to disguise themselves before fleeing.

"Most revealing from the hundreds of pages of papers was the extent to which Afghanistan had become the base for a global network of radical Islamic groups stretching from the Middle East through Central Asia to the Far East."

A month later, Peter Baker and Molly Moore, a *Post* Pentagon correspondent, put together for our readers, with the help of a half dozen *Post* reporters in Afghanistan and Washington, the first comprehensive picture of al Qaeda's five-year secret world in Afghanistan.

"While creating a loose network of terrorist cells for actions abroad," they wrote, "bin Laden created a society within a society in Afghanistan. Al Qaeda ran its own schools and grocery stores. It maintained offices, laboratories and aircraft. Shielded by a sympathetic government and forbidding topography, it housed, fed, and trained thousands of recruits in guerilla warfare at training camps and in Kabul's best neighborhoods."

The *Post*'s reporting about the early months of the Afghan war was so thorough, and independent of official pronouncements, that the Bush administration made several requests that we withhold from publication some of what we found. After careful discussion between senior officials and *Post* editors and reporters, I agreed to some requests about details that I concluded could clearly endanger American lives, disrupt ongoing military operations, or reveal intelligence collection methods. We were invariably able to do this without killing entire stories or misinforming our readers.

I ALSO AGREED TO A REQUEST FROM THE WHITE HOUSE NOT TO reveal the location of a mountainside bunker outside Washington where the president had assigned a rotating group of senior government officials to ensure survival of federal rule after a catastrophic nuclear attack by terrorists on the nation's capital.

Post reporters Bart Gellman and Susan Schmidt had discovered that the "continuity of government" plan was activated "on the fly" in the hours after the 9/11 attacks. Selected officials from federal departments and agencies were living and working twenty-four hours a day, away from their families, in the fortified secret location, rotating in and out about every ninety days. If the government in Washington were completely disabled, they would take command of federal facilities in the rest of the country.

After the reporters contacted the White House while they were working on the story, the president's chief of staff, Andrew Card, telephoned me. He did not oppose publishing the story, and I told him that I did not see any need to identify the secret location. Card had only one request: could the story not identify the bureaucrats assigned to bunker duty to prevent anyone from following them to the location when they went on duty? That was easy. There was no reason to identify them anyway.

We published the story, "Shadow Government Is at Work in Secret," on March 1, 2002. I thought it was important for Americans to know about it. At the same time, contemplating a terrorist attack with a nuclear device in Washington, where the *Post* building was pretty much at ground zero, was very unsettling for me.

By about that time in 2002, the Taliban appeared to have been all but totally defeated militarily in Afghanistan. The U.S. military stayed to support its new government. But hundreds of Taliban and al Qaeda fighters, along with Osama bin Laden, had fled into safe areas of neighboring Pakistan. The Taliban would eventually fight back, retaking portions of the country and prolonging an open-ended American military involvement for nearly two decades. The *Post* would continue to shuttle reporters into the country all that time to cover what would become the longest war in American history, a war that had killed 2,300 members of the U.S. military by the end of 2019.

18

Preparing for War

WE'RE FIGHTING TWO WARS," I SAID AT THE beginning of my September 2002 newsroom staff meeting in the *Post*'s first-floor auditorium. It was just a year after the 9/11 terrorist attacks, and months after the retreat of the Taliban in Afghanistan. We had mobilized to cover both the Bush administration's global war against terrorism, including the continuing military operations in Afghanistan, and its increasingly likely invasion of Iraq.

What seemed to be the inevitability of a U.S. war in Iraq posed challenges for me and the newsroom. We were preparing to cover what would likely be a much bigger, more costly war. We were trying to penetrate the administration's secretive preparations for launching such a war. And we were seeking to hold President Bush accountable for his apparent determination to rush into it.

We had reporters in Washington, Afghanistan, Pakistan, and Indonesia investigating covert U.S. efforts to capture and interrogate al Qaeda terrorists and their suspected allies to prevent potential future attacks. At the same time, we had reporters in Washington, United Nations head-quarters in New York, Baghdad, Cairo, London, Istanbul, and Bahrain trying to determine whether, when, and how the United States would go to war against Saddam Hussein in Iraq.

I emphasized to the newsroom staff that our goal should be not just to react to events, as we had to do after the September 11, 2001, attacks. We should set our own agenda whenever we could. On Iraq, I wanted us to pursue answers to these questions: How much of a threat did Saddam Hussein pose to the United States? What are the pros and cons of going to war against Iraq? How is the Bush administration making its decisions about going to war?

It would not be easy. In the lingering aftermath of the 9/11 attacks, many Americans and members of Congress appeared ready to support whatever Bush decided to do. And the administration was revealing little about its plans.

Bob Woodward had reported in June that President Bush signed an order earlier in the year directing the CIA to begin covert operations to overthrow Saddam Hussein. In July, the *Post* reported that administration officials were debating options for invading and occupying Iraq. In August, while Bush was still saying he was undecided about attacking Iraq, others around him were publicly testing justifications for a war.

"There are al Qaeda in a number of locations in Iraq," Secretary of Defense Donald Rumsfeld told reporters on his plane as he flew to Texas to discuss military options with Bush at his ranch on August 20.

"There is no doubt that Saddam Hussein now has weapons of mass destruction," Vice President Dick Cheney said in a speech on August 26. "There is no doubt he is amassing them to use against our friends . . . and against us."

I became convinced that Bush was going to invade Iraq. I wanted to inform our readers as fully as possible about his real, if somewhat hidden, intentions. And I wanted our newsroom to be fully ready to cover a war. In late August, foreign news editor Phil Bennett and national news editor Liz Spayd each prepared detailed prewar coverage plans for their staffs. By mid-September, I began holding frequent "Iraq crisis" meetings with key editors and reporters to go over their progress in answering the questions I had posed. I would bear the primary responsibility for how the newspaper met this challenge.

Steve Coll was in and out of the newsroom during much of 2002 while writing a six-hundred-page book, *Ghost Wars*, about the CIA's quarter-century involvement in Afghanistan before the 9/11 attacks. It would become a best seller and win Coll a second Pulitzer Prize. Before 9/11, I had continued to run the newsroom while writing a book with Bob Kaiser, *The News About the News: American Journalism in Peril*, about worrying changes confronting the news media. But Coll was working on something much more ambitious. I was impressed that he could devote any time at all to the newspaper. Much of his attention, when he was in the newsroom, was given to the foreign news staff, who took advantage of his knowledge of the region from his research and travel there for their preinvasion reporting.

I focused on the Bush administration's steady march to war. Over the next six months, we published scores of stories—well over a hundred of which were displayed on the *Post*'s front page—about how a war against Iraq was being sold to the American people and how the military was planning an attack. Story after story reported how Bush, Cheney, and Rumsfeld repeatedly claimed that Saddam Hussein had or was developing weapons of mass destruction that could threaten the United States. Initially, there was not much doubt expressed about that by American or European politicians or officials.

On October 2, a resolution was introduced into Congress, at Bush's request, to give the president the authority to use the military "as he determines to be necessary and appropriate" in order to "defend the national security of the United States against the continuing threat posed by Iraq." On October 7, Bush went to Cincinnati to make a nationally televised speech urging support for the resolution. It happened to be the first anniversary of the beginning of American bombing in Afghanistan, when Bush had also addressed the nation.

Karen DeYoung, who had asked to report on national security at the White House, covered the speech. Bush said that Saddam had stores of chemical and biological weapons and was seeking to develop a nuclear weapon. In addition, he said that some al Qaeda leaders had fled to Iraq and some al Qaeda members were being trained in Iraq "in bomb-making, poisons and deadly gases."

DeYoung pointed out in her story that "intelligence officials have played down the reliability of such reports." She also noted that some critics had charged that military engagement with Iraq could undermine the global war against terrorism, while Bush contended in Cincinnati that it could be "crucial to winning the war against terror."

Although polls showed Americans divided about going to war, Congress quickly backed Bush, with only a minority of dissenting voices. The House approved the resolution by a vote of 296–133 on the afternoon of October 10, and the Senate voted for it, 77–23, shortly after midnight.

On October 22, a front-page story by White House reporter Dana Milbank raised questions about Bush's assertions about Iraq and his justification for war. It was headlined "For Bush, Facts are Malleable."

"President Bush, speaking to the nation this month about the need to challenge Saddam Hussein, warned that Iraq has a growing fleet of unmanned aircraft that could be used 'for missions targeting the United States,'" the story began. "Last month, asked if there were new and conclusive evidence of Hussein's nuclear capabilities, Bush cited a report by the International Atomic Energy Agency saying the Iraqis were 'six months away from developing a weapon.'"

Milbank wrote that those statements "were dubious, if not wrong." The unmanned aircraft, or drones, could not reach the United States from Iraq, and there was "no such report by the IAEA."

The story, which also pointed out other misstatements by Bush, touched a nerve in the White House. Press secretary Ari Fleischer and deputy chief of staff Karl Rove each telephoned *Post* political editor Maralee Schwartz to complain. Fleischer also called me and asked if Milbank was the best person to cover the president. I said that he would be staying on the beat.

Milbank, who would later become a *Post* columnist, sometimes did put what appeared to be his own opinion into the first drafts of some of his news stories, which his editors would always take out. But he also explained in his stories how and why the president and his aides did things the way they did, including the political context for policy decisions and actions. I liked that, and I believed that our readers benefited from it.

I was not influenced by how the White House reacted to our coverage of the run-up to the Iraq war. I also ignored the strong support for military action against Iraq being expressed on the *Post*'s editorial page. In fact, I stopped reading the editorials and op-ed (opinion) columns entirely. Nevertheless, some readers believed that our newsgathering and the editorial page's opinions were somehow aligned, which bothered me.

I DID NOT FEEL ANY POST-9/11 PUBLIC PRESSURE OR PERSONAL patriotic inclination to downplay skepticism about an invasion of Iraq. Investigating the administration's rationale for war, including what threat Saddam might really pose, was a goal I had set for our reporting at the outset. The staff responded with significant, revealing stories right up to the beginning of combat.

However, in the welter of prewar coverage, I did not always keep my eye on that ball. I did not put on the front page enough of the stories questioning the administration's rhetoric. Thinking like an editor rather than as a reader, I too often assumed that they could easily be found by readers in the multipage packages of prewar stories inside the newspaper's front—or "A"—section each day. That was a mistake.

In September, I did put on the front page a story in which Dana Priest first reported that "the CIA has yet to find convincing evidence linking Saddam and al Qaeda." I did the same with a story by reporter Joby Warrick, in which government officials, weapons experts, and United Nations inspectors cast doubt on assertions by Bush and Cheney that aluminum tubes Iraq tried to buy could be used in enriching uranium for nuclear weapons.

But other stories, in which experts and unnamed intelligence agency sources questioned claims by the administration about the threat posed by Saddam Hussein, appeared inside the newspaper's A section. At the same time, I did not realize that some stories were being delayed or even held out of the paper by editors who were unsure about the reliability of their sourcing. For example, Pentagon reporter Tom Ricks wrote what would have been a prescient story in October 2002, in which retired military officials told him that senior Pentagon officials were concerned about the risks of invading and occupying Iraq. A national news editor killed the story because it relied so much on the retirees and nongovernment experts. I did not pay enough attention to reporting that raised questions about the Bush administration's justifications for going to war. That was also a mistake.

In addition, during those months, two other major news events distracted me and the newsroom: the D.C. sniper attacks and the *Columbia* shuttle disaster.

Beginning on October 2, 2002, two snipers who were later identified as forty-one-year-old John Muhammed and seventeen-year-old Lee Malvo terrorized the greater Washington area for three weeks with random fatal shootings of people at bus stops, gas stations, shopping centers, and schools. They killed thirteen people and injured three others before they were arrested on October 24. Because it was a local story for the *Post*, it did not interfere with the national and foreign staffs' focus on Iraq. But it was nearly all-consuming for me, just as it was for our frightened readers.

On February 1, 2003, the space shuttle *Columbia* disintegrated while entering the earth's atmosphere, killing all seven of its crew. Reporting on the disaster and the investigation of its cause (a piece of foam insulation broke off the shuttle's external fuel tank and struck its wing during reentry) put a strain on the national news staff. It also demanded my attention at a critical juncture in the run-up to the war.

Just five days after the shuttle disaster, Secretary of State Colin Powell made a lengthy multimedia presentation at the United Nations in New York. He said it would be a "compelling demonstration" that Saddam Hussein "is concealing the evidence of his weapons of mass destruction." I put the main news story on the front page, along with an accompanying article about Powell's unprecedented use of U.S. intelligence information.

Parts of that story, and several others displayed prominently inside the A section, reported skepticism by terrorism experts and European officials about the points Powell made. Those fact-checking stories raised important questions about the evidence Powell presented. But, again, neither they nor summary of them appeared on the front page. It was conventional at the time to put the news out front and analysis inside. That was another mistake in this instance.

Six weeks later, on March 16, as war appeared to be near, we published eight stories in our large-circulation Sunday newspaper examining the risks of an attack on Iraq. They included the military risks of the invasion plan, the political risks for Bush, the economic risks for the United States, the risks of instability in the Middle East, and the diplomatic risks of alienating European allies. The military and political stories were displayed on the front page. The rest were again packaged prominently inside the A section.

That package of stories included, on page A-17, a story that I realized later I should have put on the front page:

"Despite the Bush administration's claims about Iraq's weapons of mass destruction, U.S. intelligence agencies have been unable to give Congress or the Pentagon specific information about the amounts of banned weapons or where they are hidden," veteran reporter Walter Pincus wrote in that story. "The assertions, coming on the eve of a possible decision by President Bush to go to war against Iraq, have raised concerns among some members of the intelligence community about whether administration officials have exaggerated intelligence in a desire to convince the American public and foreign governments that Iraq is violating United Nations prohibitions against chemical, biological, or nuclear weapons and long-range missile systems."

Pincus, a dogged, irascible, then seventy-year-old reporter, had interviewed numerous intelligence analysts, government officials, and members of Congress, none of whom would speak on the record. Pincus was a former congressional investigator who had long covered intelligence and nuclear weapons issues with distinction for the *Post*. But he was not a clear writer; editing his stories could be time-consuming. This story apparently languished for days on a national news desk swamped with work.

Somehow, Pincus's story came to the attention of Bob Woodward. Woodward was doing reporting for both the *Post* and for his next book, *Plan of Attack*, about Bush and what turned out to be the beginning of the Iraq War. He told Pincus that his sources had similar doubts about the administration's claims. Woodward then talked to the national news editors and made sure that the story was published, albeit inside the paper. Both Pincus and Woodward later said that they wished they had appealed to me about putting the story on the front page. I do not remember talking to the national editors about the Pincus story or considering it for the front page. It should have been there, even though it relied on unnamed sources. By that time, the beginning of the war was only days away.

MORE THAN A YEAR LATER, AS THE AMERICAN OCCUPATION OF Iraq was going badly, and weapons of mass destruction were never found, questions were raised about the news media's prewar coverage.

On May 26, 2004, the *New York Times* published an article "from the editors" saying some of its reporting "was not as rigorous as it should have been." It cited articles that reported erroneous claims about Saddam Hussein possessing or seeking weapons of mass destruction, which were based on false information given to *Times* reporter Judy Miller by Iraqi exiles seeking to overthrow Saddam.

That prompted Michael Getler, then the *Post*'s ombudsman, or in-house critic, to review our prewar coverage. "My assessment is that the *Post* did not commit the sins of the *New York Times*," he wrote in his op-ed column published on June 20, 2004. "In fact, the *Post* had quite a few probing stories." But he concluded that too many of them "appeared inside the paper rather than on the front page."

The *Post*'s media reporter, Howard Kurtz, then independently reviewed our performance in an August 12, 2004, front-page story that was consistent with Getler's critique. In it, Kurtz quoted me telling him, "We were so focused on trying to figure out what the administration was doing that we were not giving the same play to people who said it wouldn't be a good idea to go to war and were questioning the administration's rationale. Not enough of those stories were on the front page. That was a mistake on my part."

I believe that President Bush was always determined after 9/11 to go to war in Iraq regardless of what the news media did. But that was not an excuse for my biggest mistakes as executive editor.

ON THE NIGHT OF MARCH 19, 2003, WE WATCHED ON TELEVISION in the newsroom the beginning of the U.S. bombing of Baghdad. By that time, the *Post* was ready to cover the invasion and what turned out to be the disastrous occupation of Iraq better than any other news organization. When the invasion began, we had one of the few American correspondents who stayed in Baghdad, nine reporters traveling with U.S. military units, five other reporters and two photographers roaming Iraq on their own, and seven reporters and photographers working from nearby countries, including bases for U.S. forces in neighboring Kuwait.

The architect of our war coverage was foreign news editor Philip Bennett, working with national news editor Liz Spayd. I encouraged them to select the best journalists from anywhere in the newsroom. Bennett, whom we hired in 1997, had been a foreign correspondent and foreign news editor, among other roles, at the *Boston Globe*. He was a soft-spoken, decisive, caring editor who worked tirelessly to put the right *Post* journalists in the most appropriate foreign assignments. He mentored them and, when necessary, closely monitored their safety.

Bennett began by pre-positioning *Post* correspondents in and around Iraq. In the autumn of 2002, he sent Rajiv Chandrasekaran, a brilliant, enterprising young *Post* reporter still in his twenties, from Jakarta, where he covered Southeast Asia to Baghdad. Bennett joined him in the Iraqi capital briefly in an unsuccessful attempt to get official permission to open a news bureau. Instead, Chandrasekaran was able to establish an outpost in Baghdad's Palestine Hotel, as well as a working relationship with the Iraqi officials who assigned him a minder to monitor his interviews with Iraqis.

In Washington, Torie Clarke, the assistant defense secretary for public affairs, contacted *Post* Pentagon reporter Tom Ricks to ask for "radical suggestions" about how the military could facilitate media coverage of an anticipated fast-moving war in Iraq. She said she would like to meet with me and senior editors who would direct the coverage.

Ricks told Clarke that we were "extremely skeptical" of the Pentagon's intentions. After many military leaders blamed the loss of the Vietnam War on critical reporting by American correspondents there, the Pentagon had repeatedly restricted news media access to the U.S. military during combat. It had just recently refused to allow reporters to contact American Special Forces in the war in Afghanistan.

Years earlier, the Pentagon censored dispatches from the limited number of correspondents allowed to accompany American troops during the short Persian Gulf War in 1991, when a U.S.-led coalition decisively beat back an Iraqi invasion of Kuwait. The Pentagon did not let the news media witness any of the fighting during the brief U.S. invasions of Grenada in 1983 and Panama in 1989. Reporters and photographers who tried to travel by boat to the island of Grenada were turned back or detained by the U.S. military. During the Panama invasion, journalists were grounded on planes in Miami and Costa Rica until the decisive first day of fighting had ended. I was among the news media executives in Washington and New York who repeatedly complained about all of this to the Pentagon over the years.

Clarke insisted that covering an Iraq war would be different. She said that news organizations could "embed" reporters with military units from the beginning, without restrictions on their coverage. Ricks suggested that the Pentagon provide chemical and biological warfare training for the journalists. He said they should then be assigned to units at their bases before deployment, meeting the commanders and learning how to file stories from the battlefield. That all made sense to me.

After consultation with knowledgeable *Post* editors and reporters, I sent Clarke a letter listing units of the Army, Air Force, and Marines with which we would want our reporters to embed. Clarke then met with us at the *Post* to discuss our suggestions. We emphasized that we also wanted the military to cooperate with and not harm any reporters covering the war independently of U.S. military units. Before the end of 2002, the Pentagon held several safety training sessions for likely embedded reporters and offered them protective gear and recommendations for vaccinations.

By the end of February 2003, eight *Post* reporters were designated to be embedded with various units of the U.S. Army, Marines, and Special Operations Command. Bennett also sent reporters and photographers to Kuwait, Jordan, Israel, Saudi Arabia, Egypt, Qatar, and Kurdish-held northern Iraq. Several of the *Post* journalists sent to Kuwait would later travel independently into Iraq in the wake of an invasion.

On February 24, Rajiv Chandrasekaran conducted a half-hour online chat from his hotel room in Baghdad with readers on the *Post*'s website, washingtonpost.com. He said that the city appeared calm, with people going about their daily business. He explained that it was difficult to have anyone talk frankly with him because of the presence of his government minder. It was an early use of our website to tell readers how we worked.

Chandrasekaran was soon joined in Baghdad by photographer Michael Robinson-Chavez and a new *Post* foreign correspondent familiar with the region, Anthony Shadid. Shadid was a second-generation Arab American who had studied Arabic at the American University in Cairo. He had earned a reputation as an outstanding correspondent in the Middle East for the Associated Press and the *Boston Globe*. Modest but self-confident, determined and fearless, Shadid dedicated himself to learning about and explaining Arab life to Americans. He could not have joined the *Post* at a better time.

Meanwhile, military units began contacting *Post* reporters about embedding with them. Rick Atkinson received an invitation from the 101st Airborne. The son of a U.S. Army infantry officer, Atkinson had grown up on military bases around the country and the world. He turned down an appointment to West Point to become a newspaper reporter and author. After winning a Pulitzer Prize at the *Kansas City Times*, he was hired onto the *Post*'s national news staff by assistant managing editor Peter Silberman while I was national editor in 1983. Over the next two decades, Atkinson would distinguish himself covering defense issues and politics, working as a foreign correspondent based in Berlin, and editing the investigative reporting team.

In 1989, Atkinson published a best-selling book, *The Long Gray Line*, about the tragic Vietnam War experiences of members of the West Point class of 1966, which expanded on stories he wrote while working in Kansas City. He helped cover the 1991 Persian Gulf War for the *Post* and wrote another best-selling book, *Crusade*, about that brief war. After the success of those books, Atkinson took an open-ended, multiyear leave of absence from the *Post* to research and write The Liberation Trilogy about the Allied armies' campaigns in North Africa and Europe during World War II. The first volume, *An Army at Dawn: The War in North Africa*, also became a best seller. Atkinson was researching the second volume, about the military campaigns in Sicily and Italy, when we asked him to help the *Post* cover the war in Iraq.

Ben Bradlee and I were generous about granting book leaves because the experience could professionally stretch our best journalists and keep them working for us longer. Atkinson, Bob Woodward, David Maraniss, and Dana Priest were among many *Post* journalists who stayed affiliated with the newspaper for years while writing books, some of them best sellers. Ben and I also wrote books ourselves.

Atkinson wanted to be assigned to the headquarters of the 101st Airborne Division, commanded by Major General David Petraeus. Atkinson had known Petraeus through his reporting since the time when Petraeus was a major working for the army chief of staff. It was a good example of what I often told reporters: news sources you develop early, at working levels of any institution, can become very important sources if they rise to the top. Atkinson's rapidly growing reputation as a military historian also helped him get the assignment he wanted.

By March 1, Atkinson was with Petraeus in Kuwait, where the 101st Airborne was staging with other American forces for the invasion of Iraq. On March 5, he sent a long, confidential e-mail to Phil Bennett, who shared it with me and with Steve Coll. Atkinson laid out the expected strategy for the invasion in authoritative detail. So many American troops were expected to be rapidly fighting their way north through the Euphrates River valley, Atkinson wrote, as only he could, that "traffic management up the valley is a big concern (reminds me of the attack on Rome in May 1944, with traffic causing huge headaches)."

In mid-March, with war obviously imminent, I discussed with Bennett and Coll whether Chandrasekaran, Shadid, and Robinson-Chavez should stay working in Baghdad when the invasion of Iraq began. Don Graham and Bo Jones told us that they were concerned about the journalists' safety. It was a particularly difficult decision for me. The story was important, but the safety of our journalists was paramount.

"At this point, we want to leave the decision in your hands, and to closely monitor when the moment for a decision might come," Bennett told the three of them in a March 14 e-mail. "But I want to alert you that the drift of opinion here is that you should leave. Don and Bo have made very clear to Len, Steve and me that this is their preference; they do not see costs to our coverage of leaving Baghdad that compare with the benefits of your safety."

The next day, Saturday, in an e-mail and a phone conversation with Bennett, Chandrasekaran said the three of them wanted to stay, based on their assessment of the risks, after talking to Iraqi officials. Bennett and Coll were impressed with their reasoning. I sent the exchange of messages to Don at home.

"I read the Baghdad email and think they're obviously doing their best to be rational about it," Don messaged me on Sunday. "Trouble is—this is one where there's not much information to gather. Where will bombs drop? Where's a good place not to get in a crossfire? You can't know. . . . I don't envy you the choice, and I'm not going to make it for you. But correspondents will be killed this time."

Bennett, Coll, and I reviewed how well positioned we would be to cover the invasion—with *Post* reporters embedded with U.S. military units, others ready to follow them into Iraq as soon as it became safe, and still others at the headquarters of the invasion force in Kuwait. We did not need to risk the lives of the three in Baghdad. We decided that Bennett should tell Chandrasekaran, Shadid, and Robinson-Chavez to leave Baghdad as soon as possible. Robinson-Chavez went to Jordan. Chandrasekaran went to the American military's headquarters in Kuwait, where he would write daily front-page overview stories about the invasion, with contributions from the *Post* reporters in the field.

But Shadid telephoned Bennett at 3 a.m. Washington time on Wednesday, March 19, to say he would not leave Baghdad, where he was staying in a downtown hotel. "I'm basically begging you to let me stay," he told Bennett. He described precautions he had taken, and he emphasized how important he thought this war would be for the Middle East. "I know you might fire me, but I'm not leaving," he said. "I've been preparing for this my entire career. Please let me do this."

Shadid had taken the decision out of our hands. I was worried about his safety, but I was also impressed by his bravery and sense of duty as a journalist. Getting the story, getting it right, and making a difference were his mission.

19

Iraq

HE INVASION OF IRAQ BEGAN WITH A U.S. cruise missile bombing attack on Baghdad at 9:34 p.m. in Washington that Wednesday night. It was early morning on March 20, 2003, in Iraq.

"At 5:34 a.m., explosions thundered over a city still asleep," Shadid wrote in an eyewitness story displayed on the *Post*'s front page. "The attack caught Baghdad's defenders by surprise: A minute passed before air raid sirens began to wail, and more time before the answer of antiaircraft fire. For the next hour, long pauses were interrupted by tracer bullets racing across the sky and more antiaircraft rounds."

As bombing continued in the days ahead, Shadid roamed Baghdad to tell our readers intimate stories about the struggle for survival of ordinary Iraqis. In one middle-class home, he found a family huddling in fear as cruise missiles exploding nearby shook their house. "We're in a dark, dark tunnel," one of the women in the house told him, "and we don't see the light at the end of it." Shadid wrote about the burial of a fourteen-year-old boy killed in the bombing and about a mother sending her son off to war. He reported the mixed feelings that many Iraqis had about both the Saddam Hussein regime and the invading Americans.

U.S. and British ground forces poured into southern Iraq from Kuwait on March 21. *Post* correspondents were embedded with the three largest American forces, along with other units. Bill Branigin, a taciturn but acutely observant and smooth-writing veteran of conflicts all over the world, was traveling with the Army's 3rd Infantry Division. Peter Baker, who had covered Bill Clinton's presidency and impeachment from the White House in the 1990s, was with the commanders of the Marines' 1st Expeditionary Force. Atkinson was with Petraeus and the 101st Airborne. The mission of what was called "Operation Iraqi Freedom" was to fight as rapidly as possible northward to Baghdad and "decapitate" Saddam Hussein's three-decade-old regime.

I had gone online from my office computer at noon Washington time on March 20 to answer readers' questions about how we would cover the war. In this time before social media, I often used washingtonpost.com online chats to be as transparent as possible about how we produced our journalism. In this chat, I explained that "reporters embedded with American forces are acting only as journalists and will not be engaging in any military activities."

I also emphasized that the reporting from our embedded journalists would not be dictated or censored by the military units with which they were traveling. At the same time, I told questioning readers, "we take seriously our responsibility not to harm national security or the operational safety of American forces. We have voluntarily withheld from publication so far details of current military operations that would compromise the element of surprise. We will report those details once the military action is completed."

I explained once again that our news coverage would not be affected by the *Post* editorial page's strong support for the war. Nor would it be influenced by Bush administration's assertions that the war would be over quickly, that American forces would be welcomed by the Iraqi people, or that the ensuing occupation would be peaceful. Our job was to report what really happened, not just what the administration claimed was happening. Our independence became clear just days into the invasion.

After an initially rapid advance, the American forces became stalled by the supply chain traffic jam that Atkinson had warned about, by pockets of surprisingly fierce Iraqi resistance, and by a debilitating three-day desert dust storm.

Post reporter Mary Beth Sheridan was embedded in central Iraq with the Army's 11th Aviation Regiment, which flew Apache Longbow attack helicopters to attack Iraqi tanks and other armored vehicles. She reported on March 26 that U.S. officers had to devise "new tactics to counter Iraqi fighters" who had driven off about thirty attacking Apaches "with low-tech anti-aircraft, rifle and rocket-propelled grenade fire." One of the Apaches was shot down, and its two-man crew was captured.

From the command encampment of the 101st Airborne during the dust storm, Atkinson collaborated the next day by satellite phone with the *Post*'s authoritative Pentagon correspondent Tom Ricks in Washington about concerns they were hearing from senior military commanders. They wrote that their sources doubted that the relatively small invasion force—less than half the size of the force that easily defeated the Iraqis in the 1991 Persian Gulf War—could accomplish its goal of swiftly ousting Saddam Hussein. They said that some of the military commanders "even see the potential threat of a drawn-out fight that sucks in more and more U.S. forces."

When Baghdad fell to the invaders in thirteen days, some media critics questioned that and other *Post* stories "suggesting that the Pentagon's strategy was a mess," as one wrote. But in the long run, our stories proved prophetic. What they reported about the military commanders' concerns about the U.S. strategy and force strength foreshadowed the failures of the ensuing occupation that would prolong American military involvement in Iraq for the next seventeen years and counting.

Embedded *Post* reporters repeatedly demonstrated both their independence and the value of their being eyewitnesses to the fighting. Their best stories put our readers right with the troops on the ground.

One example was Bill Branigin's March 31 eyewitness story of the killing by 3rd Infantry soldiers of seven women and children in a vehicle speeding toward troops in Bradley Fighting Vehicles at an intersection near Karbala, southwest of Baghdad. The Pentagon later issued a statement saying the driver ignored warning shots, which was not true.

Branigin reported that soldiers in the Fighting Vehicles ignored their commander's radioed order to fire warning shots before shooting at the oncoming vehicle.

"'Cease fire!' [Captain Ronny] Johnson yelled over the radio," Branigin wrote. "Then, as he peered into his binoculars from the intersection on Highway 9, he roared at the platoon leader, 'You just [expletive] killed a family because you didn't fire a warning shot soon enough.'"

The *Post's* non-embedded reporters did significant work on their own, often under even more risky and uncomfortable circumstances. They also somehow kept their good humor. In an April 1 e-mail to the foreign news editors from southern Iraq, where he was covering heavy fighting around Basra, Keith Richburg wrote that he was sleeping "under the highway overpass, outside Basra airport."

"If arranging a re-supply," he told his editors, "may I request two cases of Sam Adams beer, chilled, and a tenderloin steak, rare, with fresh veggies on the side? And how about a shower and shave? Okay, it's April fool—I can dream, can't I? Cheers."

BACK AT THE COMMAND ENCAMPMENT OF THE 101ST AIRBORNE, still on the road to Karbala, Rick Atkinson had just finished transmitting a story from the public affairs tent. It was 11:30 p.m. local time on Friday, April 4. He was ready to call it a day when he received an e-mail asking him to call the foreign news desk in Washington, where it was still afternoon. As Atkinson later recounted, "Swearing vividly at the intrusion into my sleeping time, I rigged the satellite phone, dialed the number, and was immediately put on hold."

Then I came on the line.

"We didn't know when we'd be able to get hold of you," I told Atkinson. "But we wanted to tell you that *An Army at Dawn* has won the Pulitzer Prize for history."

Not since Katharine Graham's memoir *Personal History* won the Pulitzer for biography in 1998 had I been so happy about a book being so honored. When it was publicly announced on the following Monday afternoon, we were able to reach Atkinson again on his satellite phone.

His voice was broadcast throughout the newsroom, as we celebrated his prize and two others won by *Post* journalists for work in the newspaper, one for movie criticism and the other for foreign reporting from Mexico.

WHEN AMERICAN TROOPS MOVED INTO BAGHDAD ON APRIL 8, the day before Saddam Hussein's regime collapsed completely, *Post* reporters produced for the April 9 newspaper perhaps the best single day of vivid stories taking American readers there.

Among them was an eyewitness account that Branigin wrote, about a bloody firefight between Bravo Company troops of the 3rd Infantry Division and Iraqi defenders at a key intersection in the heart of Baghdad. On their way there, "the Bravo company drove past dozens of burned-out Iraqi vehicles and charred bodies on the way to downtown Baghdad," Branigin wrote. "Civilian cars and trucks were among the blasted vehicles, some with corpses inside. One blackened body lay beside the wreckage of a motorcycle. Whether they were fighters heading south to engage the Americans or luckless citizens trying to escape the city remained unknown."

Shadid, who produced twenty-four front-page stories during the three-week war, described a bomb crater in western Baghdad where, "in the rubble, was the mauled torso of 20-year-old Lava Jamal. Moments later, a few feet away, they found what was left of her head, her brown hair matted with blood. They put both in white blankets trimmed with blue and left them against a nearby wall, where flies soon gathered. Sitting in a chair down the road, her mother cried uncontrollably into her hands, and then vomited."

The next day, Shadid described Iraqis celebrating in the streets as U.S. forces took control of Baghdad; Saddam Hussein, his family, and functionaries disappeared. But he also reported that there was no electricity or telephone service. And in conversations with Shadid, Iraqis shared their fears of either a long American occupation or a brutal takeover by the Shiite majority that had been disenfranchised and abused during Saddam's Baathist Party Sunni-minority rule.

Rajiv Chandrasekaran wasted no time hurrying back to Baghdad. He rode into the city with other American journalists in a two-car caravan from Kuwait on April 9. In Baghdad, with Bennett's and my approval, he set up a new *Post* news bureau in a downtown hotel where he and Shadid were joined by Sheridan, Branigin, and other *Post* embeds, now free of their military unit assignments. In a city without electricity, they worked at night by candlelight, and they slept two to a bed and on the floors.

As the founding bureau chief, Chandrasekaran moved the bureau as soon as he could to a large rented house in a gated compound in what had been an upscale Baghdad neighborhood. It was near the so-called Green Zone, the heavily fortified four-square-mile headquarters of the American occupation in palaces and villas seized from the leadership of the old Iraqi regime. The house had a courtyard, garden, and swimming pool. Chandrasekaran somehow managed to acquire a huge generator for electricity, along with the necessary technology, including a satellite internet connection. He even found a treadmill for reporter Jackie Spinner, who was a runner back home.

Chandrasekaran hired willing Iraqis whom he and Shadid had met in Baghdad to staff the bureau as interpreters, technicians, drivers, security guards, and even sometime reporters who ventured into places that became too dangerous for Americans. One of them was Chandrasekaran's Iraqi government minder before the invasion. One of the bureau's drivers had been an Iraqi jet fighter pilot. A former Iraqi Airways engineering director who began as a bureau interpreter evolved into a "fixer" who found story ideas and set up interviews, before he eventually reported his own stories published in the *Post*. A Muslim woman hired as an interpreter enabled the bureau's correspondents to interview Iraqi women who would never have talked to a man. Chandrasekaran found and hired a talented chef, who scoured local markets for the ingredients for three-course meals each evening.

Bennett, who visited the bureau, said it resembled a successfully functioning "start-up business." With Don Graham's backing, I authorized Bennett and Chandrasekaran to spend whatever was necessary to pay the salaries of the local staff, to ensure the best possible working and living conditions for *Post* journalists, and to protect everyone's safety.

On May 1, 2003, President Bush announced, from an aircraft carrier off the coast of California, that the U.S. mission in Iraq had been accomplished. But despite the American military occupation, Baghdad and the rest of Iraq were steadily descending into postinvasion lawlessness, including factional civil war and insurgent attacks on American forces. It became increasingly dangerous for both the Americans and Iraqis in our bureau.

Chandrasekaran hired a British private security contractor who, among other things, outfitted the bureau's guards with reliable firearms. *Post* correspondents were driven to assignments in cars with armed guards, sometimes accompanied by another car with another armed guard.

To better protect them, the *Post* bought two $90,000 silver Jeep Cherokee SUVs with lead plates in their doors and baseboards to protect against AK-47 bullets and roadside explosives. When the bureau's no-nonsense Iraqi security chief realized that American contractors for the occupation were driving similar SUVs, he sent the bureau's vehicles to a body shop to be visually transformed. One had "Flower of Lebanon Taxi" painted on it; the other had swoosh decals adorning its sandblasted exterior, carpet covering the dashboard, and fuzzy dice hanging from the rearview mirror.

Chandrasekaran required that everyone who worked there, Americans and Iraqis, check in with him regularly whenever they were away from the bureau or the Iraqis' homes. Although just thirty years old when he set up the bureau, Chandrasekaran became a kind of father figure and stern taskmaster. He established strict house rules and created safety handbooks. With teasing respect, the Iraqi staff called him "Little Saddam." Most of the dozens of *Post* reporters, editors, and photographers who came through the bureau during his time there found him to be nurturing, and the bureau to be a welcoming haven in the war-torn country.

While the entire *Post* bureau led the way in American news media coverage of what was happening in Iraq, Chandrasekaran and Shadid were its stars. Chandrasekaran reported authoritatively about the missteps of the military occupation's mismanaged Coalition Provisional Authority as it dismantled the old regime's bureaucracy, military, and law enforcement agencies.

Shadid chronicled the first signs of a religious and political awakening among Iraq's Shiite majority, foreshadowing sectarian strife to come. At great risk to himself, he revealed growing anti-American sentiment among ordinary Iraqis. In an emotional story he later described as "the most difficult to report in his career," he interviewed an Iraqi father who executed a son accused of being an informant for the Americans.

Post Pentagon reporter Tom Ricks went to Baghdad and reported with Chandrasekaran a seminal July 7, 2003, story about the rising Iraqi insurgency, which contradicted the expressed optimism of the Bush administration. "Recent Iraqi attacks on U.S. troops have demonstrated a new tactical sophistication and coordination that raise the specter of the U.S. occupation force becoming enmeshed in a full-blown guerrilla war," they wrote. "Officials and experts are debating whether the war is expanding geographically and demographically, from just Sunnis and (Saddam) Hussein's Baath Party diehards to others, such as Shiites and Islamic extremists and the average Iraqi on the street."

In February 2004, a bomb exploded in front of the Baghdad home of one of the bureau's Iraqi translators. That same day, someone in a car driven slowly past the *Post*'s bureau house took photos of it. The bureau had become a target. Chandrasekaran and the staff moved everything they could to a floor of the Sheraton Ishtar Hotel, which was protected by concrete barriers, a U.S. military guard post, and a perimeter, within which unauthorized vehicles were not permitted.

Anthony Shadid was working on a story in the bureau at the Sheraton just past midnight on April 6, Iraq time, when we reached him by telephone. We were calling from the newsroom in celebration of his winning the 2004 Pulitzer Prize for international reporting. The phone line from Baghdad crackled with static, but we could hear on the newsroom speakers Shadid's characteristic response to our congratulations and praise. "I've had four hours of sleep and ten cups of coffee and I was trying to figure out my lead," he said about the top of the story. "Then a bomb went off outside my window. Just another day in Baghdad."

As conditions in Iraq became increasingly chaotic and dangerous in the continuing war, several *Post* journalists had close calls. Dan Williams, an experienced war correspondent, ventured inside the city of Fallujah, forty miles west of Baghdad on the Euphrates River, to report on the ongoing bloody battle between insurgents and American troops there. On the way back to Baghdad, the bureau's armor-plated SUV, in which Williams and his driver were traveling, was attacked by gunmen in another vehicle who fired dozens of bullets from AK-47 assault rifles. The SUV spun out before the driver regained control, but its armor successfully protected them.

A week later, Jackie Spinner was returning to a bureau car from an interview at the notorious Abu Ghraib prison near Baghdad, where U.S. forces held several thousand suspected Iraqi insurgents, when a man tried to kidnap her. She was rescued by U.S. Marines who happened to be passing by and heard her screams.

Post reporter Steve Fainaru was riding in an armored Humvee in a U.S. military convoy when a roadside bomb killed four Iraqi National Guard soldiers in a pickup truck right in front of his vehicle. The Humvee's armor saved his life.

We rotated dozens of *Post* journalists through the Baghdad bureau for limited stays because of the danger, stress, long hours, poor living conditions, and distance from their families. They volunteered from throughout the *Post* newsroom. Many of them were in Iraq only for months at a time. Exceptions included Shadid, who was there on and off for years, and Chandrasekaran, who stayed eighteen months as bureau chief. Volunteers were carefully screened by the foreign news editors to determine whether they could hold up under the strain and keep themselves safe. We contracted with a company that offered each of them psychological counseling on their return, focusing on the challenges of reentry into "civilian" life.

I worried more and more about the risk of attacks on and the kidnapping of journalists in Iraq and elsewhere in the Middle East and South Asia. My gravest responsibility as executive editor was to chair an on-call committee that we formed to respond to the kidnapping of any of our staff anywhere in the world. The group included the *Post*'s publisher, general counsel, and financial vice president, plus an experienced outside terrorism consultant. We also had a State Department contact. We carried cards in our wallets with information on how to contact each other in an emergency. I'm still thankful that we never needed to use them.

Beginning immediately after the invasion, we attended to unfinished business from the Bush administration's rush to war. We aggressively addressed issues that were shortchanged in the run-up to the war.

Bart Gellman, who had been covering national security issues since 9/11, went to Iraq with U.S. investigators looking for any evidence that Saddam Hussein had weapons of mass destruction and was developing a nuclear capability. Over months of unmatched reporting from there and back in Washington, Gellman showed conclusively that the Bush administration's primary justification for the invasion of Iraq was simply not true.

In a May 11, 2003, story on the *Post*'s front page, Gellman detailed the fruitless extensive search by the U.S. 75th Exploitation Task Force throughout Iraq for any evidence of what Secretary of State Colin Powell had claimed in his address to the United Nations Security Council on February 5—that Saddam had tons of biological and chemical weapons and a program to build a nuclear bomb. Military leaders of the large U.S. task force of Special Forces troops, biologists, chemists, and arms control and other experts told Gellman that they searched dozens of suspected sites and found nothing.

A week later, Gellman described accompanying one of the four Site Survey Teams as it broke into a locked warehouse searching for biological and chemical weapons. They found vacuum cleaners. Gellman wrote that the twenty-five-person team also "dug up a playground, raided a distillery, seized a research paper from a failing graduate student and laid bare a swimming pool where an underground chemical weapons stash was supposed to be." Gellman reported that the team's "odyssey through Iraq is a tale of frustration and disillusionment."

In June, Gellman revealed that a covert Army Special Forces Unit, Task Force 20, had also been secretly searching for weapons of mass destruction in Iraq since before the invasion. Sources with knowledge of its mission and access to its reports, Gellman wrote, "said the team has found no working nonconventional munitions, long-range missiles or missile parts, bulk stores of chemical or biological warfare agents or enrichment technology for the core of a nuclear weapon."

Gellman and Walter Pincus then interviewed officials and analysts in and outside the government and reviewed internal documents about what the administration knew about any purported Iraqi nuclear weapons program before the war. They found a pattern "in which President Bush, Vice President Cheney and their subordinates—in public and behind the scenes—made allegations depicting Iraq's nuclear weapons program as more active, more certain and more imminent in its threat than the data they had would support." Gellman and Pincus wrote in their August 10 story that "on occasion administration advocates withheld evidence that did not conform to their views."

On October 26, Gellman reported, from records and interviews with international arms inspectors, that "although Hussein did not relinquish his nuclear ambitions . . . it is now clear he had no active program to build a weapon, produce key materials or obtain the technology he needed for either."

Gellman's work was definitive. At the time of the invasion of Iraq, Saddam Hussein did not possess nor was he developing weapons of mass destruction. The weapons had been destroyed and programs to develop them abandoned after the 1991 Persian Gulf War. We were unable to produce that journalism before the Iraq War, but we led the way in doing it afterward.

ON WEDNESDAY NIGHT, APRIL 28, 2004, THE CBS NEWS MAGA-zine program *60 Minutes II* broadcast horrifying photographs of U.S. military police gleefully posing next to naked, hooded Iraqi prisoners inside the Abu Ghraib prison twenty miles west of Baghdad. Days later, *The New Yorker* magazine posted online a story by Seymour Hersh about a U.S. military report of "numerous incidents of sadistic, blatant and wanton criminal abuses" of Iraqi prisoners by U.S. military personnel at Abu Ghraib between October and December 2003.

We covered the television and magazine revelations on the front page, along with some of the photographs. Then an enterprising young *Post* reporter obtained from a confidential source other photographs of the prisoner abuse taken by a member of the military at Abu Ghraib. On May 6, we published some of those that had not appeared elsewhere, including one showing Pfc. Lynndie England holding a dog leash connected to the neck of an Iraqi prisoner. It was the first of a series of exclusive *Post* reports about the scandal.

We published on May 9, 10, and 11 a hastily put-together series of stories by *Post* reporters, including some by Dana Priest, who had been investigating U.S. detention and interrogation of suspects around the world in the Bush administration's war on terror. Labeled "The Road to Abu Ghraib," the stories put the scandal into the context of what the reporters had been finding.

Priest and reporter Joe Stephens wrote that Abu Ghraib "is just the largest and suddenly most notorious in a worldwide constellation of detention centers—many of them secret and all off-limits to public scrutiny—that the U.S. military and CIA have operated in the name of counterterrorism or counterinsurgency operations since the Sept. 11, 2001, attacks."

In mid-May, a *Post* reporter obtained sixty-five pages of sworn statements by thirteen abused Abu Ghraib detainees and more than a thousand photographs and videotapes that were part of the evidence assembled by U.S. Army investigators prosecuting seven military police officers for brutalizing the prisoners. The statements were in handwritten Arabic, accompanied by typed translations into English. All the photos and videos had been shot by the MPs with their own digital cameras, recording their staged abuse of the detainees and some of their own consensual sexual acts.

A story on the *Post*'s May 21 front page reported that the Iraqi Muslim detainees "said they were savagely beaten and repeatedly humiliated sexually by American soldiers working on the night shift at Tier 1A in Abu Ghraib during the holy month of Ramadan." They described being kept naked for days at a time, forced to wear hoods over their heads, molested sexually, threatened by unmuzzled dogs, tortured in various ways, and ordered to pose, often naked, for humiliating photographs and videos.

We posted the detainees' sworn statements on washingtonpost.com, with a warning about their explicit content. We withheld the name of a detainee who described being sexually assaulted, consistent with *Post* policy not to identify victims of sexual assaults.

Some of the newly obtained photographs were published in the newspaper, including on the front page. Many more were posted on our website, with a warning about their content. We also posted one of the videos, showing soldiers "attempting to arrange a human pyramid with naked Iraqi prisoners."

I went online at washingtonpost.com at noon that day to discuss my decision to make public the detainees' statements and the photographs and video. I said that they showed "even more extensive and repulsive kinds of abuse than we had previously reported." I described how Steve Coll and I decided which images to publish and put online after consulting other senior editors and our photo editors. I said that we did not publish in the paper, or post online, scores of other images of naked Iraqi detainees being abused because of our concern for their dignity. We also cropped some of the pictures we did publish to minimize nudity and avoid identifiable faces.

Abu Ghraib became a dominant story in the news media during the summer of 2004. In late August, the Pentagon released investigative reports that implicated nearly fifty military police and intelligence officers in the abuse and torture. They concluded that faulty planning for the occupation of Iraq and breakdowns in the U.S. military leadership there also were to blame.

The scandal coincided with the June 28 transfer of political authority from U.S. occupation to an interim Iraqi government. More than 130,000 American troops remained in the country and retained the authority to conduct combat operations against the expanding insurgency and to detain Iraqis.

Chandrasekaran told *Post* readers at the time that the occupation "had failed to fulfill many of its goals and stated promises intended to transform the country into a stable democracy." Despite many millions spent by occupation authorities and American contractors on various recovery projects around the country, he wrote, "Iraqis continue to endure blackouts, lengthy gas lines, rampant unemployment," while "assassinations of Iraqi political leaders and debilitating sabotage of the country's oil and electricity infrastructure now occur routinely." Meanwhile, American civilians there "now face such mortal danger that they are largely confined to compounds surrounded by concrete walls topped with razor wire."

In September, before he left Baghdad, Chandrasekaran obtained from Kroll Security International, a private security firm working for the U.S. government in Iraq, its daily reports showing an average of seventy attacks a day by insurgents and other Iraqis against American troops, Iraqi security forces, and private contractors throughout Iraq. His front-page story contradicted assurances days earlier by Iraqi prime minister Ayad Allawi, at the White House and at a luncheon with *Post* editors and reporters, that his country was becoming safer.

AS THE WAR IN IRAQ DRAGGED ON AND THE DANGERS FOR AMERican and Iraqi journalists increased, many American news organizations pulled out. We maintained our Baghdad bureau, although it had to move again for security. Ellen Knickmeyer, its new bureau chief, and the other reporters bravely reported the violence that had overtaken the country. Countless assassinations, kidnappings, and car bombings occurred every day. Sunni insurgents and Kurdish and Shiite militias fought for control of neighborhoods, cities, and regions across the country. Embattled U.S. military forces found themselves caught frustratingly in the middle and under fire from all sides.

Steve Fainaru, one of the *Post*'s most meticulous reporters and engaging writers, volunteered to travel with typical army troops to see the war through their eyes. He spent much of 2005 with the 5th Battalion of the 7th Cavalry and Iraqi government troops they were supporting, and he produced what Phil Bennett later called "simply the most intimate and true journalism I've ever seen about what it means to be a soldier in Iraq."

"The physical and emotional toll of prosecuting the war in Iraq was vividly apparent in interviews, personal diaries written by the soldiers, and even songs they recorded in makeshift barracks studios," Fainaru wrote after being on patrol with the 3rd Platoon of Charlie Company of the 5th Battalion. "Weighted down by 50 pounds of body armor and ammunition, the soldiers venture out every day in 120-degree heat to find the insurgents. More often than not, they never do, even after bombs explode directly on them, a source of endless frustration compounded by what the soldiers said is the unwillingness of most Iraqis to help them."

Fainaru wrote about the drowning of four members of the platoon when their Humvee rolled into a canal, about roadside bomb attacks that destroyed other Humvees and claimed three more lives, and about how the platoon's request for a minesweeper was denied by superiors because of greater needs elsewhere. He gave readers vivid eyewitness narratives of military violence and intervening tedium, populated by soldiers who came to life—and died—on the newspaper page.

Fainaru had come to the *Post* from the *Boston Globe*, where he covered the Boston Red Sox, Wall Street, and Latin America. At the *Post*, he did investigative reporting on the sports staff and wrote about civil liberties issues and the war against terrorism before spending large parts of several years in Iraq. Many of the stories he pursued were his own ideas. It was a good example of the kind of journalistic freedom that my editors and I gave *Post* journalists, like Fainaru, who demonstrated talent and initiative.

In 2007, Fainaru went back to Iraq to investigate shootings of Iraqi citizens by private security contractors working for the U.S. military and State Department there. He found that tens of thousands of armed contractors employed by more than one hundred private security companies operated outside of Iraqi law and without meaningful U.S. oversight. Making up for chronic U.S. troop shortages in Iraq, they were hired to protect American diplomats, military installations, and supply lines, as well as convoys carrying materials for reconstruction projects and vehicles, weapons, and ammunition for the newly formed Iraqi military and police.

These contractors became deeply involved in their own shooting war. Fainaru wrote in a June 16 front-page story that "private security companies, funded by billions of dollars in U.S. military and State Department contracts, are fighting insurgents on a widening scale in Iraq, returning fire and taking casualties that have been underreported and sometimes concealed."

He rode with four Crescent Security Group contractors guarding a mile-long convoy of thirty-seven tractor-trailer trucks in southern Iraq, just two weeks before the convoy was ambushed, and the contractors were kidnapped and disappeared. Fainaru found that the security company employing them had routinely sacrificed safety to cut costs while being paid millions of dollars by the U.S. government. His moving account of conversations with them about their lives humanized his investigation.

After the killing of seventeen Iraqi civilians by Blackwater company contractors at a Baghdad traffic circle on September 16, Fainaru interviewed former Blackwater guards, other security company employees, and U.S. officials to report that "most of the more than 100 private security companies in Iraq open fire more frequently than has been publicly acknowledged and rarely report such incidents to U.S. or Iraqi authorities." Fainaru investigated several fatal shootings by contractors to show how they "operate in a lawless void in Iraq, with many shooting incidents escaping official or public scrutiny."

In April 2008, Fainaru won the Pulitzer Prize for international reporting for his investigation of the security contractors' private war in Iraq. It was the same month in which he wrote that the body of the last of the four Crescent Security contractors he had ridden with, twenty-five-year-old Jonathon Cote, was finally found in Iraq, near Basra, where their convoy had been attacked.

BY THEN, NEARLY ONE HUNDRED *POST* REPORTERS, PHOTOGRAphers, columnists, and editors had worked in Iraq for varying periods of time—four times the number of *Post* journalists who went to Vietnam to cover the war there. They were supported by the more than thirty Iraqi bureau employees, who risked their own lives just by working for an American news organization in the bureau or as drivers and security guards.

In October 2007, we lost one of our Iraqi colleagues, Salih Saif Aldin, who fearlessly reported for the bureau in places that became too dangerous for Americans. While on assignment in the Baghdad neighborhood of Sadiyah, he was shot and killed. I never met him, but he had been part of our family. We mourned him at the *Post*.

Most of what Americans knew about the war came from the work of *Washington Post* journalists and those with the other news organizations that maintained a continuous presence in Iraq. *Post* journalists reported from inside Iraqi neighborhoods, homes, shops, schools, hospitals, and morgues. They traveled the country with American troops and on their own. Their work was physically unpleasant, psychologically testing, and, too often, life-threatening. Their reporting often contradicted what was being said by American officials inside the insulated Green Zone in Baghdad and in Washington, and it stood up against criticism from the administration and supporters of the war. *Post* journalists got it right.

From the top of the *Post* newsroom pyramid, I was far removed from our journalists on the ground in Iraq. But I took pride in my role in approving the hiring of most of them, putting their amazing editors in place, and making it possible for all of them to do such outstanding work. I oversaw all the coverage, and I made key decisions when necessary. Morale in the newsroom was high, despite the demands of the story on nearly every corner of it. We were proud of our work.

As in Afghanistan, U.S. military involvement in Iraq long outlasted my time as executive editor of the *Post*, which ended when I retired in October 2008. I tried during the nearly five years that I oversaw our coverage to avoid forming an opinion about the war. But it became more and more obvious that our reporting in Iraq and Washington showed factually that the war and the occupation were ill-conceived, badly prepared for, and poorly executed by the White House and the Pentagon, despite the valiant efforts of the troops on the ground and their initial success in ending Saddam Hussein's Baathist regime.

20

Woodward and Plame

ON THE MORNING OF NOVEMBER 16, 2005, television reporters and cameras were clustered on the sidewalk in front of Bob Woodward's Victorian-style home in Georgetown when I drove up, parked in the driveway, and walked to his front door. Although I had done my share of television interviews over the years, no one in the media stakeout recognized me, which was just as well. I was there to have a serious conversation with Woodward.

The *Post*'s front page that morning revealed that Woodward had testified under oath in a federal investigation of whether Bush administration officials had illegally leaked the identity of a CIA undercover officer named Valerie Plame. In a closed-door deposition at a Washington law firm two days earlier, Woodward was questioned by Special Counsel Patrick J. Fitzgerald about what a senior Bush administration official had told him about Plame and her husband, former ambassador Joseph Wilson.

On July 14, 2003, in the *Washington Post* and other newspapers, syndicated columnist Robert Novak had publicly identified Plame, who worked on weapons of mass destruction issues for the agency, as having suggested that the CIA send Wilson to the African country of Niger in February 2002. Wilson, who had experience in Africa as a diplomat, was asked to investigate intelligence reports cited by the Bush administration that Iraq was attempting to buy "yellowcake"—raw uranium—from Niger. The CIA did send Wilson, who determined that Niger had made no such deal with Iraq.

When no evidence of an ongoing nuclear weapons program was found in Iraq after the 2003 invasion, Wilson described his 2002 Niger trip in news media interviews and a *New York Times* op-ed column on July 6, 2003. Wilson wrote in the *Times*: "I have little choice but to conclude that some of the intelligence related to Iraq's nuclear weapons program was twisted to exaggerate the Iraqi threat" before the war.

Special Counsel Fitzgerald was appointed by the U.S. Justice Department at the end of 2003 to investigate whether Bush administration officials, seeking to discredit Wilson's findings, had told Novak (and other reporters in Washington) that Plame improperly suggested her husband's Niger assignment. White House proponents of the Iraq War felt undercut by skepticism inside the CIA and the State Department, where Wilson had worked as a diplomat, about the administration's justification for invading Iraq. For a government official, revealing the name of a CIA undercover officer would be an illegal disclosure of classified information, a felony.

In his deposition, Woodward told Fitzgerald that a senior Bush administration official mentioned Wilson's wife and her position at the CIA, without naming her, in a mid-June 2003 interview with Woodward. That was a month before Novak publicly identified Plame by name in his July 14 column. Woodward said that it had come up "casually" and briefly, as "banter," in the ninety-minute interview with the official, who was a confidential source for Woodward's book, *Plan of Attack*, about what led to the Iraq War.

The problem for me—and for the *Washington Post*—was that Woodward had not told me about that interview with his confidential source during nearly two years of the Fitzgerald investigation, even though two other *Post* reporters had been caught up in the inquiry. Woodward did not come to me until late October 2005, when Fitzgerald indicted Lewis "Scooter" Libby, Vice President Dick Cheney's chief of staff, for perjury and obstruction of justice during the investigation. Woodward told me that when he read the Libby indictment, he realized the significance of the date of his interview with the official, in which the role and CIA employment of Wilson's wife had come up. He then contacted his source and me.

As Woodward knew, *Post* reporters Walter Pincus and Glenn Kessler, publisher Bo Jones, our lawyers, and I had endured months of difficult legal negotiations in 2004 when Fitzgerald sought information from the two reporters' 2003 confidential interviews with officials who were under investigation. Now, in two tense weeks, the *Post*'s lawyers and I had worked out a way for Woodward to be deposed by Fitzgerald without publicly revealing his confidential source.

I waited until after his deposition to question Woodward about keeping me in the dark for so long. Once Fitzgerald's investigation began, Woodward should have told me about his interview with the confidential source for his book, in which the CIA employment of Wilson's wife had come up. He could see how the investigation could threaten such crucial confidential source relationships.

For the first time that I could remember, I was angry with Woodward rather than just bemused by his occasional self-serving evasions while juggling his reporting for the *Post* and his best-selling books. He had watched what Pincus and Kessler had gone through, and the rest of us along with them, without saying a word about what he knew. Woodward also saw Judy Miller of the *New York Times* spend eighty-five days in jail for refusing to discuss her conversations with Libby before he personally released her from their confidential source agreement.

Woodward was aware of what a looming issue the Plame investigation had become for the principle that journalists protect confidential source relationships, a principle on which Woodward had depended during his entire career. He also knew that he had seriously violated the Bradlee-Downie "no surprises" rule. After our more than three decades of working together, he had let me down.

Woodward was prepared that morning for our conversation, which took place over bagels and orange juice at his dining room table. He insisted that he had told Walter Pincus at the time about what his confidential source had said about Wilson's wife, even though Pincus did not remember it. Once Fitzgerald's investigation began, Woodward said, he didn't tell me about his confidential source interview "because I did not want to get subpoenaed, and I thought what the source said was trivial. It was clear to me at the time that it was just banter."

"I was focused on the reporting I was doing for the book and getting the book done," Woodward said as I took notes. "I didn't want to get dragged into the investigation. Other reporters were being subpoenaed. The investigation had created an atmosphere that could make it more difficult for me to conduct confidential source interviews for my book. And I wanted to protect a source who was giving me valuable information for later use in the book and the newspaper."

"I owe you an apology," he told me with what I believed to be sincerity. "I should have told you sooner. It was a breakdown in communication, and I'm sorry."

The headline on the *Post*'s front-page story the next morning about our meeting was "Woodward Apologizes to *Post* for Silence on Role in Leak Case." Woodward "made a mistake," I told our news media reporter, Howard Kurtz, who wrote the story. "He still should have come forward, which he now admits. We should have had that conversation. I'm concerned that people will get a misimpression about Bob's value to the newspaper and our readers because of this one instance in which he should have told us sooner."

JOSEPH WILSON, WHO BECAME AN OUTSPOKEN OPPONENT OF THE war in Iraq, had begun talking to journalists about his 2002 trip to Niger in the spring of 2003. On May 6, *New York Times* columnist Nicholas Kristof wrote, "I'm told by a person involved in the Niger caper that more than a year ago the vice president's office asked for an investigation of the uranium deal, so a former U.S. ambassador to Africa was dispatched to Niger." The ambassador, Kristof wrote, "reported to the CIA and State Department that the information was unequivocally wrong."

At the *Post*, Walter Pincus read Kristof's column with interest. He found out that Wilson was the ambassador, and Wilson agreed to an interview as a confidential source "on background," a ground rule for certain interviews under which the reporter agrees never to name the source. Pincus also interviewed several CIA sources. In a June 12 front-page story, Pincus wrote that the CIA had not shared Wilson's Niger finding with the White House or other government agencies before the invasion of Iraq. The article attracted relatively little attention.

So Wilson went public. He wrote his July 6 op-ed column for the *New York Times*, agreed to be profiled in the *Post*, and appeared on *Meet the Press*.

Then came Novak's July 14 column. "Wilson never worked for the CIA, but his wife, Valerie Plame, is an Agency operative on weapons of mass destruction," Novak wrote. "Two senior administration officials told me his wife suggested sending Wilson to Niger."

Three days later, *Time* magazine reporter Matthew Cooper wrote that Bush administration officials "have taken public and private whacks at Wilson, charging that his 2002 report, made at the behest of U.S. intelligence, was faulty and that his mission was a scheme cooked up by mid-level operatives." Cooper added that "some government officials have noted to *Time* in interviews (as well as to syndicated columnist Robert Novak) that Wilson's wife, Valerie Plame, is a CIA official who monitors the proliferation of weapons of mass destruction."

The CIA struck back. Dana Priest and *Post* White House correspondent Mike Allen reported on the *Post*'s September 28 front page that, at the request of CIA director George Tenet, the Justice Department "is looking into an allegation that administration officials leaked the name of an undercover CIA officer to a journalist"—columnist Robert Novak. "A senior administration official said that before Novak's column ran, two top White House officials called at least six Washington journalists and disclosed the identity and occupation of Wilson's wife," Priest and Allen wrote. "'Clearly, it was meant purely and simply for revenge,' the senior official said of the leak."

Walter Pincus and Mike Allen stirred the pot further. "On July 12, two days before Novak's column," they wrote in an October 12 story, "a *Post* reporter was told by an administration official that the White House had not paid attention to the former ambassador's CIA-sponsored trip to Niger because it was set up as a boondoggle by his wife, an analyst at the agency working on weapons of mass destruction. Plame's name was never mentioned, and the purpose of the disclosure did not appear to be to generate an article, but rather to undermine Wilson's report." Pincus later publicly identified himself as the *Post* reporter.

The federal investigation of what inevitably came to be called "Plamegate" gathered steam. Attorney General John Ashcroft recused himself on December 30, 2003, because of his relationships with White House officials. Deputy Attorney General James Comey appointed Fitzgerald as special counsel to take charge of the investigation. Scooter Libby made the mistake of telling FBI agents that he had not disclosed Plame's job or identity to any reporter and had only heard gossip before it was publicly revealed in Novak's column. He would later repeat those denials under oath to a federal grand jury.

Numerous other administration officials were questioned by the FBI and the grand jury. Fitzgerald also sought the testimony of journalists to whom they had spoken. Fitzgerald obtained from the officials under investigation signed waivers of any confidential source agreements they had with the reporters. Most of the journalists doubted the validity of those written releases, and they did not come forward voluntarily. Fitzgerald then subpoenaed several reporters and threatened to subpoena others. He persuaded a federal judge and an appellate court to rule that each reporter was the only available "eyewitness to the crime" of disclosing the identity of a covert CIA officer.

When Judy Miller was subpoenaed, she refused to testify before the grand jury. She had not written anything about Plame in the *New York Times*, but prosecutors believed she had information relevant to the investigation of Libby. After months of legal wrangling, Miller was held in contempt of court and jailed in July 2005. Her confinement in the D.C. Jail drew a great deal more attention to the investigation and made Miller something of a celebrity.

Before that, *Time* magazine's Matthew Cooper also was held in contempt, although not yet jailed, when he refused to testify about conversations with Libby and Bush political adviser Karl Rove. Libby and Rove then each gave Cooper personal waivers of their confidential source agreements, which satisfied him. Avoiding jail, he testified that Rove had warned him to be wary of what Wilson had written in the *New York Times*, and that Rove had added that Wilson's wife worked at "the agency." Cooper also testified that, when he then told Libby in an interview that he had heard that Wilson's wife worked at the CIA, Libby responded, "I heard that, too."

At the *Post*, Glenn Kessler, who covered the State Department, was threatened with a subpoena to testify about two confidential source interviews he had with Libby in July 2003. Such subpoenas always presented a problem. It was important that none of our reporters reveal the identity of any source who was promised confidentiality, unless the source had released the reporter from that promise. But we also didn't want a reporter to risk jail for not obeying a court order to enforce a subpoena. So we had to work hard to find a way out of the dilemma.

After prolonged negotiations involving our lawyers and Fitzgerald, and with my approval, based on Libby's waiver of confidentiality, Kessler agreed to discuss only narrowly specified parts of the interviews. He told Fitzgerald in his sworn deposition on June 22, 2004, that Libby did not mention Plame, Wilson, or Wilson's trip to Niger in those two conversations.

We had to go through it all again when Walter Pincus was subpoenaed to testify about his October 12, 2003, story about being told "by an administration official"—before Novak's column was published—that Plame had "set up" Wilson's trip to Niger. Pincus steadfastly refused to identify his source for the story. However, the source identified himself to Fitzgerald and informed Pincus that he could testify about their conversation. That is what Pincus did in a September 15 sworn deposition, without discussing the source's identity.

Pincus also testified about telephone interviews with Libby "about the origins and results" of Wilson's trip to Niger on a confidential source basis. Through his lawyer, Libby had specifically released Pincus from the confidentiality agreement for those interviews. Pincus only testified that Plame did not come up in the conversations.

Once again, we were able to resolve the subpoena of Pincus with strictly limited questioning that did not force him to violate his agreements with confidential sources. "As someone who covers national security and intelligence, I depend on confidential sources more than most reporters," Pincus wrote in a public statement about his deposition. "My pledge of confidentiality to sources can only be released by them and only on their terms. Confidential sources now and in the future can rest assured that I stick by my word."

In both cases, we made it through the needle's eye without compromising our principles about protecting confidential sources, seeing our reporters go to jail, or risking a court ruling that could scare off confidential sources in the future. We benefited from the backing of Bo Jones and Don Graham and extraordinary work by *Post* lawyers and outside counsel. After months of tension and uncertainty, I felt relieved.

But it was not over.

On October 28, 2005, Libby was indicted by a federal grand jury in Washington on five felony counts of perjury, obstruction of justice, and giving false information to investigators about his discussions with journalists about Valerie Plame. He immediately resigned as Cheney's chief of staff.

After receiving a telephoned personal release from Libby of their confidential source agreement, Judy Miller got out of jail on September 29 and appeared before the federal grand jury. She testified that Libby had disclosed in a meeting with her on June 23, 2003, that Wilson's wife was a CIA employee involved in her husband's trip to Niger. According to Miller's testimony, Libby sharply criticized the CIA, Wilson, and Wilson's report on his trip to Niger. Miller's notes from a second meeting with Libby on July 8, in which he repeated that criticism, contained the misspelled name "Valerie Flame," although Miller testified that she did not know where it had come from.

In Woodward's sworn deposition in a Washington law office on November 14, 2005, Fitzgerald questioned him, by prior agreement, about his mid-June 2003 interview with a Bush administration official and two subsequent conversations with two other officials for his book. "All three persons provided written statements waiving the previous agreements of confidentiality on the issues being investigated by Fitzgerald," Woodward wrote in a statement we posted on the washingtonpost.com website on November 16. "Each confirmed those releases verbally this month and requested that I testify."

Woodward testified that he did not remember bringing up Wilson or his wife in the other two interviews, although "Joe Wilson's wife" was included in the lists of questions that he brought with him to those interviews, one with Libby and the other with White House chief of staff Andrew Card. Woodward added that nothing about Wilson or his wife appeared in his notes from those interviews.

Woodward's deposition—and the secret he had kept from me for two years—became big news on November 16. I agreed to be interviewed about it by Wolf Blitzer on CNN. At 4:30 in the afternoon, I was sitting in a chair facing television cameras and lights in the front of the newsroom, which was full of reporters and editors. I could not see them behind me, but everyone's attention apparently turned toward the television monitors mounted throughout the newsroom.

"Bob has acknowledged today that he made a mistake in not telling me about it sooner," I told Blitzer. "He's apologized to me and to the newspaper."

I pointed out that Woodward's groundbreaking reporting over decades depended on his keeping his promises to confidential sources. "He kept that promise about Deep Throat for three decades, even to the point that somebody else revealed that information," I told Blitzer. "It is sacred at this newspaper, as it is at most newspapers, and I assume at your network also, to not reveal the names and contents of conversations unless we're given permission to do so by our confidential sources."

After the interview ended, the newsroom erupted into applause. It felt good to know that I had the staff's support in my rare and uncomfortable time in the spotlight.

Again, I went on our website to chat about the issue with readers. I made clear that I wanted Woodward to continue working with the *Post*. I explained that he had often produced stories for the newspaper from his book research over the years, in addition to the multipart advance excerpts from his books that we published in the *Post*. I reminded everyone how he had immediately responded to the 9/11 terrorist attacks by providing the newspaper's readers important information from his extraordinarily well-placed sources.

Almost a year later, former deputy secretary of state Richard Armitage publicly acknowledged that he was the confidential source who told both

Woodward and Robert Novak that Wilson's wife worked for the CIA. He contended that he had disclosed it inadvertently in separate interviews with the two journalists. He said he did not know and did not tell them that Plame was a covert officer. "I feel terrible," Armitage said in a September 7, 2006, interview on the *CBS Evening News*. He was never charged in the federal investigation.

Libby's trial began on January 16, 2007. Woodward and Pincus were among six reporters who were called by his defense lawyers as witnesses on February 12 to show that Bush administration officials other than Libby had discussed Wilson's wife with reporters before her identity became public. Pincus testified that then White House press secretary Ari Fleischer was the confidential source who had been the first person to tell him that Wilson was married to a CIA officer. Fleischer had released Pincus from his confidentiality agreement to testify.

With Armitage's release from their confidentiality agreement, Woodward testified about their June 13, 2003, conversation and allowed the relevant portion of his audio recording of the interview to be played for the jury. When Woodward brought up Wilson's Niger trip, Armitage had interjected, "His wife works for the agency." In the brief discussion of her that followed, Armitage added, "Everyone knows it." Valerie Plame's name and covert status at the CIA never came up.

On March 6, Libby was convicted on four of the five felony counts and later sentenced to thirty months in prison. Bush commuted his sentence, and President Donald Trump pardoned him in 2018.

I remember the Plame case as a disturbing near-criminalization of news reporting. Some Bush administration officials, led by Libby and angered by Wilson's *New York Times* column, did set out to discredit Wilson and his Niger mission. But it was never clear to me whether they realized that his wife was a covert officer at the CIA, rather than an analyst, when they identified her to journalists. Novak was most at fault for ignoring warnings from the CIA about her covert status before he published his column.

Libby lied to the FBI and a federal jury, for which he was convicted. But neither he nor any other Bush administration official was prosecuted or convicted for disclosing Plame's identity to reporters. I believe that it was the sort of contretemps that could have been resolved through public exposure rather than by criminal prosecution. Fitzgerald's overly zealous investigation did threaten confidential source reporting often necessary in holding government accountable to the American people.

THE CONTROVERSY ALSO RAISED LONG-SIMMERING QUESTIONS about how Bob Woodward balanced his research and writing of best-selling books with his reporting for the *Post*. As I always said in media interviews and online chats with readers, I never found it to be an untenable conflict. Woodward regularly contributed to the newspaper significant information from his book research, both in his own stories and in valuable contributions to other reporters' stories. He was there in times of our greatest need, such as after the 9/11 terrorist attacks.

Woodward was only one of many *Post* journalists who became media stars through work they did at the newspaper, books they wrote, appearances they made on television, and speeches they made. In the internet age, their relative celebrity became helpful in attracting audiences to our website. Perhaps because of my own comparatively lower profile, it was relatively easy for me to manage this growing trend without appearing competitive. Most of the newsroom's star journalists kept me and their editors informed about their activities, and they followed our rules about outside compensation that avoided conflicts with the newspaper's ethics policies.

Woodward, however, was not easy for me to manage. Although I eventually knew about each of the twelve books that he wrote during my quarter century as managing editor and executive editor of the *Post*, I often didn't see or hear from him for weeks or months at a time. He worked on his books at his Georgetown home, where an upper floor was an office staffed by assistants. In turn, I and some of my editors worked with Woodward to extract newspaper stories from his book research and to select and edit excerpts from the books themselves for publication in the *Post*. I never felt that our readers were cheated.

"You knew how to keep me on a leash, but not to hold it too tightly," Woodward told me while I was writing this book. "But it was always there, and I was thankful for it. You can be a little icy, and so can I. You used me. I used you and the *Post*. And that is the core of a lasting relationship."

Earlier, when I first interviewed him for the book at his home, Woodward displayed on his kitchen table a tall stack of all the *Washington Post* stories and excerpts from his books that we published while I was executive editor. He told me that they contained nearly 150,000 words.

One of the most successful journalists of his time was obviously concerned about his legacy. It was the kind of telling detail that Woodward would have wanted to note about someone else in one of his books.

21

Exposing a CIA Secret

The 7 a.m. meeting in the Oval Office with President George W. Bush on Friday October 28, 2005, was one of the most momentous half hours of my many years in journalism. The president of the United States was asking me, as executive editor of the *Washington Post*, not to publish a story about his administration's secret war against terror in the aftermath of the September 11, 2001, attacks on the United States. My decision could end a multinational covert operation at the heart of that secret war, which raised serious legal and moral issues for the U.S. government and several European countries.

I had been in the White House many times over the years. I had participated in Oval Office interviews with presidents Lyndon Johnson, Ronald Reagan, and Bill Clinton. I had met in the Map Room with First Lady Hillary Clinton to hear complaints about our coverage of her and her husband. I had attended White House dinners and receptions. I was not awed to be there.

But this was the only time I had been summoned to the White House in this way, along with Don Graham, who had succeeded his late mother as the *Post*'s CEO and chairman. I knew that the meeting would severely test my determination to hold the Bush administration accountable for its actions, while I dealt with life-and-death national security questions. My focus was on the story, not the occasion.

The setting was formal, as though we were a visiting foreign delegation. Don Graham and President Bush were seated at an angle next to each other in the upholstered blue-and-gold Federal Stripe wing chairs in front of the fireplace, which was at the opposite end of the room from the president's Resolute desk. I was sitting nearest to Bush at the end of one of two facing beige couches. *Post* publisher Bo Jones, who had accompanied Don and me, sat on my left. A scowling Vice President Dick Cheney sat opposite me on the other couch, with the more genial director of national intelligence, John Negroponte, seated next to him. Stephen Hadley, the president's national security adviser, hovered nearby.

"I haven't made a call like this before as president," Bush began, making clear the importance of the meeting for him. "We have an enemy that still wants to kill," he said to me. "These people are psychological nuts who will kill and want to kill again. It's a real war."

It had been just over four years since the devastating 9/11 al Qaeda terrorist attacks that killed 2,996 people in New York, the Pentagon, and a rural field near Shanksville, Pennsylvania. In addition to the ensuing military wars in Afghanistan and Iraq, the Bush administration was fighting a secret war against suspected terrorists around the world.

After several years of painstaking investigation, Dana Priest, a talented and determined *Post* reporter, had pieced together an extraordinary story about a key part of the unprecedented covert Central Intelligence Agency counterterrorism program that Bush had authorized just six days after 9/11. Her story, if published, would reveal that the CIA had been hiding and coercively interrogating, even torturing, dozens of captured "high-value" terrorist suspects in covert "black site" prisons in countries in Eastern Europe and elsewhere. Three of the black sites had been secretly set up and operated outside the law in relatively new Eastern European democracies, whose citizens did not know of their existence.

CIA officials had been trying to persuade Dana to drop the story after she outlined it for them in detail, as *Post* reporters always did when national security was involved. Three days before the Oval Office meeting, Dana and I had been invited to CIA headquarters in Langley, Virginia, for what turned out to be a preview of what I would hear at the White House. Without specifically confirming the content of the story, CIA director Porter Goss argued that its publication would severely damage national security while "we're in the middle of a very serious war."

In the Oval Office, the president echoed much of what Goss had told us in trying to persuade me not to publish the story. Bush also emphasized what he said would be the consequences of naming countries that hosted CIA secret prisons.

"If any of these countries are exposed, it would make it very difficult for us to maintain allies in the war on terror," the president said as I took notes. "This program is so dark that I do not know the names of the countries—if the program exists."

"I would also add that there is a danger of retaliation," Cheney said gravely, looking me in the eye. Revealing the existence of the CIA black sites in specific countries "could elevate them on the list of targets for attack," he warned. "Lives are at stake."

I was somewhat surprised when Bush went on to describe his administration's counterterrorism activities in some detail. He seemed very well prepared for the early morning meeting. That impressed upon me how sensitive and significant this story could be.

Just as I had at CIA headquarters, I asked questions about how publication of the secret prisons story might cause harm. I listened carefully to the answers, as I conspicuously continued to take notes. I had spent hours with Dana and her editors, going over and over her extensive reporting, her explanation of the classified information involved, her assessment of the national security issues, and her reasons for feeling strongly that the CIA black site program should be revealed to the American public. I had repeatedly consulted with the *Post*'s lawyers about any legal risks involved in publishing the story, and with a senior intelligence official, whom I knew personally, about any national security risks.

At the outset, Don Graham had explained to the president that I made the final decisions about what to publish in the news pages of the

Washington Post. I did not feel unprepared or intimidated about deciding what to do. By that time I had been executive editor for fourteen years, and I had confronted many similar, if less high-stakes, decisions about the impact of *Washington Post* journalism on U.S. intelligence operations. It was an inescapable responsibility of leading one of the world's most influential news organizations with the unique freedom guaranteed by the First Amendment in the United States. My entire career was built on a motivating belief that when journalists are holding government—and other powerful people and institutions—accountable to citizens for their actions, we are fulfilling our highest purpose in our constitutional democracy.

I always went through the same deliberative process for such stories. Was it important for the American people to know that their elected government was secretly doing what we would be revealing? If it was, what would be the consequences of publication, especially any potential risks to human life or the country's security?

DANA PRIEST WAS AMONG MANY TALENTED WOMEN WHOM I EN-couraged in key reporting and editing positions in the *Post* newsroom. I worked hard to increase the diversity of the mostly white male staff I had joined as a summer intern reporter in 1964, in part because I inherently believed in hiring and promoting the best possible journalists and enabling them to do their best work. I never fully realized at the time how much my support mattered to the women themselves.

"You were editor during a big turning point for lots of great female reporters," Dana told me years later. "We were breaking ground, not as the first women in the newsroom, but as an entire generation of women who were trying to hang onto our great jobs and start families, too. Most of them succeeded, and then some."

I realized early on that Dana, who also had been a *Post* summer intern, deeply shared my mission of accountability journalism. While reporting on the federal bureaucracy, she took the initiative to investigate working conditions in the U.S. Postal Service and overcrowding in prisons. After being assigned to cover the Defense Department in 1995, Dana essentially embedded herself in the U.S. military by traveling to and with troops stationed around the world, developing valuable sources all the way up to top commanders. While traveling with them in eighteen countries in Asia, Africa, and South America, she became particularly expert about U.S. Special Forces and the Pentagon's regional military commanding officers. She revealed in stories in the *Post* how the regional commanders and their forces were effectively shaping American military and foreign policy in critical parts of the world, away from scrutiny in Washington.

In the middle of all that, in 1998, Dana was asked by her editors on the *Post*'s national news staff to help investigate President Bill Clinton's affair with White House intern Monica Lewinsky, who Dana had encountered by chance after Lewinsky was moved from the White House to work at the Pentagon. Lewinsky told Dana during a trip overseas that she had given Clinton a tie that he wore to a State of the Union speech. But Dana wanted to stay on the Pentagon beat, and her editors and I left her there, after she told other *Post* reporters what she knew about Lewinsky and Clinton.

By 2001, I was so impressed by her determination and resourcefulness that I asked Dana to take on the particularly difficult national intelligence beat. Just months after she started, on the morning of September 11, al Qaeda terrorists crashed passenger airliners into the World Trade Center in New York City, the Pentagon, and, after the courageous passenger revolt, a rural field in Pennsylvania. The CIA's ensuing all-out pursuit of terrorists, on orders from President Bush, became the focus of Dana's intelligence assignment from then on.

"I used my military reporting experience," she later recalled. "I asked the same basic questions. How is the CIA fighting this war? What are its weapons? Its battlefields? Its rules? Are its tactics achieving our strategic goals?"

But the answers were much harder to come by. Dana could not go on missions with the CIA because they were top secret. Potential sources were wary about talking to her, in part because many of them were periodically given lie detector tests to determine whether they had divulged classified information to anyone, especially reporters. She learned never to seek or discuss significant information in e-mails or to call sources at their offices. Instead, she had to contact them at home or meet them in public.

As Dana got started, other *Post* reporters were able to find pieces of the puzzle in other parts of the government. Bob Woodward reported in an October 21, 2001, story that President Bush had authorized the CIA to fight al Qaeda with the "most sweeping and lethal covert action since the founding of the Agency in 1947." *Post* reporters Rajiv Chandrasekaran and Peter Finn reported in a March 11, 2002, story that U.S. forces had "secretly transported dozens of people suspected of links to terrorists to countries other than the United States, bypassing extradition procedures and legal formalities," where "they can be subjected to interrogation tactics—including torture and threats to families—that are illegal in the United States."

By the end of 2002, Dana and another *Post* reporter, Bart Gellman, were able to piece together the first authoritative account of how the CIA itself was subjecting captured terrorist suspects to "physically and psychologically aggressive" interrogations at a secret facility inside the U.S.-occupied Bagram air base in Afghanistan. Their December 26 story was based on "interviews with several former intelligence officials and 10 current U.S. security officials, including several people who witnessed the handling of the prisoners" in "a cluster of metal shipping containers protected by a triple layer of concertina wire." They described how prisoners "are sometimes kept standing or kneeling for hours in black hoods or spray-painted goggles. . . . At times they are held in awkward, painful positions and deprived of sleep with a 24-hour bombardment of lights—subject to what are known as 'stress and duress.'"

Curiously, no one from the government contacted me before or after that story was published to express any national security concerns, as had happened in the past with stories involving covert intelligence operations. But Dana was surprised by the amount of congressional criticism, hate mail, and telephone threats she received. Although she told me that she wasn't worried, I insisted that she check in regularly with the *Post*'s security people and take whatever precautions they suggested. At the same time, I encouraged her to keep digging and assured her that I expected to publish what she found.

Ever since the 9/11 attacks, I had been actively involved in the *Post*'s investigative reporting about them and the U.S. response. But, as I have written, I had not focused enough attention on investigating the accuracy of the Bush administration's assertions of terrorist connections and weapons of mass destruction in Saddam Hussein's Iraq as the justification for starting the Iraq War. It was the biggest mistake of my career. I was determined not to repeat it in directing the newspaper's investigations of the administration's conduct in its secret "war against terrorism."

Dana's reporting for the "stress and duress" story was a breakthrough. She had found a military interrogator who had been involved in the black site interrogations and who described the techniques she detailed in her story. Unlike the well-known detention and interrogation center for terrorist suspects on the U.S. military base at Guantanamo Bay, the CIA's secret Bagram facility, along with still unidentified other places around the world where suspects were detained, were beyond the reach of U.S. law and off-limits even to other U.S. government agencies. Dana methodically set out to find where they all were and what was going on inside them. She spent nearly three years on her quest, while continuing to produce many other revelatory stories about the CIA's expanding and increasingly expensive covert war on terrorism.

Working long hours, Dana found people inside the CIA and others who had left the agency who were worried about whether it was torturing terrorism suspects and what damage that could do to the agency's reputation and to the country. She found people in other places inside and outside the government who were briefed about some of what the CIA was doing and who also were concerned. They were reluctant to talk on the telephone, so Dana met them in restaurants, cars, and "odd places where you are not going to be seen," often at night. Many of these sources were afraid or unable to tell her very much. So just as Bob Woodward and Carl Bernstein had done during Watergate, she would, when necessary, ask them simply to verify bits and pieces of information she had picked up elsewhere and add what they could.

I made sure that Dana kept me informed of her progress, along with her immediate editors. I listened carefully and asked questions during conversations in the office I had inherited from Ben Bradlee in the newsroom. I repeatedly supported her determination to keep going, despite the difficulties she faced. At one point, Dana told me that she had asked the *Post's* police reporters to buy a bunch of disposable cell phones on the street, but she decided it was too awkward to ask her sources to use them. Dana sometimes confided to me her doubts about whether she was finding out things that we wouldn't publish, but I told her those decisions would come later.

Along the way, Dana discovered that the CIA was secretly flying captured terrorist suspects from one country to another for detention and interrogation in its and foreign countries' secret facilities—what the CIA called "rendition." A *Post* researcher, Margot Williams, noticed that one Gulfstream V turbojet used for renditions was being followed around the world by plane-spotting hobbyists who found its tail number, N379P, on the internet. Dana and *Post* researchers discovered the false identities of its CIA front owners. Dana was able to describe in her December 27, 2004, story the pattern of global renditions in fascinating detail, featuring the extensive travels of that one Gulfstream V, whose owner of record was listed as Premier Executive Transport Services Inc., a front company.

Even though she had not yet completed her reporting on the overseas secret prisons, Dana revealed so much else about the CIA's covert counterterrorism war in the *Post* during 2004 that I nominated her for the 2005 Pulitzer Prize for Beat Reporting. She was later chosen as one of three finalists by that category's jury of distinguished journalists, but the Pulitzer board, the final arbiter, did not award her the prize. She was very disappointed, as was I.

"I did my best grinding, daily beat work on the CIA in 2004," Dana told me years later. "When I didn't win, Don (Graham) called me into his office to talk, and I actually broke down crying because I felt I had let the paper down."

By the autumn of 2005, Dana had put together enough of the pieces of the CIA overseas secret prisons puzzle to produce a draft story. To my surprise, it had a Warsaw, Poland, dateline, where Dana had done some of her reporting. She told me that Poland, because of its other extensive counterterrorism intelligence cooperation with the United States, was perhaps the most important of the three Eastern European countries where the black site prisons had been located. Even before our later discussions at the CIA and the White House, I had decided, without objection from Dana, not to publish details we knew about the other secret counterterrorism cooperation with Poland because they did not raise the legal or constitutional issues of the CIA's black sites.

As Dana's draft story pointed out, the black sites' secrecy, prisoner isolation, and interrogation methods—including the simulated drowning called waterboarding—would be as illegal in Poland and the other Eastern European democracies where sites were located, as they would have been in the United States. That was why her CIA sources were so worried about the legal, moral, reputational, and sustainability risks of the secret prisons program for the agency.

Dana had gone to Poland and interviewed current and former senior Polish government officials, who denied the existence of any CIA secret prisons there, while nevertheless emphasizing the fledgling democracy's close intelligence relationship with the United States. "Since September 11, we have been a very active member in all counterterrorism projects," Poland's interior minister told Dana. "I would like to make it very explicit, Polish-American relations are very special, especially in this area."

After Dana found the identity of the key CIA operative in the U.S. Embassy in Warsaw, she left a message for him with her name and hotel phone number. That afternoon, she interviewed a senior Polish official who had approved the black site program. The next morning, she was surprised by a long-distance call from CIA headquarters in Langley. "You're making us very nervous with your questioning" and upsetting Polish intelligence and military officials, she was told. "Please stop your reporting and come into CIA headquarters to talk."

She told the caller she would go to the CIA in Langley, Virginia, and discuss her reporting after she was done in Poland. This was standard operating procedure at the *Post*. On any story about the government, a reporter would talk to officials to seek comments about its accuracy, ask them for more information, and give them an opportunity to comment.

On stories involving classified information and national security, the reporter also would listen to any concerns about harm that officials contended could be caused by publication. The reporter and her immediate editors would then come to me to make decisions about including or omitting sensitive information in a story. If any issues remained unresolved, including objections to publishing the story at all, I would become even more involved. *Post* reporters and editors all knew about my strict "no surprises" rule, which I had inherited from Ben. I never wanted to be surprised by any issues in the newsroom or with stories published in the newspaper about which I should already have been aware.

When she was back in Washington, Dana first telephoned Jennifer Millerwise, then the CIA's director of public affairs, and gave her a detailed account of what was in the draft story. Millerwise asked Dana to come to the agency, where she met with Millerwise and Jose Rodriguez, then the CIA's director of the National Clandestine Service. Dana knew that he oversaw the black site prisons, and that he had never talked to the news media. But he wanted to persuade Dana to drop her story. When she asked about the legality of the black sites, he told her, "We can break laws with other countries." That was technically true for the CIA, unlike any other U.S. agency.

In making his argument against publication, Rodriguez emphasized what he described as the fragility of Poland's extensive counterterrorism relationship with the CIA. He warned that Dana's story might even force Poland to break off relations with the United States. He told her that he was already planning to go there to reassure its officials, who now knew what Dana knew from her visit to Warsaw. As Dana and I would hear repeatedly, Rodriguez also said that the story could harm American counterterrorism cooperation with many other countries if those countries could not trust the CIA to keep their secrets.

When Dana told them that I was likely to publish her story in some form, Millerwise asked for a meeting with me, Dana, the CIA director, and other intelligence officials at 4 p.m. on Tuesday, October 25. I decided to bring along my managing editor, Phil Bennett, and the national news editor, Liz Spayd, both of whom had been working on the story with Dana and me.

In a memo she sent us on Tuesday morning to prepare for the meeting, Dana said that the CIA did not want us to name Poland, Romania, and Lithuania in the story as recently democratic, former Soviet Bloc Eastern European countries that hosted CIA black sites. The memo repeated what Rodriguez had told Dana about potential damage to other U.S.-Polish intelligence operations around the world, which I had already decided not to detail in the story. Dana had drafted another story about Poland's cooperation with other European nations and the United States on secret intelligence gathering unrelated to terrorism, which I had decided not to publish at that time because it did not involve controversial or legal questions that, in my mind, would warrant exposure.

THAT AFTERNOON, OUR LITTLE GROUP DROVE IN ONE CAR ACROSS the Potomac River onto Route 193 in northern Virginia to the turnoff for the heavily wooded, three-hundred-acre campus of the Central Intelligence Agency in Langley. We cleared security at the gatehouse on the entrance road and drove past a number of nondescript buildings before parking in front of the agency's squat, seven-story headquarters. A security officer escorted us across the vast marble-lined lobby, past the wall of stars memorializing unnamed CIA agents who had died in the line of duty. He took us into a key-operated elevator that opened directly into the seventh-floor office of CIA director Porter Goss. Its large windows looked out onto trees whose leaves were just starting to turn autumn colors on a gray, rainy day.

I had listened to business-like entreaties by several other CIA directors about relatively easy story decisions, such as not identifying covert intelligence agents, which I had never done. I had found ways to publish stories about which those directors had expressed concerns—sometimes by removing details that could risk real harm to life or covert intelligence operations—without losing the import of the story. I was prepared to listen carefully to what Goss had to say so that I could evaluate the CIA's concerns about publishing this story.

We sat around a conference table that day with Goss, Millerwise, and John Negroponte, the relatively new director of national intelligence who was now Goss's boss. It became apparent to me, there and later in the White House, that Negroponte, although he said much less than the others, could be stage-managing our encounters. He was a burly, balding, tough-minded man with an ingratiating manner, with whom I had come into contact years earlier during his long diplomatic career.

The bespectacled, gray-haired Goss, once a CIA case officer, was an unimpressive former congressman who clashed often with career people in the CIA and, eventually, Negroponte. Goss had been given command of the agency just over a year before our meeting, and he was replaced six months afterward.

Goss began the business-like meeting by saying he would be speaking hypothetically because any such black sites would be part of a covert operation that "cannot be admitted to." He even claimed, at first, not to know which countries we were talking about. If any such black sites existed, he said, whatever the CIA would be doing in them was "all useful" and "all lawful." He would not discuss interrogation methods, except to say, without elaboration, "We have special legal capabilities to do what we do."

If Dana's story were to "name names and places" of secret sites in foreign countries, Goss said, it "could lead to instability and unrest" in those countries. "We would lose their cooperation," he said, which would "create a loss of capability that this country needs. There is no other way to do this."

Echoing what Jose Rodriguez had told Dana earlier, Goss added that publication of such a story could cause the CIA to "lose credibility and the ability to operate" counterterrorism programs with many other countries because they would see that the CIA could not keep secret such an important covert operation. "We deal on the basis of confidence, trust and secrecy," he said. "It could end up severely limiting our options internationally." And, he told us, he could lose credibility within the agency.

Although I did not say so then, I was not impressed by those arguments. I thought that the CIA's credibility was its own responsibility. And Goss's stature within the agency was none of my concern. If the black sites had to be closed after publication of a story revealing them, I thought, the terrorist suspects could be moved to prisons in the United States or on American military bases like Guantanamo Bay, within the reach of U.S. law. When I asked Goss about that, he said, "We only have undesirable alternatives."

"There is no other way to do this," he insisted, because "the CIA can only operate overseas" and "no other [U.S.] agency is authorized" to carry out such a covert detention and interrogation program. Disingenuously, he added, "We're not in the prison business, so we would need to find a partner who would go along openly."

Negroponte, in a brief interjection, focused on the draft story's naming of Eastern European countries secretly hosting black sites. That exposure, he contended, could endanger their other secret counterter-rorism cooperation with the United States, which he did not specify. "These are agreements of real confidentiality between heads of state," he said. "Identifying those countries frontally could cause other damage in relationships with those countries. It could end up severely limiting our options internationally."

After no other information was forthcoming, I thanked our hosts for the meeting. "We'll take everything into consideration," I told them. "We'll let you know when we're ready to publish."

On the ride back to the *Post* and, later, in a meeting of the four of us in my glass-walled office, Liz Spayd argued strongly for naming the Eastern European countries that hosted the CIA black sites. Otherwise, she said, we would be complicit in illegal activities unknown to their citizens.

I was determined to avoid unnecessary delay in deciding whether to publish the story. I doubted that any more meetings with officials would be necessary. I had learned my lesson when intelligence officials in the Reagan administration tied up Ben Bradlee and me in phone conversa-tions and meetings for nearly six months arguing about publication of the Ivy Bells espionage story in the mid-1980s.

"I CAN'T CALL IT A DAY WITHOUT SUMMARIZING MY THOUGHTS on today's extraordinary conversation," Dana wrote to me, Liz, and Phil Bennett in an 11:20 p.m. e-mail that I opened Wednesday morning.

"In the simplest terms," she began,

> that little Chinese gong, the gut-level alarm that experienced reporters learn to listen to, has been ringing about CIA detentions and interro-gations since the first time, nearly two years ago, when I learned about the CIA's secret "stress and duress" tactics at Bagram. It continues to ring today, even louder, after dispassionately digesting all that was said in our meeting.
>
> What the CIA is doing, and how it is doing it, is fundamentally wrong. That's the reason my editors have egged me on in this time-consuming, expensive quest, to be able to display the system in a finite—not hypothetical—way so that an honest debate on the matter can be

had. Naming these countries makes it nearly impossible for the CIA to continue denying that this questionable, unorthodox and even, perhaps, unproductive system exits. Hedging with generalities will produce the status quo, a continuation of their denials and continuation of the program as it is.

The people who put themselves at risk to help me are not anti-CIA. In fact, they worry deeply about the future of the agency, which, in their view, has gone so awry as to believe they can treat terrorist subjects in a way that Americans did not even treat Nazi captives, or Mafia members or leaders and mules of the drug cartels, who have collectively killed more people than Al Qaeda. Yes, this is an unconventional war, but we must hold government officials accountable for their decisions, by describing those decisions with as much accuracy and detail as we can collect. Then let the public decide.

Now I can go to bed. Goodnight,

Dana

Besides being a succinct and eloquent statement of her motivation and rationale for the CIA black sites story, Dana's late-night *cri de coeur* epitomized the role of accountability journalism to which she and I had devoted our careers. In my role as editor, I would never let her story include an opinion that "what the CIA is doing, and how it is doing it, is fundamentally wrong," and Dana knew that. She was right to want the story to "hold government officials accountable for their decisions, by describing those decisions with as much accuracy and detail" as possible and letting the public decide. It was left to me to decide which of those details accomplished that purpose without knowingly causing unnecessary harm to U.S. counterterrorism efforts. That also was the editor's role.

On Wednesday afternoon, after more conversations with me, Phil, and Liz about the meeting at the CIA, Dana summarized in another memo her answers to some of the questions we had asked her. They were based on her confidential interviews with a number of former senior CIA officials.

If the story were to be published, these officials told Dana, all the black sites would probably be closed, and it would be hard to find other countries in which to locate replacements. "There are few places in the world that will do this because it is against the law," said a former CIA lawyer. Another former CIA official pointed out to Dana that operating such black sites could not be divorced from whether the "enhanced interrogation techniques" used by the CIA amounted to illegal torture, in addition to depriving the terrorist suspects of legal rights otherwise guaranteed by the United States and the Eastern European democracies that had been secretly hosting the black sites.

"There aren't really any alternatives to keeping a detention system totally untouched by anyone but the CIA," another former CIA official told Dana. "Maybe Donald Trump could buy a boat for the CIA, and we could keep it in international seas." Trump was then a boastful New York real estate mogul.

At the same time, Dana's CIA sources were not very concerned about the story's long-term impact on the agency's relationships with other countries' intelligence operations. "Every time there have been revelations, we run around wringing our hands saying foreign governments won't work with us," one CIA veteran official told her. "But they continue to do so, sometimes after a bit. Disclosure is part of the calculus."

"Is there anyone so naïve as to think you could keep this secret?" another intelligence source asked rhetorically, according to Dana's memo. "No one does this without thinking it will come out someday. That's part of the decision, taken freely."

The sources' candor was refreshing to me, since intelligence officials had often told me that *Washington Post* revelations about covert intelligence activities had significantly disrupted cooperation with other countries in ways they could not disclose.

At the same time, one of Dana's sources did say that naming one of the Eastern European countries could be disruptive. "If this is a functioning, flourishing democracy," the source said about one of the countries, "the revelation will be huge in the country because it would be clearly illegal."

THE DAY AFTER OUR VISIT TO CIA HEADQUARTERS, THE WHITE House called the *Post* to ask Don Graham and me to meet with President Bush on Friday. I agreed that it would be the last such meeting before I made my decision about publishing Dana's story.

Don invited *Post* publisher Bo Jones, who had previously been the newspaper's general counsel, to join us. I had already been consulting Jones, along with the newspaper's in-house and outside lawyers, because he had given me invaluable advice over the years on questions of libel, national security, and government pressure on the press. Don and Jones had been close ever since they both attended St. Albans School in Washington and then Harvard, where, two years apart, they each had been president of *The Crimson* student newspaper. Jones had joined the *Post* as general counsel in 1980 and became publisher in 2000, when Don succeeded Katharine Graham as the company's CEO and chairman.

Because it was, at the time, an off-the-record meeting to help me with my decision making, we did not invite Dana to come with us to the White House. Under the deep background ground rules for the meeting, she could not have used anything said there in her story, and we did not want to risk accusations of acting in bad faith. But after all her exhaustive work, Dana was disappointed. "I was pretty pissed," she remembered years later. I would have been, too.

In the meeting in the Oval Office, the president framed the discussion of Dana's proposed story, on which he had been briefed, in the context of his war on terrorism since 9/11. "People say Bush brings up the war against terror" whenever there are political disagreements about his administration's tactics, he told us, "but this is a real war."

He continued: "To do the job of working with others to prevent attacks from coming again, we need to be able to cooperate with our allies. My concern is that a friend of the United States gets exposed for cooperating with us in the war on terror, and that government goes down, or other governments say they can't afford to cooperate with us. A story revealing the names of those countries would damage the security of the United States."

As an example of the kind of cooperation that such a story might jeopardize, the president said, such "cooperating could be [an intercepted] telephone call telling us that they're moving money. The bastards are still moving a lot of money," he added about the terrorists' finances.

"There's a reluctance, nervousness [by cooperating countries] to be on the front line in the war on terror," Bush continued. "It's all interrelated. These guys are damn smart. Fighting them requires new skills, new kinds of cooperation, different kinds of assets to defeat them. . . . Everything this country has done is within the law."

I asked the president about exactly that, in the context of the legal questions involved in what Dana's story would reveal about the CIA secret prisons. His national security adviser, Stephen Hadley, interjected to say that the captured terrorist suspects should be considered enemy combatants. "Unlawful combatants have different rights," he said, without directly addressing the legality of the black sites or what went on inside them, including interrogation methods.

"Sometimes these people are able to give us information that protects America," the president added, with emphasis. "It's really important that we succeed."

As I continued taking notes for my decision making, I asked more questions. Hadley, a bespectacled, self-effacing, Ivy League–educated lawyer with long experience as a national security staffer in Republican administrations, responded to most of them with the same generalities we had encountered at the CIA. Vice President Cheney said nothing more after his earlier warning that "lives are at stake." The meeting broke up after half an hour.

As I was leaving the Oval Office, Negroponte, who also had said little, came up beside me. He put his arm around my shoulders and asked, "You're not really going to name the countries, are you?"

Figuring that he was referring to the three Eastern European democracies, I asked, "Is that what you're most concerned about?"

Negroponte repeated his question. I said I would think about it.

I realized that was their bottom-line request. The president and the others had emphasized the possible risks to international cooperation with the United States in the war on terrorism, especially with any countries named in the story as locations of CIA black sites. They realized they would probably have to live with publication of the story, but were hoping to minimize collateral damage.

On the brisk four-block walk back from the White House to the *Washington Post*, Don, Bo Jones, and I reviewed the pros and cons of publishing Dana's story. Jones doubted there would be any legal problems for the newspaper. The government could not stop the story because the 1971 U.S. Supreme Court decision in the Pentagon Papers case made such prior restraint virtually impossible. They both noted the concerns expressed in the meeting about the impact of naming the Eastern European countries. Nevertheless, Don reiterated that it was my decision whether to publish the story and what it should contain.

I knew from our many years working together that Don was a very cautious person who worried about the newspaper ever being seen to cause harm in any way. So I appreciated his confidence in me and his protection of my independence as executive editor. It left an important decision entirely up to me. But that did not worry or delay me.

Back in the newsroom, I went over my notes from the White House meeting with Dana, Liz Spayd, and Phil Bennett. We discussed various issues in the long story, including the naming of the Eastern European countries. Afterward, Dana sent her final draft to me.

I decided that it was important for the American people and the rest of the government to know about this extralegal covert program. But I also concluded that there was enough convincing detail in Dana's story without having to identify the Eastern European countries that hosted black sites, which might risk ending their other counterterrorism cooperation. I expected that the secret prisons would most likely be closed because of the story, and I accepted that responsibility.

I removed the Warsaw dateline, along with the names of Poland, Romania, and Lithuania, and several paragraphs specifically about them. Then I took the story to Scott Vance, Dana's immediate editor on the national news desk, for line-by-line editing. Dana had been watching me move around the newsroom as she awaited my decision. When she saw me talking to Scott, she went right over to him as I returned to my office. After he told her what I had decided, she returned to her desk very upset, as she told me many years later.

But characteristic of her fierce tenacity as a journalist, Dana didn't give up. She went back to Scott and suggested replacing the names of Poland, Romania, and Lithuania with the phrase "several democracies in Eastern Europe." That was accurate, of course. And the fact that they were democracies was part of the point of the story. The reference to a "Soviet-era compound" in the story's first sentence also was a hint.

Dana and Scott proposed the change to me. I quickly agreed, wondering why I hadn't thought of it.

Dana's 2,723-word story was published on the front page of the *Washington Post* on November 2, 2005, under a big, bold headline: "CIA Holds Terror Suspects in Secret Prisons," and a subhead in smaller type, "Debate Is Growing Within Agency About Legality and Morality of Overseas System Set Up After 9/11."

"The CIA has been hiding and interrogating some of its most important al Qaeda captives at a Soviet-era compound in Eastern Europe, according to U.S. and foreign officials familiar with the arrangement," the story began.

> The secret facility is part of a covert prison system set up by the CIA nearly four years ago that at various times has included sites in eight countries, including Thailand, Afghanistan and several democracies in Eastern Europe, as well as a small center at the Guantanamo Bay prison in Cuba, according to current and former intelligence officials and diplomats from three continents.
>
> The hidden global internment network is a central element in the CIA's unconventional war on terrorism. It depends on the cooperation of foreign intelligence services, and on keeping even basic information about the system secret from the public, foreign officials and nearly all members of Congress charged with overseeing the CIA's covert actions.
>
> The existence and locations of the facilities—referred to as "black sites" in classified White House, CIA, Justice Department and congressional documents—are known to only a handful of officials in the United States and, usually, only to the president and few top intelligence officers in each host country.

The story described the open-ended isolation in which terrorist suspects were being held in the black sites, in addition to the "enhanced interrogation techniques" to which they were subjected, including "tactics such as 'waterboarding,' in which a prisoner is made to believe he or she is drowning."

The story reported the "considerable concern" within the CIA about the covert program's "legality, morality and practicality." It also pointed out that "the Eastern European countries that the CIA has persuaded to hide al Qaeda captives are democracies that have embraced the rule of law and individual rights after decades of Soviet domination."

In the story's ninth paragraph, readers were told that "The Washington Post is not publishing the names of the Eastern European countries involved in the covert program, at the request of U.S. officials. They argued that the disclosure might disrupt counterterrorism efforts in those countries and elsewhere and could make them targets of possible terrorist retaliation."

I had decided that it was important to be as transparent as possible about my decision making and about how the story was reported. The story showed how Dana had found so much information about the covert program, and it revealed as much as possible about her sources and their motivation, without naming them.

While Dana had fought hard for everything she wanted to include in the story, she told me later: "I was so glad I didn't have to make the decision, for fear that something would get blown up."

Nothing was blown up by terrorists. But Dana's story exploded in Washington and across Europe.

Secretary of State Condoleezza Rice, who was traveling in Europe when the story was published, was asked about it wherever she went. Within hours of publication, the government of Romania demanded that the CIA close its secret prison there. The black site at a former riding school in Lithuania was shut down months later in 2006. The CIA black site in an intelligence training center at a remote villa in Poland had already been quietly closed, in anticipation of our story. The European Union and national governments and news media throughout the continent conducted investigations that eventually named the three countries as having hosted CIA secret prisons. Government officials in some countries lost their jobs amidst political and diplomatic recriminations.

The terrorist suspects were relocated to Guantanamo Bay. President Bush publicly acknowledged the CIA secret prison program on September 6, 2006, when he announced that all the overseas black sites had been shut down. I expected that, and I saw no evidence over the years that it was a serious setback for U.S. counterterrorism activities.

Congressional leaders initially called for an investigation, not of the CIA's covert program, but of what they considered leaks of classified information to the *Post*. Except for some lively hearings, which did not involve Dana or the newspaper, it went nowhere. Reader reaction ranged from accusations that the story was unpatriotic to criticisms of my decision to withhold the names of the Eastern European countries.

As Dana expected, many of her sources would no longer talk to her for fear of being investigated. As a precaution, she had squirreled away information about other aspects of the CIA's covert war on terrorism that produced several stories with more details before she had to abandon the intelligence beat for a while. "I was so blacklisted that I would scare people who I would call, really scare them," Dana recalled, "because they thought the government was spying on me."

Three years later, the Senate Intelligence Committee did begin an investigation of the CIA's covert program. The committee ultimately produced a 528-page report that was released in redacted form in December 2014. It revealed that the CIA had paid millions of dollars in inducements to the countries that agreed to host black sites, whose actual locations were kept secret from U.S. ambassadors, members of Congress and, yes, even President Bush. It detailed and labeled as "torture" the enhanced interrogation techniques used at the black sites, including waterboarding, much of which was later outlawed by President Barack Obama, court decisions, and legislation. The report also concluded that torture had not produced reliable information, but it had been effectively used as a recruiting tool by Al Qaeda and had damaged U.S. standing in the world. Without our story, this may never have been known.

Dana won the 2006 Pulitzer Prize for Beat Reporting "for her persistent, painstaking reports on secret 'black sites' prisons and other controversial features of the government's counterterrorism campaign."

22

Legacy

Perhaps the most meaningful moment of my seventeen years as executive editor of the *Washington Post* came near the end. Just after 3 p.m. on Monday, April 6, 2008, I stood in front of hundreds of colleagues gathered in the newsroom to announce that the *Post* had won six of the fourteen Pulitzer Prizes awarded for American journalism published in 2007. It was, as I told everyone, "an historic day for our newsroom."

It was exhilarating for us all—and bittersweet. As the *New York Times* reported the next day, "The *Post*'s Pulitzer haul may turn out to be something of a valedictory for Leonard Downie Jr., the paper's executive editor since 1991, who is widely rumored to be considering retiring later this year." In fact, I had already been told that I would retire before the end of the year at age sixty-six. Although it would not be announced for another two months, many in the newsroom had heard the rumor. A new publisher wanted a new editor for the *Post*'s tortuous transition into the digital age of news.

For the newsroom staff, the breadth of *Washington Post* journalism that was awarded those six prestigious prizes—one each for local, national, foreign, and investigative reporting, commentary, and feature writing—reinforced a sense of purpose and pride at a time of uncertainty. The digital revolution was steadily undermining the economics of the *Post* and all of the nation's newspapers. The *Post*'s print circulation, advertising revenue, profits, and newsroom staff all were shrinking at an alarming rate. Yet another buyout to further reduce the staff was coming.

For me, the journalism recognized by the Pulitzer Prizes that year epitomized what I had accomplished as leader of the *Post* newsroom—and what I hoped would remain its mission long after I had left: Investigative reporting that made a difference. Comprehensive, authoritative reporting of big breaking news events that affected people's lives. Vivid storytelling that emotionally engaged audiences in print and online. I thought of it as my legacy.

Reporters Dana Priest and Anne Hull and photographer Michel duCille won the Pulitzer Gold Medal for public service journalism for exposing the mistreatment of severely wounded soldiers at Walter Reed Army Medical Center in Washington. Priest had come to me with complaints from relatives of hospitalized Iraq War veterans. She teamed up with Hull and duCille. David Maraniss became their editor. Taking advantage of public access to the hospital, Priest, Hull, and duCille spent four months quietly observing and interviewing soldiers and staff at the Walter Reed complex. They found dirty, unsafe accommodations and poor medical care for hundreds of maimed soldiers remaining there for treatment after surgery at the hospital. When their first articles appeared on the front page of the *Post* in February 2007, the Army immediately began with clean-up, repairs, staff changes, and improvements in care. The commander of Walter Reed, the army surgeon general, and the secretary of the army were removed from their jobs.

Bart Gellman and Jo Becker won the national reporting Pulitzer for revealing how Vice President Dick Cheney wielded unprecedented power behind the scenes in the administration of President George W. Bush. I had successfully urged Gellman to take on what he initially thought was "just too hard a target" in the secretive, combative Cheney. Gellman eventually recruited Becker, and they showed how Cheney masterminded much of the controversial counterterrorism, tax, regulatory, and environmental policies of the Bush administration.

Steve Fainaru won the international reporting Pulitzer for exposing the unchecked, often violent actions of heavily armed private contractors employed by the Pentagon and State Department during the U.S. occupation of Iraq. After the contractors' frequent fatal shootings of Iraqi citizens first made news, managing editor Phil Bennett took a walk with Fainaru in downtown Washington. He persuaded Fainaru to go back to Iraq to investigate the contractors and their U.S. government employers.

The metropolitan news staff won the breaking news reporting Pulitzer for thorough, sensitive, and enterprising coverage of a horrific mass murder at Virginia Tech University, in which a deranged student shot forty-two people, killing thirty-one and himself. Our reporting in print and online was especially important to our readers, because more than 7,000 students at the Blacksburg, Virginia, campus were from the Washington area. The newsroom mobilized much as it did after 9/11. We eventually had seventy-five journalists working on the story. David Maraniss, who had undergone hip replacement surgery just three weeks earlier while on book leave, once again responded immediately after I called. Maraniss wrote a dramatic narrative reconstruction from the surviving students' experiences, based on his telephone interviews and reporting by *Post* journalists who went to the campus.

Steve Pearlstein won the commentary Pulitzer for his strongly argued business section columns about the dangers of excessive subprime mortgage lending, which helped lead to the credit crisis that undermined the world's financial system in 2008. Pearlstein was one of the very few financial journalists in the country to raise the alarm before the crisis became apparent. He explained clearly, with passion, how excessive "loosey-goosey lending" had infected greedy giants of Wall Street.

Gene Weingarten won the feature writing Pulitzer for his *Washington Post Magazine* story describing an audacious busker performance by classical violin virtuoso Joshua Bell, which Weingarten set up during the morning rush in a busy downtown Washington subway station. Bell, wearing casual clothes, was mostly ignored by commuters hurrying to work. Weingarten's lyrical account of the extraordinary scene, along with a video, were a hit on washingtonpost.com and with the Pulitzer judges.

IT WAS ONLY THE FOURTH TIME EVER THAT A NEWSPAPER WON more than three Pulitzer Prizes in one year. In 2002, the *New York Times* won seven, most of which were for stories, photography, and commentary about the 9/11 terrorist attacks on the World Trade Center. The *Los Angeles Times* won five in 2004, and the *Post* four in 2006. Altogether, the *Post* newsroom won a total of twenty-five Pulitzer Prizes while I was executive editor, the most in the tenure of any editor in the then almost one-hundred-year history of the prizes.

Among them were an unprecedented three Pulitzer gold medals for public service journalism under one editor—the one for Walter Reed in 2008 and back-to-back gold medals in 1999 and 2000. The *Post* also had won a public service gold medal for Watergate in 1973. Each gold medal recognized extraordinary journalism that made a difference.

The 1999 gold medal was for a *Post* investigation of unwarranted shootings by Washington police officers—which we found to be the highest rate of police shootings in the nation at that time. A team of fifteen reporters, computer analysts, graphic artists, and editors were led by Rick Atkinson, who was then the investigations editor. Jeff Leen, Sari Horwitz, and David Jackson were the primary reporters. The investigation prompted the department's leadership to extensively retrain the entire police force in the use of firearms. After thirty-two citizens were shot, twelve fatally, in 1998, only one would be killed by Washington police in 2000. I believe the *Post* saved lives. Leen would then take over the investigative reporting staff, and he would direct five more Pulitzer-winning investigations while I was executive editor.

The 2000 gold medal was for an investigation by Katherine Boo of the abuse and deaths of mentally retarded citizens living in 150 privately run group homes financed by the District of Columbia government at a cost Boo calculated to be about $100,000 per resident each year. Boo found 350 documented cases of physical abuse, neglect, and molestation of mentally retarded residents of the group homes during the 1990s—and 53 unexplained deaths in just three years—all without any sanctions of the group homes' owners by the city.

A year later, *Post* reporters Sari Horwitz and Scott Higham, working with database editor Sarah Cohen, won the Pulitzer Prize for investigative reporting for revealing that, over a seven-year period (1993 through

2000), 239 children had died in Washington after they or their families had come to the attention of the city's child protection system. By documenting the names and stories of 180 of those children, Horwitz and Higham showed how government officials knew for years about the system's fatal flaws and had done nothing about it. The *Post* investigations—both of the group homes for the mentally retarded and the deaths of the children in the city's child protection system—prompted investigations, court cases, and reforms that continued for years.

Investigative reporting had also won two of the four Pulitzer Prizes awarded to the *Post* in 2006. Dana Priest won in beat reporting for her exposure of the CIA's secret sites in Eastern Europe for the detention and interrogation of terrorism suspects. Sue Schmidt, Jeff Smith, and James Grimaldi won in investigative reporting for their revelations of the corrupt lobbying practices and relationships with members of Congress of influential lobbyist Jack Abramoff. He went to prison, along with Congressman Bob Ney and nine other lobbyists and congressional aides. Congressman Tom DeLay stepped down as House Majority Leader and left Congress.

JOURNALISM, THE OLD ADAGE GOES, SHOULD COMFORT THE AF-flicted and afflict the comfortable. That is just what the *Post* did during my leadership of the newsroom. We investigated presidents, members of Congress and other officials, many government agencies, lobbyists, corporations and their executives, even local schools and churches, and sports teams, coaches and athletes. Despite resistance, we published investigations that led to significant reforms of the United Way charity, the nonprofit Nature Conservancy, and the Smithsonian Institution, organizations long unaccustomed to scrutiny.

I worked with a succession of three brilliant managing editors—Bob Kaiser, Steve Coll, and Phil Bennett—to build, on Ben Bradlee's foundation, what became recognized as one of the leading newspapers in the world. We continued to attract many of the best journalists, increasing the newsroom staff to more than nine hundred people and its budget to more than $140 million a year at its peak in the early 2000s.

The *Post* dominated coverage of politics and the White House, opened new foreign bureaus, and covered local news more extensively than any other major paper. We experimented with new features, and we rigorously reexamined every part of the newspaper at our annual editors' retreats. While always finding room for improvement, I thought our journalism got better and better each year.

However, the entire time, we were heading into a storm that put all of that at risk.

The *Washington Post* was a local newspaper with national ambitions during my early years there. Watergate first gave it national, and even international, prominence. Ben and I then built national and foreign reporting that rivaled what we perceived as our competition. But the *Post* was still a locally based newspaper, whereas the *Wall Street Journal*, *New York Times*, and *USA Today* printed and sold newspapers across the country and depended on national advertising. Nearly all the *Post*'s newspaper circulation was in the Washington area and nearby Maryland and Virginia. The lion's share of its lucrative advertising was local—ads for department, specialty, and grocery stores, and for automobiles, real estate, and employment.

When I became executive editor, it was still an enviably strong economic model. In 1993, print circulation peaked at 832,000 for the daily paper and 1,158,000 on Sunday—the largest circulation in proportion to its local market in the country. The advertising revenue made possible by that audience paid for the steady expansion of the newsroom. It also produced solid profits for The Washington Post Company, which had been a publicly traded corporation, led by the Graham family, since 1971. The company also owned *Newsweek* magazine, half a dozen television stations, and Kaplan, an expanding for-profit education company. But the newspaper was still its economic center.

In a speech about the strength of the newspaper's local revenue base, Katharine Graham once said the *Post* was about Woodward and Bernstein, but also about Woodward and Lothrop, then a Washington department store that was the paper's largest advertiser. Her good friend, multibillionaire investor Warren Buffett, who owned 20 percent of the *Post*'s stock, was an influential business mentor for both Katharine and Don Graham. At one of Don's retreats for *Post* executives, Buffett emphasized to us the value at the time of the *Post*'s audience and advertising monopoly in the Washington area.

Beginning when I was Metro editor, I had doubled the staff covering local news. As managing editor and executive editor, I steadily increased national and foreign news coverage, which was important to much of the Washington area's federal workforce and international community. We also reached a national audience through our partnership with the *Los Angeles Times* in a news service used by many American newspapers. For a time, we published a national weekly print edition of the *Post* sold by mail subscription. And we reached a worldwide audience in the Paris-based *International Herald Tribune*, which the *Post* half-owned with the *New York Times*.

As the newsroom staff and budget steadily grew, I became known for insisting that we could do it all. I emphasized that the *Post* had become a unique source of outstanding local, national, and international journalism, including more investigative reporting than any other newspaper. At the same time, Don Graham continued to emphasize the importance of the *Post*'s local circulation and revenue base. While the times were good, neither of us saw our messages as conflicting.

IN 1992, HIS SECOND YEAR AS MY MANAGING EDITOR, BOB KAISER had accepted an invitation from then Apple CEO John Scully to attend a conference in Japan at which technology company executives and leading analysts discussed the future of media in the nascent digital age. Widespread use of the internet was still a few years away. But Kaiser wrote a prescient seven-page memo to Don, me, and key *Post* executives, saying, "I was taken aback by predictions at the conference about the next stage of the computer revolution." He correctly foresaw that the news industry would profoundly change as people sought out news and information on computers.

"'Multimedia' or 'new media' is a popular idea for one possible use of these powerful computers connected by a fiber optic cable network," Kaiser wrote, foreshadowing the "World Wide Web" then still being developed. "The *Post* ought to be in the forefront of this—not for adventure, but for important defensive purposes."

He recommended that the *Post* "design the world's first electronic newspaper" and "explore the feasibility of incorporating ads" into it.

"Change is coming," he concluded. "There's a big and important role for the *Washington Post* in this new world."

Kaiser also recommended that the *Post* design electronic classified ads that could be searched by computer. Unfortunately, that didn't happen fast enough at the *Post* or any other newspaper. Instead, Craigslist debuted in the San Francisco area in 1998 and expanded nationwide in 2000. It eventually decimated classified advertising, one of the largest sources of revenue for newspapers.

Don was slow at first to explore Kaiser's vision. But the *Post* eventually became a pioneer in digital news. It first experimented with a subscription daily news and information service for personal computers through the dial-up online service provider CompuServe. The *Post* then moved to the internet and launched washingtonpost.com as a free news website in 1996.

The website began as a separate subsidiary of the *Post*. Don located it across the Potomac River in northern Virginia, a right-to-work state, to avoid union problems and labor strikes that had plagued the *Post* in the past. He and I also agreed that the website should be free to experiment digitally, independent of the newsroom, where much of the staff was at that time wary of what would happen to news on the internet. All the website's news stories still came from the newsroom, however, and I had the final say about how they were used.

Don created a new division of the company and invested tens of millions of dollars in washingtonpost.com before it began earning any significant revenue from digital advertising. I thought it could expose *Post* journalism to larger national and international audiences. Don was seeking to recover some of the printed newspaper's lost local audience and advertising.

In 1998, Steve Coll succeeded Bob Kaiser as my managing editor and the driver of the newsroom's relationship with washingtonpost.com. Kaiser wanted to return to writing. He had signed on for only five years as managing editor, and he had given me seven.

Coll soon attended a digital news conference in Atlanta, and he came back convinced, as Kaiser had been, that *Post* journalism could thrive on the internet. "The *Post* can innovate and experiment on the Web, bolstered by confidence in its old-fashioned journalistic values—accuracy, independence, completeness, honesty, depth, and a commitment to holding government and public institutions accountable," he wrote in a 1999 memo for the newsroom. "The chaotic explosion of channels made possible by the Web is driving online audiences increasingly toward credible and reliable news outlets."

He worked with the then editor of washingtonpost.com, Doug Feaver, to create an afternoon "PM Extra" edition on the website, with postings written by *Post* reporters about developing stories. Coll held "road show" meetings with reporters and editors throughout the newsroom to share his vision and persuade them to write stories for the website in addition to the print newspaper. They increasingly did so, led by reporters on the national news staff, who saw in the immediacy of the website a way to beat competitors and attract new sources. We built a television studio in the newsroom, and *Post* reporters made appearances on local and national television to talk about their stories and attract more people to our website.

The national audience for washingtonpost.com grew steadily. PM Extra evolved into a "continuous news desk" in the *Post* newsroom for day-long production of stories for the website. As I wrote earlier, readership surged for our extensive reporting online about the long count in the 2000 presidential election. At the peak of audience traffic for that coverage, washingtonpost.com had a then unprecedented six million unique monthly visitors. Coll noticed that four million of them came from around the nation, one million from abroad, and only one million from the circulation area of the print newspaper. That gave him an idea.

MEANWHILE, *NEW YORK TIMES* PUBLISHER ARTHUR SULZBERGER Jr. pressured Don into selling the *Post's* half ownership of the *International Herald Tribune* to the *Times*, ending thirty-five years of partnership. I was one of the *Post* members of the *IHT* board. Janice and I enjoyed its rather lavish annual meetings in Paris, complete with tickets to the French Open tennis tournament. But I noticed and resented that the *Times* members of the board had begun blocking changes needed to cope with new competition and other issues. So I was not really surprised that Don asked me to come to his office in late 2002, when Sulzberger telephoned him about dissolving the partnership.

What I heard was insulting to Don, if not blatantly bullying. If Don did not sell, Sulzberger made clear, the *Times* would pull out and start a competing international edition. Alternatively, he said that the *Post* could retain a small minority share in the *IHT*, and *Times* editors would decide whether to publish *Post* stories in it. From my perch on a couch across Don's office, I signaled that I would not want that to happen. Don sold the *Post*'s share of the *IHT* to the *Times* on December 30 for $70 million—money that the *Times* never recouped from the international paper.

The sale was a shock to *Post* foreign correspondents, who counted on the *IHT* for distribution of their stories around the world. I remembered that most of the stories I wrote as the *Post*'s London correspondent had appeared in the *IHT*, often on the front page. That had given me additional credibility and influence with my sources and the governments I covered. After the sale to the *Times*, Don and I were able to reach an agreement with the *Wall Street Journal* to have some *Post* stories published in its international edition. But it was not the same for our correspondents, and it did not last.

The *IHT* lost both *Washington Post* journalism and its editor, David Ignatius, who became a foreign affairs columnist for the *Post*. He and his predecessor, former *Post* deputy managing editor Michael Getler, had considerably improved the *IHT* over the previous six years. They both had been successful foreign news editors at the *Post*, and they were especially well-prepared to run an international paper. But I guessed that *Times* editors back in New York resented the influence that *Post* veterans Getler and Ignatius had in the *IHT* newsroom.

DON WAS MORE INTERESTED THAN EVER IN THE INTERNET. BUT he also invested $230 million in new printing plants in suburban Maryland and Virginia, which were producing beautiful full-color editions of the *Washington Post*. Nevertheless, print circulation was declining by 1 to 2 percent, daily and Sunday, every year. Don worried about that and its potential impact on advertising revenue. It would be on his mind when he was confronted with Steve Coll's big idea.

With my blessing, Coll created a task force of *Post* newspaper and website editors and business managers to study what the *Post*'s national and international strategy should be after the *IHT* breakup. After six months' work, its members decided that it would not be wise to try to print and distribute the *Post* nationally or to create an international print edition. Instead, they would recommend that Don invest in greatly expanding the national and international audience that washingtonpost.com was already attracting on the internet. I agreed with their analysis and endorsed their recommendation.

Coll thought Don would be pleased that the task force was not recommending a national print edition, but rather a much less expensive increase in national and international digital journalism. He was so sure of it that he did not brief Don before he presented the task force report on March 20, 2003, at an off-site meeting of *Post* editors and business managers at the Inn at Perry Cabin in St. Michael's, Maryland.

Coll found Don's reaction to be completely unexpected and discouraging. Don did not really address the merits of the task force's recommendation. Instead, he essentially accused it of abandoning the newspaper's bedrock local audience and mission. He asked Coll how the proposal would play with the proverbial firefighter in suburban Prince William County, Virginia.

After the meeting broke up, Coll met me as we walked to our cars. He was despondent. His big idea had been rejected. I tried to explain that I'd found over the years that Don often reacted in what seemed to be a hostile way to ideas for which he was unprepared, and that he often came around later, even if it required considerable argument. But Coll told someone else before we all drove back to Washington, "I'm done."

When I asked Don about the meeting for this book, he said his reaction to Coll's proposal might have been a mistake. After all, Don had presided over considerable growth in the *Post*'s national and international digital audience. What was on his mind, he told me, was that he feared Coll was too interested in long narrative stories that he thought might turn off the *Post*'s average local readers.

Coll told me that Don's reaction was indeed a turning point for him, in what became a slow-motion decision to leave the *Post*. His 2004 book, *Ghost Wars*, was a critical and commercial success, winning the 2005 Pulitzer Prize for general nonfiction. That nudged Coll further along. "I had always dreamed of writing big books," he told me. Don tried to reconcile with him on lunchtime walks. But Coll recalled that Don also told him, "Don't write another book."

"I thought it was worth giving my life to the *Washington Post* only if we're growing, only if we're going big, being a force in the world," Coll told me. "I didn't want to manage decline."

Coll resigned as managing editor at the end of 2004. He would work as a writer for the *New Yorker* magazine, head the New America Foundation, publish more books, and eventually become dean of the Columbia University Graduate School of Journalism. His vision for worldwide success for *Washington Post* journalism on the internet would eventually become a reality, but only under a new owner.

I HAD WONDERED AT THE TIME: *WAS I MANAGING DECLINE? WOULD that be my legacy?*

The slide in print circulation accelerated, and advertising revenue recovered only slowly from the 2001 recession. Don decided that the newspaper had to cut costs. At the end of 2003, the *Post* offered a generous buyout to employees over the age of fifty-five with more than ten years of service. Depending on longevity, they were eligible for up to two years' salary, increased pensions, and health care until they turned sixty-five. Fifty-four people in the newsroom took the buyout, which would be the first of several. I was able to keep on contract some people who took the buyout, and I hired other journalists for new roles. As the *Post* newsroom staff began to shrink from over 900 people in 2003, it was still one of the largest in the country.

But many editors and reporters began to worry. Too many Friday afternoons in the newsroom in 2004 featured cakes and goodbyes for colleagues who were leaving.

The cutbacks did not directly affect the much smaller website staff. In 2003, the *Post* started a lively five-day-a-week tabloid paper, called *Express*, with a separate, small staff, which was distributed free to hundreds of thousands of bus and subway riders every day. (It was discontinued in 2019 because too many transit riders were reading news on their phones instead.) We conducted a seventeen-month experiment in presenting

Washington Post news and talk on a local radio station, which ended in August 2007.

As paid circulation of the printed *Post* continued to fall, its marketing department convened focus groups and did more polling. Many people said they had less time to read the newspaper. At the urging of the marketing department, we decided to make routine stories shorter and the newspaper more physically attractive and easier to navigate for younger adult readers. We delivered slightly different newspapers to readers in the District of Columbia, Maryland, and Virginia, in which local stories about their areas were displayed more prominently. I worked on all of this in retreats with the top editors and in mass meetings with the newsroom staff, in which I repeatedly emphasized the need for change to improve readership.

In hindsight, however, I can see that most of it was an unhelpful diversion, if not completely wrongheaded. Instead, I should have been more engaged with our website, as I would be toward the end of my time as executive editor. Even after most of us in the newsroom realized the importance of washingtonpost.com, some of the newspaper's business managers still saw the website as a rival for the printed newspaper's audience and advertising, on which their annual bonuses were based. They pushed the newsroom to concentrate on what turned out to be a fool's errand of trying to shore up print circulation, rather than overall *Post* readership both in print and online. I often pushed back on or ignored pressure from the business side of the newspaper, putting me at odds with some of its executives, who resented my influence with Don and Bo Jones.

The newsroom was busier than ever, with, among other stories, the 2004 election, the wars in Iraq and Afghanistan, national security issues, and an abundance of investigative projects. Audience surveys showed that readers rated the quality of our journalism highly. The best stories attracted ever larger audiences on washingtonpost.com, where even some of the longest stories, like the Walter Reed investigation, were among the most widely and thoroughly read.

I thought that, journalistically, we were still on the right road. But I was uncertain about how to adapt to the other challenges of the digital revolution.

IN LATE 2004, I HAD TO REPLACE STEVE COLL AS MANAGING ED-
itor after he stepped down from the job. As I had in choosing Coll, I established an open process in which candidates submitted detailed memos
and endured probing interviews with me about how they would do the
job. As usual, Tom Wilkinson asked people throughout the newsroom
for their views on potential candidates. The finalists were foreign news
editor Phil Bennett, national news editor Liz Spayd, and Style section
editor Gene Robinson, an African American. The *Post* had never had a
woman or person of color as managing editor.

I saw the emergence of Spayd and Robinson as evidence of success in increasing the number of women and minority journalists in
the newsroom, as well as their opportunities for good assignments and
supervisory positions. But I found that I was still somewhat out of touch
with their feelings.

In the end, I selected Bennett to be managing editor, based in part on
his exceptional direction of the coverage of the Iraq and Afghanistan wars
and his tireless devotion to the care and safety of his correspondents. He
also had worked with some of the best journalists outside his own staff
on award-winning projects. Based on his memos and our conversations,
I believed that he could work effectively with me in reorienting the newsroom for the website, while ensuring that outstanding journalism was
our primary goal.

However, many in the newsroom were surprised that I had not taken
the opportunity to promote Spayd or Robinson. Passing over Robinson
was particularly disappointing for the African American journalists. He
was a talented reporter and editor, well-liked, and a symbol of achieve-
ment. At a newsroom staff meeting two weeks after Bennett's selection,
several African American journalists expressed their concern to me. As
it turned out, Robinson would become a syndicated *Post* columnist and
television commentator. He won the Pulitzer Prize for commentary in
2009. During the *Post* newsroom ceremony, Robinson thanked me for
not giving him the job of managing editor.

I also was involved in the 2004 selection of Jim Brady to be executive editor of washingtonpost.com. He had worked previously at the
newspaper, at AOL, and as sports editor of the website. He was becoming

a leading expert in digital journalism. When I interviewed him for the top website newsroom job, Brady kept steering the conversation toward the need for blogs on washingtonpost.com. I was mystified at first, as no newspaper journalist had started a blog by that time. I was picturing the caricature of someone in their pajamas sitting in front of a home computer.

With Brady's leadership, the *Post* soon became the first newspaper at which its journalists regularly wrote blogs for its website. By mid-2006, washingtonpost.com featured forty blogs by sports, politics, business, and Style reporters, critics, and columnists. It also conducted online chats with *Post* journalists and editors, including me. With my agreement, Brady was a pioneer in enabling website readers to attach their comments to our stories. In mid-2007, Bennett and I designated an editor on each of the newsroom's staffs to focus on journalism for the website, working with their counterparts at washingtonpost.com. Brady and I oversaw an innovative plan for the newspaper and the website to collaborate on coverage of the 2008 election.

While I was working so well with Brady, I realized that it was time to merge the newspaper and website newsrooms. I began discussing with the *Post*'s vice president for advertising, Katharine Weymouth, how we could persuade Don to merge both the news and business operations of the newspaper and the website. Weymouth was Don's niece and Katharine Graham's granddaughter. She was a lawyer who worked at the *Post*'s outside law firm, Williams and Connolly, before Don brought her to the *Post*. When he promoted her at the paper, everyone assumed he was grooming her to eventually succeed himself, as his mother had done with Don.

I thought that I had gotten along well with Weymouth while we worked together on changes in the newspaper designed to increase advertising opportunities without compromising its journalism. But apparently some people on the business side of the newspaper made clear to her that they saw me as an impediment to continued cost-cutting and other changes they wanted to make.

In November 2007, Bennett presented to me an ambitious, detailed plan—"The Post/2010"—to further reorganize the newsroom to work more effectively with the website and reduce staff and costs, while concentrating resources on our highest journalistic priorities. It coincided with the coming of the newspaper's third buyout of older employees. I was so immersed in news like the Virginia Tech shootings and projects like Walter Reed, plus preparations for the 2008 election, that I don't remember what I thought about Bennett's plan. It turned out not to matter what I thought.

23

Farewell

AS WAS MY HABIT, I CHOSE TO WALK UP THE
nearby back stairs from my fifth-floor newsroom
office to Bo Jones's publisher suite on the seventh floor
of the *Washington Post* building. He had scheduled a
meeting with me at 5 p.m. on Thursday, January 31,
2008. I figured it might be about the latest buyout offer
being prepared for scores more *Post* employees, including many in the newsroom. I had in my hand a list of
things I wanted to discuss with Jones.

When I reached the sixth-floor landing, I suddenly
wondered, almost aloud: *Do they want me to retire?*

I knew I was eligible for the buyout, which would be
very lucrative for me. But I had expected to stay in my
job until I reached seventy, as Ben had, even as he had
given me most of the responsibility for the newspaper.
In fact, Don had more than once suggested that he and
I might retire together, although Don was three years
younger than I was. I also was still deep into restructuring the newsroom to try to protect its journalistic mission and strengthen its relationship with our website,
while cutting costs and staff.

I had discussed those changes at a confidential lunch with my top editors two weeks earlier. We talked about how we could use the upcoming, still secret, third buyout to further reorganize and do some strategic hiring into some of the vacancies we expected. I had taken detailed notes and planned upcoming working group meetings with Bennett and me. I emphasized to the editors my determination to see this transition through to a successful conclusion.

In Jones's office, he came out from behind his desk to a chair facing the couch on which I was sitting. He was a tall, trim man with an almost shy, genteel Southern manner. He was holding a piece of paper. Seeing that, I held up my list and said, "I have a number of things to run by you, but you can go first, since you scheduled the meeting."

"Why don't you go first?" Jones suggested, and I did. While we talked, I noticed that he seemed unusually distracted.

Then, clutching his piece of paper, he said, without preamble, that Katharine Weymouth would be replacing him as publisher of the newspaper—and that she also would become publisher of washingtonpost .com. Jones said it would be announced in a week, at the end of the scheduled publisher's meeting with department heads from throughout the newspaper. Jones said Don wanted him "to help out at corporate" as vice chairman.

I told Jones that I thought it was time to put both the newspaper and the website under the same publisher, but that I didn't expect it to come at his expense. He smiled wanly.

Then, in a nervous, almost offhanded way, Jones added, "They also want you to retire. You should take the buyout."

I became numb as he discussed the details. I should "secretly" complete the paperwork for my buyout and make financial arrangements, he said. Weymouth would work with me on when I would announce and take my retirement.

I was determined not to show how shocked I was. I did not argue or ask questions. Jones, with whom I had worked closely for years, appeared to be uncomfortable enough.

I stumbled down the stairs to the newsroom, fighting back tears. I felt panicky as I went into my office, trying hard not to show any emotion that could be seen through its glass wall facing the newsroom. I first called Janice, who had become the rock in my life during a decade of marriage. I practically whispered so that I could not be overheard by my loyal, longtime executive assistant, Pat O'Shea, who was sitting at her desk just outside my office.

"Something big, something life-changing has just happened," I told Janice, mumbling about retirement. I told her that I would not stay in the newsroom for the Democratic presidential candidates' debate that night. I would come home early to talk.

Then I reached Don, who was out of the building, on his mobile phone. I asked if I could talk to him the next day. He knew why I was calling, and he suggested that I come that evening to his home, where we could talk alone. I again telephoned Janice, who said that she thought that would be a good idea.

I arrived at 6:30 p.m. at Don's beautiful, recently purchased, historic townhouse just north of downtown near Dupont Circle. I found it still in the late stages of renovation. Don had just moved in after separating from his wife. Plastic sheeting covered the floors, stairs, and most of the furniture. We found places to sit in an upstairs bedroom, me on a recliner and Don facing me on the edge of the bed. I was still in a sport coat and tie; Don wore a winter sweater.

He began by reviewing what I already knew in his shorthand way. "Kath," Don said, referring to Weymouth, did not know what to do about a new editor. She would need time to find one. We briefly discussed a few possible candidates in the newsroom, including Phil Bennett and several editors at other newspapers. Then Don assured me about "practical things." He would give me the title of vice president at large, like Ben's, and an office on one of the executive floors. Pat O'Shea could continue as my paid assistant. Don was talking around why I was there.

Finally, I broached the subject. Was there something about my performance that led to this? Was I not changing the newsroom fast enough?

"You've been a great editor. Very few people could have done the job you did," he told me. "Kath has never said anything bad about you. It is just time for a change—for both of us.

"Kath will do things I would not have done," Don said, "things I might not like." He noted that I, Weymouth, and others had been urging him to merge the newspaper and the website. He added that "2008 will be a difficult year for both of us." We began to cry unashamedly.

Don asked if Janice and I still wanted to have a scheduled dinner with him the next night at a nearby restaurant. "Sure, we do," I responded, knowing what Janice would say. "I think that's very thoughtful."

I went home and talked everything through with Janice. For a diversion, we watched and analyzed the Democratic candidates' debate. I woke up in the middle of the night, fretting, and she awakened and comforted me.

Somehow, the next morning felt very much like the first day of a new life when I entered the newsroom. Fortunately, it became a busy day. I did a lot of planning with the national news editors for coverage of upcoming primary elections and the Democratic and Republican national nominating conventions in the summer. They would be my thirteenth and fourteenth conventions, going back to 1984. I loved the nonstop intensity of the political conventions and election nights, when I found no story or detail in our coverage to be too small for my attention. It helped on that day to look forward to the possibility of a 2008 finale before I left.

I also started thinking about how to prepare for my exit. I could not tell Pat O'Shea yet. I mused to myself about what files and books I would keep, and what we would throw away. I had a memoir like this book in the back of my mind. I realized that I would be on two tracks for the months ahead. I felt bad about not being able to tell Bennett yet. It was hard not talking about everything to anyone besides Janice and Don. I wondered what it would be like to not be in the newsroom anymore, after forty-four years, even though I expected to write more books, having just finished a novel. Like a spectator at an evocative movie, I noticed anew the newsroom banter, the stimulating discussions about stories, and my decision making about the next day's newspaper.

At 7 p.m., I arrived at Don's favorite Italian restaurant to join him and Janice. Ever the outgoing and sensitive partner in our marriage, Janice asked Don about how he was feeling and how his grown children were. In my somewhat wondrous state of mind, I was impressed once again by her charm and empathy, her adaptation to the situation.

Don seemed awkward. He kept moving his pen in and out of a shirt pocket under his sweater. "I don't know what's going to happen next," he said, somewhat cryptically, without elaboration. I was beginning to feel uncomfortable.

Then he asked me how I felt. I told him that I was still recovering from the shock; I said that it was hard, but I was managing. "I'll make sure that everything is okay for you and Bo," he said, a promise on which he would make good. After dinner, he hugged each of us tightly, his eyes glistening. In all the years we worked together, I had never felt closer to Don, even though most of what we were feeling went unsaid.

FINALLY, AT 4:30 P.M. ON MONDAY, FEBRUARY 4, KATHARINE Weymouth invited me to her sixth-floor office, where she asked me how I was doing. My response was brief and guarded. She pressed me on a timetable for my retirement. "I'm thinking of three to six months," she told me. That would rule out running election night in the newsroom, but I didn't argue. She said she would need time to learn the newsroom and to find a new executive editor.

"We'll talk," she added. "We have to make cuts but preserve the newspaper's quality. The next three years will be crucial."

As it turned out, we did not talk very much again about the future, although she did involve me in the search for my successor. When I once suggested that I could help with strategy for merging the website and the paper, Weymouth was not interested. Outside the newsroom, my time was already over.

At seven that evening, I took Phil Bennett across 15th Street to the lounge of the Madison Hotel, and I told him everything. "I think it's wrong," he said. "The newsroom will be shocked. You *are* the *Washington Post.*"

The ascension of Weymouth, then forty-one, to chief executive of the newly formed Washington Post Media, with oversight of the newspaper and its website, was announced later that week, along with the new buyout plan. Nothing was said about my future. In an interview with *Post* reporter Frank Ahrens, I said that the newspaper and website newsrooms were already working more closely together.

Weymouth eventually told me the dates she had set for my retirement and its announcement. I told no one else in the newsroom, except for Fred Hiatt, the editor of the editorial page. He had worked under me as an outstanding local and national reporter and foreign correspondent in Tokyo and Moscow. Even though I tried to ignore editorial page opinions, he and I respected each other's journalistic values, and we sometimes consulted on staffing.

On March 28, he sent me a handwritten note that meant a lot to me. "Since you shared your news, I've been trying to imagine the *Post* without you," he wrote. "I won't engage in any long tribute. But your rock-solid integrity has been a model and an inspiration."

"On the plus side," he added, "now you can start reading our editorials."

After the announcements of the Pulitzer Prizes in early April, speculation that I might retire was everywhere. Word got around that Weymouth was talking to possible candidates to replace me. When a *New York Times* reporter interviewed me in mid-May about what had become obvious, I said, "The new publisher and I are working hard on restructuring the newsroom, and I would expect that any new publisher would eventually have a new editor, and we're working on that."

The *Times* story noted that the *Post* had just two executive editors in the past forty-three years—Ben Bradlee and me. I counted eight at the *Times*—six of them while I was executive editor of the *Post*.

AT 3:30 P.M. ON JUNE 23, 2008, NEARLY EIGHTY DAYS AFTER THE announcement of our six Pulitzer Prizes, another large crowd gathered in the newsroom. Don Graham and Katharine Weymouth were standing with me outside my office. Janice had taken a seat close to me at a nearby desk. Phil Bennett, Bob Kaiser, and Ben Bradlee stood nearby. I picked up a microphone connected to the sound system for the newsroom and our news bureaus around Washington.

"On June 22, 1964—forty-four years ago yesterday—I came to work in the newsroom of the *Washington Post* as a summer intern," I began, reading a speech I had written with care. I retraced the steps of my career at the *Post*, including my investigative reporting and various editing positions, beginning with the old city desk, "where one of my reporters was a promising young journalist named Donald Graham."

I said that the most rewarding accomplishment of my seventeen years as executive editor "is how much we have enriched—and sometimes changed—the lives of our readers with vital information and good reading day after day. Especially when we have given voice to the voiceless in our society and held the powerful accountable."

The changes now needed at the *Post* in the digital era "brought us a new publisher," I said. "A new, young publisher needs a new, younger editor.

"It is time for me to retire, which I will do on September 8."

I thanked many people: Katharine Graham and Don Graham, Bo Jones and Ben Bradlee, my managing editors Kaiser, Steve Coll, and Bennett, and many other colleagues standing before me. That was easy so far. My voice had been strong, and my delivery measured. But as I turned to the last page, I came to the most difficult part to read.

"My devotion to the *Washington Post* has been so intense that it has often crowded my personal life," I confessed. "So, I'm boundlessly thankful for the love, support and happiness given to me by my wife Janice, who is here today.

"As Janice and the six children in our blended family know all too well, this newsroom has been more than a home away from home for me." My voice was cracking, and I had to pause. "I love all of you—and I love our newspaper. I will always cherish what we have accomplished together. To everyone standing here before me and listening to me elsewhere—and everyone who worked with us over the years—I simply want to say, thank you, thank you very, very much for the experience of a lifetime."

Ben and I embraced. As Janice watched intently, Weymouth spoke, saying, "Len is incontrovertibly one of the great editors of our time."

Then Don said, "In the second half of the twentieth century, I believe I speak for all of us saying, we have worked with the best in the business." We embraced, tearful again.

The applause went on and on, as I tried to maintain some composure. I thanked everyone repeatedly. "I'll never forget this moment," I told them. "Now, get back to work."

Indulging myself, as I am now, I did read a June 25 *Post* editorial about change at the newspaper and for me. "For a generation of readers," it stated, "Mr. Downie's integrity, fierce commitment to fairness and determination to produce a compelling newspaper every single day—which, counting seven years as managing editor, amounts to some 9,000 news-papers—have defined *Post* journalism. For a generation of journalists, Mr. Downie set the standard."

THE REST OF MY TENURE PASSED ANTICLIMACTICALLY, ALTHOUGH I stayed immersed in directing the collaborative coverage of the election campaign by the newspaper and the website. On July 8, Weymouth announced that forty-seven-year-old former *Wall Street Journal* editor Marcus Brauchli would replace me on September 8. He had combined the *Journal's* print and online newsrooms, before Rupert Murdoch's News Corporation bought the *Journal* and forced Brauchli out. I was among those at the *Post*, besides Weymouth, who had interviewed him for the *Post* job.

On Saturday, October 8, after I had moved out of the newsroom to my retirement office upstairs, former *Washington Post* journalists Bradley Graham and Lissa Muscatine held an amazing retirement party for me. Hundreds of colleagues, friends, and relatives of Janice and mine overflowed their spacious home in suburban Maryland.

The party featured a skit largely written and directed by Valerie Strauss, a smart and cheeky *Post* reporter whom I had always counted on to tell truth to my power in the newsroom. Over the years, she had taken full advantage of my open-door policy, appearing in my office whenever something at the newspaper was worrying her or others in the newsroom. Before each of my many meetings with the entire newsroom staff, I would strategize about what challenging question Strauss might ask, so I could prepare an answer. She never disappointed, and her questions usually prompted helpful discussions about significant issues in the newsroom.

Many of my newsroom friends participated in Strauss's multi-scene skit at the retirement party. It satirized my accidental summer internship, preoccupation with weather stories, pursuit of President Clinton, micromanagement of political coverage, addiction to chocolate, rumored sex scenes in my soon-to-be-published novel, and what I might write about in a memoir. It was outrageous, funny, and right on the mark. It reminded me of newsroom camaraderie that I had taken for granted, and that I would miss in my new life.

A month later, on election night, November 8, I was back in the newsroom after all, at the invitation of Brauchli and politics editor Steven Ginsberg. I was assigned to run the "decision desk," and to make "the calls," for website and newspaper stories and charts, about who won the presidency and key congressional and state races, as early as possible. I worked with polling data, raw vote trends, network television projections, and assessments by *Post* political journalists. As usual, the newsroom was filled to capacity with people working on the election, including college journalism students who telephoned state election officials and experts for further information when I needed it.

It would have been an extraordinarily enjoyable last hurrah, had I not felt so harried, and at times somewhat inadequate, trying to make accurate decisions fast enough. Ginsberg was kind, but on more than one occasion, I was surrounded by a ring of political reporters and editors anxiously awaiting my next call. Fortunately for me, it was easy to declare Barack Obama the winner of the presidency relatively early.

Finally, I was able to sit back and take in all the digital technology and the video camera crews who were scanning the election night newsroom and interviewing its journalists for washingtonpost.com. I realized how much everything was changing. It was indeed my time to go, and I appreciated the thanks and best wishes from everyone who stopped by before they left the newsroom that night.

Long after midnight, some of us walked a few blocks from the *Post* building to the streets around the White House, which were filled with celebrating Obama supporters. Young and old, men and women, white and black, they crowded every street as far we could see, many of them singing spontaneously. I had not voted, of course, and I did not know what kind of president Obama would be. But I could feel the change that infused that early morning. Just as I had felt the change in the *Post* newsroom. Just as I could feel the profound change coming in my life.

24

The *Post*

I DO NOT REMEMBER THE EXACT DAY OR TIME, but I will always remember the telephone call. I was driving somewhere in Washington in early August 2013 when my Blackberry rang. I slowed down, took it out of the case on my belt, and answered.

"I'm in my car," I told Don Graham.

"Then pull over."

I did.

"This has to be absolutely confidential for now."

I agreed.

"We're selling the newspaper."

It was a complete and shocking surprise to me.

Don explained that the *Post* was being sold to Jeff Bezos, the multibillionaire founder of Amazon. The newspaper would be bought by Bezos personally, not by Amazon, a publicly traded company. I had a hard time digesting what Don was saying. Regardless of the rest of The Washington Post Company's holdings in television, cable, and education, which were not being sold, the newspaper had been Don's life. Our devotion to it was something we had long shared, even after my retirement.

It was a very difficult decision for Don. When he telephoned his long-time friend, Arthur Sulzberger Jr., publisher of the *New York Times*, the other leading family-controlled American newspaper, to tell him about it, Sulzberger burst into tears.

The *Post* had been family controlled ever since Don's grandfather, Eugene Meyer, bought it at auction in 1933. Even after it became a public corporation in 1971, the Graham family controlled the voting stock. But Don and The Post company's board still felt a duty to shareholders. In recent years, the only way to maintain the newspaper as a profitable part of the corporation appeared to be constant cost-cutting.

Katharine Weymouth had been working on the digital transformation of the *Post* and exploring ways to increase its revenue. Marcus Brauchli, my successor as executive editor, merged the print and website newsrooms while continuing to reduce the size of the staff. In an understandably difficult period, he was seen as a remote figure in the newsroom.

At the end of 2012, Weymouth decided to replace Brauchli with *Boston Globe* editor Marty Baron. He had been a strong leader at the *Globe*, who emphasized investigative reporting, while coping with budget pressure from its then owner, the *New York Times*. The *Globe* had won the 2003 Pulitzer gold medal for public service for its investigation of widespread sexual abuse of children by Catholic priests in Boston. Baron would later be brilliantly portrayed by actor Liev Schreiber in the Academy Award–winning movie *Spotlight*, an inspiring, meticulously accurate drama about the *Globe*'s investigation and Baron's leadership.

Almost immediately, Baron energized the *Post* newsroom. In June 2013, he began publishing stories by Bart Gellman and other *Post* reporters about secret surveillance of Americans by the National Security Agency, based on classified documents obtained from NSA subcontractor Edward Snowden. The *Post* stories won the Pulitzer Prize for national reporting, shared with Britain's *Guardian* newspaper, which also received documents from Snowden. Baron's decision to publish those stories showed that he would be as bold at the *Post* as he had been at the *Globe*.

However, Weymouth still faced a daunting financial future for the newspaper, and she was unable to figure a way out of it. She and Don reluctantly decided that it would be best to sell the newspaper to a private owner who could and would stop the bleeding and make needed invest-ments in digital innovation. Bezos, whom Don already knew, emerged from the search by an investment banking firm. In their conversations, Don was assured by Bezos that he would be committed to the *Post*'s sur-vival and growth as a leading digital news organization.

I attended a mass meeting of employees at the *Post* on August 5, 2013, when Don and Weymouth announced the sale of the newspaper to Bezos for $250 million. Many of the people crowded into the first-floor audito-rium cried. They realized that an era had ended, and they did not know what might come next.

A month later, Bezos visited the *Post* from Seattle. He attended a se-ries of meetings, including a town hall for the entire newsroom staff in that same auditorium. Bezos promised to invest in the newspaper with his "long financial runway." He emphasized that he considered the *Post* a vital American institution.

"I do feel that newspapers, and in particular the *Washington Post*, are important components of free societies," Bezos said. "We should think big about what is the next golden age of the *Washington Post*."

He emphasized that he would not influence the *Post*'s newsgathering or editorial policies. He would concentrate instead on the investment and experimentation necessary to grow its audience on the internet. Bezos would be in touch about that with Baron and other key *Post* leaders through regular telephone calls and periodic meetings in Seattle.

Less than a year after the sale of the *Post* was final, Bezos removed Katharine Weymouth as publisher and replaced her with Fred Ryan, a member of the Washington establishment. Ryan had worked in President Ronald Reagan's White House, served as his chief of staff after Reagan's two terms ended, and later became chairman of the trustees of the Reagan Presidential Foundation. He also had been vice chairman of Allbritton Communications, then a Washington-based television, cable, and inter-net company. Ryan would facilitate Bezos's investments in the *Post*, while leaving the newsroom independent.

Marty Baron was able to greatly expand the newsroom staff and its reporting. Plentiful cutting-edge news stories, popular new website fea-tures, and numerous online newsletters significantly increased its au-dience on the internet. *New York Times* media critic David Carr wrote in an October 5, 2014, column that "the killer app" behind the *Post*'s surging internet traffic "is real, actual news. And the *Post* has generated a ton of it."

Baron particularly fostered investigative journalism and aggressive national reporting. Under his leadership, the *Post* won the Pulitzer Prize for national reporting an unprecedented three years in a row—in 2015 for reporter Carol Leonnig's investigation of the U.S. Secret Service, in 2016 for a staff investigation of police shootings nationwide, and in 2017 for reporter David Fahrenthold's investigation of Donald Trump's charitable foundation and businesses.

At the beginning of 2016, the *Post* left its aging building at 15th and L Streets NW in downtown Washington, which was made iconic by the movie *All the President's Men*. The building was soon demolished to make way for Fannie Mae, the government-backed mortgage financing company. On the last day on which we were allowed into the stripped-down building, current and past staff members filled the barren newsroom for a farewell ceremony. We were especially moved when the uniformed marching band of Washington's Eastern High School, with which the *Post* had a long association, snaked through the crowd in the newsroom, playing "The *Washington Post* March" by John Phillip Sousa.

The *Post* moved only a few blocks away to a spacious, refitted office building at 13th and K Streets NW. Walking into the long, two-story, technologically advanced newsroom was a revelation. Computer engineers and digital data specialists worked among the reporters and editors. Huge screens hanging in a two-story atrium in the middle of the newsroom showed continuously updated data about the audiences for *Post* stories and multimedia on the internet.

While Baron and Bezos still cared about the printed newspaper and its role in the Washington area, they made the *Post* a leading national and international multimedia, multiplatform news organization. Its internet audience competed with that of the *New York Times*; washingtonpost .com would have more than 1.5 million paid digital subscribers by 2019. With Bezos's encouragement and financing, the *Post* opened software and audience development research laboratories in Washington and New York. They produced innovative digital tools used by the *Post* and sold to other news organizations, bringing in new revenue. At the end of

2016, Ryan sent a memo to *Post* employees saying that "The *Washington Post* will finish this year as a profitable and growing company."

High-quality journalism was "integral to the *Post*'s business model at a time when the future of digital journalism seemed to be veering toward the lowest common denominator of exploding watermelons and stupid pet tricks," columnist James B. Stewart wrote in the *New York Times* on May 17, 2017. He quoted Baron as saying in an interview, "We tell people what they didn't already know. We hold government and powerful people accountable. This cannot happen without financial support. We're at the point where the public realizes that and is willing to step up and support that work by buying subscriptions."

That sounded like my *Washington Post* journalism in a new age. By then, however, I had moved on. When the *Post* transferred to its new building, there was no longer room for an office for me. My "vice president at large" title disappeared with my office. The other *Post* alum who had that title, Ben Bradlee, had died in October 2014, after years of decline with dementia. I was a pallbearer at his funeral, which was attended by many hundreds of present and past colleagues and media luminaries in the Washington National Cathedral.

I became a university professor, teaching investigative reporting for Arizona State University's outstanding Walter Cronkite School of Journalism, with Janice and me dividing our time between Washington and Phoenix. I also published my modestly successful novel, *The Rules of the Game*, about a Washington investigative reporter and a U.S. president, both of whom are women.

Although I had left the *Post*, it did not completely leave me. In the spring of 2017, I was contacted by a former *Post* colleague, R. B. Brenner. He told me that director Steven Spielberg was making a movie about the *Post* and the Pentagon Papers.

Back in 2009, at my suggestion, Brenner had been a consultant on the newspaper-themed movie *State of Play*. Through the contacts he had made at the time, he was asked by an art director and the property master for Spielberg's movie to help with the design and props for a replica of the *Post* newsroom at the time of the Pentagon Papers story in 1971.

Being only ten years old at the time, Brenner had never set foot in that newsroom. But he knew it was not the *Post*'s new newsroom during Watergate, as seen in *All the President's Men*. So he researched archives and interviewed former *Post* reporters and editors, including me, who had worked in the 1971 newsroom.

Coincidentally, I received a call from Josh Singer, coauthor of the script for Spielberg's movie about the *Post*. Singer had won an Academy Award for the screenplay of *Spotlight*. One of its central real-life characters was Walter "Robby" Robinson, the head of the *Boston Globe*'s Spotlight investigative team during its investigation of pedophile priests, who was portrayed in *Spotlight* by actor Michael Keaton. Robinson had since joined the faculty of the Cronkite School, with an office down the hall from mine.

When Singer sent him a draft of the Pentagon Papers movie script, Robinson suggested that he show it to me because I had worked in the *Post* newsroom at the time. Singer did. I was pleased by the screenplay's verisimilitude and its portrayal of Katharine Graham's relationship with Ben Bradlee and her brave decision to follow the *New York Times* in publishing stories about the Pentagon Papers, in defiance of the Nixon administration. I "made notes" on the script, as they say in Hollywood, and Singer said he found them helpful.

By May 2017, Brenner and I were hired to be on-set consultants for the journalism scenes in the *Post*'s old newsroom and in Ben Bradlee's house at the time. At our suggestion, Steve Coll was brought on so that the three of us could rotate through the shooting schedule. Together, we first advised the actors, extras, and production assistants on the roles of the journalists in the newsroom and what they would be doing at various times of the day. The actors portraying the principal editors and reporters impressed us by how well they had prepared, by reading books the journalists had written, as well as what had been written about them. Meryl Streep, of course, *was* Katharine Graham every day that we saw her on set.

The 1971 *Post* newsroom set was built in an office building in downtown White Plains, New York. Replicas of the first floors of the Georgetown houses of Ben Bradlee and Katharine Graham were built on sound stages of the Steiner Studios in the old Brooklyn Navy Yard. I was impressed by their authenticity. I felt nostalgic on the 1971 newsroom set. I became misty-eyed when I wandered alone through the startlingly accurate replica of Mrs. Graham's house, where I had visited so many times over the years.

It was fascinating to watch Spielberg and his crew making the movie, which he decided to title, simply, *The Post*. Singer and Spielberg were receptive to most of our concerns about authenticity in the action and dialogue. During the frequent breaks in shooting, it was interesting to talk to some of the actors and producers about their craft and about mine. And it was gratifying to contribute ideas to Singer and Spielberg, including one very brief line spoken in the movie.

It was especially rewarding to hear Spielberg share why he was filming *The Post*, and why he wanted to finish it during President Trump's press-baiting first year in office. He did not want to slight the key role of the *New York Times* in publishing stories about the Pentagon Papers and winning, with the *Post*, the landmark U.S. Supreme Court case eventually allowing further publication. But Spielberg wanted to show the emergence of Katharine Graham, Ben Bradlee, and the *Post* on the national stage, and to depict a turning point in the mission of the American press to hold government accountable—with Watergate to come. He told me it was a labor of love for him.

I first saw *The Post* at its premier, held at the Newseum in Washington. I then hosted well-attended showings in theaters for friends and former colleagues in Washington and for students and faculty at the Cronkite School in Phoenix. Each time, I felt the movie took its place with *All the President's Men* and *Spotlight* as the most realistic and meaningful screen depictions of the importance of newspaper journalism and stories that made a difference. I relished each audience's applause when Mrs. Graham finally said, "Let's go, let's go, let's publish," and when the presses started to print *Post* newspapers with its first Pentagon Papers story on the front page. The reaction of the journalism students, especially, gave me hope for the future.

25

The Rest of the Story

$\mathcal{A}$S I FINISH WRITING THIS BOOK, THE ROLE, performance, and very existence of truth-seeking news media are under siege. Prompted by President Trump's unprecedented attacks on the press, people who do not like factual reporting with which they disagree dismiss it as "fake news." Journalists are harassed on social media and in public. Partisan media dispense malicious propaganda disguised as news. Local newspapers keep shrinking and dying across the country, as rapacious hedge funds buy many of those still standing and drain their remaining assets.

At the same time, there are some surviving, even prospering, larger multiplatform, independently owned newspapers, like the *Washington Post*, that are doing outstanding investigative and other reporting that is needed more now than ever. They have been joined by an increasing number of national, regional, and local nonprofit news organizations dedicated to revelatory factual reporting. But they all must compete for attention and credibility with steadily increasing disinformation, as Americans increasingly rely on media with which they feel most comfortable.

This book is not intended to be nostalgic. I believe that it has real relevance today. I showed how my colleagues and I worked all those years—as *Post* journalists do now—to make certain our stories were accurate and fair, even when they caused controversy or challenged authority, including presidents of the United States. We were not motivated by personal or institutional bias. We were pursuing the truth, however imperfectly at times, and holding the powerful accountable— not propagating "fake news."

I now do whatever I can to help others with that mission. While teaching investigative reporting, I helped direct for many years the Cronkite School–based, foundation-funded News21 national student investigative reporting project. Student journalists from universities around the country produced professional-quality, multimedia investigative stories about guns, voting rights, treatment of veterans, legalization of marijuana, water pollution, and hate crimes in America. Their work was published by newspapers and news websites throughout the nation. It was rewarding for me to help students learn by doing ambitious journalism in the public interest.

Before writing this book, I cowrote another, *The News Media: What Everyone Needs to Know*, and a report published by Columbia University, "The Reconstruction of American Journalism"—both about the challenges facing the news media today. I also researched and wrote "The Obama Administration and the Press," a widely circulated special report for the Committee to Protect Journalists (CPJ). It examined how President Obama failed to fulfill his promise to make his administration the most transparent in U.S. history. Instead, his administration made it more difficult for news media to do the reporting that would hold it accountable to the American people. I later undertook a similar CPJ project to examine the Trump administration's much more dangerous hostility toward the press and its habitual lying to the American people.

I am the founding chair of the journalism advisory committee of Kaiser Health News, a robust, independent, nonprofit news organization providing vitally needed reporting and investigative journalism about health issues to millions of Americans through collaborations with newspapers, commercial television, and public broadcasting throughout the country.

There are now scores of other nonprofit news organizations, including public broadcasting stations and networks, that are doing local, state, and national investigative reporting. Like Kaiser Health News, many of them are collaborating with other news media to produce important journalism that otherwise might not exist. Still other fledgling nonprofit news organizations are trying to fill gaps left by shrinking and disappearing local newspapers and television news broadcasts. To survive, those news nonprofits need public support.

News reporting that pursues the truth has not fundamentally changed during my years in journalism, although the transmission of news and information has been profoundly transformed. In the age of the internet, Americans have a wide range of choices. Everyone, every day, can decide what to read, hear, and see in the digital media universe. I believe that it is important, if not always easy, for an informed citizen to discern which news media are pursuing the truth, and which ones are offering lies.

Increasing numbers of authoritarian regimes around the world are preventing their citizens from knowing the truth. A worrying proportion of American politicians and media figures appear to be trying to do the same thing here. We all have a responsibility to prevent that from happening.

For journalists, it is, more than ever, all about the story—getting it straight, and making a difference.

Afterword

𝕴T WAS VERY DIFFICULT TO END THIS BOOK during the COVID-19 pandemic. The crisis put still more stress on the nation's news media, even as they played an increasingly important role in keeping Americans informed and holding power accountable when it was most needed. Journalists had to drastically change the ways they worked to keep themselves and their news sources safe. News media had to separate facts from rumor and especially deliberate misinformation coming from President Trump. And they had to contend with the president's continuing attacks on their reporting.

When the crisis worsened, the audience for news grew dramatically. But advertising in newspapers, after an already long decline, cratered during the crisis, when much of the country and its economy were shut down. Except for the largest newspapers, increases in paid digital subscriptions made up for only a fraction of the decline in print advertising revenue. More journalists lost their jobs as more newspapers reduced their frequency of publication or went out of business.

Meanwhile, President Trump's calculated hostility toward the press only intensified during the coronavirus crisis. The president and his supporters, including right-wing media led by Fox News, relentlessly attacked the rest of the news media and individual journalists when they accurately reported facts and asked questions that displeased the president and challenged his truthfulness.

Trump's behavior reminded me of Richard Nixon's attacks on the *Washington Post* during Watergate, his illegal wiretaps and FBI investigations of reporters, and his "enemies list" that included newspaper and television journalists. White House tape recordings eventually revealed that Nixon also raged against the press in Oval Office conversations with his aides. We at the *Post* and the rest of the press outlasted Nixon. Americans, who had been divided over his presidency, came to support a profound increase in the kind of investigative reporting that brought him down.

As I have written in this book, Bill and Hillary Clinton, and their supporters, were not happy with the reporting I directed at the *Post* about their Arkansas business dealings and the president's White House affair with Monica Lewinsky. George W. Bush and officials in his administration notably lied to the press and the public about their justifications for the invasion of Iraq after the 9/11 terrorist attacks. Barack Obama's administration tightly controlled information and access to its officials needed to hold the government accountable for its actions. Obama also began prosecutions under the 1917 Espionage Act, which continued during the Trump administration, of numerous government employees and contractors for disclosing classified information to the press.

But none of those presidents purposely sought to fundamentally destroy the credibility of the press or lied to the American people in the ways that Trump has. As he told Lesley Stahl of CBS News, when he was elected president in 2016 after relentlessly attacking the press during the campaign, "I do it to discredit you all and demean you all, so that, when you write negative stories about me, no one will believe you."

Fox News anchor Chris Wallace said in a December 11, 2019, speech, "I believe that President Trump is engaged in the most direct sustained assault on freedom of the press in our history. He has done everything he can to undercut the media, to try and delegitimize us, and I think his purpose is clear: to raise doubts, when we report critically about him and his administration, that we can be trusted."

Trump repeatedly attacked the press, specific news organizations, and individual journalists in his tweets, campaign rallies, and even COVID-19 news briefings. He urged boycotts of news organizations and their corporate owners and called for changes in libel law to punish the press, even though libel law is determined by the courts and the states. The president's press secretaries, other White House aides, and administration officials also frequently attacked the press, often parroting Trump's language about "fake news."

As I wrote in my 2020 Committee to Protect Journalists report on Trump and the press, these attacks on the news media, along with Trump's thousands of documented false and misleading statements, dangerously undermined truth and consensus in a deeply divided country. Along with disinformation in partisan media and on the internet, it became increasingly difficult for Americans to tell factual news reporting from propaganda and lies.

Changes in the norms of the news media also contributed to that difficulty. Increased analysis and journalistic "voice" in news stories, while often making those stories more informative and engaging, sometimes veered into what appeared to be opinion or partisanship. Even when clearly labeled, news and opinion were intermingled on news media websites. Cable television news networks indiscriminately mixed reporting and opinion on news shows on which newspaper and television reporters often appeared.

Opinion polls showed Trump succeeding in discrediting much of the press among his followers, even during the COVID-19 crisis. At the same time, on the other side of the divide, there were noticeable increases in digital subscriptions to major newspapers, including the *Washington Post* and the *New York Times*, and in donations to public radio stations, other nonprofit news organizations, and press freedom groups.

"One of the effects of the way Trump has attacked the press is to remind people about the importance of freedom of the press and our role in holding government accountable," Dan Balz, the *Post*'s respected chief political correspondent, told me somewhat optimistically.

Nevertheless, many of the journalists and media experts I interviewed for the CPJ report said they fear an existential threat to American freedom of the press. "Trump disrespects the press as a core democratic institution," University of Utah media law professor RonNell Andersen Jones told me. If American acceptance of the news media's First Amendment role erodes, she warned, "freedom of the press is in peril."

Attacks on the credibility of truth-seeking journalists and news organizations by Trump and his enablers in the right-wing media only increased during the national upheaval following the police killing of a black man, George Floyd, by a white police officer in Minneapolis in late May. In that atmosphere, scores of journalists covering protests across the country were physically assaulted, tear-gassed, pepper-sprayed, and shot with rubber bullets by police. At least several dozen were arrested before being later released. Many of the journalists had shown police their media credentials and shouted "Press!" before being attacked or arrested. Photographers and television journalists carried cameras and microphones; some were arrested while broadcasting live. Journalists of color believed they were singled out.

Nevertheless, much of the news media, already under severe strain from the pandemic and its economic consequences, reported extensively on the protests and the underlying issues of American policing, systemic racism, and societal inequality. Journalists investigated the Trump administration's heavy-handed response to the protests, its use of the military, and its many false assertions about the protests and how it responded to them. Not since the 9/11 terrorist attacks had the news media's role been more important.

I devoted my life—and this book—to that vital role of the press in our democracy. It is imperative that it survives pandemics, economic crises, civil unrest, intimidation, and political attacks.

Author's Note

THIS BOOK IS THE STORY OF WHAT I DID, SAW, AND FELT IN MY momentous years in journalism. It draws on my memory; contemporaneous notes I made over the years; recent interviews; my extensive personal papers; both the Benjamin C. Bradlee and the Bob Woodward and Carl Bernstein Watergate archives at the Harry Ransom Center at the University of Texas in Austin; more than fifty books, including my own; and scores of *Washington Post* stories. I did all my own research. In journalistic style, I have cited sources when relevant in the text throughout the book, rather than using footnotes.

I'm grateful for the interviews for this book that I conducted with Don Graham, Bob Kaiser, Steve Coll, Phil Bennett, Marty Baron, Milton Coleman, Karen DeYoung, Tom Wilkinson, Dana Priest, Bob Woodward, Carl Bernstein, Susan Schmidt, Larry Meyer, Steve Luxenberg, Charles Babcock, Athelia Knight, Peter Silberman, Charles Krause, and David Kaczynski. I thank Patricia O'Shea, my outstanding executive assistant during all my twenty-four years as managing editor and executive editor, for her tireless management of my time, correspondence, and papers.

I benefited from critical reading of the manuscript in progress by my wife, Janice—my first and toughest editor—and by Bob Kaiser, Tom Wilkinson, Tracy Grant, Nora James, Don Graham, Steven Ginsberg, Glenn Frankel, David Ignatius, and Tony Ryan. I'm very grateful to Peter

Osnos, my former *Washington Post* colleague and the founder of the book publishing company PublicAffairs, for making this book possible and guiding me along the way. I thank my astute manuscript editor, Lisa Kaufman, who helped me to see the book as a whole and to pull it all together, my exacting copy editor, Michael McConnell, and everyone at PublicAffairs. Once again, I thank my agent, the legendary Amanda "Binky" Urban of ICM, for unfailingly being there for me.

Many people made possible my career in journalism. My parents, Leonard Sr. and Pearl Downie, instilled their values in me and my brothers. Margaret Ann McGinty at Wilber Wright Junior High was the most inspiring of my school newspaper advisers. George Kienzle, director of The Ohio State School of Journalism, was my first mentor, believed in me, and pointed me to the *Washington Post*. Katharine Graham, Ben Bradlee, and Howard Simons shaped the *Washington Post* where I was able to grow and later lead. Don Graham put his trust in me and supported me over the years; I will forever be in his debt. Bob Kaiser, Steve Coll, and Phil Bennett were strong partners as my managing editors. Kaiser, Tom Wilkinson, Milton Coleman, and Herb Denton were influential advisers.

Hundreds of outstanding *Washington Post* journalists worked with me over decades to produce journalism that made a difference; those I was able to name and credit in these pages are representative of many, many more. Although their work did not appear in the book, I want to especially recognize Mary Hadar's leadership of the *Post*'s influential Style section during its golden age and George Solomon's direction of the *Post*'s league-leading sports section.

I thank Christopher Callahan, founding dean of the incomparable Walter Cronkite School, and many faculty members and students there for helping to make my second career in journalism so enriching.

Mistakes I made over the years are my responsibility, as are any shortcomings of this book.

Index

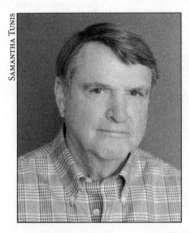

Samantha Tunis

LEONARD DOWNIE, JR. is the former executive editor of the *Washington Post*. Downie spent his entire journalistic career at the paper, where he started as a summer intern reporter in 1964. He soon became a prize-winning investigative reporter on the paper's local news staff. While deputy metropolitan news editor from 1972 until 1974, Downie was one of the editors of the paper's Watergate coverage. Downie also served as the *Post*'s London correspondent before becoming national editor in 1982. In 1984, he was named managing editor of the *Washington Post*, a position he held until 1991, when he became executive editor. Downie retired from the *Post* in 2008. Under Downie's leadership, the paper won twenty-five Pulitzer Prizes, including three Pulitzer gold medals for public service. Downie is now a journalism professor at Arizona State University's Walter Cronkite School of Journalism. This is his seventh book.